P.O. 23595
11-27-00

The Horizontal Society

THE
Horiz

Yale University Press   New Haven and London

ontal

SOCIETY

LAWRENCE M. FRIEDMAN

For Leah, Jane, Amy, Paul, Sarah, David, and Lucy

Published with assistance from the foundation established in memory
of Philip Hamilton McMillan of the Class of 1894, Yale College.

Designed by Sonia L. Scanlon and
Set in Adobe Garamond type by The Composing Room of Michigan, Inc.

Printed in the United States of America.

Library of Congress Cataloging-in-Publication Data

Friedman, Lawrence Meir, 1930–
    The horizontal society / Lawrence M. Friedman.
        p.   cm.
    Includes bibliographical references and index.
    ISBN 0–300–07545–6
    1. Group identity.   2. Ethnicity.   3. Social values.   4. Social history—
20th century.   I. Title
HM131.F736   1999
306′.09′04—dc21   98–31594
                        CIP

A catalogue record for this book is available from the British Library.

The paper in this book meets the guidelines for permanence and durability
of the Committee on Production Guidelines for Book Longevity
of the Council on Library Resources.

10 9 8 7 6 5 4 3 2 1

CONTENTS

PREFACE

THE WORLD WE LIVE IN seems to be cursed with identity wars and identity politics. National passions pockmark the earth. There is, for example, a particularly vicious kind of modern war: war in which one ethnic group, one people, slaughters or tries to slaughter another. Since Bosnia, the sinister phrase "ethnic cleansing" has entered the language. Its meaning is all too clear.

The fingerprints of identity politics are seen in violent and nonviolent issues alike. *Within* nations, identity politics is at the very center of the cultural and political stage. Affirmative action, multiculturalism, the right of Native Americans to reclaim land, water, fishing rights, even ancestral bones, the right of deaf students to choose a leader who is more "like them" (in other words, deaf) at an American college for the deaf—the American list is endless. We could compile such lists for country after country. We live in an age in which group identity *matters,* and matters deeply: the country, race, ethnic group, or religion you belong to, not to mention membership in other "nations," including the nation of sexual preference. Of course, some of these forms of identity have always mattered. The fault line between men and women goes back millions of years, to the dawn of the species, if not further. Religious identity has its pedigree as well; and so does the European habit of burning Jews or heretics at the stake. But there is a general feeling abroad that aspects of personal identity matter today in new and different ways. This feeling, it seems to me, is basically correct.

And yet this is a world that is more and more constituted by *individuals.* We live in an age of genocide, but also in an age of universal human rights, an age that sprouts charters or rights, constitutions, and declarations of rights like leaves on the trees. It is an age in which old forms and traditions seem to be breaking down—forms and traditions that trapped the individual in a cage of ascription; that fixed human beings in definite social roles, pinned them like specimens to a given position in the world, no matter how they might wriggle and fight. It is also a world that seems, more and more, to share a kind of common culture. It is a world that sings the same pop songs and seems to watch the same movies, everywhere on the globe. Benjamin R. Barber, in *Jihad vs. McWorld,* a book that (rightly) attracted considerable attention, referred to this common culture as "McWorld." There is no doubt that this also exists.

Can these tendencies be reconciled? Or is our world too complicated a case—a mass of hopeless contradictions? One aim of this book is to tie together some of these phenomena, which seem so different, so opposed to one another, yet which I feel, almost instinctively, are related. I cannot claim that my answers are the only ones possible. I am certainly not the first person to ask questions about identity, nationalism, the legal order, and individualism, or to try to answer such questions. But I do hope to add at least something to current debates.

As a law teacher, I am particularly interested in questions of law and authority, how these are structured, what they mean to our society (and other societies), and how they grow, change, shrivel, and expand over the years. Changing conceptions of identity are inevitably reflected in law and inevitably shape the law. Issues of identity lie at the base of the civil rights movement and civil rights law. They arise, to give another example, in the law of citizenship and immigration and in conceptions of human rights and minority rights. These legal and social issues will figure prominently in this book. Similarly, the decay of tradition and the rise of individualism have a profound impact on the legal order and the structure of authority.

My purpose in this book is to explain and describe. I use these two words quite deliberately. I am not trying to pass judgment. I am not making policy prescriptions. I am not predicting a golden age or, conversely, forecasting doom. I have no overt suggestions about what governments and societies should or should not do. Of course, icy neutrality on questions of policy is impossible. It is also undesirable. I do have strong opinions, and I do make moral judgments; many of these will be obvious in the following pages. Some of these judgments are simple and clear-cut and will be shared by most readers. There are people in the world who, for one reason or another, think they are justified in killing people of other races and religions; not many of those people are likely to read this book.

One simple point: the past is dead. You can never go back; for most purposes, we have to work with the world we have, not with the world we would like to have or used to have. The past does cast a shadow on the present; it may even *seem* to be vibrantly alive, compellingly alive, but this is an illusion. In truth, it is not the past as such that makes a difference. It is the past insofar as it has been inherited, accepted, and reworked and reconceived by people in the present. For better or worse, we are what we are, and what we are is *where* we are, in space and in time. The world has changed enormously over the last century or so. We—all of us—live in a world that was never here before. It is a world of mass transport and communication, a world of satellite TV, a world of computers and air conditioning. We live in what some people like to call a global village. This is a nice phrase, but it is only a metaphor. This world is definitely *not* a village, and village life, for most of us, is entirely and irrevocably extinct.

In any event, the first step toward changing the world (if that is what we aim for) is to understand what aspect of the world we want to change, to identify what it is and how it got that way. The basic function of this book is to get under the skin, so to speak, with regard to some aspects of the modern world. This book is about modernity and the modern world. It is about the conditions of modern life, and how they have fundamentally altered our sense of who we are and, in so doing, altered as well our sense of law, order, and authority.

Nobody writes a book entirely alone. As usual, there are a lot of people I need to thank. Some of them—most of them—are people I have never met. They are the people whose books I cite and quote and use and admire, the scholars on whose work I am trying to build. These are scholars who have written about immigration and citizenship or about rights and constitutions, or who have tried to explain what makes the world we live in tick. There is a rich literature about nationalism, its history, its nature. I have leaned heavily on this literature. Indeed, in some ways, what I have tried to do in part of this book is to apply the insights of this literature to law, rights, and related subjects. Hence my debt to such scholars as Benedict Anderson, Eric Hobsbawm, and Ernest Gellner. Kenneth Karst made extremely valuable comments on the manuscript. Benjamin Barber's *Jihad vs. McWorld* appeared in 1995, when I was already at work on this book. My approach and my assessment of the issue are, I think, quite different from his. But his work is stimulating and important; I enjoyed it, and I learned from it.

I owe thanks, too, to the various students at Stanford, mostly in the law school, who fell into my clutches and who scurried about to find references or supplied me with citations and bits of research here and there. Among these students were Peter Bouckaert, David Himelfarb, Brian Pearce, and Shannon Petersen.

This book was written at the Stanford Law School, in Stanford, California. I want to thank my colleagues, generally, for their aid and encouragement. My assistant, Mary Tye, was a tremendous help to me; I am grateful for her efficiency and good humor. I also owe an immense debt to the staff of the Stanford Law Library. They have been patient, cooperative, and helpful at all times. I don't think I could have finished this book without them.

INTRODUCTION

I N APRIL 1994 UNSPEAKABLE horror swept over Rwanda, a small country in central Africa. It all started after the president of the country was killed in a mysterious air crash. This accident, if it was an accident, somehow unleashed demonic violence; it seemed to act as a signal, a spark, making old hatreds burst into flame. Two ethnic groups, the Hutu and the Tutsi, uncomfortably share the national space in Rwanda. In the days and weeks that followed the death of the president, the capital, Kigali, and the rest of the country were engulfed in looting, rape, and murder of almost indescribable ferocity. Organized government disintegrated; thousands of innocents—men, women, and children—were slaughtered; mobs of young men roamed the streets with guns, machetes, and whatever they could get their hands on, to kill other human beings—their fellow citizens—like animals. Refugees—more than a million of them—fled in panic across the borders. Western countries scooped up their citizens and flew them to safety. In Kigali, as shadowy groups contended with each other, rotting corpses lay everywhere, on the streets, in churches; the dead were strewn about like rag dolls thrown in the garbage; piles of bodies were shoveled into makeshift graves and buried in indignity and haste. The flickering lights of common decency and civility guttered and went out, and Rwanda slid into a kind of ultimate night.[1] It did not emerge from this state of anarchy and absolute evil for months.[2] Later, an exhausted peace took hold; a new government came to power, which exerted at least some control over the forces of murder; many refugees filed wearily back over the border. But who can say what lies ahead for Rwanda? Furthermore, the problems of Rwanda are echoed in Burundi and have influenced the fate of the Congo as well.

Rwanda seems remote from Western experience. I suspect that many Europeans or Americans or Japanese, reading about the killings or watching it all on television screens, felt that these episodes of slaughter had nothing to do with them or their world. They might have thought that in this remote African country civilization was only a thin veneer over a basic heritage of savagery. They might have thought—with more than a hint of racism—that Rwanda was a primitive country. Algeria—another scene of bloody massacre—was, to be sure, also in Africa. But at the same time as Rwanda, another horror story was unfolding in Bosnia, right in Europe's own backyard. If Europeans could shrug their shoulders and explain Bosnia away (the Balkans were a notorious, historic mess), there was always Northern Ireland or, for that matter, skinheads in Germany. There were also vile, unspeakable, bloody wars and disruptions all around the rim of what used to be the Soviet empire, in Armenia, Azerbaijan, Tajikistan, not to mention the tower of corpses in Chechnya, inside Russia's very borders.

If Americans felt smug, as many of them probably did, one could have reminded them of how they had treated their own native peoples; how, within not too distant memory, Indians were hunted down like dogs; how settlers laid waste to Indian villages and murdered whole settlements. If the Japanese were inclined to feel aloof and superior, one could remind them of what they mostly choose to forget: how they butchered the Chinese during the 1930s, or their unspeakable savagery during the Second World War, and their bloody and oppressive imperial past in Korea and elsewhere. And in Europe, of course, Germany, the country of Goethe and Beethoven, holds a kind of sick record for absolute evil: the murder of six million Jews and countless other human beings—Gypsies, Poles, and whatever groups the Third Reich deemed unfit or unworthy to live.

Or is all that simply too much like ancient history? Is it poor taste to bring up such things to Americans, Germans, and Japanese, cocooned as they are in their current prosperity? Perhaps; perhaps not. In any event, there is more than enough in the contemporary world to be ashamed of as the twenty-first century approaches. And what ties most of these wars, massacres, and atrocities together, what binds them into one bloody, ragged bundle, is ethnicity, national feeling, race feeling, religious strife—in short, conflicting concepts of identity. In almost all of these purulent conflicts, at the root of so much of the fighting and killing, there lies a strong sense of some sort of *us,* some communal identity, which is opposed to some sort of *them,* and is in holy or unholy battle against this general or specific other.[3] All too often, these identities are so powerful, so emotionally charged, that they give men (and it is almost always men) license to kill.

What is it about the sense of ethnic identity that produces this lethal brew? Or religious identity, for that matter, where that seems (at least superficially) to be the source of the problem? Of course, the source of the problem is, in each case, complex. Religion and national feeling in themselves do not make murderers of us all. A Mother Teresa and the pope do not kill. Neither do most honest patriots. In many episodes of communal hatred, we can point to certain evil men and evil forces that stir up the population, goading and inciting for reasons of power or money. This was undoubtedly true in Rwanda and in other areas of communal war—Sri Lanka, for example.[4] But a Hitler does not rant and rave at random; the message must find an echo among his listeners; the poisoned seeds must land in the right kind of soil. If you appeal to ethnic, and religious, identity, you are likely to get a response.

But first we have to ask, somewhat naively, what do we mean by "identity?" What does it mean to identify yourself as a member of a group? Identity is, of course, a sense of self. When a person looks in the mirror and asks, who am I? the answer she gives is her identity (or part of it). To be sure, what we see in the mirror is basically our own reflection—that is, we see and are conscious of a self, a unique human being. Not even identical twins are exactly alike. We are each different from everybody else. We each have our own special fingerprints and a face that is like nobody else's. In our times, we each carry about manufactured markers of identity: a driver's license, a passport, a secret code that unlocks a money machine or allows us to make long-distance calls without coins. And everyone who is not abjectly poor or homeless in the United States has an address and a social security number. In many countries, people carry about an identity card, a residence permit, a registration of some sort or another. And no two of these are alike.

But we also can, and do, identify ourselves in terms that go beyond the self, that link the self with some other entity or group. Identity for most of us means being part of a group. An identity, as Charles Taylor has put it, is defined by "commitments and identifications"; these "provide the frame or horizon within which I can try to determine from case to case what is good, or valuable, or what ought to be done, or what I endorse or oppose."[5] Identity, then, is not just a sense of who we are—a definition; it is a lens through which we see the world.

What is that lens made out of? What are the commitments and identifications that people have in our times, and that define the way we think and feel and see? I say in our times, because it is *modern* identity, contemporary identity that we are dealing with here; and the sense of identity is very much dependent on time, space, and culture.[6] To begin with, we are almost always members of families, tied to a nuclear group—a mother, a father, children, brothers, and sisters—or to an extended group of cousins, aunts, and uncles and even more remote kin. For many people, there are no ties as strong as family ties. In non-Western cultures, these ties tend to be even stronger. Beyond the family, men and women in our societies think of themselves as belonging to bigger groups—nationalities, tribes, ethnic groups. We might think of ourselves as "American," as "Thai," as "Italian-American," or as an "Algerian living in France," and so on.

Gender is also incredibly basic to identity: nothing stamps our identity more fundamentally than whether we are women or men. Race is also fundamental—black, white, Native American, or Asian. And so (for many people) is religion—Roman Catholic, Greek Orthodox, Buddhist, or Jewish. One also defines oneself as young, middle-aged, or old; or as a lesbian, a stamp collector, or a carpenter; or as a dentist or school teacher; or as an employee of the European Union in Brussels or a doctor in Brazil.

There are, in short, countless ways of describing one's *primary* identity. But does it even make sense to talk about a primary identity? Identities overlap; everybody has many identities, like different roles in a play. We call on different identities at different times and places—again, like an actor who plays many roles. For many people no single role is primary; now woman, now American, now mother, now forensic pathologist, now grower of roses; for others, one identity dominates all others.

Roles and identities also vary culturally and in terms of time and place, as we have said. There have always been women and men, but not necessarily feminists (or men who bond with other men or run around howling in the woods); there have always been young and old, but the categories carry different meanings in different cultures. Each marker of identity has its specific history and drags with it its own tradition of meaning. How people conceive of themselves, then, is a fascinating issue in psychology, anthropology, and sociology, and in the study of history as well; it is also tremendously important in terms of law, politics, and public policy. Identity politics today is making an enormous splash in the world.

The core of this book pivots about a distinction between two kinds of identity, which I will call *vertical* and *horizontal.* Relationships in traditional families were strongly vertical. There was a clear line of authority from top to bottom. In one (ideal-typical) form of traditional family, papa was firmly in charge; mother and children were part of his domain. (Perhaps there were servants or slaves to round out the household.) Mothers were subordinate to fathers, but they had authority over their children. There were, perhaps, complex kin arrangements; in many societies, the power of a mother-in-law with respect to her son's wives, for example, or of a father's brother with respect to his nephews was sharply defined; and there were clear rules about who would inherit, who would rule, who could marry whom, and whose village or house would be home.

In a traditional village, there might be forms of vertical authority: peasants who owed fealty (or rent) to a local lord or dignitary, parishioners under the religious rule of a priest or elder. In our image of village life—in the Middle Ages, in central Africa, or in the South Pacific—people stayed close to home; almost nobody roamed about or migrated. People also stuck to the roles they were born into or grew into—roles determined by age, sex, birth order, and position in society.

In modern society, identity (and authority) is much more horizontal. In the course of this book, I will try to develop what I mean by this term. The core idea is this: modern men and women are much freer to form relationships that are on a plane of equality (real or apparent)—relationships with peers, with like-minded people. As one author put it, modern identity is "peculiarly open"; and the "modern individual is . . . peculiarly 'unfinished' as he enters adult life."[7] We are becoming "fluid and many-sided," evolving a "sense of self appropriate to the restlessness and flux of our times"—a sense of self that Robert Jay Lifton has called "protean."[8] Modern man and woman, then, seem to have a wide menu of choices. By this I mean a choice not only of friends but of men and women who share ideologies or interests. Modern technology makes this possible, of course. Consider a man who becomes a passionate collector of old bottles: suppose that he joins a club devoted to bottle collecting, becomes "active," subscribes to the newsletter, goes to annual meetings, and exchanges tidbits of information with people of similar mind. He has formed horizontal associations and made for himself a horizontal identity. It is a relationship different from the intense, vertical relationship he has with his mother and father, though it can, of course, be intense in its own right. There may be some people whose whole world is old bottles.

Collectors of old bottles are not particularly important to modern society. Affiliations of race, gender, ethnicity, religion, and politics are. When *many* people decide to make one of these their whole world, it makes a difference, politically and socially. Some of these factors (race, gender, ethnicity) seem inborn, fixed, and are nothing like joining a club of stamp collectors or bird-watchers. Harold Isaacs speaks of a "basic group identity," which "consists of the ready-made set of endowments and identifications that every individual shares with others from the moment of birth by the chance of the family into which he is born at that given time in that given place."[9] And indeed, identity does have what seems to be an inborn element. But the decision to affiliate, to focus on this element, is just as horizontal as the decision to devote one's life to old bottles. We live in a world where old, tight, vertical identities and relationships have loosened, have become less pressing, less dictatorial; the individual finds herself adrift, in search of meaning and of new affiliations. The "communities" people form can be "partial, fluctuating"; can "come in odd places and combinations"; can be fleeting, improvisational—or extremely intense.[10] Ethnic identity is one of these affiliations. But only one. And it, too, can range from a vague background murmur to a flame that consumes a whole life.

Horizontal groups can be large or small. The biggest of all, in most societies, is what is called "the nation." The nation is the king of groups, the group beyond all groups. National identity is, or is supposed to be, the identity that trumps other identities. Whatever else we are, we are all Americans (or Canadians or Japanese or Maldivians). Many people, of course, do not, and have never, identified most strongly with their nation; they never fly the flag, so to speak, or they fly it only fitfully. For others, nationalism or patriotism is a deeply embedded value, something even to die for. The political significance of this horizontal group—the nation—is abundantly clear.

Equally obvious is the horizontal nature of the nation or the ethnic group. A nation cannot sense itself as such if it cannot speak to its members, reach them, communicate with them. Before the world was transformed into what we know it to be today, there were, to be sure, tribal loyalties, clan loyalties, and religious loyalties, but there were no nations in the modern sense.

The starting point of our journey, then, is the shift from vertical to horizontal identity, from vertical to horizontal social structure. It is a *relative* shift. The old institutions are mostly still with us. The family is certainly not dead; I do not even think it is dying. It is simply different, and in some regards weaker than it was before. Arguably, in some ways the contemporary nuclear family is stronger and tighter than the old extended family—perhaps today's family makes emotional demands on its members that are more intense than in earlier times. The demands of modern marriage are surely more intense than the demands of traditional marriage. Marriages are more brittle than before because of their very intensity.[11] As we shall see, the horizontal world radically redefines the meaning of religion; but nobody with eyes to see and ears to hear would have any doubt that religion remains a vital and powerful world force. The church has not withered away any more than the state.

Power, authority, and influence, then, have become *relatively* more horizontal, though not absolutely. Think, on the one hand, of the typical person in a tiny village in medieval society. On the other hand, think of a woman in a big city in the United States—a divorced career woman, whose family relationships are loose but who has tight relationships with friends, who is an avid bird-watcher, a member of the Sierra Club, a feminist, an active Democrat, a churchgoing Catholic, and a dues-paying member of the American Association of Retired Persons. She is, relatively speaking, more horizontally inclined than her great-great-great-great-grandmother, in her German or Swedish or African village. It is because of this steady movement from vertical to horizontal that we can, in fairness, call our society horizontal.

I call a society horizontal when it allows, or puts stress on, the freedom of individuals to affiliate with larger groups. But the groups, it is important to note, are not necessarily themselves horizontal, let alone democratic. They can be, in fact, absolute dictatorships or hold their members in something close to slavery. Certain religious cults are an extreme case. But a devout Catholic recognizes the authority of the pope and the bishops, and may be as humble and obedient as any monk of the Middle Ages. What is horizontal is the process, not the group once it is formed.[12] This is even true of such "compulsory" groups as the nation or the ethnic group.

This relative shift from vertical to horizontal, in human relationships, over time, seems undeniable. But what brought it about? Obviously, we are dealing with a long-term trend, something which is in many ways slow and fundamental, like the movement of glaciers or the uplifting of rocks. The pace has, as we shall see, picked up considerably in this century. Basically, we are talking about the process of modernization. This term has been much criticized, and properly so, for vagueness, overlapping meanings, and other sins. It is, nonetheless, a useful idea, provided we use it (like medicine), in moderation, and with the correct dosage. Whatever name we give to the process, and however we define it, there are certain core elements that everyone will recognize. Modernization has been described as "the growth and diffusion of a set of institutions rooted in the transformation of the economy by means of technology."[13] Modernization has its technological side and its economic side; these also lead to political, cultural, and psychological changes.[14] All aspects of modernization move in tandem. And they tend to move in one direction: toward ending the narrow isolation of traditional life.

Modernization is above all a process of *connection*: a process of linking the small, molecular units of human life into larger ones. But as the linkage goes on, the glue between the atoms and molecules becomes weaker. This process of connection did not, of course, take place overnight; in one area, it began, perhaps, with something as simple as hacking out a road to connect this and that village. Then came the railroad, the telephone, the telegraph, airplanes and computers, radio and the movies and, above all, TV; now the long shadow of the internet hangs over the future. And when did this occur? In Europe bits and pieces can be traced back for centuries.

But the trend took hold, in earnest, though perhaps somewhat haltingly, in the late eighteenth or early nineteenth century. It coexisted with the Industrial Revolution, with the grimy mines and factories that sucked in workers from their villages. The class struggles of the nineteenth century presupposed an early stage of the horizontal society. Marxist thought, and the very concept of class solidarity, assume horizontal linkages among workers. Peasants in isolated villages have no sense of membership in a "class." The process of connection accelerated in the late nineteenth and early twentieth centuries; and now, at the brink of the twenty-first century, it seems to be rushing forward at breakneck speed.

When isolation is destroyed, the social units—the molecules that make up human life—tend to rearrange themselves, as we have said, and in the process they create what we are calling a horizontal society. People form or are aggregated into new groups—some small, some (as we have seen) as large as the nation. Clearly, too, the process is not merely one that makes it possible for nations to form; it is also (paradoxically) a process of international *convergence.* It brings about a kind of global uniculture. That much is clear on the level of technology. A telephone is a telephone is a telephone, whether in Japan or Finland or Uganda. Technology is also the *carrier* of a global mass culture. This means that convergence has taken place in many ways and has taken many forms. After all, a society in which people use telephones—and computers, and jet airplanes, and antibiotics—is not simply the same old society, with a few new gadgets pasted on. It is different in culture, in personality, in social structure—fundamentally different from past societies, and from past ways of living, thinking, and behaving.

Different: but how? What are the results of this form of the great transformation—what does it mean to have a horizontal society? The consequences, we think, are profound. Literally *everything* is changed. Significantly, the nature of group and individual identity is altered. In a horizontal society, identity becomes, perhaps for the first time, problematic. It becomes, in short, a matter of (apparent) choice. Most of us think of our primal identities as completely given—inborn, in fact. To be sure, we know that not all the basic markers of identity come to us this way. Some people are born deaf or unable to walk; others get there later. People can change religions, and many do. Absolutely nobody is born elderly. What most people do not realize is the heavy element of choice for other forms of identity—even "natural" identity, like gender or race. It isn't that we decide, all of a sudden, to be male rather than female, or black rather than white—or that this is even (socially) possible. I cannot easily decide to be a Norwegian; but if I happen to be born in Norway and speak Norwegian, I can decide what I will make of this fact—perhaps nothing, perhaps everything. That is, I can be born black or Hispanic or Estonian; whether I choose (or think I choose) to pivot my life around this inborn element is another question. Even with regard to the "nation" of men, or the "nation" of women, there is a similar element of (apparent) choice and of horizontal affiliation.[15] We have, in short, a certain degree of control over identity: over which identity to put on top of the pile. Or, to be more accurate, we either have this control, or, what comes to the same thing socially, we think we do.

In fact, we have *more* choice than we imagine in certain matters, and less than we imagine in others. More, in that we can put certain inborn identities in the forefront of our lives or try to smother their consequences, if we wish. Less, in that many of our "free choices" are dictated by social forces or hidden norms that we are totally unaware of, or are exercised within limits and boundaries that we never think about. We *think* we choose a dress or a shirt solely because we like this particular dress or shirt. And so it is: but we never stop to ask why this color or style is so popular or why we cannot or do not decide to wear a toga or a sari instead. Nothing much turns, of course, on what kind of dress or shirt we choose. Decisions to join the Nazi party, on the other hand, can be fraught with consequence, in the aggregate at least. The appeal of the Nazis in Germany in the 1930s depended on social facts and traditions that were missing in England or Switzerland. These differences among countries were and are terrifically important. But there is still a level at which *all* modern countries, in a horizontal world, are subject to the same kinds of forces.

Senses of identity, in that horizontal world, are complex, and they seem, on first blush, to be moving in every direction at once. As we noted, there is more individualism—more choice, more of a culture of personality, personal satisfaction, and self-realization; and yet group identity seems as virulent as ever, if not more so—we see greater tribalism and more nationalism. The world is thus fragmented into a herd of clans, nations, solidarity groups, religious and ethnic groups, clubs, cabals, and so on ad infinitum; yet there is also more consensus than ever before about universal human rights. At a deeper level, we will argue, all these tendencies are in fact quite consistent, are in fact linked with each other in a chain of cause and effect.

The point is that all this tribalism is a *consequence* of individualism and is not in contradiction to it. The individual, let loose from traditional moorings, does not float aimlessly in a sea of products and decisions. He or she looks for new moorings, *has* to look for new moorings. The new affiliations have a million different faces. Some of them lead to conflict or even take people down the dark road to war. Some are politically neutral— most of them, perhaps. Others lead to a demand for multiculturalism in its various guises.

The nation as a horizontal group is one of the sources of ethnic conflict. Inside countries, since the sense of being a nation is so often tied to a particular language, history, and culture, the act of binding a nation together also breeds a sense of exclusion, and hence the formation of subnations. Minorities become restless; they rebel or demand more space or more power or more voice. What kind of a nation is Canada? If it is English-speaking and has a queen, then what about Quebec? Is Quebec a separate nation? And if it is, and if that nation is defined by the French language and Francophone culture, then what role do Mohawks have in Quebec? And what about the people inside Quebec who speak English? And what about immigrants from Greece?[16]

In country after country, these subnations define themselves and become disturbers of peace. Some of these subnations are old ethnic fragments; others are strange new conglomerates of people, forming and transforming themselves into pressure groups. The story of these fragments, and what they mean for politics and law, is also part of our argument.

A horizontal society is a society of mobility—a society of rolling stones. People all over the world are on the move. There is more migration, more visiting, more tourism, more travel than ever before. Yet, even stay-at-homes indulge in a kind of virtual travel—whether or not you go to the world, the world comes to you. Images of far-off places flood in on the television screen. Instant communication, throughout the developed world and beyond, is a commonplace of the end of the twentieth century. Somehow, some way, there is access to TV and the world of news and entertainment absolutely everywhere. Sometimes it seems as if no jungle is so thick, gloomy, or overgrown that the magic eye fails to penetrate its depths. There are still exceptions, no doubt—remote villages in the Amazon or on the roof of the world in Nepal. But almost everybody else is exposed to a vast global culture that sweeps around the world.

These forces operate in a curious, double-edged way. They promote a kind of universal tribalism. They also promote a tribal universalism. They spread a common culture. This is, on the whole, a culture of entertainment and images. But it is also a culture of technology and a culture of ideas and ideals. How else can we explain the fact that the natives have become so restless? Why are certain basic concepts of human rights, which we can trace probably to the West and to the Enlightenment, now common coin in country after country—as an ideal, of course, and sometimes as a reality? Why are there free-speech movements in countries that never knew such a thing before?

Everybody knows that world economies are now tightly linked, for better or for worse.[17] Nobody is self-sufficient anymore. Giant corporations spring up and operate on a global scale. They buy and sell on world markets. This is not just a matter of free trade. It is a matter of culture. It is not just grain, steel, oil, and automobiles that travel from country to country. Consumers buy and sell bits and pieces of culture as well. As American movies flood world markets, soap operas made in Argentina enthrall audiences in Mexico. Movies and TV shows arouse global desires. A boy in Hungary sees American-style sports shoes on his TV set, and his heart lusts to possess them. The shoes might be made in Malaysia, following an Italian design, for a German company. If he—and his pals—become desperate enough, the shoes are bound to appear in the shops of Budapest. World trade, in goods, services, and forms of entertainment, is constantly expanding; the horizontal society promotes it, and it in turn promotes the horizontal society.

Every country is therefore linked to almost every other country. This fact in itself creates a kind of global culture. After all, merchants and manufacturers cannot deal with each other, cannot haggle and contract, without a certain degree of cultural understanding—some language in common, some common notions of law, some common norms of commercial practice. Otherwise, international trade would be like meetings between European explorers and "natives" in Africa, America, or Oceana, where misunderstanding was absolute, one side or the other ended up cheated or murdered outright, and no commonalities bound the parties together. The world of international trade, in our times, is entirely different. Common markets "demand . . . a common language"; and they produce "common behaviors of the kind bred by cosmopolitan life everywhere."[18] There is in fact a common normative language, a basic framework of understanding. Bankers have become jet-setters; business is now increasingly transnational, which means it has to cope with dozens of countries—which means, in practice, finding a common denominator. The very practice of law has gone global.[19] American megafirms have branches in dozens of world cities. In 1995, the biggest of such firms, Baker & McKenzie, with over 1,750 lawyers, had affiliates in more than fifty cities, including a branch with 146 lawyers in Hong Kong; Sullivan and Cromwell, the big Wall Street firm, had branches in London, Paris, Melbourne, Tokyo, and Frankfurt, among other cities.[20]

Apart from this important development—though not unconnected with it—there is also a middle-brow and middle-class world culture, a culture of culture, the culture of global longings and desires, and a mass culture than both depends on, and feeds, the elite global culture of banks, big corporations, and high-powered lawyers. Television is the basic engine of this new, horizontal culture. Television is an engine of cultural mobility. Thanks to television, people can change, move, alter, respond—even buy—without getting up from their couches. And, as we just pointed out, in this horizontal world, there is also a great deal of actual mobility: the planet is awash with tourists, refugees and, significantly, migrants. History, to be sure, has many stories to tell of migrations and wanderings—Goths, Vandals, and Huns; Bantu peoples in Africa; natives drifting down from the Arctic and slowly populating the Western hemisphere. But these old migrations were mostly movements en masse. Modern immigration is quite different. It is much more disjointed. It consists of individuals or small family groups, young men (and women) seeking their fortunes, cousins crossing borders to share a pad with a cousin and to hunt for honest work. Whole nations—Australia, Argentina, Canada, and the United States—grew up as immigrant countries; immigration supplied them with workers and citizens. These countries had at one time what looked like open doors (though never quite as open as they seemed, as we shall see); they had vast empty spaces (ignoring, as settlers almost always did, the claims and needs of native peoples); they wanted strong hands and new blood, rising real estate values, and growth, growth, growth.

The very life of these countries rested on cultural pillars that assumed a developing and horizontal society. In traditional society, people in general stayed put; they were born and died in their little villages; they did not leave the nest, either for pleasure or business, or as emigrants or immigrants. This kind of fixity has changed—and radically so, in the horizontal society. In our world, the glue that binds people most firmly to their place of birth is cracked and dried; it no longer works its adhesive magic.

Yet migration takes place in a world made up of nations; and the nation is a concept that both gathers in and shuts most definitely out. Modern nationalism, itself a creation of the horizontal society, collides with the desperate movement of millions, people shaken loose from their moorings by the very forces that created nationalism and the even stronger forces that created a common global culture. Many countries (Germany is a prime instance) have defined themselves as closed, ethnic communities—communities of history and blood. In these countries, the laws of citizenship and immigration are not just technical questions for lawyers; they are at the heart of public policy and are political dynamite. But Germany is not alone. Tens of thousands, even millions, from Third World countries are now banging on the doors of the rich and developed countries. Thus, questions of immigration and citizenship disturb the political peace in country after country. In fact, for a century or more, even the so-called immigration countries have been furiously debating *who,* and how many, should come.

Authority changes meaning, too, in a horizontal society. Authority is no longer vested in the holders of vertical power—at least not to the same extent. It is more diffuse—more horizontal. Leaders are no longer distant, awesome, and unknown; they are familiar figures on TV, and they are joined to their subjects in a symbiosis of symbols and images. Very notably, the horizontal society is a celebrity society. The men and women who get and hold power become celebrities; and they exercise their power in a celebrity way.

Celebrity culture is not just a matter of famous people and certainly not just a matter of rock stars, movie stars, and soccer players. It is also a frame of mind that affects the very essence of authority. It affects the way we do business, affects who we elect to office, and how we run our countries as well. The difference between a "celebrity" and an "authority" is fundamental: a celebrity is someone we know, or think we know, through the media, through publicity, that is, vicariously. A celebrity is a familiar image—a face on television. People in modern society—ordinary people, people who sit in front of the TV screen—*seem* to have a horizontal relationship to celebrities. Appearances here are important, but extremely misleading. Still, by contrast, traditional authority was vertical, and the higher up the authority, the more stern, distant, and remote it was.

The other side of the coin is that the celebrity, who seems so close to us (visually at least), can also reach *us* more easily, can speak to us. In a horizontal society, which is also a society of choice or apparent choice, the masses of the people are in a sense unformed, malleable, protoplasmic. This is thus a society of the black arts of manipulation—a society of propaganda, focus groups, public opinion polls. If people can choose, if they have options, then other people can, and do, try to influence their choices. This is obviously true of consumer goods; there are dozens of brands of toothpaste in our world. But it is also true of the market for ideas—and the market for identities. This was a century of globalization but also a century of rabble-rousers, of demagogues, of fiery orators—an age of men (and an occasional woman) who tried to create, out of an inchoate mass, an identity army, ready to march against whoever or whatever was labeled the enemy of the day. This process is still going on.

These themes will be taken up in more detail in later chapters. The horizontal society, like all forms of social ordering, has its problems and pathologies. I can offer no obvious cures. I do think that it helps to *understand*, to know what makes society tick. The issue of remedies and cures will be touched on in the final chapter.

I

The Way We Live Now

IN THE INTRODUCTION, I BROUGHT in the concept of the horizontal society. I made a few general points about where it came from. It is not easy to say much about origins; and I will not try to fill in details or provide an elaborate theory to explain the world we live in. That would be quite beyond my powers, or maybe anybody's powers. Clearly, whatever produced modern society—the Industrial Revolution, surely, and whatever created *it*—is the motor force behind the developments we are discussing. Once the process got going, it fed on itself, fueled by the astonishing growth of science and technology. Something in the history of the West somehow unleashed forces that burst open the cages of ignorance and set science and technology free. Science and technology in turn unleashed powerful forces of their own. These transformed the world. In the process, they created what we have called the horizontal society.

It is science and technology, and what they mean to society, that make our lives so different from the lives of our distant great-great-great grandparents. These tools, machines, techniques, and products have revolutionized every aspect of life. Their importance culturally, socially, and economically is beyond calculation. Just imagine what computers, jets, air conditioners, antibiotics, and television have done to, for, with, or against the human species in a short space of time—a mere moment of history. And these recent advances have occurred on top of earlier, equally revolutionary inventions and discoveries: automobiles, trains, the telegraph and telephone; vaccinations and the germ theory of disease; evolution and the descent of man.

Above all, then, the modern world is the world of science and high technology. Technology and science have turned the world upside down and inside out. Technology and science have made and remade social structures—transformed them totally. After all, an automobile is not just a faster horse that runs on gasoline instead of hay; a computer is not just a rapid, foolproof adding machine or typewriter. The medium not only changes the message; it also reconstructs the context of the message. The television world, the world of visual images, is profoundly different from the print culture it replaces, as Neil Postman has argued. Images replace written language "as our dominant means for construing, understanding, and testing reality"; these images undermine "traditional definitions of information, or news, and, to a large extent, of reality itself."[1] Postman points out the way television structures reality; it emphasizes *images* rather than ideas. Television, he feels, creates "the illusion of knowing something," while in fact it leads the viewer "away from knowing."[2]

It is important, too, to emphasize the sheer intrusiveness of television—coming on top of the telegraph, telephone, radio, and movies—as the king of modern communication. Television has completed the process of breaking down the barriers of time and space that separate people. It is a prime instrument of horizontal communication. Television can (and does) broadcast in many languages and in many styles; but there is a deep, subtle, underlying sameness to its message. It can, of course, be boring, but overall it is vivid, engaging, full of color. Its universal message stresses fun, image, entertainment, buying, selling, and consuming. Its powerful beam spreads an ideology of individual wants, desires, and fulfillments, an ideology of choice—the ideology of a horizontal world. Electronic mail and the Internet—new means of instant communication—also break down borders. They accelerate what Peter Berger has called the "urbanization of consciousness"; in the modern world, the individual is "bombarded with a multiplicity of information and communication."[3] We probably have only the dimmest sense, right now, of what the ultimate impact will be. But the Internet can only heighten the tendencies that make society more horizontal. The Internet makes it possible to send and receive messages across great distances and to communicate with strangers—that is, to form and cement horizontal groups.

All this technology, in turn, has revolutionized culture—and perhaps, in the process, has even affected personality. In this chapter, I want to look at a few of the cultural changes that make up a horizontal society and relate them to changes in authority, governance, and social structure. I discuss four basic aspects of culture in contemporary society, and refer briefly to their echo in the world of public affairs.

First, and perhaps most basic, is the perception of change itself. People today are aware of the fact of change and of the lightning speed at which change takes place.[4] People see technology changing the world before their eyes. Nothing seems impossible any more—walking on the moon, scooping rocks from the surface of Mars, curing AIDS, even balancing the budget. Change does not happen magically, but through human agency. Despite all the grumbling about government, people expect government to perform. Authorities are expected to have programs—ideas about what to do and how to make meaningful change. Nobody expected a program from Louis XIV or from the emperors of China and Japan.

Second, technology creates a global culture—high and low. Mac-Donald's and Disney Productions circle the world. In a high-tech, horizontal society, real communities decline and virtual communities arise—bound together by norms, images, and ideas peddled through the airwaves. In our societies today, old bonds of trust and reciprocity—what some have called "social capital"—are under siege; newer electronic bonds promote the rise of interest groups and pressure groups (local, national, and global), which need not be, and often are not, based on face-to-face contact. Politics gets transformed in the process.

Third, the global culture, in its vividness and immediacy, promotes what has come to be known as celebrity culture. Leaders are no longer distant and remote. They are as close (we think) as the dial on our television sets. The voices of the stars penetrate our living rooms; their images flicker in our bedrooms. Authority itself gets converted into celebrity status. The president is a kind of national rock star; citizens are more likely to recognize the face of the prince of Wales or the president of France than, say, their own first cousins once removed or, perhaps, their next-door neighbors in an apartment complex. Celebrity culture gives rise to what we might call the public-opinion state: a polity where spin doctors are constantly taking the public pulse. Image, short-term popularity, and communication skills become of sublime importance to politics.

Fourth, the ubiquitous camera creates the need for boundaries—for protection of the self against ultimate intrusions. Celebrities may be as familiar to us as family, but they also feel the need to hire bodyguards and hide themselves behind iron fences and burglar alarms. A horizontal, celebrity society gives birth to the concept of privacy; for the first time in history perhaps, there is serious discussion of a right of privacy. People worry about, and debate, ways to protect and preserve zones of intimacy and seclusion in a world with satellite eyes. Privacy is a major problem for big and small people alike.

Finally, in this chapter, I discuss how pervasive these phenomena are. Are they mostly American or the product of American influence? Are they exclusively Western, and thus a poor fit in Asia, Africa, and other parts of the world? Or are they (as I think) *modern* rather than Western. If I am correct, then the real differences between, say, societies in Japan and Spain are less than they seem. They are like dialects of a common language rather than totally foreign tongues.

I take up each of these themes now in turn.

Change and More Change

One of the most obvious things about the world we live in is the sheer speed of change. Our world is not the same as the world of our grandparents, or even the world of our parents. Theirs seems a quaint, antique, and slow-motion existence. Today, the ground is constantly shifting underfoot. There is no fixity; nothing stays the same.

Change is cumulative. The further back we go in time, the less we recognize the landscape and the more exotic and foreign life seems. Think of a medieval or ancient city—Rome or Nineveh, for example—cities without cars, skyscrapers, television antennae, airports. The social landscape was equally foreign—maybe more so. How many of us would feel at home in the Middle Ages—in what William Manchester has called a "world lit only by fire?"[5] If we were projected backward in time, at least our sense of strangeness would be cushioned by what we learned in school about history. But an ancient Roman or a Chinese of the age of Confucius who slipped through a time warp into New York or Beijing today would be utterly baffled. Perhaps this would be almost as true of Thomas Jefferson or Catherine the Great.

Compared to older, traditional societies, we live in a period where change is constant, unremitting, and the pace of change seems to be accelerating. Of course, other societies—ancient kingdoms or feudal states or the societies of "primitive" tribes—were not really completely static and tradition-bound; they only *seem* that way, to us and perhaps to them as well. No society is or can be truly changeless, however; it is simply a question of degree. The Old World suffered through wars, plagues, and vast nomadic movements. But these events took place within a mind-set, a mental framework, of greater fixity and stability than would be true today.

It would be too pat, perhaps, to say that modern people, men and women, expect the unexpected. But they certainly expect, or are inured to, constant change. People's ideas or perceptions of what is changing, and how it changes, and the speed of change, can be seriously distorted; change can even be, at times, a figment of the imagination. Most of us are like passengers on a ship at sea, in the middle of a raging storm; we see a little bit behind and a little bit sideways or ahead, but we cannot grasp the total dimensions of the storm, or of the ocean itself. Each of us experiences only a small part of reality. Another part of reality we read about or watch on television. Unquestionably, people sense constant movement, change, alteration, and "progress." Even clothes are supposed to change from year to year: there is this year's fashion, and last year's fashion, and the fashions of the year before.[6]

Then there is the idea of "news," that is, of something novel happening every day, something worth reporting. Millions of people wake up in the morning and watch the news on television; they may also listen to radio news throughout the day and later catch the evening television news. It would be unthinkable to read in the newspapers or to hear on television that "nothing much happened today." There is always news, always something going on, always change. Some days bring major headlines; other days are quieter. But there is never *no* news: the message we get every day is that things are never exactly the same.

Many of the changes in life are not man-made: floods, earthquakes, droughts, hurricanes, forest fires, and other natural disasters. But all these do have a human dimension: they affect some community, some country, some wedge of the economic system. And they bring about or imply a demand on government (or somebody) to *do* something—provide disaster relief, help in the rebuilding process, or improve regulations—*something*. This is, in part, because we conceive of change as largely under human control. The average citizen, who has no idea how (for example) a refrigerator works, still feels that scientists, if they worked hard enough, could cure AIDS or the common cold, or get electric power out of turnip juice, or send a satellite zooming off to Pluto.

The average citizen, too, who may have trouble balancing a checkbook, may also feel that economists, and other mysterious persons working on the payroll of the government, should be able to do something about unemployment, the adverse balance of trade, high rents, or the price of cheese. Or, for that matter, crime rates or sex discrimination. A world of rapid change is a world of high expectations—public and private. This is why every government or regime, no matter how conservative, is supposed to have an agenda, a scheme for reforming the world. It is supposed to improve the public business. It is supposed to fix the economy and tinker with the law. Doing nothing is not a conceivable option. Some of us might think of this or that public program as a step backward; but this is only a metaphor. There is no going backward. There is only one direction to go, and that is full steam ahead into the future. To govern at all is to commit oneself to change.[7]

The Global Culture

The new technology—especially technology that lets us communicate with each other—has incredible power and immediacy. Of course, it is not easy to measure the effect of television or E-mail. But whatever the effect is, it is clearly global in scale. A single world culture—the culture of modernity—has sprung into existence, and technology is largely responsible, first, for creating it and, second, for spreading it wherever its long arm can reach. Nowadays, that means absolutely everywhere.

This culture has not, however, totally displaced the older print culture or the even older forms of narrative and learning. Books and magazines are still hanging on. Nor has television gotten rid of local cultures—human differences remain and will remain. The Irish are not the same as the Chileans or Japanese. But the culture of modernity has modified all existing ways of life; it coexists with all of them, and none have been able to resist its influence. What is distinctively Irish or Japanese or Chilean is distinctively *modern* Irish or Japanese or Chilean. The global culture "is what gives the local culture its medium, its audience, and its aspirations."[8]

What does this global culture consist of? Very striking is the dominance of *popular* culture. All over the world, there is a shared interest in professional sports; in rock and roll and other forms of contemporary music; in ways of eating and dressing, and in things to eat and wear. The audience for the Olympic games or for the World Cup in soccer can run into the billions. I hardly need mention that in the days before television, no such vast audience was possible. There was radio, of course, for a few decades, but radio, for all its power, never had the vividness and strength of television images. And it was local. Before the age of satellites, short-wave radio was feeble and squawky and hardly made a dent on the world.

Television and movies, however, changed the type, the scope, and the scale of entertainment. These really do replace the local experience in the realm of information and fun. On television, entertainment can come from far away, and it can resonate all over the world. A popular singer can be popular wherever there are antennae. Michael Jackson or Elvis Presley become familiar names and voices in India or Venezuela. Pop music respects no borders. Meanwhile, Russians can watch soap operas made in Brazil.[9] There is no practical limit to the number of people who can watch a television show—especially if it is dubbed and subtitled and transmitted around the world. At the same time, nearly everybody seems to be watching the same movies. And they are, it so happens, mostly American—and usually fast, explosive, and macho. What is clear, though, is that entertainment has become much more global and much more horizontal.

In short, technology has more and more turned the world into a single, linked system of culture. Local cultures never leave the stage entirely, but they have to share it with the common culture of pop music, movies, and television. TV, in particular, spreads the common culture to the far corners of the world; it is a kind of global pandemic, but it spreads at a speed that makes the old plagues and pandemics unbearably slow.

World culture is primarily a culture of leisure and entertainment: it is soccer, movies, rock and roll. It is also a culture of fast food: McDonald's, Kentucky Fried Chicken, or pizza. There is an astonishing uniformity of clothing worldwide, especially among young people. Fashion is notoriously fickle and hard to reduce to a science; but clothing is not randomly chosen. There is always an underlying message in the way people dress. Take, for example, blue jeans: once they were humble work clothes; now they are a symbol of youth, informality, and American values. The clothes people wear today express comfort, casual freedom, leisure, and youth. They are universal—the very opposite of native dress. They are emblems of choice. They have become the official costume of a horizontal society.

There is a lot to deplore in global mass culture, if we feel in the mood to deplore: vulgarity, mindlessness, empty conformity, sometimes sheer ugliness. We should remember, however, that this culture is a mark of relative affluence. People close to the edge of starvation do not play video games; they squat in their huts over a bowl of rice or a handful of grain, not over a bottle of Coca-Cola and a pizza. We live in a world where, in a large club of countries, an enormous middle-class mass has come into being. Yet even in countries mired in desperate poverty—and the poor, after all, still number in the billions—mass culture finds a way to reach much of the population. This mass culture—global, immediate, accessible, buoyant, with shared heroes, models, and goals—is immensely intoxicating. Ayatollahs fulminate against it; dictators censor it; mandarins try to slam the door on it. Yet this culture, like an odorless, colorless gas, manages to seep through every screen or barrier put up against it. No Great Wall can keep out these northern barbarians.

In some ways, the worldwide craze for professional sports represents both the local and the global. There is nothing quite so tribal, for example, as the World Cup matches. Fans go wild over their teams: whether Brazil or Italy wins or loses can set off riots or celebrations and affect political and economic life. The team embodies the very soul of the country; the games are ritualized war, without the buckets of blood. Yet the sport is truly global. The whole world gets to watch it on TV. A single sports culture binds all the listeners. In addition, there is a single hierarchy of authority: the rules of the game are the same all over the world. Audience and players know the same regulations and conventions. They "understand their application in the same way." In a sense, then, spectators at the games, and the audience of millions watching on television, "have come to share a common language."[10] The sports world is a portable, transnational, and profoundly horizontal culture.

High culture, too, has shown its power to encircle the globe. Orchestras in Tokyo play Bach and Mahler; Korean violinists are as much at home in the classical repertory as their colleagues in London and Prague; museums in the United States eagerly build collections of Japanese and African art. On a more visceral level, you can find sushi bars and Indian restaurants in Paris and London,[11] " 'Mexican' cantinas in Copenhagen, 'Italian' trattorias in Amsterdam . . . and 'Spanish' tapas bars in Berlin."[12] Somewhat more subtly, there is also a convergence in governmental cultures—in politics and modes of campaigning; these too have been "Americanized." This is true of systems of law and legal cultures.[13]

This convergence, of course, is most obvious in countries that are more or less democratic. And, once again, we can point a finger at TV as the power that pulls these political traditions together. All politicians have to reach their voters, and the voters are sitting at home in semidarkness, watching the tube. Television is both vivid and expensive; and the medium definitely affects the message. In the legal realm, the global economy is a world of transnational deals and deal makers. The lawyers and businesspeople who are part of this world have developed or learned a common culture. Otherwise, they would find it hard even to talk to each other. But this common culture puts pressure on the legal order, which would otherwise be quite parochial.[14]

The players in the world of international trade are genuine jet-setters: their marketplace is the whole world. These players are multinational corporations and transnational law firms with a base in New York or London and branches in every continent. These are elites who develop a strong, co-hesive horizontal culture. They tend to speak the same language (usually English) and, like soccer fans, abide by the same rules and conventions, even though their aims and habits may remain intensely local. The global village is a reality both at the top, among these legal and economic jet-set-ters, and at the bottom, at the level of fans of basketball, rock and roll, Dis-neyland, and *Jurassic Park*.

When we say that the main global culture is a mass culture, we must be careful not to confuse two meanings of the word *mass*: mass refers to or-dinary citizens but can also imply a large group of people physically as-sembled in one place. Mass culture in the first sense does not necessarily imply mass culture in the second sense. Of course, popular rock groups and soccer teams can draw tens of thousands of screaming fans into the world's biggest stadiums. But mass culture is in some senses lonely and individu-alistic. The reasons for this can be summed up, as usual, in a single word: television. More and more, entertainment is about observing and absorb-ing, not about participation. It is a matter of millions of atomized individ-uals, each on a solitary couch, clutching a solitary beer, with the set turned on and the zoom lenses beamed at the singers or players or stars.

What does this kind of isolation do to a society? Robert Putnam, for one, sees a drastic decline in the United States of what he calls "social cap-ital." He defines this to mean "features of social organization, such as trust, norms, and networks, that can improve the efficiency of society by facili-tating coordinating actions."[15] According to Putnam, membership in all sorts of social and leisure-time groups has declined. People are "bowling alone"—that is, they are no longer joining leagues, clubs, and associations the way they used to do. Presumably, this atomization sends ripples up and down the river of social life. Putnam is not sure what has caused the decline in social capital; but he is tempted to pin the blame on television, for the reasons we have already mentioned: television is profoundly individualiz-ing, profoundly antigroup.[16]

Putnam's article on "bowling alone" concerned the United States, but Putnam has done extensive research on social capital in Italy as well. If there is, in fact, a decline in social capital, and if television is to blame, then such a decline must be taking place everywhere in the Western world, if not globally. Putnam's facts and figures can be (and have been) questioned; but I feel he has nonetheless put his finger on a real phenomenon. Whether it is a problem—a source of social malaise—is another story.

What Putnam calls the decline of social capital is clearly connected to the horizontal society. To be sure, people still form attachments; they still join clubs, leagues, organizations, and informal networks. But many or most of these are "groups" in a very different sense. In a bowling league, people meet each other face-to-face. It is a *physical* community. In a horizontal society, there is a proliferation of virtual communities. People communicate less through word of mouth than through other means. Many lobbies, interest groups, and associations gain their power through mass memberships; but the "members" are mostly people who fill out a form and mail in a check in a stamped, self-addressed envelope. The National Rifle Association, the American Association of Retired Persons, and many other pressure groups, including most environmental organizations, are horizontal entities.

Of course, interest groups and pressure groups existed long before the invention of television. America has apparently always been a nation of joiners. As de Tocqueville pointed out in the nineteenth century, Americans "of all ages, all stations in life . . . are forever forming associations"; these were "of a thousand different types—religious, moral, serious, futile, very general and very limited, immensely large and very minute."[17] At the time de Tocqueville wrote, America was already at least quasi-horizontal; one expects interest-group politics in a mobile society with free elections. The new ways to communicate simply make it easier to put associations together. The latest toys—E-mail and the Internet—will only accentuate the trend. Virtual groups multiply like rabbits. Whatever "cyberspace" may mean, and wherever it is (in a sense it is everywhere and nowhere), it constitutes a forum where people talk to each other across great distances, in other words, horizontally. They can get to know (or virtually know) other people, whether in Montana or Turkey or Saigon, who share their interests, their doctrines, and their goals. The process is wonderful for people with hobbies—owners of pet salamanders who want to reach other people with pet salamanders. But cyberspace is also a powerful tool of politics, a simple, costless way of reaching like-minded people.

The Celebrity Culture

Popular culture is also celebrity culture. At the core, it revolves around celebrities. Some are local figures who are unknown outside Russia or Japan or the United States. But an increasing number are truly global personalities, people known in the most remote village as well as in the great urban centers. Many American rock stars are as famous abroad as they are at home. Two cities in Germany both claim to be the second home of Elvis Presley (he served in the army in Germany); one of the towns, Bad Nauheim, has erected a black marble monument to its hero. The "Elvis Association of Germany, Austria and Switzerland" proudly claims to be "the largest Elvis fan club in the world outside of the United States."[18] Movie and TV stars and a number of sports heroes, many of them American, are also known throughout the so-called civilized world. For whatever reason, the United States seems to be particularly good at creating, and marketing, trash with a global appeal.

Celebrity culture, as we will argue, is more than a matter of idolizing popular singers, soccer players, and movie stars; it affects authority and the structure of politics itself. In this day and age, presidents and prime ministers are or become celebrities themselves; celebrity worship, its habits, and its frame of mind have penetrated deeply into the marrow of public life. In Putnam's world of declining social capital, men and women focus less on their immediate surroundings, their face-to-face groups, and more on horizontal groups; they focus also on the physically distant figures they see on TV—in other words, on celebrities.[19]

What is a celebrity? A celebrity is, of course, someone who is famous, but not everyone who is famous is a celebrity. According to one (cynical?) definition, a celebrity is someone who is famous for being famous—who is "well-known for his well-knownness," a "human pseudo-event."[20] The essence of celebrity is "high visibility." Ordinary people—that is, non-celebrities—are basically invisible. They have a small network of people who know them—family, friends, people at work; and that is that. When they walk on the street, stroll in the park, or drive down the highway, nobody pays attention, no heads turn, no one takes their picture. The celebrity, however, is dazzlingly visible, a shooting star flashing across the sky. The celebrity transforms every occasion; she sets off vibrations in any room or locale she enters. The celebrity commands attention. A celebrity is defined as a person "whose name has attention-getting, interest-riveting, profit-generating value."[21]

This description is incomplete, but it makes an important point. The difference between fame and celebrity is clear-cut. There are famous people who are not highly visible: they are never in the newspapers, never in the gossip columns, never on talk shows. They are never *seen*; they project no familiar images; they have no fan magazines and are never written up in *People.* No one in Japan is better known than the emperor, yet the emperor of Japan is not a true celebrity. He is (or was) distant, mysterious, godlike, unseen.[22] The present queen of England, on the other hand, is a celebrity of the first order. Her face is familiar to all—it appears on millions of coins and postage stamps—and her picture is everywhere. Her voice is familiar, too;[23] in fact, everything she does, every move, every occasion, finds its way into the media. I hardly need add that the members of her family are even more famous. Tabloids and celebrity magazines all over the world feed hungrily on news about the goings-on of Prince Charles and the rest of the royal crew. The celebrity of celebrities was Diana, princess of Wales; her death touched the hearts of millions of people precisely because they felt they knew her, that she was almost a member of their family, even though she was rich and royal and lived behind closed doors in a palace.

The English sovereign, in fact, was once a distant and remote presence. Henry VIII never appeared on TV. Most of his subjects never laid eyes on him. Authority for the ordinary peasant was far-off and magical. Its nature was reflected in popular literature and mythology. The princes and princesses of fairy tales were not drawn from the stuff of daily life; they were miraculous, otherworldly. The touch of the king cured scrofula. Cinderella could be transformed into a princess, but only through magic. A true princess was different in kind from the ordinary run of humanity.

The princes and princesses of the late twentieth century continue to live fairy-tale lives (the cliché lingers on), but the tales told about them are dramatically different. Instead of magic coaches, they drive expensive cars—which, of course, any of us could drive, provided we had the money. The lives of royalty, and of the stars, illustrate a heightened form of the everyday—the proverbial "life styles of the rich and famous" of television and magazines. The vast audience has the illusion of a peep show: what goes on behind the scenes is revealed before their very eyes. Instead of fairy tales, we have tabloids and soap operas (including the "telenovelas" of Spanish-language television), in which the characters are rich but ordinary, leading lives drenched in romance and scandal yet almost obsessively mundane.

Indeed, a celebrity is never remote and mysterious—the essence of celebrity status *is* familiarity. This is why the age of television is also par excellence the age of the celebrity. A celebrity is not the Wizard of Oz behind a screen; a celebrity is someone who can be watched, whose face can be instantly recognized, someone who is as close as the nearest TV set.[24]

Of course, this familiarity is, for the most part, a deception, an optical illusion. People on the street do not really know the queen of England, and they did not really know the princess of Wales; they do not really know the president of the United States, his wife, his daughter, and his pets, any more than they know the real life of rock stars and basketball players. They think they know these people because they watch them walk, talk, and express themselves; because they see the insides of their houses, what they wear, and how they live. It is precisely the illusion of familiarity—the images, the show, the projection on public screens—that makes a celebrity what she is. Celebrities are, to be sure, glittering and magical; they have an aura; talent or luck or tragedy or chance has anointed them. Yet at the base, there is something amazingly ordinary about them.

The emperor of Japan was a god until he renounced his godhood after World War II. The queen of England is not a god and never was; instead, she is an ordinary person—a hausfrau (though a very rich one, to be sure, and with royal blood), a mother of four, and a lover of horses and dogs. But she happened to be the oldest daughter of a king of England who had no sons, and because of this accident of fate she became queen of England when her father died. The greats of sport and popular music are also, in most regards, completely mundane, just like you and me—except, of course, for the way they twang a guitar, shoot baskets, hit a ball, or sing a song. All of these are perfectly ordinary activities. The average person can easily picture himself in their position; and, in fact, most people have tried their hand at some of these popular skills.

Great scientists and great industrialists, however, are usually not celebrities, and partly because their work *is* remote and hard to understand. There are a few exceptions. Albert Einstein, in his day, was a deviant case—famous in part because his work *was* so remote and obscure. His theories were said to be so complex that only a handful of geniuses could figure them out. Still, much of the Einstein folklore stressed how much he was like everybody else—for example, he played the fiddle, got married, produced children. In addition, people loved the idea that this genius did badly at school.[25] He was, in short, an ordinary person with one freakish talent. That, indeed, is another form of celebrity: an ordinary human being who has been born with two heads, has given birth to quintuplets, or has won a twenty-million-dollar lottery. The one thing a celebrity is *not,* however, is austere, private, far-off, godlike, or arcane.

At least celebrities who play basketball or singers are supposed to have talent. But many celebrities have no obvious gift—talk show hosts, for example, who make millions of dollars and are among the most famous people in the United States. Others have tiny talents, blown up out of all proportion by gurus of public relations and marketing. Still others, as we have seen, become celebrities by accidents of fate.

Criminals can be celebrities in their own right: if all else fails, one can become a celebrity by committing some unspeakable crime.[26] Whatever appears on TV in prime time is, after all, potentially the stuff of celebrity. In the notorious trial of O. J. Simpson (1994–95), everybody involved in any way with the case turned into a star, indeed, a celebrity among celebrities. The judge, Lance Ito, was surely better known than any member of the Supreme Court of the United States (who are themselves minor celebrities). Obscure forensic technicians, people who were walking their dogs at the right time of night, a limousine driver, a maid at a neighbor's house—all these bit players and spear carriers of the Simpson trial became famous beyond their wildest dreams. Indeed, anyone who plays a part in a sensational trial is likely to end up at least a transient celebrity.

It is also possible to manufacture a celebrity out of whole cloth, just by spending enough money on publicity. Celebrity feeds on itself. When this spiraling process occurs, it becomes literally true that a celebrity is a person who is famous for being famous. The accidentally famous, like the witnesses in the Simpson case, may write books, appear on talk shows, and, in so doing, attract even greater public attention. This type of celebrity status, of course, is brittle and evanescent.

The true celebrity, however, embodies a paradox. She is different, yet she is just like us. Jib Fowles, in his study of American stars, tells a story about Mae West, a famous (or, more accurately, notorious) movie star during Hollywood's glory days. During an interview in a restaurant, a man came up to West and "interrupted and spoke to her familiarly"; when the man left, the interviewer asked "who he was and was told she had no idea. 'He sounded as if he knew you,' the interviewer persisted. 'They all do, dear,' she responded."[27]

This story captures the essence of celebrity status: the sense of familiarity that comes from seeing the face and hearing the voice, from feeling as if one could reach out to the screen and actually touch the star. Of course, celebrities, often enough, *make* this sense of the familiar come about, through publicity and public relations gimmicks. The public is bombarded with information about the lives of the rich and the famous. Much of this "information" is a tissue of lies, but it is vivid and concrete. The familiarity, oddly enough, is part of the magic. The celebrity is knowable, yet just beyond our reach. The look, the sound, the habits, the way of life: we *know* them intimately. We watch these personalities as they come and go; we can buy a list of their addresses and gawk at the iron gates around their mansions. Stars, then, are both familiar and inaccessible, at once.

The familiarity breeds a sense of entitlement: we have a right to know celebrities and a right to gain access to their lives. Candidates for president are supposed to reveal everything—their income tax returns, their private lives, even what underwear they wear. Stars have no apparent right to privacy at all. Thousands of print pages and thousands of images, each week, purport to tell us everything we want to know, and more, about their most intimate secrets. The zoom lens and the loose tongues of friends and employees make it possible to peek into their very bedrooms. In the United

States—perhaps the most advanced case of celebrity culture—the greedy stare of the television camera has even invaded the criminal courtroom, reaching a kind of hysterical climax in the O. J. Simpson trial.[28]

At one time, the Supreme Court was quite dubious about letting TV invade the halls of justice. In 1965, the court reversed the conviction of Billie Sol Estes, a notorious swindler, because his trial had become a media carnival—part of it was even carried live on radio and TV.[29] In the Simpson case, tried during a less bashful era, the camera was under no such inhibitions. Millions of people absorbed "gavel to gavel" coverage—until boredom set in. In fact, the TV audience saw more than the jury did. The jury was censored and sequestered. At critical times the jurors were shooed out of the room, like children, while the lawyers wrangled with each other. The cameras, of course, kept right on rolling.[30]

Because celebrity status is so personal, it is also infectious. It rubs off on those around it. There are second-hand celebrities and even third-hand celebrities. Anybody who knows a celebrity intimately—the president's first cousin, Princess Diana's nanny, former dates of Elvis Presley, or hairdressers, dentists, or plumbers to the stars—becomes a satellite celebrity. Such people bask in reflected glory. Once again, it would be hard to find a clearer example than the O. J. Simpson case. According to one report, Donna Shalala, Secretary of Health and Human Services under President Clinton and one of the most powerful women in the country, finding herself at a party attended by Kato Kaelin, asked him for his autograph. And who was he? A Hollywood wanna-be whose sole distinction was that he lived at the Simpson place and was around on the fateful night of the murder, when he heard a strange thumping noise. That thump was enough to make him an object of frantic media coverage.[31]

Since celebrity status is infectious, like the flu, fans collect autographs, hang out at the stage door, cluster at the entrance to the hotels, wait outside the church at celebrity weddings, file past the body at celebrity funerals, and heap flowers on celebrity graves. The public is eager to express a kind of solidarity; they want to feel part of the family of stars, so to speak. They aim to catch a spark or two of the magic fire that celebrities emit all around themselves—sometimes even after death. When the estate of Jacqueline Onassis went up for auction in April 1996, a wild buying frenzy ensued. Bidders paid hundreds of thousands of dollars for worthless gew-gaws—fake pearls, ashtrays, golf clubs—merely, one supposes, because they were touched by the hand of this celebrity of celebrities.[32] And the death of Diana, princess of Wales—*the* celebrity event of 1997—touched off a volcanic eruption of mourning and grief.

The Simpson case, which rocketed into the headlines in 1994, repre-sents the celebrity culture at its highest (or perhaps its lowest) form. Simp-son was a star athlete, familiar to millions for that reason and also because of TV commercials and movie roles. He may have been the greatest show-business figure ever charged with murder; the comedian Fatty Arbuckle, charged with killing a girl in 1921, is a distant runner-up.[33] In an atmos-phere of unbelievable ballyhoo, Simpson went on trial for the murder of his wife, Nicole, and a friend of his wife's, Ronald Goldman. The prosecu-tion had what seemed to be a powerful case, complete with blood and DNA; yet many people (especially black Americans) refused to believe Simpson could possibly be guilty. He was, after all, a "hall of famer"—a great celebrity, in short. It was simply too discordant with his image to think of him as a double murderer. Perhaps some people simply didn't care; a celebrity like O. J. Simpson was, in some sense, above the law. Although a mountain of evidence seemed to point to Simpson's guilt, the jury ac-quitted him with almost flippant speed.[34]

The Simpson case also illustrates something quite remarkable about celebrities. They are, in an important sense, immune from moral judg-ment. Mike Tyson, heavyweight champion of the world, served three years in prison for rape. When he emerged, blinking in the daylight (so to speak), he was just as much a celebrity as before—perhaps more so, since he now had two strings to his celebrity bow. He was welcomed in grand style by two thousand people in Harlem and lionized after donating $1 million to charity.[35] Tyson later got into trouble again, when he bit the ear of a boxer during a championship match; but he shows signs of bouncing back from this scandal as well. Convicted felons are shunned and despised in polite society; but a Mike Tyson—a celebrity who is, after all, a convicted felon—does not seem to suffer this fate. After all, some people become celebrities precisely because they have been accused of some truly outrageous crime—Amy Fisher, the high school girl who shot her lover's wife; or the Menendez brothers, who did away with their parents; or the "Mayflower Madam," the blue blood who ran a call-girl business. O. J. Simpson has, in fact, been shunned (to a degree), but in general, celebrity status is incredibly powerful. It is like the light of a thousand suns; millions of people seem ready to suspend their sense of right and wrong in the presence of these blazing luminaries.

What brought celebrity culture into existence? This is not an easy question to answer, at least with any degree of precision. But it is obvious that the role of the media is crucial. Without mass media, especially TV, celebrity culture would wither and die. The story starts, of course, with the print media; in some ways, they promoted celebrity culture in a blatant and flagrant way. It is enough to mention fan magazines devoted to movie stars.[36] Yet the most egregious celebrities come from the world of film and TV, with generous additions from sports and popular music. The hunger for news about celebrities, too, is a market force of considerable importance. People will buy books and magazines and watch programs about celebrities; celebrity status has an obvious market value. Again, the Simpson trial represented some kind of climax: participants, witnesses, lawyers, ex-jurors (not to mention the defendant), all busied themselves getting their thoughts and their flashing insights into print. If anything topped it, it was the death of Princess Diana, which produced whole shelves of books devoted to her short, tragic life.

The media are both conduit and cause. They did not create this form of culture by themselves; rather, their work reacted chemically, so to speak, with deeper social forces. A mature horizontal society is inconceivable without the media; it depends on the media, but it takes on a life of its own. And a horizontal society is one in which the individual occupies the center of social meaning; the individual is the focus of attention—not the group, not the family, not traditional authority, not the state. People choose to attach themselves to celebrities; this is not an order from above. These attachments are fickle, shifting, and intensely mobile. Moreover, because the celebrity, in a vital sense, is a person who is not essentially different from the ordinary person (in all aspects but that one special ingredient), the ordinary person can become a celebrity, or dream of it. A celebrity society is a society of mobility. The boy from the ghetto can earn millions as a basketball player. The kid next door can become a rap star or a talk-show host. The girl down the block can become another Madonna or a Hollywood star. Celebrities can communicate easily with ordinary people. They do not speak an arcane, elitist language. This is because they *are* the ordinary person. Or were, when they were children, or when they are at home, relaxing at Balmoral or in their mansions. And, indeed, anybody can win the lottery or become an involuntary celebrity, through some accident of fate. Part of modern life, as we saw, is change, and expectation of change. Novelty is routine. Fixity has vanished. Lightning can always strike. Anything can happen. Anything does.

Worship of celebrities is thus deeply rooted in modern culture and is tightly bound to the structure of authority in society; it has, in turn, an obvious impact on the structure of authority. To begin with, celebrities have displaced other role models. When people (especially young people) adopt idols today, these idols come from the world of the celebrities rather than from the world of traditional authority. At least this is so in Western societies. In one study, American teenagers, in 1986, were asked who they admired the most. Out of the top ten names, no less than nine were "stars" or celebrities—movie and TV figures, for the most part. One political figure made the list of the top ten—that was President Ronald Reagan. And he himself was a former movie star.[37] No religious leader, no business leader, no scientist or scholar, made the list.[38]

Most world leaders are not movie stars, of course. But in fact, in the modern world, politicians start to look more and more like ordinary celebrities, and political authority and the charisma of the stars begin to overlap. A campaign for president or prime minister looks a lot like show business, or the selling of show business, with its live appearances and TV interviews, its spot advertisements on TV, its market research and focus groups. When Bill Clinton campaigned for the American presidency in 1992, there was "little to distinguish" his appearance in San Francisco's Mission District "from a movie premiere," as one author put it. The "production setting in which political figures come to public attention mimics, and sometimes borrows techniques directly from, entertainment celebrity."[39]

How could it be otherwise? In modern Western societies, presidents, prime ministers, mayors, governors, and major political figures in general have all turned into celebrities. This was a gradual process. The media make all the difference. Few Americans ever saw George Washington in person or heard his voice. Franklin D. Roosevelt was one of the first true celebrity presidents—he made masterful use of radio, for example. Before the invention of radio, there was no way for the president to speak to the country. Once TV entered the picture, all presidents became celebrities. John F. Kennedy was an outstanding example of the new genre. The Kennedy era was also a television era; the "major events" in American history were "inextricably intertwined" with their coverage on TV.[40]

Kennedy was a striking figure: young, handsome, telegenic. But even the most dreary presidents since Kennedy have been celebrities. World leaders today are not and cannot be distant, remote, mysterious, or charismatic in the traditional sense. They seem as close as the nearest TV set. The average American—and the average citizen of a Western country—devours hours of TV every day. This average watcher literally sees the president, king, queen, prime minister every day, and perhaps the spouses, children, cousins, friends as well—even the president's cat. The American audience can observe what the president is wearing, how he does his hair, the way he walks and talks. The audience can hear the sound of his voice, his accent, his patterns of speech. In magazines and newspapers, they can absorb dozens of details about the lives of their leaders; these leaders become so familiar that they are known as "Bill" or "Maggie" or "Boris." The citizen is sure she really knows what they are like, whether they are good characters or bad. They speak to us directly—through the media, of course. In their public appearances, "intimacy is offered and identification fostered through accounts of personal traumas or idiosyncrasies or stories."[41]

The process seems to break down the barriers between "traditionally onstage and traditionally backstage activities," as Joshua Meyrowitz has pointed out; or, to put it another way, it blurs the roles that "rely heavily on mystification and on an aura of greatness." The media "reveal too much and too often for traditional notions of political leadership to prevail." The eye of TV "invades politicians' personal spheres"; it "watches them sweat. . . . It coolly records them as they succumb to emotions." The camera "minimizes the distance between audience and performer." The political leaders are "stripped of their aura" and "brought closer to the level of the average person."[42] This is the case with every celebrity—indeed, it is the very definition of a celebrity; and the politician, in our day and age, is only one celebrity among many.

Politics creates enemies as well as fans. It personalizes; and it can do so in either direction. There were, after all, plenty of men and women who resisted the irresistible charm of Ronald Reagan. And the celebrity status of political people does not mean that *government* is popular. Government is an abstraction, a process; and the right wing in many countries has been able to demonize it, to blacken its reputation, quite apart from the particular people who staff it and run it. Trust in *government* seems to be at a historic low.[43] This is true for the United States, and perhaps for other countries as well.

There are many reasons for this decline in trust. I want to mention one. In a horizontal society, politics and policies become radically disjointed. Attachment is toward the leader, not toward what he stands for; he stands (in a way) for nothing but himself, his personality, his picture on the screen. It then becomes possible (as has been more and more the case) to run for office by running against politics and politicians: politicians are bad, but I, your candidate, am good. I am different; I am an outsider; you can trust me. The administration, that giant workhorse, that machine of a million gears and levers, recedes into the background, and all that is seen is a smiling and jovial face on the television screen.

Some—and perhaps a lot—of the cynicism about government is, to be sure, pretty amply justified. People on the fringe carry this mistrust to a lunatic extreme. The United States may have a particularly rich crop of these loose screws: men (and a few women) who take their ideas of liberty, rights, and individual autonomy smack up to the point of madness—and then rush past it. They insist on their guns, their absolute right to do whatever they want with what they think they own: to reject the income tax and everything else about government; to rant about Jews, blacks, and the United Nations; to glorify a kind of Rambo image of the macho male and dream of a white utopia in Idaho or the like. But even these people have their leaders and their horizontal groups; they are as much a product of the media society as the society whose rot and decay they claim to detest. And even when they gather in communes, fortresses, and intimate barricaded camps, they reflect the media-drenched culture that allowed all these rolling stones and half-mad zealots, drawn from all parts of the country, to talk, meet, and cluster into paranoid groups.

This is one form of the camp of rejections. Others, at the opposite extreme, become so entranced and engulfed by celebrities that they lose all sense of mental balance. They become obsessive groupies or even stalkers of the stars. For some of them, the screen has become a kind of two-way mirror; reality and illusion blur together. It is as if their celebrities had walked off the screen and into their brains; virtual reality becomes more real than reality itself.

Of course, trends and tendencies are rarely if ever universal. There are always countertrends and countertendencies, always exceptions to the rules. Some people are immune to celebrity worship. Many people are immune to popular culture. There are pockets of resistance, islands in the ocean of modernity: some scholars and intellectuals, for example, along with the Amish, Christian fundamentalists, cloistered nuns, and others who have opted out of the consumer and infotainment society.

Still, all in all, few people can resist the force of the modern media and the blandishments of the horizontal society. Some political leaders play the game eagerly; some are reluctant. But all prime ministers, mayors, presidents, and other politicians, whether they like it or not, are part of the world of celebrity authority. Sovereigns, religious and secular, have traveled the same road. Particularly striking has been the evolution of the Roman Catholic papacy. The pope was once distant and august; by tradition, he never left Rome. The current pope, John Paul II, is a genuine celebrity; he travels the world, holds press conferences, appears on TV. He is a master at publicity and the dark arts of public relations. Even the Dalai Lama, once a distant, god-like figure in the remote fastnesses of Tibet, is now a famous religious leader, well traveled, urbane, politically active, and—no disrespect intended—no novice in the art of getting his name in the paper and his message across.

Of course, there are celebrities and celebrities; a photo of the pope in his underwear would shock his public and would probably never get printed (at any rate, not so far), while a German tabloid made headlines out of a photo of the naked prince of Wales.[44] Obviously, it took a zoom lens and other technological marvels to give the public a chance to see the penis of a prince. That would have been impossible until recently; it would also have been unthinkable at, say, the turn of the century. Thus has humanity progressed.

The new emperor of Japan seems to be following, slowly, in the footsteps of the pope and the Dalai Lama, and abandoning the older traditions of his role. The emperor is no longer a god; he renounced that position at the end of the Second World War. But Emperor Hirohito remained for the most part invisible. The new emperor is another story. He wears ordinary Western clothing, and in June 1994, he and his wife traveled to the United States. The empress wore tennis shoes and pants at Rocky Mountain National Park (which "shocked the royal retinue"), and the pair mixed with common folk at various times and places. A sociologist called it part of the "transformation of a faceless role into a bourgeois monarchy"; the royal couple was "doing the mom-and-apple-pie thing" to make people feel good, to normalize the monarchy.[45]

If leaders become celebrities, and there is no particular difference between leaders and celebrities, then why not take the next logical step and make leaders out of celebrities? More and more, this seems to be happening. Nothing is more important in elections than name recognition. A Rockefeller can be successful in politics not only because he has money but also because Rockefeller is a household name. Ronald Reagan, who went from movie star to president, is an extreme, but not an isolated example. Melina Mercouri, a movie star, served in the cabinet of Greece. Worn-out Hollywood actors run for Congress. Clint Eastwood was elected the mayor of Carmel, California. Dennis Martinez, a Nicaraguan who struck it rich in American baseball, was so popular in his homeland that there were "calls for him to run for President" in the 1996 elections (the calls went unheeded).[46] Since one crucial point of a political campaign is to make the public familiar with the candidate—face, bearing, voice—the celebrity starts with a built-in advantage.

The celebrity cultulre is a culture of immediacy; at least it gives the illusion of immediacy. There seems to be no barrier between the star—or the leader—and the fan club, or indeed between the celebrity and the mass public. The miracle of technology, the ever-present eye of the camera, makes it possible to peep into the bedrooms of the rich and famous (and the powerful). Thus the celebrity culture is not hierarchical in any histori- cal sense; it is not mediated through chains of command. It is direct, in- stantaneous, and it operates on individuals in their individual roles: we watch TV as single, isolated humans. Of course, the fans can and do ag- glomerate; they form clubs, political parties, associations of every conceiv- able sort. But these groups are both horizontal and ad hoc.

In short, political authority flattens out in contemporary society. It be- comes more horizontal and less hierarchical and deferential. The public may worship celebrities, but people do not *defer* to them. They may wait in line for eight hours in the rain to shake hands or buy tickets, but they call their idols "Bill" and "Julie"; and old-fashioned bowing and scraping are definitely out. This is not just a way of saying that modern societies in the West tend to be democratic—they are parliamentary or presidential systems, with free elections and all the apparatus of a republican system, and an absence of traditional authorities. Democracy *is,* after all, compat- ible with a good deal of deference to authority; in the nineteenth century, voters often had the choice between two aristocrats, one conservative, one somewhat more liberal. It is still the case that British leaders, including left- wing leaders, tend to come out of the same elite background. And in many European countries, leaders are still expected to be (more or less) intellec- tual—a Ph.D. does not hurt.

The United States long ago began to reject this kind of elected elite. Washington and Jefferson were aristocrats, American style: they lived in mansions and owned gangs of slaves. But it soon became something of a vogue to have the common touch, to be born in a log cabin, like Lincoln. For modern American politicians, it is *essential* to be just plain folks; politi- cians cannot be (or seem to be) intellectuals. Their tastes, as one columnist put it, cannot "go much beyond pork rinds and Big Macs," and it would be fatal to like Mozart and Shakespeare, "as distinct from watching bas- ketball on TV or heading for the duck blind."[47] The president of the United States is rarely, if ever, seen at a symphony concert or an opera, but he throws out the first baseball of the season.

Americans have peculiar attitudes toward the life of the mind. There is a rampant strain of anti-intellectualism in the country, to put it bluntly. This cultural trait has many roots and facets; but surely one of them is the worship of celebrities, who are always heightened forms of the everyday.[48] Celebrity worship has led to a strange turn of the wheel in American politics, which seems, on the surface, to contradict the old Abe Lincoln myth. It is still essential not to be an egghead, but the log cabin has lost a lot of its luster. In fact, the rich are very in. Millionaires swarm all over the political scene, and the public seems to love them. It is not because they are aristocratic—self-made millionaires are just as good if not better than people who inherited their money. Aristocrats are acceptable, but only if they do not act aristocratically; to do so, to be an elitist, is political death. People say they trust rich politicians, because they are not in the game for the money, but essentially they love them because they are celebrities.[49] The name of the game is the name.

In the horizontal society, political leadership is based on image, on personality, on communication skills, much more than on actual policies or programs. Voters seem to respond less to candidates' ideas (if they know them at all), than to their personalities, how they project, what the public imagines they are really like. This one seems sincere; this one seems wooden or contrived; this one seems slick and deceptive. Personality trumps ideology for more and more voters in the modern world. Of course, policies still make a difference, but hordes of voters—and "swing" voters at that—seem to vote for candidates they trust, candidates who are "real leaders," or have a ring of truth to their vocal chords; and never mind the legislative agenda. This was one of the secrets of Ronald Reagan's popularity. Many of the positions he took were not really popular, but it hardly mattered. The public loved him. Politicians, aware of the facts of political life, react accordingly; they turn themselves over to their political handlers, to men and women who manufacture images the way plastic surgeons make noses. As a consequence, the media (especially TV) become even more dominant in political campaigns.

The result, in the horizontal society, is what we might call the public opinion state. This is a political system in which leadership *seems* to be entirely open and transparent, seems to be amazingly sensitive to what people think and want. In classic parliamentary systems, the public of course has a vital role—it *votes*. But in between elections, government traditionally has massive, almost unrestrained power, especially in a country with a two-party system (like England) and a firm majority. Naturally, governments have to pay attention to public opinion, insofar as they can sniff out what this consists of. But for much of the nineteenth century, and well into the twentieth, leaders were supposed to lead; they formed a kind of political aristocracy. In any event, it was hard to know what the voting public thought—at least not in any detail.

Here is another area in which technology has transformed the world. Today, leaders can explore public opinion instantaneously. Modern social science, and modern communications, have given us polling, focus groups, telephone surveys, and the like; data are tabulated and counted, miraculously fast, by computer, and then broken down, if one wishes, by age, race, sex, or religion, not to mention postal zone. Hence there is immediate information about what people think, or what they say they think. Some politicians become like human wind chimes, making tinkling noises as each puff of air from the polls pushes them this way or that.

In any event, in the public opinion state, the regime becomes utterly dependent on what it considers the whims and wishes of the public. It bends every muscle to read the public mind in advance; and it monitors reactions to its every crucial step, as soon as the step is taken. In short, it does nothing without at least *seeming* to respond to public desires and demands. Hence all the trial balloons, the leaks, the unattributed comments—devices to try to tease out a public reaction, to find out which way the wind blows without commitment or risk. But at the same time, regimes shamelessly manipulate public opinion through every trick of the trade: propaganda, public relations, media blitzes, outright lying. Thus both leaders and followers are, as it were, locked into a single reciprocal system. The media come to exercise enormous, crucial power, since they are the essential link between the governors and the governed. The leadership is helpless without the cooperation and connivance of the media. Nobody can run for office without scads of money to buy time on television, not to mention billboards and flyers: candidates engage in a desperate search for funds or for free publicity in the form of "news."[50]

Presidential politics in the United States is an egregious example of these trends, but the parliamentary systems of Europe seem to be traveling in the same direction. A British or French election campaign is not quite so bald an exercise in TV and show business as an American election, but the play of personalities is becoming more and more evident. Technically, voters in Great Britain and many other countries vote for a party, not for a prime minister, but increasingly the public really votes for a Margaret Thatcher or against her; or for or against Helmut Kohl. Opposition parties in European countries (and in the United States) also make use of the same wiles and tricks as the governing regimes. They may have less access to the media than the government parties, but it is not for want of trying.

The public in a celebrity government is all-powerful (in theory); yet it is also systematically cheated and misled. The public gets the illusion that it knows all and sees all; it is bombarded with information—perhaps it would be more accurate to say images of information. But the information is twisted and filtered and distorted. The public gets slogans, stock stories that are rich in rhetoric, cautionary tales, and parables pandering to the most common social prejudices. They get press releases masquerading as fact. All governments lie and conceal information, but they do it in characteristic ways. Dictatorships simply ignore the truth and censor the press. A modern democratic government, for example, does not and cannot do this—or at least cannot do it as well. Rather, it lies by pretending to be telling the truth; it suppresses its own suppressions. It does not always get away with it, however. The press, for example, has an interest in scandals and exposés; these can sell a lot of newspapers. If there are enough of these scandals and exposés, the public can turn cynical and mistrustful which it does, in many countries.

The Declining Significance of Class

Another consequence of celebrity culture—notable in the United States, perhaps less so elsewhere—is its effect on the politics of class. Franklin D. Roosevelt, a "traitor to his class," used to inveigh against "malefactors of great wealth." Politics in the Western countries, as the franchise spread, became strongly redistributive. No historical event of the past century is as important as the rise of the welfare state. In a country like Sweden or Great Britain, despite the strength of class divisions (or partly because of them?), labor parties rose to power, social programs spread the gospel of equality, and taxes on income and inheritances rose until they became nearly confiscatory. It became almost axiomatic in certain circles that the rich and powerful were enemies of the people. All over Europe there were openly Marxist or socialist parties committed to some form of class struggle. Socialism was itself a kind of backhanded tribute to the emerging horizontal society. In a traditional society, the very idea of a class, made up of workers and peasants, is unthinkable. Class solidarity presupposes not only mutuality of interest among members of a class but ways of spreading the word and of mobilizing.

But the late twentieth century is not a good time for socialist internationalism and the politics of the class struggle. Socialism is in full retreat. There are many reasons for this. For one thing, big business has learned to behave itself; it is much less blatant than it was in the nineteenth century. Government regulation and relentless criticism have tamed the robber-baron mentality, or driven it underground. Nineteenth-century labor law—if one can speak of it at all—basically let the boss do as he pleased; he could hire and fire at will; and courts and legislatures made sure that management had overwhelming power.[51] Comparatively speaking, workers in the richer industrial countries are fat, pampered, and sleek. The workers in Germany or Australia have cars, television sets, and some money in the bank; they have health benefits and paid vacations; they have rights to overtime pay and unemployment compensation. Most people in the first world think of themselves as middle class, and that includes factory workers, carpenters, secretaries, miners, and other people who, in the nineteenth century, lived hand to mouth, always teetering on the edge of destitution. Indeed, almost anybody with a decent job can enjoy some of the benefits of middle-class life. At least for now.

Rich economies, and a welfare state, put a damper on any inclination to back a socialist revolution. Why risk what you have for an elusive ideal? Besides, socialism has been tried in the Soviet Union and its satellites—hardly an inspiring role model. In fact, what these countries did model was ruthless tyranny, air pollution, and a sour and lifeless economy. In Western

Europe, in the period after the Second World War, taxes and welfare policies marched ahead and were genuinely popular—until they reached a
point where they became drags on the economy. Global competition put
a premium on lean and mean companies, on high productivity, on belt-
tightening. Meanwhile, the Soviet Union collapsed, and almost nobody
mourned. More and more people had second thoughts about a policy of
soaking the rich. Raw capitalism seemed the only way to go—the only
hope for protecting the standard of living. The class struggle was a luxury
people could no longer afford.

Thus, there is no more political gold in bashing the rich. For strong
economic (and ideological) reasons, the public seems to have taken a dramatic turn to the right in recent years. Cultural elements, it seems, figure
in this shift as well. The United States may be a particularly egregious example. Almost no one talks anymore about malefactors of great wealth.
Class consciousness presupposed class ideology. But no such ideology can
flourish in a rich consumer society. In such a society, there are no workers;
instead, there are consumers. There is "no class interest, only a global pop
culture."[52] Moreover, the very *image* of the rich has changed. Celebrities
are rich. Movie stars are rich. Baseball players are rich. Their magic aura
spreads over the whole of their (moneyed) class. Very rich people are
celebrities, and the public is in awe of celebrities. People eagerly follow the
"life styles of the rich and famous"; they find the glitter, the spending, the
conspicuous consumption, ineffably glamorous and seductive. People read
People and other celebrity vehicles; they read fan magazines and soak up information about the rich like sponges.

Nor does the hunger for celebrities seem to be solely an American
habit. In many Western countries, there are gossip magazines crammed
with pictures of the stars; and there are talk shows and other spigots of
celebrity information. Germans seem almost as eager as Americans to learn
the dirt about Michael Jackson; Italians may be almost as eager as the
British to devour every detail about the prince of Wales and the dead
princess.

Hence this is no age for the politics of envy; it is an age of the politics
of stars and their fans. Since leaders are celebrities, and celebrities are leaders, the glamour of celebrity status can spread easily to anyone who is

wealthy—certainly anyone who is *very* wealthy. After all, wealth itself is a source of celebrity status, just as celebrity status is a source of wealth. Magazines eagerly draw up lists of the richest people in the country and the world. If you are on the list, you are an automatic celebrity.

Very little seems to be left of the old class-based rage—rage at the cruel, unfair way the world distributes its goods; it has been extinguished, except for a few dying embers. Not many people, it seems, connect their own sufferings and privations, their own hunger and longings, with the wealth they see all around them. To the contrary, the money of the rich smells sweet to them. For Marxists, capitalist wealth was blood money, money squeezed from the sweat and muscles of starving workers, money poisoned by poverty, disease, and death; money was greed, exploitation; it was man's oppression of man. Contemporary money is radically different; magically, it has been washed clean of these bad associations. The public mind connects it with fun: with the world of sports and entertainment. The new (and glamorous) rich are movie stars, rock-and-roll musicians, baseball and soccer players, heroes of TV sitcoms. These are indeed the most visible rich. They breed no resentment. Indeed, the masses seem all too eager to contribute their share of the rents and the tributes.

What may be critical here is that the ordinary person in the West lives in a wealthy society. Even the lower middle class has leisure. Some people, of course, have a lot less free time than others: a single mother, slaving away at a nasty and unrewarding job and caring for three or four kids, is strapped for time; finding the right hobby is not her main problem in life. But there are millions and millions in quite a different position—after-school teenagers, retired people, nine-to-five office workers—people who do have time to kill. These hordes are avid consumers of fun. The economy looks more and more like a giant engine for producing entertainment—the software and the hardware of fun.

All this has a profound effect on politics as well as on policies. It explains why, in the 1990s, a politics of low taxes, flat taxes, or even no taxes has become so popular; the progressive income tax has been radically flattened out; death taxes are cut or (in California) eliminated; yet masses of people, who themselves barely scrape by, who have no job security, let alone an estate to worry about, go to the polls and reelect the rich and the representatives of the rich. They refuse to throw the rascals out or to storm the Bastille. Indeed, these masses direct their hatred and disgust, in the main, not against the blatant rich but against those who are worse off than they are: the poor, racial minorities, immigrants, and everyone who is the total inverse of a celebrity.[53] The lifestyle of the rich and famous is the opium of the masses.

The Rights of Privacy

In a celebrity culture, the private lives of the stars (in entertainment, business, politics) are projected directly into everybody's home. These stars have, in a real sense, no right to privacy (or so it appears). Yet the whole concept of privacy, like the celebrity culture itself, is distinctively modern. And along with the concept goes a huge body of doctrines, rules, provisions, lawsuits, all turning on this "fundamental right." The United States Supreme Court has read a right of privacy into the federal Constitution.[54] The Spanish Constitution of 1978 guarantees the right to "honor, personal and family intimacy."[55] An elaborate French law protecting privacy was passed in 1970.[56]

These various laws, doctrines, and provisions have quite different meanings in different contexts; and the body of law in question is a jumble of complexity. American constitutional law on the right to privacy includes a lot of doctrine that, on the surface, seems to have little to do with privacy in its usual sense—for example, the right to buy and use contraceptives or, most notoriously, a woman's right to have an abortion. As many commentators have complained, whatever you want to call this right to certain life choices, it is not privacy in the sense of quiet isolation or the right to be left alone.[57]

In fact, privacy in constitutional law seems in some way almost the opposite of the right of privacy that the law of torts protects. The constitutional right of privacy is concerned with "zones of privacy" (a phrase the court uses at times)—areas in which the state is not allowed to interfere with private choices. In tort law, the use of the term *privacy* is more in line with the common sense definition of the word. A person can try to sue if some other person or some company reveals intimate, embarrassing facts about him or her that the public does not have the right to know.[58] This privacy, however, has to bow to the demands of a celebrity society. The courts tend to hold that the public has a *right* to private facts, even information about a person's sex life, with regard to anybody who could be called a celebrity by any stretch of the imagination—including involuntary celebrities. In one case, in 1976, a certain Mike Virgil of San Diego, whose claim to fame was his "daring and dangerous style of body surfing," sued a magazine for printing a story which told a breathlessly waiting world that Mike Virgil ate insects, put out cigarettes in his mouth, and dove off stairs "to impress women." Virgil lost his case: as a celebrity (of sorts) in the world of body surfing, his antics were of "legitimate public interest."[59]

All the meanings of privacy have in common an emphasis on individual choice and individual space.[60] Tort law, however, balances those meanings against the ravenous appetite of the public for information about celebrities, including their private lives. In a celebrity society, the eating habits of a body surfer or the sexual behavior of a member of Congress is enormously relevant; a celebrity is someone whose personal life is public property (or seems to be).

Privacy as such was almost an unknown concept in traditional societies. In tiny villages, in huts and cottages where families were crowded together, there was not much room, physically speaking, for any such right. Nobody talked about personal space. Village life was small, enclosed, gossipy; everybody knew everybody else's business. Yet the community as a unit was relatively isolated; for the most part, the outside world never intruded on its privacy.

In this regard, the world has been turned upside down. Today, millions of people want isolation and distance, not from the outside world but from the world immediately around them. They want a room of their own, space of their own, some sort of psychic barrier between them and their families, a kind of inner womb where they can curl up and be themselves. They want choice, the right to develop on their own, the right to be themselves. Relationships with the wider world are different and quite complicated. People, I think, often feel a need to defend themselves against intrusions—to wrap themselves in a cloak of anonymity. Other people, of course, are only too eager to appear on some TV talk show, revealing their most intimate secrets to the whole watching world. This, after all, makes them a celebrity, at least temporarily. This is a personal choice. Yet the same people may not take so kindly to electronic surveillance, credit monitoring, wiretapping, exploitation of their images, government intervention, telephone solicitors, and other unwelcome visitors. For most people, the TV screen is, and ought to be, a one-way mirror.

In other words, in traditional society, there was no privacy at home, but privacy in the larger world was taken for granted. Now the tables are turned. The state and other large institutions have the technical means to insinuate themselves into our very bedrooms; they can pry, investigate, seduce, interfere. More to the point, these institutions can scan our credit cards and peek into our bank accounts. They know what we buy and what we eat, what we like and what we watch on TV. This invasion of privacy is in fact another aspect of the horizontal society. Communication flows freely from person to person on a horizontal plane; we can project ourselves, our words, or personalities, across great distances; we can buy and sell and deal without restrictions of time and space. But the danger of intrusion into our lives is also very great. Men and women in this society want their window on the world, but they also want to keep their fingers on the buttons of remote control. The technical, social, and legal problems of privacy are likely to multiply in coming years.

East, West, and America

The spreading celebrity culture has, to no one's surprise, caught the attention of scholars, pundits, and other people who worry about the future. Celebrity culture looks peculiarly Western; certainly no one imagines that it hails from China or India or Zimbabwe. Then, too, it seems peculiarly focused in the United States, which has come down with an especially bad case of popular culture.

But the phenomenon itself is surely worldwide, and in Western countries it is positively epidemic. Newsstands in any Western country are crowded with celebrity magazines. The cover of *Paris Match* for June 13, 1996, displayed a picture of Sharon Stone, the (American) movie star, and the words "The men I love," in English and French. (These men included

Magic Johnson, the Dalai Lama, Octavio Paz, Gérard Depardieu, and Jack Nicholson). The celebrities chronicled in this particular issue were an international bunch: Simeon, of the Bulgarian royal family, and the princess of Lichtenstein, for example.

Yet there is an American odor hanging over the whole business of a celebrity society. In part, this is because America is so vast a producer and exporter of popular culture. The new, global culture, dominated by television and films, *is* basically American, according to some authorities.[61] Certainly, American foods, fads, customs—and, above all, American movies, TV shows, and music—have incredible appeal all over the world. The French can scream and rail; the Canadians can try to keep these invisible immigrants from polluting their culture, but the fact is that the world wants to hear, see, and smell American cultural products (if culture is the right word). In 1991, the top-grossing film in Argentina was *Terminator 2;* in Egypt, *Dances with Wolves;* and in Sweden, *Pretty Woman.*[62] The American juggernaut, in country after country, has driven out the local product; no Western country can compete with Hollywood in the manufacture and marketing of schlock.

Why should this be the case? Why this American dominance? Is it a form of imperialism? The United States, after all, is the richest and most powerful country in the world. After the Second World War, it was the glittering survivor among the ruins; the model for prosperity, enjoyment, luxury, in a destitute and exhausted world. Its influence was, perhaps, particularaly strong in (West) Germany, where American troops were part of the Occupation.[63] The American army was also stationed in Japan; American influence was pervasive there and in Korea as well. A certain undercurrent of resentment was evident in all of these countries, and that resentment is by no means gone. But the American image has been, and continues to be, incredibly seductive.

Seductive, yes: but distinctively American? Or did the United States simply reach a certain stage first, for various historical reasons? Arguably, global (popular) culture is modern rather than purely American. America was the first middle-class society; it was geographically and socially mobile, peopled with immigrants who were rootless, restless, on the move; American society blurred the lines between classes—it was, in short, on the way to becoming a horizontal society—at a time when most of Europe and Asia were moving much more slowly or not at all, when society in many countries remained stubbornly vertical.[64] Perhaps, then, the influence of America spreads over the world not by force but by example—and perhaps also because its culture moguls understand what people in a horizontal society want better than do the laggards in Europe and elsewhere.

After all, if American movies sweep French ones into oblivion, if Italians, Germans, Japanese, and Macedonians flock to see Sylvester Stallone and Clint Eastwood, it must be because, somehow, American moviemakers have (consciously or unconsciously) tapped into some deep craving of ordinary people in this day and age. Words like *imperialism* do not help explain what is happening. The problem—if there is a problem—is of two distinct sorts. One sort is (perhaps) curable; the other is not. The curable part may be the monopoly factor: the threat to, say, French cultural industries—to jobs in the film business or in recording studios. The French can conceivably react in two ways. They can try to create a better product—and this means a product that does what American products do, only more so. Or they can follow the protectionist route: they can forbid American imports, insist on home-grown products, limit the number of hours of American-made television, and so on. Such tactics are not unknown; and various countries have tried them.[65] The European Union decided in early 1996 that TV programming must be, in its origin, mainly European.[66] The Canadian Broadcasting Corporation—in a country hard-pressed to keep or even define its identity—has also decided to purge itself of American commercial programs.[67] It is hard to see how this tactic, in the long run, can possibly succeed. Cultural borders are weak and porous, particularly in the age of satellites and receiving dishes that sprout like iron flowers from peoples' roofs.

The second problem is the destruction of classical French culture (or Japanese or Bulgarian or Portuguese culture), however defined. Here restoration or protection is probably impossible. Nobody has yet invented this kind of fence or barrier: one that would not only shut out products that came physically from America but would also defeat Coca-Cola, whether bottled in France or not. What policy could succeed in blotting out blue jeans or French versions of TV quiz shows or rock-and-roll music, even if sung in French? The Chinese government, at one point, liked to use a striking metaphor to illustrate its attitude toward Western influences. Its policy, it said, was like a window screen. Window screens let fresh air in but keep bugs and vermin out. The Chinese planned to absorb the good, the powerful, the useful from the West but to screen out all the evil influences. This, of course, is easier said than done. Iran, too, has tried to ban the poison of the West. Most of us in the West think that this policy is doomed to fail. The ayatollahs may be powerful, but they are like King Canute commanding the waves, and modernism and its habits and ideologies are as strong as the waves of the sea. Benjamin Barber predicts that, in their war, "the mullahs will lose, because against satellite television and videocassettes they have no long-term defense."[68] He is probably right.

Modernism and the consumer culture may start in the West, but they are no less seductive elsewhere in the world. In short, one can argue that popular culture, global culture—celebrity culture—is not an American product as such. It is not a subtle form of imperialism. Nor are the tools, traits, and institutions of modernity specifically American. New technology and new social facts create new personalities and cultures. All this may have gotten a head start in the United States, but it spreads wherever the same social factors come to exist, which is bound to be almost everywhere. Modernity is a force, a movement, a set of values and circumstances, which modern life and modern technology produce and continue to produce. The sweep of modernity includes the whole of the Western world—and far beyond.

A Revolution of Rights

IN CHAPTER 1, I TALKED about some cultural aspects of our horizontal society and the general effects of these cultural aspects on social structure and political life. In this chapter, I will briefly discuss two direct (and closely linked) consequences of the horizontal society, the legal and the political.

The first is the so-called *rights revolution*. A right is a legal empowerment. In the broadest sense, we can call any legal claim a right, provided it seems justified and likely to win out. So, if a careless driver smashes into my car, I can collect money from him or his insurance company, and we can (and do) say that I have a right to damages. Similarly, I have a right to make out a will or to have custody of my minor children. On the other hand, when people talk about a rights revolution, they are in general not thinking of these ordinary kinds of claim; rather they have in mind fundamental rights or human rights, like free speech, freedom of religion, and so on.

Of course, ideas of fundamental rights are not brand-new; they have a fairly long and distinguished pedigree. To talk about a rights revolution implies a change in aspiration and achievement; it implies that people lay claim to more of these rights or that they are broader, deeper, or more important than before. In contemporary society, rights are also profoundly more individual than in the past. They are individual in the literal sense: they belong to and reside in individuals, not in groups or classes or strata. They are therefore (conceptually) portable: they follow us wherever we go, wherever we are; they are part of us, like our hair or our skin.

What follows from this is the notion of *equality* of rights. This is inherent in what was just said: rights inhere in everybody and are the same for everybody (at least the basic rights). Rights do not differ for upper and lower classes, men and women, Christians and Muslims and Jews, rich and poor, or short and tall. Equality is an individual idea; a society that makes legal distinctions of race, gender, class, and status, that believes in nobles and commoners, or that has an official state religion is not likely to be a society of individualists (or one in which individualism flourishes); the advance of the notion of equality is also the advance of the idea of basic, human, individual rights. (Later we will have to see how this development squares with what is equally obvious: the tribalism of modern times.)

Whose concept of equality are we talking about? Whose notion of rights? I am *not* thinking of formal philosophy or high mandarin thought, whether political or ethical or legal, but rather of ideas in the heads of broad masses of people, mostly (though not exclusively) middle-class people in Western countries. Nor am I arguing (how could I?) that concepts of basic human rights are working realities all over the world, or that many countries even come close to realizing such rights. The concepts are, however, widely accepted ideals.

There is a huge literature on the rights revolution—for, against, and about; all I hope to add in this chapter are some words about its connection with the horizontal society. Such a connection, I believe, exists; it is therefore important to argue that the rights revolution is not some artifact of the West, not something irretrievably culture-bound and hopelessly out of place in the tropics. On the contrary, I will argue that this is an aspect of modern life, one that has responded to fundamental social change—notably by virtue of change in the technologies of speed and interaction. In the previous chapter, I argued that our celebrity culture was basically modern and global rather than Western. In this chapter, I make the same argument for the rights revolution.

The second phenomenon is *constitutionalism.* Constitutions are the legal vessels that embody the charter of fundamental rights in most of the countries of the world. Almost all countries today have constitutions, and a fair number of them actually mean something. In many countries, these constitutions mean something in part because there is an institution that has the power to give body and flesh to the words of the document. This institutional role, in many countries, falls to the courts.

I will discuss these two phenomena in what follows. Most people see the story of the rights revolution and constitutional government as a story of progress, evolution, as a slow but sure movement toward liberty, justice, and dignity for everybody. But we have to be careful not to be too optimistic. Hence the chapter ends with a coda on success and failure in the horizontal society.

Rights and Their Lineage

The argument, as I have said, is that the concept of human rights or fundamental rights is an aspect of modernity, and specifically of the horizontal society. To make this argument is to deny—or downplay—the specifically Western character of rights. It is to deny the claim that the current trends can be ascribed to particular Western philosophers or the Enlightenment or Western high thought in general.

It would be wrong to ignore the history of these ideas entirely. America's founding fathers were men of intelligence and learning; historians have often pointed to the influence of John Locke and other Enlightenment thinkers on these men, on the ideology of the American Revolution, and on the progress of democracy and equality in modern American history.[1] Clearly, though, the idea that there are universal human rights, rights that inhere in everybody regardless of birth, race, sex, or identity, has particular resonance in contemporary times; all over the world, "political discourse is increasingly imbued with the language of rights, universal, inalienable, inviolable."[2] This raises the question: What makes these ideas so attractive, so salient, in the twentieth century? Why are the ideas of other great minds, men who glorified autocracy or monarchy or theocracy, relegated to the status of historical curiosities? This is not a question that can be answered from inside the world of intellectual history. To answer it, we have to step outside, into the dirtier and messier world of events and situations, into the world of new technology and the rapid, quicksilver transformations of culture.

This is indeed the century of human rights, equality, and individualism. It has also been, one should quickly point out, the century of dicta-torship and the slaughter of innocents on a truly awesome scale. The cen-tury seems likely to end with the same crazy contradictions it began with, only more so: on the one hand, countries dedicated to constitutions, laws, and official pronouncements expressing ideals of liberal democracy; on the other hand, countries in which rivers of blood pour out of a thousand wounds. As the century ends, most of the kingdoms have given up their kings, and the kings and queens who are left are not what they used to be. The old monarchies are now republics or (what amounts to almost the same thing) constitutional monarchies. Nonetheless, dictators and warlords still abound. There may even be more of them than at the beginning of the cen-tury, though mainly because there are more sovereign countries to tyran-nize than there were in 1900. The great empires have gone the way of all flesh, and the great emperors along with them; but small despots still grow like weeds in the soil of the postimperial world.

Nonetheless, in the twentieth century, the ideology of human rights—and especially an ideology of universal human rights—has become more and more salient to the general population. As far as we know, nobody de-manded freedom of speech or freedom of assembly during the long cen-turies of Egyptian or Chinese dynasties—or for that matter in medieval Sweden. Of course, neither in fact nor in theory has the progress of this ide-ology gone uncontested. The question of where these rights come from, and what culture they belong to, is a talking point in debates and discus-sions of the rights. They have been attacked as bourgeois freedoms by the Left and as weak-livered decadence by the Right. The Communist Left and the fascist Right are both in some decay at the moment, but the critiques have been taken up by what we might call the cultural Right and the cul-tural Left.

Hardly anybody dares mount a total, frontal assault on the idea of hu-man rights—verbally, at least. Even the worst dictators pay lip service to them. Still, in their extreme forms, they are regularly denounced as West-ern interventions, unsuited (presumably) to other parts of the world. It *is* a question whether universal human rights are quite as universal as, say, many Americans seem to think they are (or ought to be). Everywhere there are honest (if heated) debates about the boundaries of these rights—how far they go. Can the state clamp down on hate speech? Can it regulate or ban pornography? Can it stop home-grown Nazis from marching about in Jewish neighborhoods? In socialist countries, the official line (now mostly rotting away in the gloomy attic of history) insisted that the rights to a job, three square meals, a place to live, and medical care were much more important than such mundane rights as the freedom to move easily across borders or to denounce the ruling party as a gang of rascals and pigs.[3] Polls in what used to be East Germany suggest that the average person in that country absorbed and internalized at least some aspects of the official ideology.[4] Everywhere, too, there are dilemmas that come from the collision between "universal" human rights and claims based on cultural practices.[5] Is female circumcision, for example, brutal and sexist; or is it an aspect of African culture, which the West should not interfere with?[6]

In short, what, if anything, are the core values that go to make up the list of basic human rights? From Asia come arguments, sometimes subtle and thoughtful, sometimes a bit crude, that Asia has to grow its own particular style of democracy; concepts of human rights cannot be imported wholesale like a boatload of calculators or videocassettes. Rights must fit the culture; they need their own, special, Eastern flavoring. Tommy Koh, of Singapore, argues for a more moderate position. He thinks there *is* a common, universal core: "Genocide, murder, torture and slavery should be universally condemned." But the West, he argues, is too doctrinaire about rights; the West is too insistent on every detail of *its* definition of freedom. If Singapore thinks that the police, in their war against the drug menace, should be able to demand a urine test from suspicious people, why not let it? Why should the West "condemn such a decision as a violation of the individual's liberty?"[7]

He has a point. One size definitely does *not* fit all. It would be a miracle, or some kind of divine revelation, if in fact the ideal set of universal, timeless, bedrock human rights just happened to coincide with certain doctrines of the United States Supreme Court as of the 1990s, or with the platform and programs of the American Civil Liberties Union, or with some European declaration of the rights of man. Ideas of rights are undoubtedly time-bound. (What would John Locke or Thomas Jefferson have said about pornography or women's rights?) They are also, beyond a doubt, culture-bound. If so, how can we claim that they refer to "universal features of the human existence?" Rainer Bauböck gives one answer: they are "historically but not culturally relative." In other words, they are tied to the "social and political conditions of modernity." This means that they are "highly relevant for all present societies." Thus, these rights can be "defended from within each of the major cultural traditions."[8] This means West and East.

Historical relativity is easy to show. Koh denounces slavery and torture as violations of universal human rights; yet slavery and torture were once common, and accepted, both East and West. Slavery lasted until the 1860s in the United States, even later in Brazil, and still later in the Near East and Africa. I suppose one can argue that these practices were always evil; the evil was simply unrecognized. But it is important to remember that there were respectable people who defended slavery. Yet nobody openly defends it today—in whatever culture. As Bauböck put it, there is a core of agreement, common to all modern nations. Cultures differ, and so do ideas about rights. But within the single, overarching culture of modernity—within the horizontal society—the elements of agreement have been spreading and growing and converging.

The claim that bourgeois freedoms were a sham, a mask to hide the leering face of capitalism, was often heard during the Cold War. It is true that the West often used human-rights arguments as elements of Cold War politics. The West tended to magnify the evils of left-wing countries, while covering up (or helping out) vile dictators of the Right. All this made the idea of "human rights suspect as an emancipatory script."[9] But the Cold War is over. It is clear that millions of people had longed for a chance to enjoy these bourgeois freedoms.

Arguments against Western rights now come mostly from the Right. There is the claim that the economy comes first, and economic progress demands a firm hand at the steering wheel. A newspaper in Singapore asks, "Do you give a starving man a loaf of bread or a milk crate to vent his spleen on the passing world?"[10] I vote for the loaf of bread: but do we really have to choose? Why can't the starving man have both? Even if there is not enough bread to go around, how does it help him to deny him his soapbox? Would it really interfere with breadwinning and GDP if a government decided to allow opposition newspapers? It hardly seems likely.

The *cultural* case against Western freedoms also has its weaknesses. To be sure, Western rights and freedoms rest on certain assumptions—about individualism, about human nature—that are historically contingent and are still, despite the sweep of modernity, far from culturally universal.[11] Samuel Huntington has argued, vigorously, that there is in fact a sharp line between what is modern and what is Western. The "image of an emerging homogeneous, universally Western world" is "misguided, arrogant, false, and dangerous."[12]

Surely there is such a line, but it is fading rapidly. Modernity was historically Western; it no longer is. Since Africans and Latin Americans listen to rock and roll, go to the movies, and eat pizza, since they watch TV obsessively, why should Western rights and democratic institutions strike them as culturally alien? It is now a one-world world. The cultural arguments for Asian democracy or Eastern values are just too pat, too convenient: any tyrant in Asia or Africa can dismiss freedom of speech or women's rights or free elections as foreign and unsuitable to the culture of his people. What they *are* foreign to is his arrogance and power. As Jack Donnelly has pointed out, the "practices of an Amin or Bokassa do not rest on an alternative conception of human dignity, but rather deny the very concept."[13]

Moreover, we can ask: How Western *are* these rights, in the last analysis? To begin with, the West itself is hardly a monolith; it is a mélange of peoples and countries. Each people had its customs, languages, habits, ways of life, religious beliefs, its traditions. For centuries, the West was no more modern than the East (in technology and habits of mind). Indeed, as Eugen Weber has shown, rural France, peasant France, remained isolated, primitive, premodern, until deep into the nineteenth century.[14] What was true of France was surely true of the other peoples of Europe.

Indeed, a kind of mass extinction of traditional cultures has taken place in the West in the last two centuries. Modernization, with its ruthless hammer blows, has killed off these old ways of life. Compared to the way we live now, these ways of life were as foreign or exotic as anything in Burundi or Iraq. There were certainly no bourgeois freedoms in feudal Europe or in Finland in 1600 or in Sicily under the Normans. Koh mentioned rules against torture as universal; torture, today, *is* universally condemned. It is a real denial of due process and human dignity. Yet at one time, torture was "a normal part of criminal justice in most, if not all, parts of Europe." A movement to abolish it arose only in the eighteenth century, as part of the Enlightenment.[15] Before this time, to call torture an institution deeply imbedded in Western legal culture would not be far off the mark.[16]

In other words, Western society, or what we call Western society, is arguably not Western at all. Rather, it is *modern* society—urban, industrial, mass-media society. It is the horizontal society. It is the society that technology created, and as machines changed the world, ways of thinking and acting changed along with them. It is part of the process of converting the world "from old to new . . . from kayak to jet."[17] Of course, it is certainly possible that Western tradition, Western thought, had something in them that made modernity a more *likely* development in Europe than in, say, Asia; after all, the Industrial Revolution began in Europe, not in China or Africa.[18] For our purposes, it does not matter whether technology made the West, or the West in some subtle way made technology happen. In either case, the general idea stands firm.

What happened in the West is now happening all over the world. We can, if we want to, call the process by which the West spreads its tentacles over the globe colonial or imperial. Colonies and empires were real enough. The expansion of Europe brought massive social change to societies that had been isolated and traditional. The process, very often, was not a pretty one. Cultures were dragged into the modern world kicking and screaming. Imperial Europe and North America killed and enslaved; they ruthlessly destroyed whole cultures. Mexico City was built on the ruins of Aztec temples. The list of the defeated is long and depressing: the tribal cultures of the prairies and plains of North America, the peoples of the Caribbean and South America, the Maori, natives of Australia and Tasmania, Hawaiians and other Pacific islanders, and many peoples of Africa. Today there is more respect for minority cultures. Indigenous peoples have found their voice in many countries. They want to preserve their traditions or, in some cases, bring these traditions back from the grave.

It is not an easy job. Minority cultures are still in mortal danger. Imperialism itself is just about dead in its classic form; but modernization is now the real enemy—not armies and missionaries but the mass media and Western pop culture. Today's imperial power is the satellite, the jet airplane, the television set. From these, there is nowhere to hide—not in Nepal, not even in the Amazon basin; no one can escape horizontal influences, not even those peoples who were never truly colonized.

Nineteenth-century imperialism was a powerful social force, and it has left its mark on the world today. The European powers imposed their laws, their languages, their ways of life; they shifted people about, moving East Indian workers to Fiji, for example. They imposed their religion on millions of natives. Today's cultural imperialism, if we want to call it that, is profoundly different. The old rulers in the British Raj or the German colonial office had no interest in conducting a dialogue with the natives. The natives had nothing to teach them; they were savages. Imperialists with good intentions tried to convert the natives to civilization; the bad imperialists exploited their labor, stole their land, or, where the natives became disruptive or rebellious or got in the way, simply wiped them out.

Imperialism was different from, say, the conquests of the Vandals or Attila the Hun. Some imperialists sincerely believed they were not merely conquerors, but were bringing enlightenment to people who lived in primitive darkness. The clearest case is religion. Missionaries, peddling Christianity in Samoa or in Africa, were convinced they possessed the one true faith: the Western God offered the only path to salvation. This was a precious gift, and it belonged to everybody, even poor savages, if they would only see the light. Today, the idea of basic human rights has in a way replaced the old-time religion, as a universal good.[19] These rights belong to everybody, so that (for example) those who battle for the equality of women feel justified in spreading their message to Togo or Korea. Religion, on the other hand, has become a matter of personal taste and choice (fundamentalists dissenting, of course); each man and woman has the right to decide which path to the divine is most suitable. In polite society, it is no longer

nice to call Third World religions "pagan" or "primitive"; and the same goes
for Third World cultures. The nineteenth-century missionaries often had
their work cut out for them. In many countries, they made little or no
progress with the "savages," who adhered stubbornly to their traditional
ways. Today, paradoxically, when many more people are willing to buy into
the idea of cultural relativity, and are willing to let tribes, peoples, groups,
cultures, and clans maintain their ancestral ways, those cultures are melting away like butter in the sun, under the glare of modern ideas and arti-
facts. And this despite sincere and desperate attempts at preserving and reviving. Fairly soon, if this keeps up, nothing will be left in the world but
the modern and a handful of quaint old customs, maintained like bones in
a museum.

   Of course, modernity is not a monolith. The habits of mind and body
that we think of as modern can be, for all we know, only skin-deep. Exactly
what does it mean to "borrow" or to "Westernize" or to fall under the "influence" of modernity. How real is the transformation? The contrast between the new and the old is a cliché of the media. They love to show scenes
of tribal people, for example, at the fringes of the jungle, wearing T-shirts
and jeans, listening to transistor radios, or eating pizzas. Presumably, these
people at the edge are not very modern; they have picked up a product or
two, a habit or two, but underneath they are still deeply embedded in traditional culture. But do we really know? At the very least, we can see that
this group no longer lives in total isolation; they are becoming, for better
or for worse, part of the global system; they are almost certainly walking
down a road from which there is no turning back. What we do not know
is how far down the road they have gone.
   In any event, whether Western or not, modern culture is ubiquitous.
And part of this culture is an orientation toward rights, freedoms, individual dignity. No community can totally escape this legal or political culture,
because no community can escape the technology, the habits of mind, the
very products of modernity. The taste of Coca-Cola, or the sight of MTV,
forever alters the soul. Even the revels and backlashers, the fundamentalists, the preservationists, are distinctly if paradoxically modern; they rebel
in distinctly modern ways. This is because resistance *has* to take on forms

and symbols of the culture it most detests. Soysal, for example, points out that Muslims in Europe "redefine and reconstruct religious symbols, such as veiling, as cultural or political expression, and defend them on the grounds of human rights." These European migrants, she argues, express and understand their Islamic identity in ways that are "necessarily modern, as opposed to traditional"; they frame their cause in "universalistic, rather than particularistic arguments."[20]

This is no isolated example. Fundamentalists everywhere use modern tools—television, civil rights litigation—to advance their cause. This, I think, goes beyond mere strategy. They cannot help themselves. These are the tools of modern organized life. There is no alternative. No one can organize except through the modalities of the horizontal society. Whatever the cause—bird-watching, sexual liberation, Catalan nationalism, or traditional Islam—its adherents will use fax machines, telephones, E-mail, videocassettes; they will travel by automobile and by jet. They will have to use the technology of the enemy and, unconsciously, absorb some of its habits of thought. The forces of modernity, and the enemies of modernity, are like prizefighters inside the ring; they fight to the death, but the techniques, the rules, and even the physical location are common to both and predetermined for the two of them.

It would be too much to hope that people would stop talking in terms of Western and non-Western values. In important ways, there no longer is a West or East (or South); what there is, instead, is modern and less modern, and, more and more, different dialects of the modern. Any issue in current debate will illustrate this point. Take female circumcision in Africa, for example—an issue we have already mentioned. Some feminists in Europe and America criticize the practice bitterly. But they speak in tones very different from the language of nineteenth-century colonialists. They use a modern, horizontal language—the language of universal human rights, rights that belong to women as well as to men. People who defend the practice, on the other hand, talk in terms of cultural autonomy. They attack the West, using words and ideas that also talk about rights—words and ideas which are, in short, almost as Western as the words and ideas of their opposition.

Martha Nussbaum tells how, at a meeting of anthropologists, some

Western scholars flagellated themselves, wallowing in guilt for imposing such Western devilry as vaccination on indigenous cultures. (Vaccination in India had resulted, according to one anthropologist, in eradicating the cult of a goddess who used to have jurisdiction over smallpox.) This horrified Nussbaum—she was appalled that these "intelligent people . . . deeply committed to the good of women and men in developing countries" took positions that made them allies of "ill health, ignorance, and death."[21]

Not to worry. The complaints of these intelligent people are unlikely to have any effect on the world. The cult of the goddess was probably doomed to decline, just as older, traditional customs, beliefs, rituals, rites, and habits passed away in Belgium or Norway or France as these countries, too, entered the modern world. Vaccinations, along with the other trappings of the twentieth century, came to India by way of the West, especially through their colonial masters, the British. It was not medieval Britain, however, but modern Britain that exercised this influence. Britain brought modern tools, modern practices, modern values, and modern ways of looking at life. As India, too, began to modernize in an increasingly horizontal world—as more and more of its population was exposed to movies and TV, in particular—the modernity began to take.

There is also some irony in the complaint. Western imperialists, after all, were the ones who carried smallpox to places like Brazil in the first place. This was only one of many diseases and dislocations that the expansion of Europe brought with it. Once the isolation of a community is shattered, the old world, like Humpty Dumpty, can never be put together again. A second irony is the sheer modernity of the appeal to tradition. That the cult of a goddess is worth preserving because of some idea of cultural rights, or cultural relativity, is itself a product of the horizontal society. Whatever happens, the goddess will never be the same.

Soysal, whose work was mentioned earlier, studied "guest workers" in Europe and found, somewhat to her surprise, that these workers, who lacked "formal citizenship," were nonetheless "incorporated into various aspects of the social and institutional order of their host countries." She came to the conclusion that "national citizenship" was "losing ground to a more universal model of membership, anchored in deterritorialized notions of persons' rights," a model she called "postnational."[22] David Jacobson sees the same trend; he points to the growing power of transnational organizations, especially in Europe, to the flock of treaties, charters, and conventions on human rights; he talks about the decline of the "territorial" state. The state, he says, with some exaggeration, "is in the process of becoming a territorial administrative unit of a supranational legal and political order based on human rights."[23] Sovereignty, like many other things, is not what it used to be.[24]

Obviously, there are limits to this "postnationalism"; in some ways the countries Soysal studied (Sweden, the Netherlands, Germany, France, and Britain, primarily) may not be typical. Jacobson, too, has focused his attention mainly on Europe. Millions of people still live trapped in despotic societies—in countries governed by rulers who are callously indifferent to the noble declarations of universal human rights and whose own appetite for money and power is their main concern, sometimes their only concern. Nevertheless, Soysal and Jacobson have pointed out a real aspect of modern legal and political culture. There is no question that the idea of a universal code of rights, a basic charter for every human being, is a powerful and seminal idea in our times. Consider, for example, the concept of asylum. Many countries feel an obligation to admit refugees or asylum seekers, people with a fear of persecution. Yet why should, say, a persecuted Cambodian have the right to live in France?

Asylum and refugee law is highly charged, politically speaking. In the United States, Cold War politics ensured that asylum was "a privilege to be accorded only to anti-Communists." As a result, Cubans were accepted into the country in droves, but Haitians were definitely not welcome.[25] Haitians had the misfortune, too, to be black. Uganda, to its discredit, expelled its Asian residents; some of them who had British nationality were able to resettle in the United Kingdom.[26] But no one would say these refugees were warmly welcomed. If we go back a little further, to the 1930s, we find that few countries (certainly not the United States) were willing to accept Jews fleeing from Hitler's clutches.[27] A right to asylum was embedded in the fundamental law of (West) Germany and interpreted, for a while, quite liberally.[28] But what (West) Germany had in mind mostly was refugees from the east—their German blood brothers in the Communist zone. When large numbers of people from Third World countries started knocking on the door—indeed, walking right into the house—the Germans began to have second thoughts. By now, Germany's generous and humane asylum policy is seriously frayed; economic stringency, unemployment, and the growing pressure of numbers, mixed with plain old-fashioned xenophobia, have wreaked havoc with the policy.[29] Yet despite all this backsliding and backlash, refugee and asylum policies remain relatively liberal in many countries—strong witnesses to the idea of universal *human* rights.[30]

In fact, the flood of asylum seekers in Germany and other Western countries is yet another reflex of the horizontal society. Why are there so many refugees, so many people looking for safe havens? Persecution is nothing new, after all. Bierbrauer talks about "jet-age asylum-seekers."[31] It is relatively easy, thanks to technology, to flee from Sri Lanka to Germany or Sweden—an almost impossible journey in the past. Bierbrauer also mentions the decline of "natural barriers";[32] he refers not to mountains and rivers but to cultural barriers—traditionalism, illiteracy, ignorance, fatalism. Once upon a time, these barriers kept people anchored in their ancestral homes. No longer. The global culture has broken through these barriers. The effect is cumulative. Today, it is no longer unthinkable to leave Guatemala or Sri Lanka. Moreover, once pioneers have established a beachhead in Frankfurt or New York, there is a diaspora community for Sri Lankans or Guatemalans to escape to. They can find familiar food, language, friends, in a new environment. And the "schooling" they absorbed from movies and TV makes their encounter with the streets of these cities less terrifying and less arcane.

A Pride of Constitutions

Rights, of course, whatever else they may be, are legal claims; and in modern societies, they are expressed as legal norms. Fundamental rights or human rights, quite typically, get elevated to some kind of special or overriding legal status; they become entrenched in written constitutions. Hence, in our period, the constitutional habit spreads throughout the world.

The idea of a written constitution is not particularly new. The American Constitution, one of the most influential, is also probably the oldest constitution still in effect. It has lasted more than two hundred years. It has set some kind of record for stability and has served as a model for dozens of other world constitutions. To be sure, many countries adopted constitutions in the nineteenth century, but the constitutional habit has gotten much more powerful in the contemporary world. The "spirit of constitutionalism," we are told, "has so dramatically soared of late that it seems poised to achieve a worldwide sweep."[33] Almost all countries, in fact, now have a written constitution or some expression of fundamental law (Great Britain is a prominent holdout; Israel is another; a third is New Zealand). And almost all of these constitutions contain a bill of rights or some equivalent catalog of fundamentals.

Constitutional *systems* are much harder to study than the texts themselves. Very few, if any, countries really live up to the aspirations expressed in their constitutions. Many constitutions are not worth the paper they are printed on. Words and texts have never stopped a military coup in Latin America or Africa. The Soviet Union, before its collapse, had a wonderful constitution;[34] and there are constitutions in all sorts of one-party and authoritarian states. Still, it must mean something that even the worst military dictators in our times give lip service to democracy, and to constitutions; and a growing number of world constitutions, one hopes, actually *mean* what they say.

To make a constitutional system work, some mechanism is needed to put muscle behind the rights of the citizens. Otherwise, they are exposed to the tender mercies of the people in power. There are a number of such mechanisms. The American contribution to this delicate art is judicial review. This takes, in the first place, independent courts—powerful, proud, and determined, and detached from governmental interference. In the second place, it takes a doctrine or norm which allows (or encourages) these courts to say no to actions that violate constitutional principle.

In the period after the Second World War, judicial review has gained enormously in popularity.[35] In some ways, this looks like yet another American habit or invention, on a par with Coca-Cola. In the case of Germany, Italy, and Japan, Americans played a major role in restructuring these societies when the war ended. In each case, the new scheme of government included a court with the power of judicial review. In Japan and Italy, the courts have been rather reluctant to exercise the power, although they have gotten less timid over time. Germany, on the other hand, has been a notable success; here the vaccination definitely took. The German constitutional court has been described, probably correctly, as the most powerful and active court in the world, next to the Supreme Court of the United States.[36]

Each country has its own history and experience; there are in fact good reasons for treating the German court as an exception. But the trend toward stronger and more active courts is not a fiction. We find it on all continents, including Asia, where the judiciary in India has also been labeled the "most active" in the world.[37] Indeed, judges in Italy, in their war on corruption, have perhaps rocked the boat as much as the German constitutional judges, though in a different way. The trend we are describing is also true of the motherland of judicial review, the United States. One can trace judicial review back to the early nineteenth century, and every schoolchild knows (or should know) about John Marshall and the case of *Marbury v. Madison* (1803).[38] In this case, the Supreme Court asserted the right and the power to strike down even acts of Congress if they violated the norms of the Constitution. But in fact, the court exercised this power very rarely. It was only much later—after the Civil War—that judicial review was regularly and powerfully used.[39] And it is only in the last fifty years or so that the United States Supreme Court and other American courts have created, out of their power of judicial review, a mighty sword wielded on behalf of minorities, deviant lifestyles, and rights of privacy.[40]

Meanwhile, in our times, country after country has chosen to adopt some form of judicial review quite on their own. They have either granted the power to regular courts or have set up special constitutional courts as repositories of the power. (Germany is an example of this latter model.) Judicial activism in enforcing human rights is thus a startling, worldwide movement.[41] To a degree, it is independent of structure. Thus, even in a country like Israel, which lacks a constitution altogether, the highest court has found a way to enforce fundamental principles of right.[42] The United Kingdom is perhaps the outstanding example of a country fumbling its way without a basic charter. Even in this case, there has been in recent years "a dramatic growth in the use of the courts to challenge decisions of local and central government."[43] And in France, another country whose legal culture strongly disfavors "government by judges," functional equivalents of judicial review have made important inroads.[44] Canada, which also lacked a regular constitution, reformed its basic law in 1982 in such a way as to "entrench" a code of fundamental rights. Under Canadian law, the courts have the power to enforce these rights, and any law "inconsistent" with the basic law is "of no force and effect."[45]

Rights and Identity

We have briefly discussed the rights revolution and what goes along with it, the constitutional revolution. We have also pointed out that rights are increasingly defined in universal terms—terms that transcend all borders, physical and conceptual. The rights revolution, on the other hand, coexists with raging, rampant nationalism. In part this is because, curiously enough, the politics of identity is just as much a product of individualism and modernization as other aspects of global culture. The state of the world promotes horizontal groupings. Horizontal groups are organized along many dimensions, but identity lines are among the most powerful of all. Identity, in a horizontal society, is fluid and open; one feels the "right to plan and fashion one's life as freely as possible."[46] As people plan and fashion away, however, they often tend to look for kindred souls. They look for those with whom they share a common standard, a common language (literally and figuratively); they arrange themselves in categories that they find psychologically convenient.

Individual choice is the message spread by the media, but individual choice makes these national and subnational groupings possible. No one is forced to become a fundamentalist or a Welsh nationalist or an ardent devotee of the Kurdish cause. These are all choices that people make from a menu put on the table by newspapers, books, movies, TV and radio programs; through word of mouth; and by travelers' tales.

In describing horizontal societies, we stressed the importance of mass communication and of modern ways of traveling (methods of incredible speed). But before the revolution in communication, there was the Industrial Revolution. The Industrial Revolution vastly expanded the domain of cheap, mass-produced goods. Mass production created, in a way, the masses themselves. You would not refer to peasants in a medieval village as a mass, nor even the peasants in all of, say, Germany or France. Mass *is* a way of describing people who live in a world where one can of soup is exactly like a billion other cans. It describes people in a world where a working class exists—uprooted peasants who toil away in factories, who live in cities, and who have, or *can* have, class consciousness. It is not only the conditions of work that make these workers into a class or a mass. Daniel Boorstin talks about the rise of "consumption communities," invisible "communities created and preserved by how and what men consumed"; communities of people who shop at chain stores and eat their food out of cans.[47] And, to be sure, just as there is a world culture of sports and entertainment, there is obviously a world culture of consumption. It is enough to mention blue jeans, pizza, and Coca-Cola.

TV and the other mass media spread images throughout the world, and these images, like all images, are not just pictures: they carry ideas, values, opinions, messages. The messages are often implicit, unconscious. One of these implicit messages, speeding about the world through the eyes of the TV camera, is nothing more or less than the idea of the autonomous individual. Almost every TV commercial, almost every program, carries this secret slogan. True, the products are mass-produced and are sometimes as identical as peas in a pod. But there are competing products, competing brands; TV asks us, explicitly, to buy the products that are advertised and, less explicitly, to buy the way of life and the consumption habits of the men, women, and children who live in the world of the TV shows. Moreover, TV is an isolating, individuating medium. It speaks to us one by one; the audience is a horizontal audience, and it watches in small groups or in fragments, together but separate, passively, and often in profound isolation.

From a central point of broadcast, wherever that is, the media send out their messages—to people in their houses, in bars, or at the houses of friends. There are many different messages, of course. But on the whole they are not messages of traditional values. They are not messages of community or community spirit. Indeed, the main "community" that the media address is the community of consumers. Neither in substance nor, perhaps more significantly, in style does television reinforce time-honored, inherited values—not even when (in the mouth of a TV evangelist or the mullahs who control TV in Iran) traditional values are the *substance* of the message. Even in these cases, the message is peculiarly modern. It calls on the audience to mobilize, to adhere to the cause. It is a message of propaganda, and it is delivered to a mass audience, but the mass is made up of individual listening atoms. Hence, almost inevitably, whatever the substance, the message is also a message of expressive individualism, of consumerism, of individual choice.

It is the individual who uses, who buys, who wears the clothes and listens to the music, who goes to the store and gets the goods. It is also the individual who decides to join (or not join) a militant Islamic group or who gets seduced by images of big city life in the West and emigrates. Politically, it is also the individual who *votes;* it is the individual who is the bearer of rights. Modern individualism has fostered the regime of rights and the spread of constitutional government, with guarantees, at least on paper, of liberty and equality and justice for all.

Traditional authority flourished and grew in small communities. The tight environment protected them. Villages were self-contained. The outside world was far away. Within a village community, people lived in close-knit family groups. There was less privacy, less individual space than in modern life, especially big-city life. In villages, local authorities—fathers, mothers, and grandparents, local notables, priests and elders—wielded power that was, in the aggregate, immense. The individual, *as* an individual, counted for very little; roles and statuses determined rights. Modern men and women (and children) *are* individuals, though not the atomized and rational individual that economic theory talks about. Rather, the modern man and woman tends to embrace what has been called *expressive* individualism: the notion that our highest need, our highest goal, is to develop or realize ourselves; to craft for ourselves a uniquely textured, satisfying life; to achieve *personal* success, personal salvation, personal achievement and happiness.[48] This is the individual who is pictured on TV; it is the consuming and choosing individual. The individual, in a world of expressive individualism, is less attached to status groups, less attached to the community, the neighborhood, or village, less attached to "knowing one's place" than in more traditional societies.

But we also live in a period of strong ethnic movements. This trend seems to run in the opposite direction—away from individualism. People seem to be showing a powerful instinct to agglomerate in nations or clans. What they do in these groups looks very different from the picture of the behavior of individualists; what we seem to see is mass behavior, group behavior—people behaving like sheep in a herd or fish in a school. But this impression, I believe, is somewhat misleading. An individualist is not necessarily somebody detached from affiliations or someone who believes in the futility of nationalism, who is a "one-worlder," a devotee of the brotherhood and sisterhood of humankind. The individualist is not necessarily—or even primarily—a rootless and free-floating cosmopolitan. In fact, the ethnic eruption is, in one sense, the equivalent on the level of the *group* of the expressive individualism of the ordinary woman or man.[49]

That is, these two aspects of modern life do not contradict each other; on the contrary, they fit together like two pieces of a jigsaw puzzle. A village peasant, enmeshed in family, chained to a cycle of planting and harvest, doing his devotions at a local church, praying perhaps to a local God, paying rent to a local Lord, is the least likely candidate for ethnic fervor. Such a person never felt he belonged to some (larger) ethnic group beyond village or family or clan, had no idea that he was French or Italian or Thai. That much is clear from the historical record. Set this person adrift, in search of attachments in a horizontal society, a modernizing and modernized society, and he or she will set sail for many different islands and harbors. He may choose to fight free of all the classical markers of identity. She may bury her consciousness in work or family or hobby. But national identity, patriotism, a profound attachment to king and country or to the group—these are among the more fateful and more popular destinations.

Contemporary individualism is also the enemy of fatalism and passive acceptance of one's lot. It encourages active struggle—whether the struggle is to amass the biggest coin collection on the block, to make a billion dollars, to gain freedom for the Slovaks, or to advance the rights of gays. It also encourages and promotes the demand to be treated fairly, regardless of nationality, ethnic origin, religion, race, or personal identity. Out of this comes "rights consciousness"; and rights consciousness itself is a soil in which rights can grow and flower. There are great variations in rights consciousness from country to country. Americans are supposed to be vigorous and feisty in sticking up for their rights, while the Japanese are supposed to mediate, defer, and compromise.[50] Exactly how much variation exists can be disputed, but the *direction* of change seems, on the whole, to be moving toward the "American" style.

As the forces of modernity shatter traditional society and traditional ways of thinking, like so many panes of brittle glass, the human fragments of old arrangements may appear as atomized individuals, lost and deracinated souls (there are many of these); or they can rearrange themselves, clump themselves, in groups that are primarily horizontal. People are social animals; they cannot live without connection. Individualism is not the negation of connectedness; it is only a way of describing the *source* of human connection, the way in which people connect and how they feel about their chances and possibilities. Is identity ascriptive, fixed at birth, determined absolutely by immutable characteristics? Or is it more and more the product of what appears to be a person's choice? Often enough, people choose to connect to their national identity—they elect to be strong patriots. We will deal with this in more detail in the following chapter.

The cult of the individual is also profoundly unsettling—especially on the psychological level. It puts success and failure into people's own hands, or seems to. Of course, the sense that we are masters of our destiny is often only an illusion. In many ways life is still a lottery. For millions of people— billions, perhaps—owning the good things of life is completely beyond reach. Millions of people scratch the soil trying to make a living or dwell in miserable urban shacks, hoping for a job that never comes or remain trapped within ghettos, cracking under the load of poverty and discrimination. From their hovels, they can still see the neon and the glitter of the consumer society. Intense disappointment, disaffection, anomie, grow in this kind of soil. The slums and barrios breed crime and other forms of social pathology; family structures crumble into dust.

Modern society is intensely mobile, in many senses of the word. People quite literally move about; they are not tied to a stake in some small patch of dirt where they are born, grow, suffer, and die. This is an age of migration—of massive movements from villages to cities, from little cities to big cities, from big cities to other big cities, and from country to country. There is also social mobility, movement up and down the social scale, in all democratic societies or perhaps all capitalist societies. American mythology is full of stories about the rise from rags to riches or from the log cabin to the White House. The same sorts of myths, though perhaps somewhat more muted, are found in Europe. Mobility is especially salient in a celebrity society. Many celebrities were not born rich and famous; they were ordinary people, born into ordinary families—sometimes poor and disorganized families. They are role models for a culture of rapid, overnight success. Even the lowest of the low can dream about a breakthrough on the guitar or about earning millions of dollars from shooting baskets; anybody halfway good-looking can dream about being discovered and launched on a movie career. People without any other hope can always dream of winning the lottery. Images of this sort of Cinderella story pour in every day on TV; they penetrate the gloom of the most miserable housing project, the worst wasteland of empty lots, beer cans, and broken glass.

Mobility can also be understood in a cultural sense. A person can be "mobile," in an important sense, without ever going out of the house. A person is mobile if he or she can imagine some possibility of change—of place, of form, of ideas, of culture. A small tribal society in the midst of the jungle was never completely static—all societies change and evolve—but it was much less *conscious* of change, less open to outside influences and ideas than a modern society; its individuals were cradled and cocooned in established habits, until they were old enough to leave the nest. Modern men and women, from early childhood on, are open to change, to new modes of thought, new products, new trends. And this is so whether or not they ever walk out the door of their houses. Ideas, desires, images, flood in from the outside world. For most people, of course, mobility means going out to meet the world, but it can also mean the opposite process: bringing the world in from outside, into your own room, hut, or cottage. Both processes are central to a horizontal society. And the virus of rising expectations creeps in to places that appear, from the outside, to be hermetically sealed.

Success and Failure. A mobile, changing society, a society that worships success, that exalts consumption, and that idolizes celebrities, is also a society that cannot satisfy all its members, cannot meet their expectations. In this lies a terrible trap. Millions of people may come to think of themselves as failures. The life of a peasant or a slave could be, and frequently was, a life of misery and oppression, of intense human suffering. But it was not necessarily a life of failure, in the twentieth-century sense. People were ruthlessly assigned, by birth or otherwise, to certain shelves of status; success or failure was measured *within* each category. Rising or falling from shelf to shelf was very hard (though probably not totally impossible).

A mobile society makes it easier to climb from the bottom of the ladder to the top or to stop anywhere along the way. It is also possible to start climbing and lose your way, or to begin at the top and fall all the way down to the bottom. A success society is also, necessarily, a failure society; and in a celebrity society, necessarily, most people are not stars, never will be stars, and may consider themselves insignificant. A mobile society is a society in which a person *can* be born poor and end up rich and famous. Obviously, most people born poor end up poor. This was always true, but now it may have different consequences. Poverty was once, perhaps, "perceived as being part of the human condition"; but in a horizontal society, it may look, instead, like injustice, and the result *may* be "social dissatisfaction and revolutionary consciousness."[51]

Studies of life in the squalid barrios and ghettos of the world show what havoc, what social disorganization, comes out of stunted expectations. The issue is not poverty but hopelessness. There are, and always have been, "slums of hope": areas in town where the people are very poor but are spurred on by their expectations. The immigrant sections—the Jewish ghettos at the turn of the century in the United States, the Chinatowns in Western cities—were often seen by their residents as halfway houses on the (hoped-for) road to success.[52] But more and more what we find in many big cities—in the United States less so than in Western Europe, but perhaps more so in the developing world—are slums of hopelessness. The jobs are gone; nobody has the right skills or education to get jobs; and as the years go by, hope oozes out of the tenements. Stunted expectations are not the only source of crime, drug addiction, and general anomie, but they are powerful contributors.

In vertical societies, traditional institutions were supposed to cushion the psychological shocks of calamity and poverty, and often enough they did. But where are these institutions, now, in the vast, swarming, hydrocephalic cities that have mushroomed all around the world—places like Calcutta, or Mexico City? There is an important difference, psychologically and socially, between (modern) hopelessness and (traditional) fatalism. Today, television, movies, and the celebrity culture train men and women in habits of desire and aspiration, but this same media culture—this horizontal culture—often leaves people helpless and enraged when the dreams die out and the habits of desire curdle for lack of fulfillment.

The respectable public today seems to be alarmed by the decline of family values, judging from the noise in newspapers, magazines, and TV stories in America and elsewhere. There is a lot of nostalgic sighing for the world that was lost—a world of traditional marriage, traditional families, traditional virtues, at least in their nineteenth-century versions. Life then seemed simpler and better. The nostalgia, of course, is mostly based on myth. There never were any "good old days." But in any event, the past, good or bad, can never be recaptured.

To be sure, something can be said for traditional values. Take, for example, traditional marriage. Husband and wife had (more or less) fixed roles; what they owed each other was, from our standpoint, rather narrow and confining. In many marriages women enjoyed love and respect, but they were definitely subordinate. In our times, traditional marriage has been replaced by what has been called companionate marriage. Husband and wife are supposed to love each other romantically; they are supposed to be partners, friends, confidants, sharers of life. Marriage is supposed to be personally fulfilling; husband and wife should be deeply and thoroughly compatible if they want to craft a rich and satisfying relationship.[53]

Traditional marriages, and especially arranged marriages, were vertical marriages; companionate marriage is horizontal marriage. Each person seeks out an individual soul mate from a vast horizontal pool. People do not marry the girl or boy next door, and often not even a girl or boy who shares their religion and background. Of course, if you insist that your spouse be a soul mate instead of (for men) a good cook, a good mother, and somebody who darns the socks and is not too tired for occasional sex; or (for women) a good provider, a man of decent hygiene, and not a heavy drinker, it is much harder to get what you want. Millions of marriages snap under the strain. Divorce rates in Western countries that allowed divorce at all increased dramatically in the late nineteenth and early twentieth centuries.[54] (In countries that did not allow divorce, family disintegration increased correspondingly.)

Divorce, however, has always been controversial; Catholics did not approve of it at all, and Protestants were only slightly less suspicious. The determined opposition of the forces of morality made it hard to reform the law in the nineteenth century; any move toward cheap and easy divorce was bitterly resisted.[55] Yet the change in the ideology of marriage was an irresistible force. Divorce, once rare and difficult, became more and more common in the late nineteenth century. Divorce laws varied greatly in detail from country to country. But the trend was inexorably toward easy divorce. The dam burst in the late twentieth century. Even the no-divorce countries gradually capitulated: Italy, despite the fierce opposition of the Vatican, adopted a divorce law in 1970;[56] and in the 1990s Ireland, one of the last holdouts, followed suit.

Indeed, in California, either partner, man or woman, can get out of a marriage, essentially, just by asking the proper court to dissolve the marriage.[57] The other party's consent or permission is irrelevant.[58] This is called no-fault divorce. In the United States, the California syndrome spread to other states with amazing rapidity. By 1977, only three states still retained the old system of divorce; all the rest allowed *some* form of no-fault.[59] The no-fault idea took over in Sweden after passage of reforms in divorce law in 1973.[60] In Germany, "disruption of marriage" is grounds for divorce, and divorce for "fault" has been abolished, although judges can still deny a divorce under some circumstances.[61]

These are, to be sure, purely formal changes. The reality is equally striking. There is a positive epidemic of divorce in Western countries (and a rising rate in Japan as well). The United States has, perhaps, the worst record (more than fifty divorces per one hundred marriages); but other countries are hurrying to catch up: there are about thirty divorces per hundred marriages in Canada and France, and almost forty-five in Denmark.[62]

But divorce, considered a monstrous evil in the nineteenth century, is not the worst of the troubles that plague the traditional family. Marriage itself has lost some of its magic. Vast numbers of people now cohabit; some of these relationships are stable and long-term; some are not. Illegitimacy rates are rising in many Western countries—the rates in the United States can be described as staggering (more than one birth out of four); but the percentages are even higher in northern Europe, and they are rising in eastern and southern Europe as well.[63] Only Japan, with an illegitimacy rate of a mere 1 percent, seems to be resisting the trend.[64] The stigma attached to illegitimacy has almost disappeared. Of course, "illegitimate" is a label that can be attached to many different life situations. Some illegitimate children have two parents in a stable relationship who simply never bothered to get married. These children are at no particular risk. The problem for societies lies in illegitimacy of quite a different type—children with no father, an absent father, or a casual or unknown father. There is an appalling rise in the number of households headed by a single parent, usually (though not always) the mother. This is particular true—tragically true—in poor families. It is the reason why many of these families are poor in the first place. A horizontal society, with its emphasis on personal fulfillment, its (relative) rejection of traditional sexual morals, its vastly increased mobility, and its emphasis on buying and enjoying, puts an enormous strain on marriage and family life. Discipline, loyalty, commitment, become scarcer goods. The bonds of family life stretch and ultimately fail in millions of cases.

Thus, the social fabric frays and tatters in the horizontal society. The horizontal society is also a challenge to the economic order. As everyone knows, the economy has become truly global in the contemporary world: people, goods, ideas, and fashions stream across borders. So too does labor and capital. Any economist can tick off the advantages—the wonderful virtues of free trade, the efficiencies of free transfer of capital. Everybody gains, goods are cheaper, countries produce or sell what they make best, and everybody gets rich, or at least richer. Whatever the theory, there are also risks, dangers, and disruptions. Migration and immigration threaten cultures as well as jobs (we will take up these issues in more detail in a later chapter). The global market, as it expands, even seems to threaten the future of the welfare state. It is all well and good if markets open and expand in India, Mexico, or China, but these are still low-wage countries. Investment flows into these countries, factories get built to make shoes, steel, and automobiles, and workers in Holland and Italy and France (and Japan and Canada) lose jobs they thought were secure.

In the past, distance and expense built stronger walls than any tariff to protect against countries with cheap labor. Cheap labor was also bad labor, inefficient labor. A truly underdeveloped country is no competition for the West, because its workforce is premodern. We worry about Malaysia or China, not about Bhutan or Chad. What the Chinese worker gets for an hour's work on the assembly line or at the computer terminal has an impact on the structure of wages in advanced countries. It even influences whether there are jobs of certain kinds, at *any* wage, in the richer nations.

Physical risk has also been globalized. As the German sociologist Ulrich Beck has pointed out, we live in a "risk society."[65] In our times, we are exposed to risks that pay no respect to national borders; these risks leap over "national states as well as classes and military alliances"; they present us with "completely new challenges."[66] Chernobyl is a recent and striking example; it is, in fact, the example that first inspired Beck's work. A defective nuclear plant in what was then the Soviet Union spewed its poison through the winds into all the neighboring countries.[67] This was no freak or isolated example. Threats to the environment are less dramatic, perhaps, but in some cases even more dangerous: global warming, holes in the ozone layer, spoliation of the high seas, destruction of rain forests. In terms of international law, the Amazon forests "belong" to Brazil, and Brazil can do as it pleases with its own green wilderness. But the loss of habitat, the destruction of the natural world, at least *seems* to diminish and endanger everyone on earth, including billions of people who have never been to Brazil and never plan to go.

3

A Wealth of Nations

ONE BASIC FACT ABOUT OUR world, so obvious that we take it for granted, is that the world is divided into countries, or to put it a shade more technically, sovereign nations. It is also obvious that nationalism generates powerful emotions and can arouse powerful political energy, and that it has caused, or been associated with, innumerable wars and conflicts, past and present.

This chapter will briefly discuss what nationalism is, where it came from, and how national and ethnic conflicts relate to the horizontal society. One fundamental point is that nations and ethnic groups are largely an invention of the nineteenth century; they are not natural phenomena but are (in a way) fictitious beings. They arose out of the wreckage of traditional society, and their development is intimately connected with the rise of the horizontal society.

In other words, the sense of nationhood or the sense of belonging to an ethnic group—being Turkish or French or Brazilian—is rather new in human history. It would be unthinkable without modern ways of traveling and communicating. Modern transport and communication make it possible to give the nation a capital, a government, a means of mobilizing the population. Also, the nation gets defined in such a way as to make it a kind of superethnic group—it becomes the horizontal group of groups. This makes possible a politics of mobilization and of mass inclusion. But all too often this is also a politics of exclusion and even a politics of hatred, genocide, or war. These are the main themes that will be dealt with in the following pages.

What Is a Nation?

I begin with this rather basic question. Exactly what do we mean when we refer to a *nation?* And what does *nationalism* consist of? Other related terms include *nation-state, motherland, ethnic group.*

Most of these terms lack a clear meaning, or, at any rate, a meaning that scholars can agree on. This is certainly true of the concept of nationalism.[1] Different scholars use it in different ways. At its core, it seems to refer to a patriotic feeling, a passionate attachment to a country or to the group that makes up the nation.

In ordinary English, a nation is a state, a sovereignty. It is also a place, a geographical entity—that is, some fragment of the globe, a slice of land and water tied together by an invisible barrier called the border, which usually snakes along ridges or mountaintops, or perhaps runs along the middle of a river channel.

Every country has borders, but many of these are culturally meaningless or artificial—a rope tied loosely around a lumpy package. In any event, nobody could be really attached to a nation in the sense of a country, despite all the national anthems and poems about the hills and mountains, sparkling lakes, amber fields of grain, and what not. People do get attached to places; but nobody actually fights and dies for sparkling lakes and rushing rivers; nobody gives up life for the sake of verdant forests or glistening meadows. In fact, *nation* and *nationalism* are terms that describe an emotional bond among people within a country. This bond is either real and actual or an ideal, a goal, a striving. Nationalism, according to Charles A. Kupchan, is "an ideology that calls for the merging of the sentimental nation with the functional state."[2]

In other words, *nation,* though the term often refers to a political entity, implies a kind of ethnicity, a feeling of kinship and belonging.[3] It is a much more highly charged term than *country.* The focus of passion is not the (physical) country, not the land as such, and certainly not the government but rather the group within the state—the people, the tribe, the clan, the collective.[4] Nationalism is, and has to be, a blood brother of ethnicity. The nation is a kind of ethnic group. Small nations are small groups; big ones are big, complicated groups. There is always some kind of intensity, some feeling of kinship, among its members. As Pierre van den Berghe puts it, the "primordial" ethnic group is "an extended family." It is the "outer limits of that inbred group of near or distant kinsmen whom one knows as intimates and whom therefore one can trust."[5] This is, perhaps, a shade too literal. Many of these groups are simply too big. There are more than a billion Chinese. Kinship is to be taken with a grain of salt. But there is usually a sense of oneness—a sense that everybody is in the same boat, that everybody shares a common allegiance. And this requires, of course, the technologies of the horizontal society—without these, the oneness cannot be sustained; indeed, it cannot even be created.

The *state* is not irrelevant; it plays an important role in the concept of nationalism. As Ernest Gellner put it, nationalism is "a principle which holds that the political and national unit should be congruent."[6] A "nationalist," therefore, is not simply somebody who is attached to "his people" but somebody who thinks that his people ought to be a sovereign entity. A person may be fervently Welsh, in the cultural sense—that is, speak Welsh, think Welsh, struggle for the survival of the language and culture— but a Welsh nationalist is someone who also desires a free or autonomous Wales.

Like other key social terms, *nation* and *nationalism* have meant different things in different times and places; an American nationalist and an Estonian nationalist may well be rather different beasts. Most people, however, take it for granted that the world is made up of nations. They may also think that the nation is something exceedingly real and concrete, and something that has always been there—if not actually, then potentially, as if it was always the destiny of Geneva to end up as part of Switzerland or the destiny of California to detach itself from a mismatch with Mexico and join the United States.

No doubt the average person in France or Italy thinks there is something quite specific about French or Italian nationality; that these are clearcut categories of the world, as real as mountains and rivers; and that somehow the nation was always meant to be. Partly this comes about because of the conventional way people teach history to children (and adults). If you think there is and always has been an Italian nation, then the unification of Italy, taking bits and pieces and making Italy out of them, seems like a natural process—and a Good Thing, too. The end result was to take all these lost and scattered "Italians," stitch the fragments together, "liberate" the ones who suffered under (say) Austrian rule, and provide, at long last, a national home for all (or almost all) true Italians.

But in a crucial sense, nations are much less real than people think. Nationhood, in fact, has nothing inevitable about it, either in general or in particular. It is, in the first place, a social construct; or, to use Benedict Anderson's striking (and influential) phrase, nations are "imagined communities." There is nothing natural about the nation-building process at all. Even in the "smallest nation," as Anderson puts it, the citizens do not "know most of their fellow-members." They never see them or meet them or even hear of them; "yet in the minds of each lives the image of their communion."[7] The idea that everybody (of a certain type) belongs to one nation was basically concocted in the nineteenth century. It is part of a very special chapter in political history.

In an important book, Eugen Weber has described the process that turned "peasants into Frenchman." This transformation took place, he argues, between 1870 and 1914.[8] Well into the nineteenth century, peasants inside what is now called France had no idea they were members of the mighty French nation. Their world was small, narrow, isolated; their "country" was the village they lived in and the surrounding countryside. They did not read or speak "French"; rather, they spoke Provençal, Breton, Flemish, Basque, or one of many "French" dialects—some as different from Parisian French as Dutch is from German, or Catalan is from Spanish; in any event, peasants knew almost nothing about "France" and its history; the concept of the nation was completely absent from their mind and from their lives.

What was it, then, that turned peasants into Frenchmen? Road building, which ended the extreme isolation of the villages; schools, which forced the French language down their throats and opened up a somewhat wider world; the army, which conscripted peasants, made them into soldiers, and forced them to communicate in a common language (standard French); and the tools and machines and cultures of modernity. "Roads, railroads, schools, markets, military service, and the circulation of money, goods, and printed matter" were the engines of change; they "swept away old commitments, instilled a national view of things in regional minds, and confirmed the power of that view by offering advancement to those who adopted it." French culture, by the end of the nineteenth century, was becoming "truly national." It was a process of "acculturation." Urban France, metropolitan France, absorbed and civilized the local communities; modernization disintegrated local cultures, and education taught the villagers that they were part of an entity called France.[9]

One can quarrel with the exact dates, of course, and with a detail here or there. The pace of change may have been different in different parts of France: Flemish-speaking northern France, for example, perhaps changed more slowly and responded to somewhat different forces;[10] Brittany had its own rhythm of development and change.[11] But the main story line is powerful and convincing. What was true of France was true of other countries, though each had its own special history and followed its own special line of development. In many regards, these histories are strikingly divergent. In France, it is said, the state preceded the nation, while in Germany, the nation supposedly preceded the state. France, in other words, was bigger in size than the world of the French; it had to absorb and homogenize. Germany, on the other hand, did not exist as such until the middle of the nineteenth century. Instead "Germans" were divided into many states and statelets; "Germans formed a community only in terms of speech; they lacked any kind of united political structure. But this "community" nonetheless developed a sense of self, of nationhood, based on its "common possession" of language and tradition.[12]

Yet, despite differences in the process of nation building, that process everywhere took the same general form: that of dissolving or weakening traditional ways of life and traditional authority. What replaced them were powerful currents of modernity emanating from the center, the capital. The messengers of the new national consciousness were education, newspapers, the army; the process was, in short, profoundly horizontal. Once the forces of modernization were unleashed on the world, once the technological revolution began, the outcome was perhaps inevitable. But nobody could have predicted the exact configurations—nobody could have guessed which "nations" would emerge at the end of it. Nobody could have foreseen that the Netherlands and Switzerland would be nations, but not Scotland or Wales or Catalonia, or that French and Latvian would be official languages, but Provençal would become a dying patois.

Most of the modern nations emerged in the nineteenth century. Often, intellectuals formed a kind of vanguard in the process; they were the foot soldiers of nationhood. In a country like France, they were centralizers, carriers of high culture—and enemies of the dialects, subcultures, and minority languages. In other places, they were members of an elite subculture. Many of these elites took on the job of national liberation (as they defined it), but they had to begin by liberating the minds of the people, who did not always know they had to be liberated. The elites had to teach the ordinary folks, farmers mostly, that they were part of a larger entity, instead of simply clods of earth in some village, people whose horizons never extended past a few miles of dusty road. As we mentioned, schools and armies were important tools of this development, but there were others—even choral groups and clubs.[13]

In the nineteenth century dozens of smaller ethnic groups in Europe seemed to wake up from their sleep to think of themselves indeed as being a nation, just like England or Russia or France, the big boys on the block. They acquired a sense of commonality, a sense of kinship. But this consciousness developed slowly, as it had even in France. Small circles of committed intellectuals worked hard at the job—trying to create, for example, national languages out of rainbows of dialects (more of this shortly). They also theorized about the *Volk*, collected folk songs, lovingly chronicled customs, and published propaganda about the nation. Last but not least, they often agitated for national independence. In any event, what came first was the sense of commonality: religion, language, culture, or all of these. Language was often a crucial factor, though not always. A passion for sovereignty did not *cause* nationhood; it was, in fact, a consequence.

This was the journey traveled by Czechs, Estonians, Latvians, Poles, Catalans, Icelanders, the Irish, Basques, and so many others; most of these peoples have their own country today; others have been able to elbow their way to autonomy inside a larger nation. The latest spurt of nation making, in our times, occurred when the Soviet empire disintegrated; after the dust settled, more than a dozen new "nations" climbed out of the rubble. Each of the Soviet republics is now a free nation, with everything that goes with nationhood—a capital, a presidential palace (or the like), an ambassador to the United Nations, flags, songs, and the rest. Other potential nations are still waiting in the wings. Ideas that once seemed ridiculous—an independent Abkhazia or Chechnya or Moldova, an independent Nauru or Seychelles, for example—have either come to pass or are now no longer out of the question.[14]

No scholar of nationalism has been more significant, perhaps, than Ernest Gellner. Gellner's account of the rise and meaning of nationalism puts heavy stress on the needs of industrial society.[15] Industrial society, unlike agrarian society, demands a "new *kind* of division of labour." In these modern economies, people have to be "ready to move from one occupational position to another, even within a single life-span." The workforce has to have a shared culture and preferably a shared language. Workers have to be able to "communicate contextlessly and with precision with all comers . . . through abstract means of communication." The social units, therefore, have to be "large and yet culturally homogeneous." But this means there has to be a *state,* a "centralized order-enforcing agency," a "high culture," an educational system, and a way of spreading the culture through the entire population. In short, there is a necessary linkage between modern society, industrial society, nationalism, and the nation-state.[16] In other words, nineteenth- and twentieth-century man "does not merely industrialize, he industrializes *as* a German or Russian or Japanese. . . . Modern industrial High Culture is not colourless; it has an 'ethnic' colouring, which is of its essence."[17]

Gellner, of course, is talking about horizontal societies. He is talking about societies in which the tiny, primary groups have tended to disintegrate and in which a larger unity gets cobbled together. This is the nation-state. Nationalism is the glue that keeps it from flying apart.

We should not exaggerate how *new* it is to feel part of a nation or an ethnic group. Obviously, people have always been aware of other people, different people, just beyond the bend in that dusty road or in a village in the next clearing in the woods—people who might speak a strange language or dialect or look different or follow different ways of life and worship different gods. The idea of the nation is a social construct, but it is not a total invention. It has its roots in the sense of ethnicity, and that sense is not *entirely* a nineteenth-century invention. It goes back much further in time. Something like a sense of nationhood, or peoplehood, is certainly to be found in the history of the Jews, as recounted in the Old Testament, and among the classical Greeks.[18] Indeed, it could be argued that "modern nations and nationalism have only extended and deepened the meanings and scope of older ethnic concepts and structures." This point has been powerfully argued by Anthony D. Smith.[19] National feeling has to have something to build on. That has to be admitted. There must be something there, some consciousness of like and unlike, some sense of a common history and a common destiny. It cannot be *wholly* invented. But what gets made out of the raw materials—how they come together to form the idea of the nation—this is, indeed, largely the product of modern times.

All horizontal groups are both real and artificial. Even myths have to have something to go on. There obviously are Hispanics, and they share certain traits of culture and language. There obviously *is* such a thing as gender; and there is something quite concrete about being blind or deaf. Today, there definitely *is* such a place as Romania. It is on the map; it has borders and embassies and membership in the United Nations and all the rest of the trappings. These things do not make a nation, but once the nation is in place, they help to strengthen it. And they tend to succeed all the more if there is something real to build on. It is a fact, for example, that most people in "Romania" speak a Romance idiom, in the midst of a sea of Magyars and Slavs, and that for the most part they share a religion and (perhaps) a way of life.[20]

These bedrock facts construct a foundation on which one can erect the temple of Romanian national identity. What Romanians worship in the temple is quite another story. Romanian history and propaganda endlessly tout the noble connection between the grand old Roman province of Dacia and modern Romania, which is depicted as a kind of direct descendant.[21] Dacia, which was a piece of the greatest empire of all times and shares its reflected glory, seems much more *worthy* somehow than most of the rest of "Romanian" history, which is, after all, a dreary tale of impoverished peasants, conquered and reconquered, and living and dying in Balkan obscurity for centuries on end.

The Language Issue

Language is at the very core of culture or ethnic identity, or seems to be. This is certainly a strong impression in places like Estonia or the Czech Republic or Korea. The true borders are not rivers or mountain ridges or lines on the map but linguistic frontiers: where Czech ends and German or Slovak begins. What could be more real, more concrete, than the fact of language?

Yet in some ways, languages are like nations: all modern languages are both real and nonreal. As Eric Hobsbawm has pointed out, national languages are in fact "almost always semi-artificial constructs. . . . They are the opposite of what nationalist mythology supposes them to be, namely the primordial foundations of national culture."[22] Indeed, the national language (the standard language) is something cultivated, grown, worked on, fashioned. The process took place in waves: the Reformation, for example, brought about one wave because of its enthusiasm for translating the Bible into ordinary languages. But the process accelerated in the nineteenth century.[23]

Again, there was nothing inevitable about the creation of any *particular* national language—and nothing inherent or a priori to tell us *what* that language would look like. Dutch is an independent language taught in Dutch schools, with a literature and a tradition and a great deal of pride and prestige. Across the border, in Germany, people speak low-German dialects; these, historically, were closely related to those speech habits now called Flemish or Dutch. The differences are not really linguistic; they are historical and political. The Netherlands is an independent country, a nation; it uses its language in schools, on TV, and in court; Dutch is a culture language, a standardized and literary tongue. The German dialects, on the other hand, are rural speechways, with no prestige and no hope for advancement; socially, they are defined as substandard and stamped with the stigma of low status. They are dying out rapidly. Nothing in the languages themselves doomed them to extinction. History and politics have made all the difference.[24] Swedish, Danish, and Norwegian are distinct languages even though they are closer to each other than many dialects of Italian; this is because Sweden, Denmark, and Norway are distinct countries and get to control and define their official language.[25] A language has been defined, cynically but accurately, as a "dialect with an army and a navy."[26] One might add: and a TV station and control of the schools. If Quechua can get itself made official, if it can get teachers and announcers and programs, it can make its way in Peru, even against mighty Spanish, and *without* an army and navy.[27]

It took hard work and dedication to make standard languages out of some spoken jargon, which is what every official language was at one time. It would probably insult the French to describe their language as a hopelessly mangled vulgar Latin larded with barbaric borrowings, but that would be rather close to the mark. A similar comment could be made about the other Romance languages. Or English could be described as a creolized Germanic tongue, crammed with a flock of mispronounced words from Latin and French. English might have died out completely if the Norman conquerors had come in droves, instead of dribs and drabs—if they had succeeded in swamping and outreproducing the Anglo-Saxon peasants. In that case, the mighty English language would be as marginal today as Frisian or Welsh—or even extinct, like Cornish and Manx.

In the history of standard languages, as we pointed out, intellectuals often played a key role, gathering up bits and pieces from various dialects, listening to peasants, collecting folktales, inventing new words, establishing a norm out of speechways that were, in the past, sometimes so different that one speaker of Italian could hardly understand most of the others. They labored like ants, patiently creating their national languages and the national sense of identity along with it. They pieced together something firm, standard, uniform, and often rather new: Nynorsk in Norway, for example—now one of the country's official languages. Of course, the emerging languages were not pure inventions—they were syntheses. In the case of, say, French or German, the standard was there already; the problem was how to get the masses to speak it, and speak it properly. Other, submerged languages (Basque, Breton, Finnish, Czech, Albanian) were in more serious difficulty. A few had sunk to the level of a local patois; without standards, without a center, nothing prevented a language group from splintering into fragments. This is, after all, what happened to Latin when barbarian hordes ate out the heart of the empire. Latin shattered into dozens of pieces—which were patiently reassembled and aggregated, much later on, into entities we today call Italian or Romanian or Spanish.[28]

Clearly, reviving or exalting a standard, national language also meant getting rid of its rivals: extinguishing local differences and ruthlessly suppressing those dialects and minority languages that lost out in the race for dominance. French has largely defeated Breton, Flemish, Catalan, Basque, Provençal, German, Italian—minority languages within France; but its main conquest was the conquest of other forms of French. In fact, French was a foreign language for almost half of all children who reached adulthood in France in the last quarter of the nineteenth century.[29] English has driven Manx and Cornish to extinction and threatens Welsh, Irish, and Gaelic; but again its main victims have been the dialects, including the speechways of Scotland, which might have evolved into a national language if Elizabeth I had been survived by children, instead of a cousin who happened to be the king of Scotland.

Language, though crucial, is not the only element in nationhood. Sometimes, as in the case of the German nation, the language element was early and powerful; there was a standard (High) German language, which influenced builders of ethnic solidarity perhaps more than the nationalists influenced the formation of a standard language. The process took different twists and turns in other places. In Belgium, the Flemish movement at first wanted nothing more than recognition for its language, which the movement defined as identical with Dutch. After 1890 or so, there was a "shift from language to ethnicity." That is, the Flemish movement came to emphasize culture, "group solidarity," and "development of the Flemish nation."[30]

A common language is crucial because language carries culture. A nation is not a nation without something it can call a culture. If the language is small and confined to one country, then the culture and the language are pretty much coextensive, at least psychologically. There are many examples: Estonian, Icelandic, Samoan. Obviously, the case is different for countries that share their language with others—countries speaking English or Spanish or Arabic. In these countries, language is important but it has to share the stage with other carriers of culture. Among these world languages, there are forces keeping them together and forces pulling them apart. Nationalism, of course, is one of the latter. At times there has been talk about the "American language"; H. L. Mencken wrote a book with that title.[31] One finds differences in spelling and pronunciation between England and the United States, not to mention Barbados or Australia. But in a horizontal world, TV, the movies, and print media tend in the opposite direction: they prevent the fatal splintering of English. A similar story can be told for Spanish. For Arabic, the immense power of the Koran is a factor. On the other hand, in war-torn Bosnia, each of the three ethnic groups (Serbs, Croats, and Muslims) have taken to insisting that each speaks a separate language, although the differences are basically trivial—less than those between the English of Queen Elizabeth II and that of the American president.[32]

In other places, language will not do as the chief vehicle of national identity because there are too many languages, and no clear candidate for primacy. The language question in India or Nigeria—with dozens of languages—is thus quite different from the language question in Belgium or Canada. In India, religion—particularly militant Hinduism—takes the place of language as the cement of national identity; at least this is what the Hindu movement would like. It seeks to forge a "pan-Hindu identity, facilitated by modern mass communications," and this may result in an "increasingly self-conscious religious community capable of transcending its own heterogeneity."[33]

As the example of India suggests, religion is another possible building block for national identity. Some small ethnic groups do not share their religion (or language) with anybody else; for them, language (or religion) can occupy center stage as a basis of national identity. Christianity, Buddhism, and Islam, however, are world religions. Hence, in, say, Islamic countries, religion can be *part* of the basis for national identity, but not all of it. The same is true of Protestant Christianity in, say, Barbados or New Zealand—they share this with many other countries, just as they share the English language. National identity can be cobbled together out of many elements. What they all have in common is that they must base this identity on the tools of a horizontal society. They all depend on techniques and tactics of mobilization that are distinctly modern or at least take on a heightened form in our times.

Ethnic Identity and Historical Memory. As we have seen, in discussing national languages, it takes hard work to create, and maintain, a sense of ethnic identity. This is why the efforts of nineteenth-century nationalists were so crucial. Ethnicity was, in a way, *there,* as a possibility, a block of marble unshaped by the sculptor. It was inchoate, like the standard languages. There were dialects of blood and religion and custom, and dialects of memory, folklore, and historical experience. Out of these, a sense of identity could be, and often was, patiently stitched.

Other symbols and practices were also mobilized, in order to give cohesion to the nation. There were rituals, parades, customs, costumes, ceremonies—carefully nurtured, often enough, by nationalists, central governments, and whoever stood to gain from nationhood. These gewgaws and trappings serve to bind the members of the nation together emotionally, to provide a basis for unity, to provide common experiences and references, and to give the illusion of a common past. Effort is necessary because the nation is, for most people, the largest horizontal unit of them all. And it tends to be somewhat remote and abstract—or runs this danger. The nation, after all, is hardly a natural unit, like the family or the village community is. The nation has to be massaged into life.

Customs and rituals often carry with them supporting legends and tales. Many are supposed to be hoary with age, inheritances from the distant, misty past. In fact, they are often pure legend. It would surprise most Scots to know that clan tartans and kilts are, to be blunt, fabrications concocted in fairly recent times; and it would surprise most of the English to know that much of the time-honored pomp and circumstance that surrounds the royal family is also recent—and rather manipulative at that. As Eric Hobsbawm put it, rather baldly, these are "invented" traditions.[34]

But artificial or invented does not mean unimportant. A flag, after all, is more than a random fluttering rag. It is a symbol; it is supposed to carry meaning, and for many people it does—it is enough to mention the ruckus over flag burning in the United States.[35] Legends and stories also carry meanings. Many countries (and ethnic groups) have myths of origin: tales of some murky common ancestor, stories about their descent from a god or gods, or some heroic, defining saga that is at the heart of a national history. Hobsbawm has remarked that modern nations "generally claim to be the opposite of novel"; they assert that they are "rooted in the remotest antiquity, and the opposite of constructed." They claim to be "human communities so 'natural' as to require no definition other than self-assertion."[36] If everybody in the nation is descended from some primordial god or ancestor, then they are all members of the same huge family; they are all children, or children's children, of the same primitive father or mother.

All over the world, we find these defining myths: myths that "provide the means of collective location in the world and the charter of the community which explains its origins, growth and destiny."[37] Most self-conscious groups have, in fact, an official history, that is, stories they tell about themselves, whether or not they have a descent myth, literally speaking. Indeed, in the words of Stephen Van Evera, "chauvinistic mythmaking" is a "hallmark of nationalism." Evera classifies these myths into three categories: self-glorifying, self-whitewashing, and other-maligning (the third category, which is quite important, refers to myths that denigrate nonmembers).[38] Such myths have little enough to do with history as a professional historian would understand it today. But even professional history was, until quite recently, drenched in chauvinistic myths.[39]

The history that nationalists write is, therefore, a social construct, an interpretation masquerading as a collection of bald facts. Of course, in a sense all histories are constructs of this type. But there are constructs and constructs. Nationalist movements, in general, aim to create a "truly living past," a past full of wonderful or heroic or tragic tableaux; the point is to strengthen the notion of a single people with a single story, a story that unites the whole country in a common experience. Thus we have William Tell and his apple, "Alexander Nevsky slaughtering the Teutonic Knights," Joan of Arc, the Jewish people weeping by the "waters of Babylon," and the "last Welsh bard lamenting on a crag above King Edward's advancing army."[40] These myths and stories continue to be created. In the United States, there is Afro-centrism. Some Native American scholars claim that the "roots of democratic ideals, such as free speech and participatory democracy," are to be found "in Native American traditions" and that "Native Americans influenced, rather than experienced, colonial political institutions."[41] Many countries tell tales of great victories, battles that were won and were turning points in the glorious tapestry of history—Waterloo, Agincourt, Gettysburg; these are particularly common in the big and successful countries, which, after all, have a history of winning and swallowing up their rivals. Other people, like the Jews and the Armenians, have to make do with stories that include murder, defeat, and oppression. But these too have great power. Israel celebrates the heroic resistance of Jews against Romans at Masada, even though it ended in a bloodbath.[42] The United States has its own tales of glory and virtue: Paul Revere's ride, the Alamo, and so on.

Of course, this phenomenon—heroic, didactic history—is not particularly new. Myths of glory are found among ancient peoples, too. The Old Testament is a magnificent anthology of origin stories. The Bible tells a history of the Jewish people that makes them descendants of wonderful, miracle-working ancestors, and it assigns them a special relationship to God. The Romans also had their myth of origin: two boys raised by wolves. The stories told by dozens and dozens of cultures, ancient and modern, though they are supposed to be historical, basically express "ideology in a narrative . . . structure"; they symbolize the "moral consciousness" of the country.[43] Since these stories emphasize *common* experience, it puts an almost genetic stamp on nationality.

More surprising than the myths of preliterate, tribal peoples, about the Great Turtle God or the like, are the ways that modern nations, up-to-date contemporary countries, preserve the functional equivalents. American history is taught as a myth of origin—what "we" did, the wars "we" won, the glories of our ancestors, the wonders of our Founding Fathers, the suffering of the Pilgrims, whether or not little Korean-American or Irish-American or black children in the classroom have any actual link to the people who made up the "we" at the time. (The children in the classroom might even be descendants of people "we" were fighting against.) Jews recite "we were slaves in Egypt," without taking into account the thousands of years since Egypt and the thousands of people marrying and converting in and out of Judaism. These matters fall by the wayside.

History is a serious subject, but popular and nationalist history is another thing entirely—idealized, half mythical. As we noted, the Romanians celebrate the ancient Roman province of Dacia—and would just as soon forget most of the centuries in between then and now. The Israelis dwell on Davidic Israel and give short shrift to the Diaspora; Mexicans tend to treat the Aztecs as their true ancestors, even though the great majority of Mexicans speak Spanish and only Spanish, and many of them have Spanish blood or a mixture of Spanish and Indian blood. History gets constructed and reconstructed in the name of the national myth. Most countries have legends, too, that take the form of silence: past embarrassments are omitted; injustices and cruelties, which might ruin the parade of virtue, are ignored. Most students in the United States, who are forced to swallow large draughts of American history, have never heard about the wanton killing of Native Americans; the Japanese gloss over the rape of Nanking and similar indiscretions. Inconvenient, shameful, embarrassing periods are inevitably reconfigured. It all ends up as a tale of glory or, when that would be too much of a stretch, a sorrowful tale of suffering, inflicted by others. History, unlike the Father of Our Country, can definitely tell a lie.

History, in short, ends up as *national* history, as a celebration of the nation, a story that defines what the nation consists of, that recites its experiences, its common past.[44] In fact, these fantasies are not about the past at all; they are really stories about the present—and the future. They assume or advocate a future in which the members of the group will enjoy greater prosperity and glory precisely because of their share in the honorable past. The alternative is a kind of extinction, which people cannot face, either for themselves or for some larger grouping which claims their identity.

Origin myths, of course, do not have to stand the test of truth; the actual nations that are supposed to be descended from a sun goddess or from two boys raised by wolves, or whatever, are never actually made up of a single line of descent. Nations are stewed mixtures of all sorts of people, thrown together by history, accident, conquest, and random fornication. Modern countries, to be sure, have no truck with the more blatant origin myths, which are out of place in an age of science and skepticism. Nor do they work in the same way in immigrant countries—places like the United States or Australia, where the population has nothing to do with goddesses or wolves, and everything to do with transatlantic and transpacific passage. These countries cannot claim that their citizens are members of a single giant family in the literal sense; and they are far too recent to have the kind of origin myths the Romans had. In many cases, there was a basic stock of early immigrants who seized on and captured the high ground of nationhood; later immigrants, who tend to be more heterogeneous, have the job of assimilating themselves into the social patterns of the "natives."

Obviously, in Australia or Argentina, nationhood has to be based on something different from the *Blut* and *Volk* of the Germans and similar countries. The immigrant nations have their own myths of unity, their tales of glory and victory, and their modified version of descent as well. In Australia, it is even an honor to trace one's ancestry to convicts dumped in Botany Bay. In the United States, it was for a long time taken for granted that the real Americans, the Americans of Americans, were white Protestants whose great-great-great-great-grandfathers (or grandmothers) "came over on the *Mayflower*"; arrival on some leaky tub in the nineteenth century would not do. The honor goes to the pioneers and the people who share their blood. Still, nationhood may, in fact, be slightly weaker in these immigrant countries than in the Blut and Volk variety of nation. Despite this—or because?—these countries seem to be prone to outbursts of ferocious patriotism, and even nativism. At least this is true (unfortunately) in the United States.

As we shall see, nowadays, in the high period of multiculturalism, the pretensions of the early settlers no longer go uncontested. The *Mayflower* crowd has been taken down a peg or two, and the leaky tubs have developed their own myths of suffering and redemption. There is a reaction against official history. Still, it remains very popular in majority circles. Historians or others who attack the received and glorious narrative of American experience stir up a hornet's nest. They are accused of defiling the temple, or even of something close to treason.[45]

Immigrant countries, like all the rest, write history in terms of patriotic glory, with heroes, noble battles, martyrs, and villains, and they have their own standard lists of defining and important events. Even when these events are not pure inventions, they get a chauvinistic spin: the wars are always justified, land grabs were the working out of manifest destiny, and so on. Until very recently, did any teacher of history at the high school level, anywhere in America, *seriously* question the rights and wrongs of the war with Mexico? Or the war with Spain?

Constructed history is useful, because it helps to answer the question What *is* the nation? The answer it gives is this: the nation is a group that has traveled along the same historical road, made the same journey together. A nation is a kind of superclan, a grotesquely extended family. It therefore shares, as it were, the same childhood, the same affective experiences. The language of nationality, like the language of ethnicity, "is the language of kinship."[46] This is why origin myths, ethnic symbols, and ethnic histories survive in the global society. Whatever their meaning in the ancient world, they live on today because they have a profoundly modern function: they provide, or try to provide, a common denominator in a world of horizontal affiliation. The nation is the largest of the horizontal groups, and these myths and symbols help to define it, mark its boundaries, and describe its history and traditions.

New and Artificial Nations

We have talked about how nations were made, mostly in the nineteenth century, out of an inchoate mass, a potential lump of ethnicity. In some cases, however, the trip has gone in the other direction. That is, the nation came first—as a political and legal entity, as a sovereignty—and nationalism, national feeling, and true nationhood came only later. This is very much the situation in large parts of Africa. As colonial powers pulled out or were driven out, they left behind a flock of new countries. But these were little more than lines on maps—administrative districts. The lines meant nothing in any cultural or ethnic sense; they were drawn as a result of the machinations of the colonial powers, and little more.[47]

These countries, then, as they staggered out of the dungeon of imperialism into the sun, were themselves as much prison houses of nations as the old Austro-Hungarian empire. That is, they were typically made up of a bewildering array of language and culture groups. African countries tend to be mad mosaics of splinters and fragments, mélanges of small and large groups speaking in many tongues; the boundaries of language groups, clans, and ethnicities, are often vague or undefined and in any event have nothing to do with the boundary lines drawn by colonial powers.

Yet, however artificial these borders were and are, and however little sense of nationhood there was in Africa, it seemed only "right and natural" that Africans would be organized into nation-states "on the European pattern."[48] This was one point on which colonial rebels and colonial masters were in agreement. As independent countries, they seem much less likely to break up than the old empires of Europe. Their subnations on the whole have as little cohesion as the country itself, and they lack the kind of national feeling that leads to independence movements, rebellions, disintegration. The few exceptions only prove the rule. The Ibos tried to secede from Nigeria, but the central government clawed its way back to unity over a mountain of corpses.

Nation building became a special task for almost all African countries, as the colonial empires disintegrated. It is far from an easy job. In the West, the forces that produced the horizontal society were also the engines of nation building: roads, schools, a national language, and (most powerfully) modern means of transport and communication. The countries of Africa are dirt-poor. Many of them lack decent roads, or roads of any kind. Much of the population lives beyond the reach of the central government. Under these conditions, it is hard to build a nation. Extreme poverty also retards the forces that make some kind of horizontal unity possible. Still, there *is* radio and TV, and in many of these countries people as a whole are far less isolated than, say, the inhabitants of a French village in the twelfth century. Yet in the larger countries—say, Nigeria or the Sudan—there are too many different groups inside the borders; weaving them together, under current economic and social conditions, and with the inevitable scramble for scarce resources, seems almost impossible.

In much of Latin America, the problem is somewhat different. The borders seem artificial not because there are too many ethnic groups but because the people on the other side of the border are often a lot like—or identical to—the people on this side. What is it that makes a self-conscious nation out of Honduras, for example, as opposed to El Salvador? The two countries hardly constitute distinct ethnic groups; the people speak the same language, enjoy the same climate, grow the same crops, suffer from the same cluster of insoluble problems. They do have separate histories, of course—every independent country, after all, has its own history. They also share a joint history of conflict, sometimes rather bloody.

But where did Honduras come from in the first place? The answer lies in part in accidents of the old Spanish empire and in the rather artificial boundaries it drew for administrative purposes; and in part in certain twists and turns of Central American or Latin American politics. These factors never had much to do with ethnicity, let alone with nationhood. Venezuela, according to one scholar, was basically not a state at all in the nineteenth century but merely a collection of squabbling vicinities.[49] Of course this was hardly unique: one wonders what Ethiopia or Nepal meant to most people who lived in Ethiopia or Nepal in the nineteenth century—even assuming it means very much today. As we saw, it was also a question what France meant to the people who lived within its borders. In 1800, or 1820, probably not very much.[50] Perhaps this hardly mattered in nineteenth-century France or Venezuela—but it matters greatly today, since modern governments, for their own sake if nothing else, feel that they cannot survive without some sort of unity and nationhood.

In any event, when the dust settled in Central America, a country called Honduras appeared on the map. It acquired the trappings of a nation and (in time) a history of its own, not to mention a certain amount of shared experience. Out of such materials, one can *maybe* create the sense of a distinct community, which at least some people who live in Honduras might possibly feel. Unquestionably, there *is* a Honduras today; it is a legitimate member of the community of nations. It has a seat in the United Nations; it has embassies here and there; it has (unfortunately) an army; it has all the outward signs of a nation; and it meets the minimum condition for entry into the community of nations.[51] There is most certainly a Venezuela and a France. Whether in any meaningful sense there is a Liberia or an Afghanistan, to mention two unhappy, fragmented countries, is at the moment a more difficult question.

Today, in international politics, a situation in which one state tries to gobble up another is considered dangerous and unsettling. This feeling in the international community tends to keep alive various "fictitious" nations, a term used by James Mayall, who applied it to such countries as

Chad or Lebanon. At any other time in history, Mayall remarks, "They would have long since fallen prey to the ambitions of imperialist neighbours [or] . . . disintegrated into smaller units." But today, "territorial revision is . . . regarded as anachronistic." The secretary general of the United Nations, U Thant, stated in 1970 that "the United Nations has never accepted and does not accept and I do not believe will ever accept a principle of secession of a part" of a member state.[52] This attitude, and the geopolitical fact it reflects, serves as a kind of life-support system, a collection of tubes and ventilators that keeps certain states alive, even when they are (in Mayall's view) "manifestly not viable."[53] When Iraq tried to swallow up Kuwait, a fictitious country if there ever was one, the United States responded with force, and most of the world cheered from the sidelines. This was not the only factor that led to the Gulf War (Kuwait sits on top of a huge pool of oil), but the war would not have had the sheer legitimacy it garnered if masses of people had not been convinced that it was intolerable to allow Iraq to violate Kuwait's sovereignty through aggression.

But perhaps, like Honduras, Chad, and Lebanon—and probably even Kuwait—after a while fictitious countries start to become less fictitious. In a curious way, the fictitious nations strengthen the general thesis about "imagined communities." Although historical accidents produce these nations and preserve them through their comatose states, still, if they last long enough, they tend to regenerate themselves. That is, a sense of nationality somehow gets contrived, and in the end, they too can and do become as real as the true nations—all of which, after all, are themselves imagined communities. In all of these real nations, too, there is a heavy element of historical accident—or, if we do not like the word *accident*, a heavy element of contingency. But for this or that turn of the wheel, France could have been two countries or six countries or no country at all. As Harold Isaacs has pointed out, there is no law of history, no formula, that can explain why "little Gambia and the tiny islands of Fiji, Nauru and Grenada could become 'nations,' while big Biafra could not"; or why tiny Bahrain is a member of the United Nations and all that, while the poor "Kurds must still fight on to establish their own Kurdistan."[54]

Among African countries, it is rarely the case that a single ethnic group monopolizes or dominates the whole country. (One exception, ironically, is Somalia.) Almost every country struggles with the problem of multiplicity, sometimes peacefully, though often not; yet central governments are determined to hold the country together. In many cases, at least the outlines of a kind of nationhood can already be perceived. These countries by now have a common history, colonial or otherwise. Their tribes, groups, and language communities, then, are like partners in a bad marriage who have stuck it out for many years. They may not like each other, but they have accumulated a longtime stock of common memory and experience, and this forms a makeshift bond or perhaps scar tissue, crusting over ancient wounds.

Something similar happens in what we might call splinter nations. Between the two world wars, Austria was a small rump state, a hunk of German-speaking people left over when the Austro-Hungarian empire was stripped of its captive nations. Nobody expected the country to last; indeed, few Austrians thought of it as a country at all. *Anschluss* with Germany was a foregone conclusion. But then came an actual Anschluss, as their native son, Adolph Hitler, entered triumphantly into Vienna. Austria suddenly ceased to exist as a nation; the very name was obliterated. Then war broke out, followed by the defeat and dismemberment of Germany. Austria was reconstituted as a country and has been independent ever since. Anschluss no longer seems like a real option; and Austrian nationalism may be in process of formation. There is, after all, a glorious imperial past to work with. Austria is by now most definitely a nation; at any rate, its population certainly thinks so.[55] Moldova is another splinter country—a small fragment of what used to be the Soviet Union; largely made up of Romanian speakers, it remains to be seen whether it stays independent or hitches its wagon to Romania.

In any event, it is assumed today that the whole world is and has to be divided into nations. Some of these nations are so feeble and artificial that they split in two (like Czechoslovakia). Where this is not possible or desirable, then nation building is a necessity. Everything can be mobilized for this noble end: banners, national songs and colors, patriotic blather, TV messages, schoolbooks praising the nation or its leader or its past. Whether this works, and under what conditions, is hard to predict with any accuracy.[56]

In any event, it should be clear by now that a nation is less a matter of (legal) sovereignty than a state of mind, an attitude, a concept. And this concept is very much the creature of modern culture—a culture of horizontal groups; and of horizontal groups that nest inside other horizontal groups. The nation, as we have said, is the largest of these groups, the most inclusive. There are good nations, bad nations, pluralistic nations, monolithic nations, nations that work as nations, and nations that are falling apart. But they all struggle with the problem of unity, of parallel action, of legitimacy, within a horizontal society. They all use the same horizontal means—notably the media—to attack their problems. And they all feel, instinctively, the same need to mobilize the population, and for the same reason. A king of medieval France did not worry about the loyalty of peasants to France—or even to the king. Famine, pestilence, or religious differences could bring about unrest, but rarely was unrest based on divided loyalties or the problems of ethnic belonging.

Nations and Subnations

As we noted, the literature on nationalism and the nation is awesome in size. Some basic insights are widely accepted: Anderson, for example, is often cited, and his point about "imagined communities" has won a good deal of acceptance. The insights of the literature also apply to subnations—to groups inside countries: the Québecois, for example, with their distinctive spin on who they are and what their history consists of. The Québecois have a common language and live in a compact, and distinctive, place.

But there is also a growing tendency throughout the world for ethnic solidarity, even among groups that are scattered here and there within national borders, like raisins in a cake. In the United States, for example, Poles, Italians, Greeks, Jews, and other immigrant groups have shown a tendency to grow their own brand of imagined brotherhood. This, of course, is a relatively new development. The "masses of immigrants brought no sense of nationality to America with them, only local identities and allegiances." Solidarity came later—as a result, really, of what happened in America, not what happened in the old country.[57] Originally, there was a strong impulse to assimilate—to dive into the famous melting pot. (I return to the concept of the melting pot in a later chapter.) For many children of the children of immigrants, a sharp sense of ethnic belonging sprang up only *after* they had, in fact, almost totally assimilated. Immigrant ghettos were once compact and organized more or less vertically—they were, in some regards, outposts of the old country and carried over many of the customs, habits, and ways of thought of traditional society. Now most of the older ghettos are no more, the ethnics are strewn about the suburbs and the exurbs, and their solidarity, such as it is, is purely horizontal.[58]

In some cases, a new kind of ethnicity develops, which has no real counterpart "outside." This is true, as we shall see, of the panethnicities. "Asian-American," for example, is a recent construct. The people who collectively are called Asian-American certainly did not cohere in any meaningful way in Asia itself.[59] Indeed, some of the groups that make up Asian-American roundly hated each other back home. In Asia, there was no pan-Asian sense among Koreans, Japanese, and Chinese; to the contrary, they were historic enemies. And any notion that they had anything in common with Samoans or Cambodians would have struck them as bizarre. Of course, most Americans do not make fine distinctions between, say, Koreans and Chinese. A sense that "white people" are prejudiced against all people from Asia has turned these distinctive groups into generalized "Asians."[60] Anti-Semitism created a sense of beleaguered solidarity among Jews who had almost nothing else in common but the fact that Christians hated them. In Germany, people tended to lump all "guest workers" into a kind of panethnicity, mixing together Greeks, Turks, Spaniards, and Italians.[61]

Immigrants, of course, do not "automatically or inevitably" become ethnic minorities. That comes after a process in which "dominant groups in society ascribe certain (real or imagined) characteristics to the newcomers" and use these to "justify the assignment of specific economic, social, and political roles."[62] This quote refers to "guest workers" in Europe, but it is equally true of, say, Hispanics in the United States, a category that throws Cubans, Salvadorans, Puerto Ricans, Mexicans, and Bolivians, among others, into the selfsame pot. Panethnics are not necessarily groups scraping the bottom of the melting pot; they may even be elites. In nineteenth-century Shanghai, and in other Chinese cities, a kind of panethnicity formed in the European enclaves. The Chinese did not make fine distinctions between Americans, Russians, Germans, or the British and French; in the foreign compound, where they all lived, they became part of a single social entity—they were all "Europeans" or perhaps all "foreign devils."

If the lumping process goes on long enough, the panethnicity will very likely begin to "take" among the objects of the lumping, and they will begin to feel their commonalities as never before. Each nation, then, and each subnation, is an imagined community. The imagination of the group goes beyond the group itself; it constructs and imagines the outsiders as well. These outsiders constitute the "other," or, if we want to put it this way, the imagined *non*community.[63] The national myths, in a complex process, build up a view of the outside world—often enough in the guise of an enemy. The minorities themselves think of the majority as some kind of huge panethnicity. African-Americans talk about "whites," Jews talk about "gentiles," Hispanics talk about "Anglos," gay people talk about "straights," as if these entities—we might call them *fictive majorities*—were actual and cohesive groups, with common goals, habits, and customs. In many countries, foreigners are objects of suspicion, and particular groups of foreigners may be identified with some historical and inveterate enemy. These processes feed the ethnic wars that so disgrace the earth today. The Bulgarians have their minority Turks, the Turks their Kurds and Armenians. Attitudes toward foreigners, very obviously, are decisive in shaping laws of immigration and citizenship (of which more later)—laws about which people to let in and which to keep out of the national community.

There is also an important class of what we might call metaphorical nations. These nations have no borders and no basis in blood or descent, but more and more they are elbowing their way toward the center of modern political and cultural life. I refer to such nations as the gays, the elderly, or feminists. These subnations use symbols, myths, claims, and rituals different from those of the "real" subnations: people in wheelchairs, for example, do not claim to be descended from some common ancestor. They know that their group is, in a way, artificial; their solidarity is based on common experience and feelings. These groups could never come alive without the skills and technology of a horizontal society. But once we realize that the true nations are also horizontal groups—indeed, they are, as we said, the group of groups—and are also artificial in much the same way as, say, the nation of the deaf, then we can see why it is important to draw the connection. A deaf person can choose to join the nation of the deaf or the nation of Islam—or the nation of America, for that matter.

The nation of the deaf, like all nations, can construct for itself potent symbols, sagas, myths, and histories. It can fight its own wars and celebrate its own heroes and victories. For example, during the 1988 "revolution" at Gallaudet University, an institution for the deaf, the students rose up and demanded a president drawn from among their "nation."[64] Many of the subnations—notably, gays and lesbians—have consciously or uncon- sciously gone about creating a history, celebrating landmarks and heroes, and working to establish tools and symbols of nationhood.

The women's movement is too important to pass over without adding a few words. Obviously, women have always been aware that they were women and that they were most definitely not the same as men. Gender has always been an element of identity—indeed, it would be hard to think of a more powerful and basic distinction, in all human societies, than the line between women and men. What is different in the horizontal society is the concept of "women" as an interest group, an identity group, or even as a kind of "nation," united by certain core women's issues. In a horizon- tal society, women can bond or connect *as women,* just as coin collectors or Asian-Americans or the deaf can bond or connect in *their* terms. The struc- tural aspects of the horizontal society make this kind of bonding possible, but the *culture* of a horizontal society makes such bonding not only possi- ble but real. In particular, the trait of modernity that most fosters feminism is individualism—the idea that all human beings share basic rights, and the concurrent idea that the task of each of us is to craft our own way in the world. Individualism attacks the old traditions that put women "in their place" and allows them to create a new self out of the rubble left behind when the old roles ruptured and exploded.

The Politics of Exclusion

Nationhood has to do with allegiance and connection, with a hori- zontal unity that binds all true members into one enormous group. The symbols, myths, stories, flags, and so on, are all means to that end: national kinship. Modern nations, as we said, are unlikely to insist that all its citizens are kin, in any literal sense, but they have their own, more subtle myths, mostly unexamined, about being French or Latvian or adhering to the "American way" or the like. In all these myths and slogans, there is at least a vague hint of a kind of family relationship—if not biological, then adoptive or voluntary.

The idea of the nation, in any event, is fraught with consequences. And the myths, very obviously, serve to exclude as well as to include. What nationalism does most effectively is create boundaries; and the social boundaries, the cultural boundaries, are as sharp and divisive as any physical borders. Whoever is outside the line is a foreigner—someone who can be shut out or simply ignored. There are worse things, of course, than being ignored. Far too often, those who are excluded, who are defined as the "other," are dehumanized, even demonized. Hitler's wild theories about the Volk, about the superiority of German blood, were embodied in policies of genocide. Millions of the non-Volk—Jews, Gypsies, Slavs—died in the gas chambers, in front of firing squads, or in slave labor camps.[65] There are arguments over whether the Holocaust (the slaughter of the Jews) was a unique event, or whether it makes sense to compare it with other monumental slaughters, of which there is a plentiful supply. That the question can even be asked is ineffably tragic.

Thus the nation, the ethnic group, the imagined community, for all its positive features, casts a dark shadow over the world and haunts our consciousness. It is the poisoned source of much of the wrangling—and the killing. Indeed, Daniel Moynihan has pointed out that "national states no longer seem inclined to go to war with one another"; but world peace nonetheless remains a dream. This is because, as he adds ruefully, ethnic groups *do* "fight all the time."[66]

Moynihan's observation seems, alas, all too true. There is no nation called Serbia, no country by that name, if *nation* means sovereignty and embassies and postage stamps and the United Nations. But there is a self-conscious ethnic group that thinks of itself as Serb, and so much of the murdering and expelling and suffering and raping in Yugoslavia in the 1990s came out of this self-righteous Serbian consciousness of self. What was probably just as important was how the Serbians saw the other peoples who once shared their territory. They were demons—blood enemies bent on destroying the dream of a national home for Serbs. The Moslems of Bosnia? Wild fundamentalists, monsters, implacable foes, modern day Turks. The Croats? Fascist beasts. And so it went. The Serbian case is not unique. Nothing is so depressing as to discuss Greeks with Turks, and then Turks with Greeks.

Few countries in today's world are so lucky (if that is the word) as to be ethnically pure—or even to claim that they are. Very few have only a single ethnicity inside their borders: Korea, perhaps, is one such country. Most have at least two, and many countries (Nigeria and India are good examples) have more than anyone can count. Of course, purity is partly a matter of definition. The Japanese consider themselves extremely pure and homogeneous. But there exists in Japan a Korean minority, a handful of Ainu (in the far north) and more illegal immigrants than the Japanese care to admit, not to mention "internal" minorities, like the Burakumin.[67]

In any event, the Japanese situation is not the norm. The country called Japan is made up of a group of islands. Japan has no real borders; it has a seacoast instead. In a sense, mother nature—or mother ocean, at least—drew lines around Japan, protecting the Japanese from the rest of the world. Most countries got their borders in a more sinuous way—through a long, historical process, punctuated by war after war. Maps get drawn in blood, not ink. The United States swelled to fill its continent through wars of conquest (against native tribes and against Mexico).[68] It swallowed up Hawaii and Puerto Rico. In Africa, as we said, it is notorious that the borders pay no attention to culture lines and ethnic lines; they meander crazily along routes the imperial countries laid out.

Actually, every country of any size is, in a way, a kind of minor-league empire. Not everybody in Thailand is Thai; not everyone in Iran is Persian-speaking—not even close. The world is a mixed-up place, demographically speaking. You need to know a lot of history to understand why people who speak a kind of German at home and live in Strasbourg are French or why so many people in the Fiji Islands or in Trinidad speak Hindi or why there is no country called Kurdistan even though there are millions of people who speak Kurdish and call themselves Kurds.

Most countries are mixtures of peoples, a rich stew of faces and body types, languages and religions. And in most countries, this mixture is chemically explosive—a source of conflict, trouble, often war. A dominant group, fired up with nationalism and a sense of ethnic brotherhood, eats the poisoned apple of hatred and decides that the minorities who jostle for space in their country are a danger to culture or to sovereignty or to domestic peace. In the old multinational empires, there were definitely ruling groups—the Romans or Austro-Hungarians or Ottoman Turks. But they did not usually threaten their subjects with extinction. In some cases, they even managed to grant to these peoples some spheres of autonomy—their own customs or laws, for example, or limited self-government. Of course, there is no reason to romanticize the past. In Europe, in the Middle Ages, heretics were burned at the stake; there was the periodic game of killing Jews; in early modern times (and later), settler communities in the New World and in the Pacific dealt out death to indigenous people with absolute ferocity. Nationalism in the twentieth century, however, has at times reached levels of bloodshed that dwarf anything the past has to offer. It is enough to mention Hitler's name.

But the majority culture is not always to blame. Sometimes, the trouble seems to start from underneath: a minority group (or groups) demands equality of rights, equality of power, or a share of both. This demand rarely comes out of thin air, so to speak; the minority usually has something concrete to complain about: American blacks, with their history of slavery and oppression; native tribes in Canada or aborigines in Australia, with histories of land grabs and cultural oppression; the Kurds in the Middle East, divided among at least four countries, and welcome in none of them, to say the least;[69] and the Catholics in northern Ireland. Often what is involved for both groups is the bitter residue of the process of defining insiders and outsiders inherent in the modernizing and nation-building process.

There are dozens of variations on the basic themes. Each country has its own story; each is unique, whether the country is Canada or Chad, Afghanistan or Albania, Latvia or France. The majority oppresses to express, in a perverted way, its own sense of nationhood; the minority takes up arms, in turn, in reaction to the majority and to express *its* nationhood. Minority demands, in turn, may frighten the majority and lead to crackdowns and other excesses. This happens most often in authoritarian countries; they lack democratic vents to let the steam escape. But the minority can itself be ruthless and bloody: the Tamils in Sri Lanka, for example.

In our times, the globe is pockmarked with bloody conflicts; the wars tend to be small wars, compared to the mass slaughter of the two great World Wars, but they are vicious and bloody nonetheless. The corpses lying in crazy positions on battlefields, in ditches, and on city streets are just as dead, the streams of frightened refugees just as desperate, hungry, and forlorn as they were in the pitiless years of the Second World War. These new wars are, however, rather different from classical wars of conquest. Nobody is trying to build up an empire of the Roman or British type, or even of the Soviet type. These are not wars to expand the domain of this or that king or to increase the personal fiefdom of some charismatic leader. Perhaps Hitler and Stalin were the last dictators to wage wars of outright conquest, and even Stalin saw fit to cover his plunder of nations with a figleaf of socialist internationalism.[70]

In fact, old-style imperialism seems to be rather dead. In the nineteenth century the great powers of Europe spent enormous energy building and managing colonial empires. They seized great chunks of Africa and Asia. In the process, they tended to worry far more about rival European powers than about the indigenous people they were swallowing whole. It was a race between England, France, Germany, and other countries. But none of the empires of the nineteenth century has survived to see the dawn of the twenty-first century. The British Empire, which once ruled a quarter of the world, is history, except for a few pitiful fragments in various oceans. The last substantial plum, Hong Kong, slipped away from British grasp in 1997. The French, the Spanish, the Portuguese, the Dutch, have all lost their colonies—again, except for an island here, an enclave there. The Soviet Union was probably the last of the great world empires—and a somewhat deviant example; it insisted that it was a union, not an empire, though hardly anybody was fooled. The Soviet Union seemed impregnable; but it too has crumbled into dust.

The new wars, then, are not imperial wars. They are often civil wars—wars within nation-states, or wars between ethnic groups, wars inside and outside some sort of border. These are wars between Tamils and Sinhalese, in Sri Lanka; or between Croats, Serbs, and Muslims, in the "former Yugoslavia;" or between Chechens and Russians, inside "Russia." The goal is not to subjugate and colonize other peoples in the old-fashioned way; rather, these are wars of liberation, which degenerate, at times, into ethnic cleansing and outright annihilation. The goal of a "greater Serbia," for example, is to amass a chunk of land for Serbians, getting rid of all the foreign elements in the process, and to make sure that no Serb, God forbid, is trapped within the cage of some other sovereignty. The two factions on Cyprus, ethnic Greeks and ethnic Turks, are now separated by a de facto border; the two pieces of the island have been ethnically cleansed. What Turkey is trying to do to the Kurds within Turkey is nasty, but somewhat more complicated. Turkey does not seem to want to get rid of the Kurds—which, at any rate, is impossible—but it would like their Kurdishness to wither away. Something similar goes on in many other countries with national minorities—the Slovaks with their Hungarians, for example.

The point is that modern Turkey does not act at all like the old Ottoman Empire, another of the prison houses of nations. It does not want simply to rule over the Kurds, the way the Ottoman Empire ruled over Greeks, Slavs, Romanians, Arabs, and Jews. It does not want to be an imperial power but to convert itself into something monolithic, if possible. The Kurds are an obstacle to this ambition, and the "problem" calls for drastic steps of (forced) assimilation and other forms of cultural oppression. Apparently, there is room in Turkey for only one authentic nation. Czechoslovakia also came to the conclusion that two was a crowd; Ethiopia divested itself of the Eritreans; and it is still an open question whether two is one too many in Canada and Belgium.

Increasingly, then, when wars break out, the fighting is between ethnic groups, between "us" and "them," and it reflects all too often a kind of primitive savagery. The war in the "former Yugoslavia" has been an unusually depressing example, and the war in Sri Lanka another. This book began with a brief description of one of the most awful recent tragedies: the struggle between Hutu and Tutsi in Rwanda. This is, to be sure, an extreme case. Usually, it is not millions who die but a few victims of scattered and sporadic murder—Turks in Germany, at the hands of skinheads, or victims of race riots in the United States. Nationalists in Quebec agitate for independence from Canada; so far, no blood has been shed, and perhaps none ever will be. Ethnic disputes range, on a continuum, from the most bloody, on one end, to quiet arguments within an umbrella-state, on the other.

Yet overall, the sense of national and ethnic identity seem to carry seeds of violence—more, perhaps, than the efforts of the "virtual" subnations (feminism, gay rights, the handicapped) or of most religious identities (though this was not always true). It is the intensity of ethnic feelings—or "nationalism," as some would have it—that stirs and boils and cooks so much of the witches' brew of large-scale violence.

Not that ethnic identity is *always* negative, harmful, hateful. Group feeling is extremely meaningful for people, therapeutic sometimes; group identity helps give value and purpose to life. People do not thrive in isolation. True hermits are rare, and perhaps pathological. People need to belong: we belong to families, clubs, and informal groups; there is also a sense (among many people) of belonging to the nation as well. Patriotism may be the last refuge of a scoundrel; but official policy in most countries treats it otherwise—as something valuable, to be nurtured and encouraged. Treason is a heinous offense in most criminal codes. Thousands, maybe millions, seem willing to die for the motherland, at least in times of crisis. National identity, race identity, religious identity—all these can be forces for good as well as evil. Religion, for example, is a consolation and a source of moral strength—it *can* be an excuse for burning heretics and throwing bombs, but I would hate to argue that murder is the primary role of religion in human life. The same is true for many other forms of personal identity.

Nationalism, then, is not an unmitigated evil. Indeed, it has been argued that democracy is impossible without some kind of national sense.[71] In theory, there could be democracy on a global basis—a kind of one-world system; but this utopia is so far in the future, if it comes at all, that we can ignore the idea for now. Democracies are, and have to be, organized on a *national* basis, like every other form of government. And this means that, democracy or no, the ethnic question can never be ignored.

Ethnic labels, and identity labels in general, are without a doubt a defining element of modern public life. In the United States, and in many other countries, it is impossible to understand what is happening in politics, and in cultural life, without understanding the racial, ethnic, and religious labels attached to people—white or black, notably; brown, Hispanic, Native American, Chinese, or Irish-American; born-again Christian, Buddhist, or Roman Catholic. Hardly anything has given rise to more heated debate within the academy (and to a degree outside of it) than the nature and value of "multiculturalism." Exactly what this means is never terribly clear and depends on the context and the speaker.[72] But at the very least it refers to identity and identity politics. A multicultural society is a society in which more than one culture (or language or race) has legitimacy and authority.

Each country has its own precise mix of multicultures. The United States has black and white and Native American and Hispanic and Asian-American; it has a rich mix of religions; it has an overwhelmingly dominant language that somehow feels threatened by Spanish. Canada has its native peoples, its ethnic minorities, and the great divide—the abyss—between French speakers and English speakers. India, Nigeria, Belgium, Spain, Fiji, Trinidad, Peru—each has its own special rainbow of cultures.

The Declining Significance of Class

Every country also has its rich, not-so-rich, and poor. Economic *class* is, of course, another form of identity, and one with political and social consequences. It is still true in, say, England that there is a vast gulf between the working class and the others in society. Disraeli talked about the "two nations," rich and poor.[73] In the nineteenth century, this divide, between haves and have-nots, seemed to be the most fundamental divide of all. It has not, of course, gone away. The gap in some countries—the United States, for example—has apparently widened in recent years.

For nineteenth-century Marxists, the classes were indeed "two nations," and they were in a state of war. Workers and peasants needed to unite; they needed to overthrow the evil ruling class. The first, and necessary, step was class consciousness, class solidarity. Without this sense of unity, workers and peasants were nothing. Marx and his followers worked hard to imbue the toiling masses with this ideology of struggle.

Many writers have pointed out that Marx and his disciples have proven to be very poor prophets indeed.[74] (Marxists are certainly not alone in that department.) In the nineteenth century, writing at a time of raw, ruthless capitalist expansion, they foresaw a world divided along lines of rich and poor, between owners of capital and landless, impoverished, exploited labor; they looked in their crystal balls and could imagine a united army of factory workers and peasant toilers united in a war against the bloodsucking class of oppressors. They were aware that other great fault lines—national identity, for example—split the world into pieces. But these would wither away, to be replaced by this single, master identity, and producing a single, cleansing Armageddon. The "nationality of the worker," said Marx, "is neither French, nor English, nor German, it is *labor.*"[75] He and his followers had plenty of evidence on their side: a convergent, capitalist world of riots, strikes, hunger, labor unrest. Yet, a century later, on the whole, the class war seems to have ended, not with a bang but with a whimper.

Or so it appears. One possibility, of course, is that the end of the class war is only an illusion. Any good science-fiction writer could concoct a plausible script about a future apocalypse, in which class war erupts into flames. If obscene population growth destroys the thin veneer of prosperity and propriety, if air, water, grass, and trees are consumed by the rag-tag army of new bodies, if the animals languish and die, if the oil and the coal dribble away, if there is mass starvation, pollution poisoning, global warming, an ozone catastrophe, then anything is possible.

But for now, for the moment, class war, of any sort, seems grossly unlikely and distant—at least in the richer countries. One can much more easily imagine race war or ethnic war. To be sure, whether a person is rich or poor remains overwhelmingly important. Is anything, in our societies, more significant than money? It is too early in a world so full of hunger, suffering, and oppression to write off the battle between the haves and have-nots. But even if a fiery dragon of class war does emerge from its lair, it will probably carry a distinctive ethnic overlay. It will come disguised as "north versus south," or "third world against first world."[76]

In short, there is a distinct impression that class seems to be fading fast as a marker of identity in much of the West. Overt class conflict, as such, seems to be on the decline in most Western societies. There are the usual strikes in Italy and France, but nothing compared to the labor unrest of the nineteenth century. Hardly any militant unions remain. The Left is in disarray everywhere, or has redefined itself in ways that hardly seem "left" any more. Nobody has the slightest interest in state ownership of steel mills and airlines or even banks. Indeed, the trend is all in the other direction—a rage to "privatize." Telephone companies, gasworks, railroads, state enterprises, and even prisons and roads are for sale. Meanwhile, taxes on the rich are falling, not rising.

Moreover, the ranks of Marxist countries have thinned and retreated to a few small outposts. There is China, of course, which is hardly a small outpost, but it certainly no longer qualifies as orthodox Marxist. In many parts of the West, what survives from the traditional Left? Not much. The Left has shattered, like a pane of glass, into a thousand fragments; and these fragments come labeled, not with class markers but with other markers of identity—race and gender, ethnic identity, religion, even sexual preference.[77] That is, there are black militants and radical feminists and animal-rights extremists, and so on; but they do not cohere into a single Left. Nor is there, similarly, a single Right; we have the Christian Right, the Jewish Defense League, survivalists, Nazis, creationists, flat-earth believers, and others.

What happened to class consciousness? Its defeat is partly a matter of mobility: it is easier than before to cross class lines through education, training, luck—even by winning the lottery. In capitalist societies, the rich are simply that: people with money. They are not aristocrats by birth; there are no structural barriers that make it impossible to make the transition from poor to rich. In these societies, money is always at least *potentially* around the corner. But mobility seems to me only part of the story. The decline of class has deeper roots.

Of course, to a large extent, race acts as a stand-in for class in the United States. More blacks are poor, proportionately, than whites; Hispanics and Native Americans also, on the whole, lag behind whites. Race is also something of a stand-in for class in other countries—England and Brazil, for example—and racial minorities in Australia are as poor as one can get in that society. Religion may be a stand-in for class in Northern Ireland. In the United States, the categories of race and class overlap. When Americans rail against welfare mothers and the like, they tend to be thinking of blacks. Perhaps this is why there is so much vehemence against the undeserving poor—poor whites do not arouse so much antipathy.

But if Marx was a bad prophet, then, perhaps, so too were the free-market liberals. Some of them also believed that nationalism was primitive and atavistic. Free trade and free markets would make the world into a single, large bazaar. Capitalism would be good for everybody. Tariff walls, protectionism, and other forms of economic nationalism were pathologies; they were out of step with the times; and they had to be overcome.[78] Free trade has, indeed, progressed enormously, and capitalism (at this writing) has no real rival in the world. But the disappearance of nationalism and tribal identity seems to be lagging far behind.

The fact is that any form of organized government, any kind of "nationhood," whether socialist, democratic, or dictatorial, requires cultural unity, communication with the citizens, a common language (or languages), and modes of mobilization. Whatever the ideology, it has to make its peace with the horizontal society. Hence "socialist internationalism" was bound to be a pipe dream. Similar comments can be made about any working economic system. Free trade—or *any* kind of trade—can be carried out only within a framework of common words, norms, and understandings; and these require (at the local level) the tools, techniques, and *culture* of the horizontal society. That much seems clear.

Out of One, Many

As we have pointed out, despite all the loose talk about a global village, nothing remotely resembling a global identity has emerged. It would be hard to find anybody whose primary identity was to everybody, all humanity, the whole earth, rather than to some single country (or institution). Any predictions about the brotherhood and sisterhood of men and women seem way off base. Just as a worldwide class consciousness among workers and peasants never developed, no worldwide consciousness of common humanity, based on *any* ideology, has come into being. And this despite the rampant growth of consensus about "fundamental human rights." What we have instead is Rwanda and Bosnia and Northern Ireland and Iran. Poisonous nationalism seems stronger than ever; we see fundamentalism—a narrow, bigoted intolerance—creeping into the right wing of Islam, Judaism, and some of the Christian churches; we see genocide and ethnic cleansing. We see a multitude of nasty, vicious little wars all over the face of the globe. Many students of society, as we have noted, are startled at the way ethnic war has survived in the modern world. To them, this behavior is primitive and premodern, a throwback to the law of the jungle. They had expected a single world order, a kind of cosmopolitanism. This would be the natural fruit of modernity. Progress and globalization would sweep humankind into a single integrated whole.[79]

Yet modernity *seems* to have done nothing to contain these volcanic tribal energies. Indeed, there is something grimly ironic about the current situation: Bosnia, Rwanda, and mass murders elsewhere were featured on television screens and broadcast into millions of homes. Perhaps the killers even stopped their killing long enough to watch themselves on the evening news.

It is not easy to explain why history has taken this particular turn. Part of the explanation may lie in the nature of "globalization." Roland Robertson has described this as a double process: it is a process of the "universalization of particularism," but at the same time it is the "particularization of universalism."[80] In other words, one of the new, universal ideas is precisely the idea of ethnic particularity. After all, ethnicity is itself in large part a modern idea. As we noted, people in the Middle Ages did not think of themselves as French or Lithuanian; they had more parochial ways to label themselves. Just as there was no French nation, there was also no French ethnicity. "Ethnicity" is a pandemic, as it were, an idea spread over the globe, like nationalism; and, as we have seen, the two concepts are tightly linked. Modernization, as a process that universalizes, is guilty of spreading it. At least this is the point Robertson is making. And what does it mean to modernize? It means accepting a cluster of modern ideas that spread horizontally, through the media, through the channels and conduits of modernity. It turns out that identifying with a more or less tribal group—ethnicity—is one of these ideas.

If we look to the *internal* politics of some Western countries, we see a development that is vaguely parallel. *Class* politics, in the United States at least, has dwindled to a mere shadow of its former self. Soaking the rich is out of fashion. Union membership has been sliding downhill for decades. Worker solidarity, if it ever existed, is only a memory. There are similar tendencies, if a bit weaker, in many European countries. Certainly, socialism as a political force has almost disappeared, and with it the idea of class struggle. No labor or socialist party in Europe looks on business—on capitalism—as the enemy.

What has replaced class politics is, in part, a kind of politics of national or subnational identity. In the United States, there is talk about a new, or reborn, populism, but it has almost nothing in common with the populism of a century ago. Take, for example, the populism of Patrick Buchanan, which burst like a rocket in Republican politics in 1996. Buchanan wanted the Republican nomination for president. He preached social conservatism, but also xenophobia, hatred of immigrants, and a kind of wild-eyed economic nationalism. He tried to attack what he considered a broad consensus among elites in favor of unrestricted free trade and economic globalism. Buchanan's attacks shocked many of these elites, conservative and liberal alike, and his wide appeal proved even more shocking.

Like the old-time populists, Buchanan fulminated against greedy corporations, especially multinational ones. But it was not the money or the power of the multinationals that bothered him. Rather, it was the looseness of their allegiance to America. The greed was fine, as long as it stayed at home. What he preached was not income distribution but a jihad against Mexico and Japan. No class struggle here; business and labor shared a common enemy: the world. Moving a factory abroad was betrayal.

Generally speaking, the politics of identity has largely replaced the politics of class. The unified nation dissolves, politically and culturally, into many little subnations, into bits and pieces. There is a serious question as to whether the nation in the sense of the group of groups, the loyalty of loyalties, still exists in any meaningful way. This is still one more paradox: "national" identity is stronger than ever, but in the United States, a case could be made that the "nation" is not a nation anymore. What commands allegiance is not the "United States" or "my country" but the various subnations. And this is clearly true elsewhere—say, in Canada.

Indeed, some sort of cultural evolution seems to be in progress, re-defining the nation, recasting the very idea. Some kind of pluralism, a rough-and-ready federalism of subidentities, seems to be replacing the na-tion. Exactly how this will play out, in the future, socially, culturally, or legally, is not easy to say.

The paradox is the same on the level of the *country* as it is on the level of the world. In the United States, there are no longer any small, isolated villages, no Appalachian valleys cut off from the larger world, no tiny en-claves of outcasts, no lonely islands drifting off the coasts. TV antennae sprout above the rudest huts—in the bayous of Louisiana, tiny towns in New England, Mormon settlements in Utah, snow-bound villages in Mon-tana. Schools, roads, the armies, radio, TV—all these engines of homo-geneity have been at work in the United States, as they have been elsewhere. The president speaks on TV from the Oval Office, in Washington, D.C., and his words (and his face) travel to the farthest corner of the country, all in a nanosecond. A person can travel by jet from Honolulu to Bangor, Maine, in much less time than it took to get from New York to Philadel-phia two centuries ago. Unity is the only reality. Oneness is a fact. Yet all over we hear voices moaning about the loss of American unity, about the splinter state, about fragmentation: we hear people asking, Where has *America* gone?

It is possible, realistically speaking, that the America that is gone never really existed. Perhaps the concept of the "nation" was always a fiction, al-ways an ideology—a form of dominance; it existed only in the minds of a smug, swaggering class of people whose dominance went unquestioned. Maybe it always rested on suppression of minorities and dissenters. Be that as it may, even in *that* sense, even in the sense of hegemony, some time in this century the unity of the nation began to decay and moved toward the brink of extinction. What replaced it was a cluster of subnational identi-ties, which have steadily grown in number. One might have predicted a woman's movement and a black-power movement, perhaps, or even gay liberation. But Gray Panthers? Or the revolt of the deaf?

I have used the word *subnations*. This is not just a metaphor. Many peo-ple, in fact, use the word *nation* in a subnational or nonnational sense. Mil-itant gays speak of themselves as the "Queer Nation." There is the "Nation of Islam," among black Muslims. There are even large gangs that call themselves "nations." The Native-American peoples are, all of them, "nations"; and they come closest to the classical definition, with their native courts and modes of self-government. Many other groups, even if they do not use the word, *act* as if they were a kind of colonized subnation, a subordinate group struggling for its place in the sun. Each subnation, at times, behaves like (say) one of the ethnic groups in the Austro-Hungarian empire or like some sort of inmate in a prison of nations. Each struggles for some form of independence (mostly metaphorical).

The point should not be exaggerated. There is plenty of old-fashioned patriotism left—even superpatriotism.[81] America is still a nation of flag-wavers. Loyalty to the center, to the nation, still commands a wide constituency. It is a question of changes at the margin—of more or less. And the United States may not be typical. Each country has its own brand of pluralism. Still, unless I am drastically mistaken, the same tendencies can be seen in every country of the modern, Western, industrial world.

The subnations, and their subidentities, are also, to be sure, complicated and problematic. "Identity" and "ethnicity" are slippery concepts—as slippery as the idea of the "nation." They are also in constant flux, constantly changing colors and shapes. Nobody can pin them down exactly or keep them pinned down. Each has its own special history—whether we are talking of the Navajo nation or gays or blacks or people in wheelchairs. What does seem crystal clear is the dramatic impact the rise of the subnations has had on politics. Nobody can make sense of political life in the United States without taking these nations into account. A similar case can be made for Canada, France, Britain, and many other countries. Identity is destiny (for the moment), and we have to try to fathom it as best we can.

Big Fish and Little Fish
Nation Against Nation

IN THE LAST CHAPTER I talked about the meaning of such terms as *nation* and *nationalism* and mentioned the troubling facts about the spread of rather virulent forms of nationalism—in particular, the spread of more and more nasty little wars. A good many of these are civil wars, and many of them bring about if not mass murder then at least the ugliness and cruelty of ethnic cleansing. Some of the worst of these wars take place outside the confines of the rich, comfortable world. But what happens at the fringes is dangerous, even to that rich, comfortable world. And the blood, torture, and degradation are no less cruel because the people who suffer live in places with a low GNP.

In this chapter, I explore this theme further. First, we look at the various *types* of ethnic conflict, then briefly probe some of its *sources*. Behind the blind hatred is a feeling of endangerment, sometimes vague, sometimes naked and raw. What brings this about? There is an irony here, perhaps. The horizontal society, modernity, the global culture—all these, as we have seen, foster a sense of ethnic identity; they create it, and they give identity the tools to communicate and keep a sense of oneness alive. But these forces, at the same time, also put ethnic identity in peril. Ethnic identity, in short, comes to look like competition, like "we" against "them." There are winners and losers; it is a zero-sum game. And the enemy is not only *other* groups; the enemy is modernity itself.

Hence, in the modern world, there are countless examples of backlash, counterrevolution, and (apparent) revolts against modernity. Some aspects of the ethnic movement, as we saw in the last chapter, look backward, romantically, fixated on a heroic past or a golden age. But the search for tradition is not itself traditional; it is distinctly modern. All ideologies that "seek to control or contain modernity," after all, rest on the assumption that "the course of human events can be deliberately manipulated," which is a "specifically modern notion."[1] In this sense, at least, no culture today is or can be truly "traditional."

There has always been tribal warfare. Modern "tribes," however, make war not only in jungles but also on city streets or in a countryside already ravaged by the forces of modernity. The wars take place not in isolation from the modern world but in reaction to it. Except through heroic measures—which usually fail—no group can hope to be immune from TV, mass communication, radio, movies, and tourism, all of which create a single world system and tend toward a single world culture. Autonomous communities, sealed-off cultures—"hermit kingdoms"—are no longer possible. Hence the fundamentalist aspects of ethnic conflict are not as fundamental as they seem. They are quarrels *within* modernity. Often these quarrels take the form of struggle over norms, meanings, customs, and the search for souls. It is in this light that we have to consider the disputes over Islamic law in various countries with Islamic populations and the ups and downs of customary law.

Ethnic Conflict: Genus and Species

A number of scholars have tried to classify wars, conflicts, and other grown-up games, and the groups that take part in these endeavors. The work of Gurr and Harff is, I think, of special interest. They drew a distinction between four types of "politically active ethnic groups."[2] The first two types, which they call "ethnonationalists" and "indigenous peoples," want either to separate from the state or to wrestle more autonomy out of their central governments. "Ethnonationalists," like the Kurds, the Quebec separatists, or the Tamil Tigers, perhaps, want their own country. "Indigenous peoples" are "mainly concerned with protecting . . . traditional lands, resources, and cultures." Many of the native "nations" of the United States and Canada, or the Miskito people of Nicaragua, fall into this category.[3] The other two types, which they call "communal contenders" and "ethnoclasses," simply want "greater access or participation within existing stages." Communal contenders are "culturally distinct groups" in "plural societies," competing for a share of power; ethnoclasses (guest workers in Europe, for example) are groups that want "equal rights and opportunities to overcome the effects of discrimination resulting from . . . immigrant or minority status."

These distinctions are useful even though, of course, other distinctions are possible.[4] But the boundary between types is not always very clean. Independence is, often enough, a goal groups turn to out of desperation, that is, when "communal contending" fails, or simply does not deliver the goods, and "access" can be combined with "separation" to form a kind of apartheid among equals. A lot depends on whether the group has its own compact area—a Kurdistan—or is dispersed about the country. This last situation obviously applied to the virtual nations—the deaf, for example. But "Balkan" situations, with ethnicities jumbled together, are sources of trouble all over the world. Ethnic cleansing is a device for sorting people out—violently, to be sure.

What the group is striving for—whether independence, access, or something in between—can have economic, cultural, or political dimensions, or all of these. A small country like Estonia has achieved political sovereignty, which means also a chance at cultural sovereignty. Estonia can make Estonian the official language, can insist on teaching children in Estonian, can broadcast the news and run the courts in Estonian. A free country has economic sovereignty as well—or at least as much as the global system allows. The Estonians are probably quite willing to give up a bit of this—by joining the European Union, for example, and, in the process, losing *some* of their political independence as well. Economic independence is a luxury few countries can afford. Political sovereignty is largely a means to an end: cultural sovereignty. And for cultural sovereignty, Estonia will fight to the death.[5]

Estonia is certainly not unique. In Quebec, too, culture (and language) is all. Again, political sovereignty there is only a means to an end: the end is preserving the culture of French Canada. Many French Canadians would not mind some sort of link to Canada, if they could have enough autonomy. Even the most rabid nationalists seem willing to continue economic ties with Canada; they would, in other words, be willing to give back some of the independence so long as they could conduct their affairs in French.[6]

The Double-Edged Sword

The horizontal society created national movements, but it is also the greatest threat to their existence. The world system is a juggernaut, a power measured in megatons. Its incredible strength, its pervasiveness, endangers every culture that stands in its way. Many cultures survive by clinging to sovereignty, or by manufacturing it. But flocks of little cultures vanish into extinction like flightless birds on small Pacific islands. People worry about the Javan rhinoceros or the giant panda, but the human cultures and languages of the rain forest are just as threatened; many are on the brink of doom. Hundreds of ways of life have already slipped off into some kind of black hole of history. Languages are disappearing at a rapid rate. Some sixty-five hundred languages are spoken in the world today (for various reasons, no exact count is possible), but most of them are doomed. More than half are spoken by fewer than ten thousand people. Hundreds of languages are dead or dying—remembered only by a handful of old people whose children have lost the language. For hundreds more, there are too few speakers to ensure their survival. Only a few hundred languages are likely to survive into the twenty-second century.[7] The rest will be only memories. Most will not last another generation; for example, almost all the Papuan and Australian languages; all but two dozen or so languages in Africa; all but a handful of the native languages of the Americas. And whether the Welsh language or Basque or Frisian or Irish will exist a century from now is very much in doubt.

Nation building and the formation of "imagined communities" always meant exalting one form of the "nation" over others. To stitch together a France or a Germany or a Spain meant swallowing up almost all of the minor entities within the borders. Everything but the language of the capital became a "dialect" and was sentenced to stigma and suppression. Many of these dialects have already disappeared. Television is probably killing off the rest. Plattdeutsch and Provençal, among others, may be heading down the dusty road to nowhere. It would take heroic measures to save them.

Nationalism, as we saw, was fostered by self-conscious groups, often struggling against imperial forces that threatened to push them to the wall. The struggle was particularly acute within the Ottoman or Austro-Hungarian or British or Soviet empires. How could the submerged languages and cultures prevent the imperial rulers from smothering captive "nations"? The only way, it seemed, was political sovereignty, independence, autonomy, "national" media, and control over what was taught in the schools and what the judges said in the courts. If sovereignty was not the first goal, it rapidly moved to the fore when other measures failed. "Communal contenders" turned into outright independence movements. Today, cultural independence movements have the same goals as before; and the mechanisms are much the same, except that control of TV, that huge colossus dominating popular culture, is now a vital aspect of the struggle.

The lesson learned was that cultural sovereignty was dependent on autonomy or political sovereignty. So the same process that created Spain and Spanish nationalism also created Basque and Catalan nationalism. In this instance, the present Spanish government has been flexible and enlightened (Franco of course was not). In Russia, Russian nationalists confront nationalism among the Chechens, the Tatars, the Mordvinians, and dozens of other culture groups.

Modernity is not merely a threat to language and ethnicity. It is also a threat to religious cultures. And the sense of danger helps fuel the many examples of resistance and reaction to modernity: the various forms of backlash, fundamentalism, and return to tradition. Fundamentalism, particularly in the Islamic world, has become a major force in world politics and culture.[8] After the overthrow of the shah, Iran created a fundamentalist state: severe dress codes for women, a campaign against Western influence, and a return to Islamic law. The goal was to roll back modernity (or at least *cultural* modernity) and to install what the ayatollahs considered Islam in its undefiled form. The Taliban in Afghanistan have instituted an extreme form of Islamic state; and fundamentalism is powerful in Saudi Arabia and the Sudan as well.

At their most extreme, the fundamentalist regimes are trying to cut the ties that connect their populations with the global mainstream. Music, movies, and TV come under censorship or ban. Satellite dishes, those evil rooftop flowers, are forbidden. The specter that haunts Iran, and fundamentalists everywhere, is satellite-borne poison; the invisible enemy that creeps like a smoke into the nation, polluting the very air people breathe. The devil has many shapes; they include cassettes, videos, Western music, movies, and television. These, indeed, are the very body and soul of the Great Satan.

Fundamentalists realize, quite correctly, that the culture of modernity is seductive and powerful, that it can bewitch the young, and that it will win out in the end, unless it can be banished or contained. They realize, too, that it is a difficult enemy to fight. It is everywhere and nowhere. It is, for one thing, truly global. It laughs at borders. In this regard, it is like the radioactive winds of Chernobyl or acid rain or the hole in the ozone. It is like the English words that sneak into French, corrupting its purity. It is like the blue jeans and hamburgers that helped bring down the evil empire.

Fundamentalism has elements of nostalgia, but it is inadequate to describe it solely as a longing for the past. It is, of course, a genuine if desperate response to many of the real discontents of civilization. All contemporary countries are porous and vulnerable; all are exposed to the culture of modernity; and no defense is likely to succeed unless it is total and draconian. Any degree of slippage is fatal. And even when extreme measures are taken, how long can the dams hold back the flood?

Some fundamentalists recoil against the whole idea of the "nation," which is a modern, secular concept. There are Jewish fundamentalists who refuse to recognize the state of Israel as legitimate. They are waiting for the Messiah to come and establish his kingdom; short of that, they do not care to participate in government. Yet, usually, fundamentalism often goes hand in hand with nationalist zeal. In some Islamic countries, Islam becomes one of the symbols of the nation, an authentic aspect of tradition. Modern culture is defined as an alien, Western intrusion. The enemy of the chador, quite clearly, is the T-shirt and the bikini.[9]

There is nothing new or strange in this mixture of tradition and national fervor. Nationalist movements, including those in the nineteenth century, were always eager to invoke traditional ways, even when they had to invent them, as we have seen.[10] These movements were always a mixture of the old and the new—mostly new, with a dash of tradition added for spice. Fundamentalism, too, is a mixture. The modern world is, after all, only *selectively* rejected. The rulers of Saudi Arabia see no reason not to have automobiles (no women drivers, please), air conditioning, jets, computers, and the like, not to mention modern fighter planes and submarines.[11] Indeed, these are essential trappings of sovereignty.

Old Wine, New Bottles

At bottom, the struggle of Iran or Saudi Arabia is not entirely different from the struggle of Estonia, or the Basques and Catalans, to save their language and culture. One enemy is mass culture, global culture. Without sovereignty, the tools of a horizontal society will smash minority cultures. They are too exposed to the big, the dominant cultures. Sovereignty gives small cultures the right to build a fence and keep the enemy out. Of course, there are fences and fences; the Iranian fence is not the same as the Estonian fence. One kind of fence keeps out global mass culture; the other keeps out Russians and the Russian language. But it is clear in both cases that some kind of shield or protection is needed to save language and culture.

But if we save Estonian, Basque, or Catalan culture, we are of course saving a *modern* form of Estonian, Basque, or Catalan culture. Preserving "ancient traditions" turns out to mean nothing of the sort. Romanians, Navajos, and other peoples all over the world may talk about keeping ancient traditions alive, but in fact, no group can really afford to reject modernism or nationalism. Cultures cannot reject modern technology. They cannot banish popular music. They cannot avoid becoming modern. And, for the most part, they do not even want to; they simply want to be modern *as* Basques or Cherokees or Latvians or Kurds.

This is one reason why religion plays such a strong role in the reconstruction of tradition. Religion—like language and art—is not a creature of modern technology. But religion also evolves, and contemporary religion—no matter how fundamental—is inherently a creature of its times. Good citizens of the American Bible Belt, who may insist that every word of the Scriptures is literally true and represents the word of God, nonetheless do not have many wives, as the patriarchs did, or hold slaves or sacrifice goats and lambs to the Lord. The intensity of their feelings, its rapturous subjectivity, is itself distinctively modern.

Part of the appeal of religion is its claim to timelessness; it is a haven, an island, a sanctuary, in a turbulent, changing world. By definition, it goes beyond the merely human; and it is also, to a degree, beyond culture and history. Nonetheless, even religion has to pursue its claims within the matrix of modern politics and culture. Traditionalists must press their claims through modern channels. So, for example, claims of native peoples in the United States, Canada, and Australia for sovereignty or autonomy, sacred sites, landholdings, hunting and fishing rights, rituals, and distinctive languages and customs are carried out through modern mass means. Of course nothing in tradition as such gives these people what it takes to bring a successful lawsuit. Tradition does not tell them how to hold a press conference, voicing demands for bones stolen by anthropologists or for the return of a holy mountain.

To say this is not, of course, to criticize these movements of indigenous peoples. *All* contemporary movements—whether conservative, reactionary, liberal, radical, or whatever—must carry on in a contemporary way, using contemporary weapons. There is no choice. If your enemy has a gun, you cannot use a spear and hope to win.

The big fish and the little fish are thus in constant battle—for possession of this or that patch of modernity's acreage. Ideologies may differ, but not the arsenal of tools. The struggles can turn into violence, sometimes of the most vicious and murderous form, but (happily for the world) more often than not, the wars are peaceful wars of propaganda and agitation. The violent battles get most of the newspaper footage and make the most striking images on television. But (again, more often than not), the truly decisive battles get fought over control of the educational system, the networks, and issues of political representation.

The Battle over Law

The law courts are another arena of battle—indeed, a citadel that must be taken. Native Americans, in the United States and Canada, have demanded, and gotten, a measure of legal autonomy, including tribal courts. These courts have a long, complex history; what they can decide, and what they cannot, how much power they have, and how much they must share with the states—these are knotty, tangled questions that even experts have trouble resolving.[12] The federal government has, of course, consistently meddled in tribal affairs in the United States; but the federal courts (and Congress) have, in recent years, become much more sympathetic to tribal autonomy, which includes vesting more power in native courts.

At the same time, Congress has felt the need to insist on certain basic civil rights. The tribal courts must respect these, under the Indian Civil Rights act;[13] still, the tribes are allowed, to an extent, their own cultural understandings of what is and what is not a civil right. This issue echoes an issue we discussed earlier: the universality of human rights. How thorny the issue can be is illustrated by the well-known case of *Santa Clara Pueblo v. Martinez.*[14] Julia Martinez was a member of the Santa Clara pueblo, but she married a Navajo man. Under trial law, their children could not be members of the pueblo. On the other hand, if Santa Clara *men* married out of the tribe, their children were members of the tribe. Ms. Martinez felt that this amounted to discrimination on the basis of sex, in violation of the equal-protection clause of the federal Constitution. The Supreme Court denied her claim, largely on technical and procedural grounds. Allowing the claim would amount to an "interference with tribal autonomy and self-government," which Congress had not (in the Court's opinion) authorized.[15] But the underlying issue was the conflict between two types of claim: one based on a more universal standard, the other on cultural autonomy.

Customary law has survived, in one form or another, in these American tribal courts, in courts and courtlike processes in many parts of Africa, and elsewhere in the world. The various peoples of Africa, of course, had their own systems of law before the European powers carved up the continent into colonies. They had ways of handling trouble cases and settling disputes. These systems were, generally speaking, unwritten and uncodified but were sometimes quite sophisticated.[16] On the whole, the colonial powers looked down on these systems; they considered them primitive and debased, like everything else about the indigenous peoples. These foreign powers imposed their own legal systems, at least on the commercial and modernized sectors of society. But customary law survived in the countryside and in some countries—Nigeria, for example—had some degree of official recognition.[17]

Colonialism has come and gone, and the countries of Africa are independent states. A great deal of law—an enormous amount, in fact—remains in place from the colonial period. Some of the new countries accept it and reject customary law; others have tried to preserve customary law or to integrate it into their systems (Zimbabwe, for example).[18] Customary law is in some countries taken as a valuable trapping of sovereignty or as a form of African ethnicity. The customs wear the cloak of history and are markings of culture, like the native languages.

This much is ideology; the reality is more complicated. In fact, the customary laws are not at all the same as the ancient and traditional law-ways of the group or tribe. No such thing is possible in the twentieth century, just as it would be impossible for the feudal common law to survive in New Zealand or Barbados, or for that matter, England.

The search for customary law, like the search for tradition, is itself a product of modernity. How could it be otherwise? As Stephen Innes has put it, "Trying to recreate traditional forms is at bottom the very opposite of traditional behavior."[19] This is generally true of traditionalism; and customary law is no exception. Customary law has, to be sure, certain roots in the past—and so does the common law, or French law. Customary law has more survival power in matters of family law than in economic transactions. But "customary law" is necessarily modern, necessarily shaped by modern conditions and modern problems.[20]

Customary law in Africa was, to begin with, a highly artificial construct. Of course, there were customary norms and practices, patterns of judging and dispute resolution, among the various peoples of the continent. But customary law, as it appeared in the law books, did not represent those patterns with any degree of accuracy. The codified customary law consisted of "systematic, neat and fixed rules from ideal reconstructions," stitched together from various sources[21] and set out in such a way as to conceal the subtle, shifting, complex reality of the culture that gave birth to these practices. Western observers tend to look at customary law rather romantically, as ancient, unchanging, deeply rooted in hoary folkways (a century ago, they would have looked at the same legal systems as unbearably primitive and crude). But old legal practices cannot survive unless they adapt to modern exigencies. Customary law rested on ways of life that are mostly gone with the wind. A cash economy, jobs for wages, the market system, modern armies and airlines—these have been far more destructive to customary law than any alien codes the foreign devils might have imposed.

In one interesting case, tried in the District Court of the Navajo Nation, a driver of a "Navajo tribal vehicle" ran over and killed a three-year-old girl who was crossing a dirt road. The girl's mother sued for damages. The defendant claimed that such a lawsuit was "foreign to the custom and tradition of the Navajo people." The court admitted that in the past payment had been in terms of horses, sheep, a belt, or a strand of beads. But times "had changed. More Navajos work for money today. The concepts of payment have changed. The law of Navajo tort has also changed."[22]

The points made here are not specific to customary law. Reconstructions of, say, Barotse law are no more artificial or alien to the working legal order than the German Civil Code or the American Restatement of Torts. It is, for example, usually said that the "ancient common law of England" is the formative element in Anglo-American law. Bits of it are there, to be sure, as a kind of ghostly presence; but the vast bulk of the law has to do with zoning, income tax, copyright of computer software, environmental protection, workers' compensation, food and drug regulation, and civil rights, including sex discrimination—tons of raw material and living law that have almost nothing to do with the legal concerns, procedures, and habits that were at issue at the time of the War of the Roses. Similarly "Roman law," or what is left of it, has little to do with modern French or German law. A certain amount of raw material, presumably, was there or is still there, but it is twisted completely out of shape and buried under the rubble of massive concerns of the same type as those that have buried the remnants of the ancient common law.

All this was totally inevitable. Every system has to adapt; this is as true of customary systems as it is of any other legal system. And adapt they do. We owe to Mari Matsuda a dramatic account of the way in which market factors transformed native culture—and native legal culture—in Hawaii in the nineteenth century.[23] Even before Western law was actually *imposed* on Hawaii, traditional patterns (of communal ownership, for example) had weakened, under the ruthless hammer blows of social change. When merchants and missionaries swarmed ashore in the Hawaiian Islands, they undermined (for better or for worse) the way of life on which Hawaiian tradition rested. Americans completed the work and snuffed that tradition out almost totally. But in its customary form, it was doomed in any event.

Cultures of Modernity

It is often said that law in China, Japan, and Korea is basically different from Western law because of its Confucian basis or heritage. Or that the Japanese, as one German scholar put it, resist modern law because of some "mystical sentimentality" rooted deep in their historical traditions.[24] Traditional Japanese culture does seem persistent and deep-seated. The Japanese formally adopted codes of European laws in the nineteenth century, as part of their drive to modernize. But these laws (it is argued) never really "took," and the Japanese system, or some sort of inner essence, remains much as it was.

Many scholars (and laypeople) would argue that what is Western about Japan (or Korea) is only skin-deep. Underneath is that irreducible core, which constitutes Japanese (or Korean) culture; hoary with age and exerting a powerful presence, this essence rules modern men and women from beyond the grave. Similar arguments are and can be made about China and other Asian countries—Singapore, for example.

Yet any visitor is struck by the fact that people on the streets of Tokyo act and dress like people in Paris or Chattanooga; the tall banks and hotels of Seoul, not to mention the rush-hour traffic, do not seem different in kind from the banks, hotels, and traffic in New York or Buenos Aires. Is it possible that it is the *survivals* from the Japanese past that are shallow and irrelevant rather than the Western overlay? We could certainly make out the case. These survivals might be no more meaningful than the wooden shoes of Holland or the changing of the guard at Buckingham Palace. In Japan (as in other countries) there is a tendency to treasure survivals, for sentimental reasons; they attract tourists, and (very significantly) they form part of the architecture of national identity. They are building blocks, as we have seen, in the construction of the imagined community. Yet these survivals, in many (most?) cases may be merely marginal—exotic, like rare animals displayed in a zoo; what is powerful and entrenched in daily life— what is truly real—is the culture of modernity.[25]

Obviously, this point can be exaggerated. The truth surely lies somewhere between these two polar positions. It would be absurd to argue that Japanese traditions have no meaning today. They do help account for palpable differences between modern Japan and (say) the countries of Europe. Any European or American who spends even a day or two in Japan (or Korea or Taiwan) senses such differences. But it is not easy to describe these differences precisely—or to measure their importance. Scholars disagree, for example, as to whether Japanese and Western styles of conflict resolution are fundamentally different.[26]

What seems most plausible to me is that culture and traditions help shape particular modes of modernism. All the dialects of modernism—the Japanese, the Israeli, the English, the American, the French—are mutually intelligible. There is no mistaking the gulf between life in Tel Aviv or Paris or Helsinki or Bangkok and life in, say, a remote village in the Amazon jungle, or life in ancient Babylon, for that matter. The similarities may be the crucial thing: the air conditioners, wristwatches, ATM machines, traffic jams, skyscrapers, rock-and-roll concerts, and all the rest. And there are deeper similarities as well: in business life, in sexual behavior, even in the architecture of the family. The differences may be mere details—some of them quite significant, some merely colorful (like the occasional elephant in downtown Bangkok). But they are all details nonetheless, rather than essences or cores.

But it is pointless to argue whether some cultural trait is an "essence" or not. There is no real answer. In any event, one thesis of this book is that modernity has two faces: it homogenizes and differentiates at one and the same time. It pulls people apart and pushes them together. It accentuates ethnic differences, but in the context of a single (and powerful) world culture. In one obvious sense, ethnic differences cannot be dismissed as superficial. Subjectively, they produce volcanic emotions. Passions that generate riots, disorders, even savage wars, are obviously not mere bagatelles.

Within ethnic groups, the ties that bind seem crucially important. They make possible life as we have to live it. People need a common language even to make small talk to each other. Economically speaking, it also makes sense to deal with people who "speak the same language," ethically and ethnically. It is efficient to do business with people you can trust because they are "family," or members of the same clan, group, or religion, as Janet Landa has pointed out in her studies of Chinese traders in overseas markets.[27] By the same token, it is hard to have a sense of kinship with people whose language we can't read, whose words we can't understand. As we have pointed out, the process of inclusion implies exclusion as well. (In later chapters, we will explore in more detail the process of inclusion and exclusion.)

Developed societies—whether in the East or the West—do have, in a sense, a common language and a common culture. That common culture is the culture of modernity. To put it another way, they are all, in their own way, horizontal societies. They are all bustling, complex communities, with millions of people who are part of a working, interconnected world. They have burst out of the womb of village life. They still have (for the most part) families and intimate connections, but they also have the capacity to form other kinds of ties (some weak, some strong), which are profoundly different from their ancient ties—and which are, in our terms, profoundly horizontal. The process has gone further in some places than in others. Perhaps connection has crumbled more in America than in Europe or Japan; perhaps there are more rootless, unattached, unattachable souls here than elsewhere. It may be, too, that Japan and other Asian countries, even the most developed ones, have proceeded more timidly, more tentatively, than other societies and have relaxed the chains of tradition a bit more slowly. This is one source of the perception of difference. Another is national pride: the sense of being different.

Yet another source of the perception of difference is the fact of conflict and competition. It is hard to admit strong ties to the people you are vying with: people who want to drive you out of business, steal your factories, or, in the extreme case, murder you and your kind. Yet modern countries, no matter how competitive, follow, and recognize, a common set of rules, norms, and goals. There seems little doubt to me that all societies today, wherever they are, whatever their histories, are marching in the same general direction, following the same road map on the way.

Insiders and Outsiders

IN THE LAST TWO CHAPTERS, I discussed the idea of nationalism. Whatever else it means, nationalism implies membership in, and attachment to, the nation. We discussed the meaning of the concept of the nation, some of the consequences that flow from ethnic identity, and how ethnic identity is related to the development of nations.

We pointed out that nations both include and exclude. This means that each nation, and also the subnations and virtual nations, must address its own question of *identity:* who is, and who is not, a member? This chapter focuses on the question of membership, of belonging. It asks, How does the label of membership get attached to a human being?

The process has two stages or two aspects. One of them is purely subjective—a person's feeling, sense, or choice with regard to affiliation: her willingness to say "I am Greek" or "I am a feminist" or "I am black." The other is external: how society chooses to label people—never mind how they label themselves. Of course, the two are closely connected. Panethnicity, which we have mentioned, illustrates that process. White and black Americans tend to lump Chinese, Japanese, Koreans, and Vietnamese into a single category, "Asians." This is not, of course, the way these peoples have historically defined themselves; yet what other people do by way of definition ends up *creating* a subjective category of Asians within the United States, a subsidiary melting pot into which these very different peoples are thrown.[1]

The *external* labeling process can be formal or informal. The informal would include the many and various social norms and definitions about who belongs and who doesn't belong, and to what; what it means to be a man or woman or a Jew or a black or a Honduran; who is part of the mainstream and who is "different."[2] The formal part is the legal or structural process of defining ins and outs. Again, the two aspects are closely interconnected. This chapter will talk mostly about *social* definitions, though not exclusively: in discussions of race, for example, the social and the formal are so intermixed that the various strands cannot be easily disentangled. The next chapter will deal with formal and legal definitions of identity, that is, laws of citizenship, naturalization, immigration, and related subjects.

The first proposition, which is obvious but needs to be said, is that all the definitions and categories *are* social. They are constructed, man-made. By now, it is almost a cliché among intellectuals to say, airily, that all reality is socially constructed. This is the going faith in the academic world, but the big bustling world of the streets does not share it. The average person thinks of various boxes and labels as real, concrete, inborn, immutable: one is either black or white, for example, and it is biology, plain and simple, that makes a person one or the other. This opinion (though wrong) is far from ridiculous. The categories are not figments of the imagination, and the process of social construction takes place within real limits. It would be hard to convince people (and why should we try?) that the differences between men and women are entirely a matter of definition and social custom. After all, men and women do tend to look, dress, talk, feel, and act differently; they have different bodies and occupy different social roles in every known society. How much of this is biology, and how much is not, remains, as we know, hotly controverted.[3]

It was once taken for granted that the races were extremely clear-cut biological entities. Race was genetic destiny; moreover, notoriously, the races had different talents and powers. They could be ranked; white people were the most advanced, evolved, or civilized. The science behind this thinking was always suspect, but it was socially powerful. Of course, there *are* physical differences among people, some very visible, some less so. These differences are not random but patterned: the skin color and hair of Ghanaians are systematically different from the skin color and hair of Norwegians. Today, most educated people believe that these variations on a common human theme have no fundamental significance, though they track cultural patterns that mean a great deal to modern societies. Still, there are rearguard battles over whether intelligence varies according to race;[4] and large segments of the white public, as opposed to scientists, probably still cling to older racist notions. We will return to this theme.

How the public defines a category has vast policy consequences. If something is thought of as inborn, then it cannot be changed; if it is immutable, it cannot be altered. A religion can be chosen (and more and more people seem willing to switch faiths); race or gender cannot be. This, most people would say, is as plain as the nose on one's face.

Obviously, the balance between "social construction" and "reality" is not the same for each category of identity. That someone is labeled "blind" or "female" is less a matter of pure social construction than that someone is labeled "black." Moreover, we can (and should) remember the legal or formal construction of reality—a special and significant form of social construction. That someone is "French" depends in part on what the French laws of citizenship say on the subject. This in turn affects *social* views of Frenchness, though, of course, the legal and social definitions of "French" are not necessarily the same.

How does reality get socially constructed? If race, ethnicity, or gender is socially constructed (or mostly so), how does this process take place? This is never an easy question to answer; but whatever the answer, in modern times, that answer must lean heavily on the processes that create the horizontal society.

In a horizontal society, the realm of the chosen vastly increases. People are simply more mobile—they take in so much more from the outside world and are so much freer to respond to outside images and stimuli. What is less obvious is that inborn identity also becomes, in a way, a matter of choice. What happens in a horizontal society is that the *consequences* of inborn identities diminish. One is born either a man or a woman; but to be born a woman does not mean one is condemned to darn socks and wash dishes for a man. Free choice means the right to shed the *consequences* of being black, gay, Chinese, American, Jewish, or a carpenter's son. The *sense* that this choice is real is crucial in modern society.[5] In advanced, industrial societies, this feeling leads to pressure on policy and law, which move—though always in the face of opposition—toward removal of barriers that impede life choices.

The choice of identity is profoundly individual. As we said, identity is a matter both of self-definition and of external definition. And, as we also said, the two aspects interact. People have always had identities; language and religion have always been important in people's lives—vital aspects of their sense of self. But in a horizontal society, it becomes more and more important *who* you are; whether you are white or black; whether you speak Spanish or English; whether you are Catholic or Muslim or Pentecostal. This is because local, minor identities have decayed and because the dramas of politics and culture play out on a national or regional stage. In a horizontal society, groups form, mobilize, and communicate with the speed of light. The village explodes, and its fragments splatter all over the countryside. But the struggle to remove barriers against choice often requires group action; and this in turn requires mobilization and group identity. The goal of most feminists, in a way, is to make feminism obsolete and unnecessary. But that Emerald City is far off in the dim horizon.

Defining Race

As we argued, inside and outside definitions of identity interact. On identity issues, too, it matters greatly how people *evaluate* identities—which ones are good and bad, beautiful or ugly, intelligent or stupid. It is hard to think of an idea that has wreaked more havoc in the world than the idea of race—and especially the poisonous concept of higher and lower races.[6]

Hitler's fanatical hatred of Jews was perhaps the most rabid and destructive example of the pseudoscientific idea of race. (He hated blacks as well, but there were almost none available in Europe to murder.) The Third Reich had elaborate laws defining who was and who was not that most dangerous of non-Aryans, a Jew. This was one of the tasks of the infamous Nuremberg laws of 1935.[7] Ultimately, the lowest non-Aryans—Jews and Gypsies—who had not gotten out of Germany or who had fallen into Hitler's clutches in occupied Europe ended up in the death camps. Nationalism, under some conditions, degenerates into chauvinism, xenophobia, and race hatred. There is a depressing tendency for people to define their own group as the best, the finest, the noblest of human beings. Other peoples, races, ethnic groups, and religions are defined as lower down the scale of humanity, intellectually or morally. They are defined as stupid and primitive, ineradicably shiftless and criminal (like the Gypsies), cunning and devious (like the Jews), or, in the worst cases, downright subhuman, or implacable enemies who must be destroyed in a kind of self-defense. India is famous for its caste system, which divides the population in a systematic and rigorous way into "ranked hereditary kinship groups associated with a division of labor and organized into a unified and integrated whole."[8] Caste systems operate *within* a nation or culture, but they often have an ethnic or racial origin. Less formal versions of caste are found in many countries and cultures. The Boston elite, indeed, proudly carried the nickname "Brahmins." The American race system is often called a caste system, and with some justice. Many countries, perhaps, have the functional equivalents of "untouchables."

What is inborn cannot be changed; and, if that inborn quality is rotten, dirty, or inferior, a polity feels itself entitled to act harshly with regard to these pariahs, these children of a curse; it feels free to discriminate against them. A flood of books and "scientific" studies in the last nineteenth and early twentieth centuries told the public what much of it wanted to hear: humanity was divided into higher and lower races.[9] The "science" of eugenics held out the hope that we could improve the human race through selective breeding. This method, after all, had worked wonders with cows. The true believers in eugenics seemed to spend less time and energy on how to breed superior people than on how to keep inferior people from reproducing their kind. For example, some American states passed laws that allowed the state to sterilize the feebleminded and the criminal.[10]

Many scholars (and many laypersons, too) believed there were born criminals, men and women with a hereditary taint, a genetic tendency toward weak intellect, criminality, prostitution, and social pathology.[11] "Criminal anthropologists" mapped out the physical and racial signs of inherited degeneracy. Writing in the 1870s, the Italian penologist Cesare Lombroso founded this dismal science. He was inspired when he looked at the skull of a bandit and noticed "atavistic anomalies." For Lombroso, the criminal was a throwback to some primitive past.[12] His bones, his eyes, the shape of his head, betrayed him. As late as 1939, the anthropologist Earnest A. Hooton was writing about body types, explaining that "Nordic" criminals had "sloping foreheads and less rolled rims of the ear"; Mediterranean criminals, on the other hand, had "compressed and more flaring cheek bones" and "more slightly rolled ear helices." Bootleggers "persistently [had] . . . broad noses and short faces with flaring jaw angles"; sex offenders were "shrivelled runts," while thieves and burglars tended to be "sneaky little constitutional inferiors, either physically stunted or malnourished."[13]

Almost from the outset, there were scholars who denied and exposed the theories about higher and lower races. But the theories proved tenacious; they stood at the very center of Hitler's house of murderous ideology. In 1945, Hitler's empire dissolved in an sea of rubble and blood. The cruelest racist ideas are no longer respectable. They have mainly gone underground. In the late nineteenth century, racist and eugenic ideas drew heavily on the intellectual side of Darwinism and various mutations of nineteenth-century science; among other things, these pseudoscientific notions gave intellectual support to the imperial adventures of the great powers. (Imperialism would probably have made its way without them, but they helped.) These ideas were also a reaction to the turmoil and dislocations of the industrial world: the loosening of old ties; the decline of the village world; the vast movements of peoples from homeland to homeland and from countryside to city slums; and the feeling, most acute in the middle and upper classes, that a brutish underclass threatened their values and their way of life. They were reflections, in other words, of a mobile society and its discontents—a society becoming more horizontal.

Racist ideas still survive, in one form or another, and they may reach their most virulent forms in societies with a rich mixture of ethnic groups, races, and populations. They may be most dangerous when the fault lines in society are sharpest. Caste and class differences are a lurking danger, a threat to civic order, when they coincide with differences in race, religion, or ethnic origin, as the majority group in society defines these.

To most people, whether racist or not, race still seems to be, next to gender, the most inborn of identities, the most immutable. This is of course profoundly misleading. There is no better example of how society imposes meaning on categories of identity. Race definition has a rich if unhappy history in the United States. Blacks have been split off from whites for centuries. But who is black? What label should we put on a child if, out of eight great-grandparents, she has one who is black while the rest are white? The child probably looks more white than black, although Americans (black or white) tend to be extremely good at detecting "blackness." Most of the genetic stuff inside this child's cells come from white people (if this means anything). Perhaps the child was raised exclusively by whites, in an all-white neighborhood, and associated only with whites.

Despite all this, as far as Americans are concerned, this child is definitely black. Moreover, as the child grows up, she will almost certainly identify as black—will be forced to do so, in fact, because society will define her that way. This may be true even if the admixture of black blood is so attenuated that she can "pass for white." One scholar has estimated that between 75 and 90 percent of American blacks "apparently have some white ancestry" and about 1 percent of the genes of the white population "are from African ancestors."[14] To say, as the phrase has it, that "one drop of black blood" makes you a black in American society is a bit of an exaggeration, but only a bit.[15]

At various times in American history, states adopted official definitions of blackness. In Louisiana and North Carolina, anyone with one-sixteenth or more of black blood was defined as black; in nine states, the proportion was one-eighth; in Oregon, only those with one-quarter or more of black blood qualified as black.[16] During the era of slavery, children of slave mothers were themselves slaves and therefore black—never mind how white they looked (or what proportion of their blood was white).[17] In Mark Twain's novel *Pudd'nhead Wilson,* the plot turns on a mistaken exchange of two babies—the black baby is raised as a white, the white baby as a black. Obviously, both children could pass, or the novel would make no sense.

Miscegenation was always against the law in the southern states of the American union, but many slaveholders apparently had no qualms about sleeping with slave women or taking slave mistresses.[18] The results were mixed-blood children. The more light-skinned ones were quite apparent to the naked eye. As one writer reported in 1851, the whole South was fill-ing up "with a mixed race, where every shade of color is represented between the jet black of the African and Anglo-Saxon whiteness." The slave population was undergoing "a rapid whitening," and slave owners were holding "thousands of . . . slaves who are white as their own wives and daughters."[19]

Slavery was an economic and a social system, and it obviously made sense to define race this way; otherwise, if a slave mother gave birth to a mixed-blood child, that child would have some claim to freedom, which the southern slave system was disinclined to tolerate. Socially speaking, black blood trumped white blood; or, to put it more realistically, any black inheritance, even a small one, was a kind of inborn taint that labeled a child as a member of an inferior caste. Slavery ended more than a century ago, but the social definition of race did not die out. In part, this was because slavery was replaced by a labor system in which black workers were still subordinates, reduced almost to a kind of serfdom.[20] In any event, even today, when race discrimination is officially outlawed, and segregation is against the law, the old social definition of race persists.[21]

In other words, the definition of race in the United States has been determined by specific historical, cultural, and economic factors. But there are other possible patterns. For the most part, race is an either-or matter: You are either black or white. This follows from the one-drop rule. "Mixed" has not usually been a meaningful classification. "Mixed" in this country still means simply black. In the 1990s, however, this either-or situation has been, for the first time, seriously challenged. Many people feel strongly, for example, that the census ought to include a "multiracial" category, so that people can assign themselves to it if they wish.[22]

The number of people who feel this way is rising, as is the number of people of mixed race. According to the Census Bureau, interracial marriages are much more common than in the past; the bureau counted 310,000 mixed-race couples in 1970, and 1.3 million in 1994.[23] More and more, the products of these marriages feel themselves to be special—neither black nor white, but something distinctive in between.[24] By 1998, pressure from people of mixed race was strong enough to spark a change in census policy: beginning in 2000, Americans will be able to check off as many racial categories as they wish. Either-or is out.[25]

Elsewhere in the world, there are other racial categories and other ways of defining race. In South Africa, before the end of apartheid, "coloreds" (people of mixed blood) constituted a racial classification quite distinct from blacks.[26] (Colored people, to be sure, were also different in language and culture from black South Africans.) But if a colored South African came to the United States, he or she would be lumped together with blacks and would share their social fate.

In Latin America, race is not always an either-or matter. In Brazil, to be black (according to Carl Degler), a person has to have "no white ancestry at all." A person of mixed blood is not black but mulatto. The emphasis in Brazil is "upon appearance rather than upon genetic or racial background." In that country, then, "there is a continuum or spectrum of colors from white to black, rather than a dichotomy as in the United States."[27] In some Latin American countries, race may even depend on behavior, education, and culture, particularly in countries with large Indian and mestizo populations. Here an "Indian" is someone who lives within Indian culture; that same person, living in the city, speaking Spanish, dressed in Western clothing, and working as a store clerk, would no longer be considered an Indian. In parts of Latin America, there seems to be much less consciousness of race than in the United States and less in the way of racial politics.

Yet even in Latin America the situation seems to be somewhat fluid. An account in the *New York Times* in 1995 chronicled the efforts of Piedad Córdoba de Castro, the first black woman to become a senator in Colombia, who was eager to build "a black consciousness movement in Latin American." What stood in the way was "the low level of racial identification among blacks and mixed-race people." Senator de Castro hoped to change all that. She herself had the "lighter skin of someone with Spanish, Indian and African ancestors," but the senator was "emphatic" that "she is black, an Afro-Colombian,"[28] She had, in short, adopted for herself the American definition of black.

In the United States, black and white are not the only important categories of race or ethnicity. There is, for example, the large Hispanic minority. Defining who is Hispanic is not a simple matter. This is a very heterogeneous category. After the Mexican War (1846–48), the United States swallowed a big chunk of Mexican territory, and many Spanish speakers found themselves on the American side of the border. Around the turn of the century, the United States grabbed Puerto Rico from the dying Spanish empire. Since then, the country has possessed an island with a compact, Spanish-speaking population. Puerto Ricans are American citizens and can travel within the United States freely without a passport; by now, millions of Puerto Ricans live outside the island, on the mainland. In the Southwest, besides the descendants of the original Mexican-Americans, there is a large and growing Chicano population, made up, for the most part, of recent immigrants and their children. The smaller but very potent mass of Cubans has made southern Florida in effect bilingual. These are the main components of the Hispanic population in the United States; but hundreds of thousands of Central American immigrants have swelled the total in recent years. Dominicans, Guatemalans, Nicaraguans, Panamanians, and other Latin populations all have substantial colonies in the United States.

Each group of Spanish speakers is, of course, distinctive, but there are definite signs that a panethnic sense is developing among the Spanish-speaking minority. It is hard to say what binds them together. A sense of discrimination is certainly one factor, but discrimination on what basis? Language is another common denominator. Yet many Hispanics of the second or third generation have lost the language or prefer English. Racially, Hispanics can be black, white, Indian, or mixed. And although most Hispanics are Catholic, there are also Hispanic Jews and a growing number of Protestants. A directive from the U.S. Office of Management and Budget (OMB) defined as Hispanic "a person of Mexican, Puerto Rican, Cuban, Central or South American or other Spanish culture or origin, regardless of race."[29] But this kind of vague designation poses obvious problems. There is certainly no one-drop rule for Hispanics; there is certainly no such thing as an exclusively Hispanic look; nor is it clear how many Hispanic ancestors a person has to have before he or she can claim to be Hispanic for census and other purposes.

It has been just as troublesome to decide who is and who is not a Native American, at least officially. The same OMB directive suggests a category it calls "American Indian or Alaskan Native." This includes any "person having origins in any of the original peoples of North American, and who maintains cultural identification through tribal affiliation or community recognition."[30] This is a striking definition. It clearly implies that some people can *choose* to be "American Indian or Alaskan Native," or choose not to be—this is what "cultural identification" means. ("Community recognition" implies the views of outsiders.) No black, presumably, can decide not to be black. But a mixed-blood "Indian" living in New York or Wichita is presumably not really a Native American without "cultural identification through tribal affiliation or community recognition." Behind this definition is the assumption that an Indian can assimilate, can adopt the culture of the majority and, in so doing, cease to be an American Indian. The one-drop rule definitely has no place among Native Americans either.

This assumption—that assimilation is possible—is one factor that makes the recent history of Native Americans sharply different from that of African-Americans. Once the tribes were no longer a military threat, and most of their land had already been taken away, official policy leaned, in fact, toward *forced* assimilation. The infamous Dawes Act, of 1887, aimed at the destruction of tribal land systems;[31] the idea was to carve up the land into nice little family farms—the "civilized" and "American" form of land tenure. In exchange, native families would be offered the blessings of assimilation and citizenship. Meanwhile, the Bureau of Indian Affairs did its best to "civilize" the tribes. This meant, of course, a valiant effort to turn them into English-speaking Christians who held real jobs or worked on real farms. The results, for Native Americans, were catastrophic. They were robbed and cheated of yet more land; the cultural consequences were equally disastrous. The civil rights movement of the 1950s and 1960s, however, set off explosions that spread to the reservations and led to a revival of native culture and religion. But as we have pointed out, traditionalism is in fact anything but traditional. The demands of Indian activists for separation and autonomy are superficially backward-looking; but, like all such movements, they are essentially the product of modernity and the horizontal society.

No reservation, no matter how remote, is truly isolated; people come and go; they marry in or marry out; the boundaries, social and physical, are porous; the modern world reaches in, with TV and other deviltries. This makes the task of defining and preserving a culture more difficult and more *necessary* at one and the same time. The United States government, for various purposes, finds itself forced to grope toward some sort of definition of Native American. Each of the native peoples, on its own, faces a problem of definition: who is, and who is not, a member of the tribe? This was, of course, one of the issues in the Martinez case, discussed earlier.[32] Membership is, basically, a matter of blood: but how much blood? And how much weight can be given to choice? Obviously, one does not stroll into Navajo country and join up. But there are men and women who marry members or who, for whatever reason, settle in a Navajo community. Are they allowed to affiliate? How much weight should be given to way of life? Is a person still a Navajo if he or she lives in a big city, speaks English, and follows no Navajo customs? And who decides?

These classifications are not mere exercises in theory. They have consequences. Whether a person is accepted as a member of the group has obvious meaning for the person and the group. Nor are the outside classifications unimportant. The OMB directive is not an essay in social theory; on issues of race discrimination, affirmative action, and the like, these classifications matter. Being a Native American in American society may have disadvantages, but for some purposes, and for some people, it can be an advantage. If you check the Native American box on an application for the Harvard Law School, your form unquestionably floats to the surface, and your chance of admission rises.

The Dawes Act, and official policy, aimed to break up tribes. Today, detribalization is definitely a thing of the past. If anything, we now hear of *re*tribalization and of efforts to recover and revive vanished or vanishing cultures. The Bureau of Indian Affairs has promulgated rules to determine whether a group of people is or is not entitled to be recognized as an Indian nation or tribe.[33] Tribal groups living in compact areas and maintaining their ancient language are an easy case. But there are gray areas. Some interesting, dramatic lawsuits have turned on the question What is a tribe? Perhaps the most notable was the case brought by the Mashpee Wampanoags, in Massachusetts, who asked for the return of ancestral lands.[34] The defense was that the Mashpee were not really Native Americans—they had lost their language, had intermarried, had assimilated, and no longer even looked like Indians.

The Mashpee plaintiffs ultimately lost their case. Many commentators bitterly criticized the decision, calling it insensitive to the deeper layers of Native American culture.[35] Everybody would concede that a tribe has to be socially defined. The question is, Who does the defining? Is it the members, the government, or the wider society? It is also worth mentioning that the issue in the Mashpee case was not an abstract issue of ethnicity and cultural pride. It was a dispute over very concrete, very definite rights to land.

Partly for cultural reasons, then, and partly for reasons of affirmative action, new identities emerge on the political horizon. It might be more accurate, perhaps, to speak of most of them as old identities pushing themselves forward. Some of these identities are panethnic—for example, "Arab-American" or "people from the Middle East."[36] It is fairly obvious why this identity emerged. As Americans from the Middle East meet discrimination, as they watch movie after movie in which Arabs play dark, sinister villains, a kinship develops between, say, Lebanese Christians and Muslim immigrants from Egypt. In the Old World, some of these groups were hardly on speaking terms. But the outside world does not draw these fine distinctions, and this puts a premium on solidarity. As Martha Minow put it, the construction of identity is a "mutual" process, "by self and others, insider and outsider."[37]

Asian-Americans and Arab-Americans feel this outside pressure, but most other American ethnic groups, at present, do not. Being Italian-American or Swedish-American does not matter much, legally or socially; it certainly carries very little stigma, if any. It was not always this way for, say, Italians—and most definitely not for the Irish.

In the case of race, socially speaking, there is no such thing as free choice: as we pointed out, you are black, white, or Asian, and it does not matter whether you would prefer to be something else.[38] Not so in regard to ethnic belonging. People of mixed descent can, in a way, pick and choose among ethnic options. They can decide who they want to identify with. This makes ethnic identity less stubbornly rooted and more a matter of what David Hollinger has called affiliation.[39] Because there are literally millions of people in the United States whose backgrounds are all mixed up—German-Italian-Irish or Greek-Swedish-French, and so on, endlessly—there are millions of people who can decide to emphasize one or another of their "components." What this entails is largely a matter of diet and attitude. Very little else hinges on it.

Who Is a Jew?

Religions form another of the major horizontal "nations." Today, interestingly, it is more and more a matter of choice. What does it mean to be a Roman Catholic or a Baptist? In most cases, nothing turns (legally) on the answer to this question—at least not in the United States.[40] Ordinarily, religious affiliation is a question of behavior, church attendance, and sometimes a formal ceremony. People can and do pass easily from one religion to another. Especially in the modern world, religious cultures "are sustained by voluntary affiliations."[41] You are Presbyterian if you consider yourself Presbyterian. Nobody will call you on it.

In a mobile, horizontal society, as we have said many times, identity is a matter of choice—to a degree most people do not realize. But they clearly recognize that religious affiliation *is* choice. Separation of church and state means among other things, freedom to elect whatever religion appeals to one (or none of the above). It is ironic, then, that in the modern world people are still killing each other on the (ostensible) grounds of religion. But in most such cases—Bosnia, for example, or Northern Ireland—this means that religion has been converted into a form of ethnic belonging, a form of national identity.

It is also something of an irony that in Israel, unlike any other Western country, the question Who is a Jew? becomes a contested matter, a litigated matter, and a hot political issue. Who is a Jew was, of course, an issue under Hitler's vicious anti-Semitic laws.[42] Israeli law has very different goals, to say the least. The Law of Return gave Jews the right to settle in Israel and to acquire citizenship more or less automatically.[43] This made "Jew" at least potentially a legal concept. Under strict rabbinic law, only the child of a Jewish mother is Jewish. To be sure, rabbinic law does not necessarily bind the secular courts.[44] The case of Brother Daniel, a monk, born Oswald Rufeisen, in Poland, of Jewish parents, raised a delicate question for the Israeli courts. Brother Daniel had, indeed, acted heroically during the Second World War, saving the lives of many Jews. In 1945 he became a Carmelite monk. The order had a branch in Israel, and Brother Daniel, when he entered Israel, asked for an immigration certificate under the Law of Return and for registration as a Jew. The Ministry of the Interior denied this request, and Brother Daniel went to court. The Supreme Court of Israel, in a case that clearly troubled the justices, turned Brother Daniel down. Brother Daniel, despite his Jewish mother, had separated himself from the body of Judaism by converting to another faith; the Law of Return did not apply to him.[45] A later case posed the question from the other side: Anne Shalit was not Jewish, but her husband was. The family lived in Israel, they all spoke Hebrew, and they were part of Israeli Jewish society. The question was, Were the children Jews, for internal purposes? The court here (reluctantly) said yes, but the legislature overturned the decision, under pressure from the Orthodox community.[46]

The decision in the Brother Daniel case conforms to the general understanding in most religions (not just Judaism). A person can claim to be a Catholic if she was born into a Catholic family, even if she never goes to mass and ignores all the sacraments. The default rule, for religions, is that your religion is the one you were born into, unless you move in some other direction. Formal conversion into a rival faith will sever the tie. But in a horizontal, and plural, society (like the United States), formal conversion may not be necessary. Many people "shop" for religion, going from church to church, until they find one that satisfies their needs. A person like this might say, "I was born Catholic, but I go to a Baptist Church," drawing a line between inherited and chosen religion. But the line is getting more indistinct all the time.

Who Is a German?

German law no longer asks who is a Jew; but, in another historic irony, it does ask who is a German? Germans have their own version of the Law of Return. Germany long claimed not to be an immigrant country; this was not the image it saw when it looked into its cultural mirror. Germany (under German law) was basically only for Germans. This includes people living outside Germany who are "ethnically" German. As Germany got rich, it became a magnet for ethnic Germans scattered about Eastern Europe. In particular, it attracted Germans from the territory that was once the Soviet Union. It gave a ticket of entry, say, to remote descendants of the German settlers who Catherine the Great (herself a German princess) imported into Russia. Such a "German" might not, perhaps, speak a word of German, but memories, the right blood, and perhaps a name like Schmidt or Schultz would be enough.[47] This "German" is likely to gain access to the promised land, at will, and achieve full citizenship.[48] Meanwhile, a Turk born in Germany, the child of other Turks living in Germany, speaking German, going to German schools, watching German TV, and eating German sausage, remained in limbo as a resident alien.

Who Is a Latvian? (and Similar Questions)

The German and Israeli laws are, perhaps, extreme. Some other countries use a mixture of blood and culture to define true members of the community. Latvia, for example—a small country only recently released from the grip of the Russian bear—struggles to keep its language and culture alive. The threat comes from a sizable Russian-speaking minority; indeed, most of the people who live in Riga, the capital, speak Russian, not Latvian; in 1991, ethnic Russians made up one-third of the total population of Latvia.[49] Latvian law makes it very hard for these ethnic Russians to become citizens; on the other hand, anybody with real Latvian blood can qualify for citizenship—and even aspire to high places in government. Indeed, in 1995, a German right-winger was playing an active role in Latvian politics, as the head of a reactionary party. The man spoke not a word of Latvian. But he had a parent of Latvian blood, and this made all the difference, both legally and (apparently) socially.[50] His followers probably assumed that he would assimilate (if he assimilated at all) into Latvian culture. The Russian minority, which is dangerously large, is the one to be kept at bay.

Somewhat similarly, in Quebec, foreign immigrants *must* enroll their children in French-speaking schools; only native speakers of English can opt for English-speaking schools. Foreigners as such do not threaten the culture of Quebec, so long as they can be kept from flocking to the camp of the Anglophones; they can be absorbed into the culture of those who speak French. Dispersed minorities are usually less of a threat than a single, compact minority.[51]

Who Is a Woman?

Generally speaking, people consider gender a clear-cut case. We are almost never in doubt as to who is a woman and who is a man, putting to one side the small numbers of transvestites and transsexuals. Aside from differences obvious to the naked eye, there are also, in every society, important cultural, economic, and social differences between men and women. Scholars argue about *where* these differences come from. Are they inborn, biological—part of the essence of women and men? Or are they entirely the product of social learning, culture, and the like? One group of scholars, sometimes called "biological determinists," argue that "all and only women are 'feminine' and all and only men are 'masculine.'" "Nurture" or culture theorists, on the other hand, "flatly deny" this proposition and explain differences "by appealing to factors 'outside the body,'" factors that are "environmental."[52]

This scholarly split mirrors a similar split among ordinary people. I would guess, if I had to, that *most* people think biology has more to say about gender roles than most experts would be willing to concede. Most men, and probably quite a few women, consider the gulf between the sexes unbridgeable; it is part of God's or nature's plan. But if the "essentialists" are wrong, then, in an important sense, one chooses to be a woman (or a man). Not literally, of course. Rather, we each choose, or think we are choosing, clusters of behaviors and attitudes and ways of life—even in such matters as what to wear and how to talk; these choices are labeled male, female, or doesn't-matter, for historical, cultural, and social reasons. One certainly chooses whether or not to be a feminist. In the family, a man can certainly choose to do dishes and diaper the baby and take care of his elderly mother, or choose not to. Women in particular face major constraints. Many women have a similar choice: they may stay home with the kids or perhaps not have children at all and instead throw body and soul into their career.

Of course, choice here is not to be taken in a naive and literal sense. These choices are constrained and shaped by powerful social factors and in fundamental ways. For women, many possibilities in life are preempted by the men who dominate their lives and society in general. For both women and men, many attractive choices require the money to buy them with. But social forces also force our hands in ways we are not even aware of. It is very expensive, as it were, to go down a road that society condemns or your peer group laughs at. A young male who swaggers down the street acting tough has probably not made a conscious decision to adopt this macho way of life. He might carefully decide which design he wants to tattoo on his arm, but he is unaware of what made him want this tattoo or any tattoo in the first place. He never considers for a moment turning away from a gang fight or collecting CDs of Mozart symphonies or taking up knitting. Yet in his mind, he and he alone has decided what to do. A similar point can be made for the young woman obsessed with clothes or whose whole world revolves around pleasing and attracting men.

All the areas we have discussed—race, religion, gender—have social and legal definitions; formal and informal definitions; definitions inside the group and definitions from outside. These various definitions influence each other. What makes a person black in the white community is likely to make him black in the black community. As we mentioned, panethnicities are almost always the result of outside pressure. There would be no such thing as an Asian or an Asian-American if Americans did not combine most Asians into a single racial hodge-podge.[53] In any event, in the horizontal society, many of the ways that people clump together are, in fact, highly volitional; other components of identity, like ethnicity, are a mixture of choice and social compulsion; for some—and race is a prime example—social dictates and compulsion far outweigh choice, at least so far.

Just about everybody recognizes that these identities and affiliations are important—politically, economically, and culturally. Much less attention, I feel, has been paid to the question of where they come from. Of course, there is no single complete answer, and I have not attempted one. Nonetheless, modern identities are clearly a product of what we have called the horizontal society, and they could not arise, flourish, and sustain themselves without the technological tools of that society—or the mind-set which that society brings about.

Citizens and Strangers
Legal and Social Definitions

IN PRIOR CHAPTERS, I DISCUSSED the rise of ethnic identity and its relationship to the horizontal society, mostly in cultural and political terms. I also looked at how such categories as race are officially and legally defined. This chapter will explore, briefly, ways in which the basically subjective and cultural concepts of identity get molded into legal structures—specifically, laws of citizenship and naturalization.

Probably all identity groups draw a line between people inside the group and people outside the group, between those who belong and those who definitely do not belong. Every group has devised some way to test inclusion and exclusion. For a club, the criterion might be as simple as whether a person has paid dues. The matter is much more complex for the largest of the horizontal groups—the various nations. In modern societies, tests of membership—originally social, customary, or subjective—tend to harden into a network of rules. Practical politics, of course, not political theory, is what brings these laws into being and pats them into shape. And the ideas rattling about in people's heads, their concepts about what makes somebody a "citizen," are in turn the raw material of practical politics.

A citizen is a legal member of the political community. Only citizens can vote; generally speaking, citizens cannot be deported. What else flows legally from citizenship is a matter of local law. In some countries, and in some states of the union, only citizens can hold certain jobs, especially civil service jobs. It would certainly seem odd to let a foreigner become president of the United States or prime minister of France. But whether an alien should be allowed to deliver mail or collect tickets on the national railways is another question.

The laws of citizenship affect millions of people and are obviously important. Still, in Western countries, citizenship has lost some of its magic in contemporary times. As we have seen, more and more people subscribe to the idea that there are basic human rights—rights that are universal and inherent in humanity, in personhood. But if this is true, then at least *resident* aliens ought to enjoy these rights, since they are just as much members of the human race as natural-born citizens.[1]

In the United States, the Supreme Court has held that resident aliens have a right to civil service jobs, a right to practice law, a right to work as civil engineers, and, in Texas, a right to become notaries public.[2] (Other cases have held or hinted that a state could require police, public school teachers, and probation officers to be citizens).[3] In Europe, guest workers, even when they are ineligible for citizenship, enjoy most of the basic civil rights and to a great extent share in the bounty of the welfare state.[4]

A brochure put out by the Norwegian authorities, "Information on Norwegian Citizenship," illustrates this point. It contains the following interesting line: "Your life will probably not change noticeably when you acquire Norwegian citizenship." Norwegian citizens can vote and hold office, and are required to do military service; otherwise "there is little difference between the rights of Norwegian and foreign nationals." The right to "national insurance," among other benefits, "depends on how long you have lived" in Norway, not on whether you are a citizen.[5]

The law of citizenship, like all aspects of law, is strongly influenced by social norms and opinions, by what people think it means to be German or Ugandan or Panamanian. As we will see, there are certain gross differences between legal theories of citizenship—for example, the distinction between jus soli, which emphasizes simply whether you were born in a given country, and jus sanguinis, which emphasizes ethnic identity. Behind these Latin phrases are distinctions in the social situation, history, and traditions of various countries. There is, for example, a fairly fundamental split between immigrant countries like the United States and countries that export people to those immigrant countries.

Despite these and other differences, *all* the theories of citizenship reflect, as they must, the realities of life in a horizontal society. It was the rise of ethnic consciousness, and the creation of a world of sovereignties, that created the need to define citizenship by law. Thus, the history of the law and practice of citizenship is a history of the spirit of national identity. Each country has its own story to tell, of course; in this chapter, we will look mainly at the United States, and its regnant theories of national identity. These fall into three rough but distinct phrases—the age of tolerance, the age of assimilation, and the age of plural equality.

The last of these is *our* age: the age of multiculturalism. The old hegemonies have broken down. The United States is a big, sprawling, complicated country—a nation of many horizontal groups, all of them bound together by modernity and imprisoned in the cage of American popular culture. Under these conditions, many different groups and cultures are forced to live together more or less as equals (or aspiring equals). This generates tremendous stresses and strains and engenders countless controversies. This chapter will also take a brief look at some of the contested areas of national identity.

Citizenship

The concept of citizenship has a long history; Roman citizenship was highly valued, and Roman law reflected this value.[6] The meaning of citizenship blurred considerably in the Middle Ages. It came to life again, and sharpened, in the age of the nation state.

Every country has its own laws on citizenship. Underlying these laws are two basic principles. The first is the so-called jus soli, the territorial principle (*solum* means "land" or "soil" in Latin). The extreme case is the United States: everyone born here, no matter who the parents are, or what they were doing here, is automatically a citizen. This is not based simply on an act of the legislature; rather, it is part of American higher law—it is embodied in the Fourteenth Amendment to the Constitution, as interpreted by the Supreme Court of the United States.[7] The second principle is jus sanguinis, or the principle of "blood" (*sanguis* in Latin). Citizenship in countries that follow this line is based on some sort of ethnic or racial principle: citizens are those who have the right mixture of national blood.

Most countries combine elements of both principles in their working law of citizenship. The choice is far from arbitrary. For example, immigrant countries—Australia, Canada, Brazil, the United States—tend to favor jus soli. These countries, historically, have gotten their stock of citizens through in-migration. Traditionally, these groups do not constitute a "people." Citizenship is measured in terms of commitment to the national territory, physically speaking, and perhaps to the national credo; ancestral blood counts for far less.

For much of their history, immigrant countries were desperate to grow. They wanted bodies. They held out a hand of friendship to new settlers. They made the process of becoming a citizen as painless as possible. The United States advertised abroad for immigrants (in the right European places, to be sure). Argentina created an immigration bureau in 1869, the Comisión Central de Inmigración. In 1876, the bureau began to send agents to Europe to recruit immigrants for Argentina. The bureau offered free rail transport to their jobs and several nights' free lodging in Buenos Aires. More than 4,000,000 eager foreigners crowded into Argentina before the First World War; more than 2,400,000 of these immigrants stayed on and became permanent residents.[8]

Other immigrant countries—for example, Chile—are also firmly in the camp of jus soli. Anybody born in Chile is automatically a citizen, with few exceptions.[9] Immigration into Chile is also relatively easy, and resident aliens who want to becomes citizens of Chile are encouraged to do so; there are few obstacles in their path.

In short, the basic policy in all those countries that adhere to jus soli has been, at least in the past, to encourage, welcome, and absorb large numbers of people from abroad and from lands that were perhaps somewhat different from the mother country. There was at least the appearance of a welcome mat. Of course, none of this really meant a commitment to what we would now call multiculturalism or pluralism (as we shall see). A legal regime structured along the lines of jus soli could and did cohabit nicely with a smug sense of cultural superiority. Only the most naive could describe the United States as a country free from chauvinism. France is another illustration of this point. Nobody has ever accused the French of being too attached to cultural relativity and of warm understanding of other people. Yet French law definitely leans in the direction of jus soli. Children born in France, even to foreign parents, are citizens when they come of age; all they have to do is actually live in France.

In France, citizenship means being French, but to be French is a matter of culture more than a matter of blood. "French" means, in other words, speaking French, acting and eating French, and pledging allegiance to the French nation. A black African who abandons negritude for "Frenchhood" can become French more easily than he could become, voluntarily, English or German. The French have, generally speaking, welcomed foreigners who qualify—that is, who are willing to be French and to abandon their foreign ways. [10] (Recent events, to be sure, have put a strain on this attitude, as we will see).

In countries that follow the principle of jus sanguinis, citizenship laws stress kinship, blood ties, descent from a common ancestor, or (less flamboyantly) parents and grandparents who, beyond any doubt, are part of the nation. Germany is one of the clearest examples. German leaders repeat, over and over again, that Germany is not an immigration country. The German homeland belongs exclusively to the German nation. Of course, Germany is just as much an immigration country as most of its neighbors. Ethnic purity is vain illusion. Indeed, many of the family names of the aristocratic Junkers, those most (Prussian) German of Germans, are obviously Slavic in origin. In the nineteenth century, Polish workers immigrated to Germany in droves. [11] Many German Jews lived in Germany, too, before Hitler decided to make his country *Judenrein*. Today, Germany has millions of foreigners—especially Turks—living inside its borders. But the official line has remained quite strict: one either was or was not German by blood, and that made an enormous legal difference. There is no easy road to *becoming* German. German law has been—at least until the 1998 election—inhospitable, even for foreigners who live in Germany and are willing to molt their original citizenship for a brand-new German skin.

The treatment of Turkish guest workers is the most egregious example. In the high, palmy days of economic growth after World War II, Germany suffered from an acute labor shortage. It dealt with the crisis in the usual way: by importing foreign workers—Spaniards, Italians, Yugoslavs, and especially Turks. Today, there are 1,800,000 Turks and their descendants living in the Federal Republic. On the whole, they are still legally foreigners (noncitizens), even if they and their families have been in Germany for a long time—for generations in fact—and even if the children are more at home in the German language than in Turkish or speak little or no Turkish. Yet, as we have seen, *Auslandsdeutsche* (Germans living abroad), whose ancestors might have left Germany centuries before and whose connection with German culture might be tenuous, are entitled to settle in Germany and claim citizenship on a very fast track.[12]

Germany welcomes these "ethnic Germans" with open arms and with hardly any restrictions; they are people who "belong to the German *Volk*" as the Fundamental Law of Germany puts it.[13] Originally, this provision of the Fundamental Law was meant for refugees from East Germany, granting them automatic citizenship. After the Second World War, Germany was split in two. The Soviet Union dominated the eastern half, which became the German Democratic Republic. West Germany (the Federal Republic) never really recognized East Germany as a legitimate country. Hence it refused to recognize East German *citizenship*. East Germans were simply Germans living under Soviet occupation. Millions of East Germans escaped to the West during the Cold War. They were treated automatically as full citizens the instant they crossed the barriers or vaulted over the Berlin wall.[14] The special situation of a divided country did lend strength to jus sanguinis, but it can hardly be a full and satisfying explanation of the preference for German blood. After all, Germany adhered to jus sanguinis long before there was any such entity as the German Democratic Republic.

The United States and Germany may represent polar types with regard to principles of immigration law. Many countries mix the two principles and fall somewhere in the middle of the two camps. The child of a Swedish mother, for example, is a Swedish citizen; if the father is Swedish, that too does the trick, provided he is married to the mother of the child. An alien who has lived in Sweden "without interruption" from age sixteen on, and who had spent at least five years before that "domiciled" in Sweden, can pick up Swedish citizenship at age twenty-one by applying for it in writing.[15]

Naturalization

For most people living in a country, the question Am I a citizen? never comes up. They are obviously citizens, under any theory. They were born in that country, as were their parents, and they belong to that country, whatever the definition of belonging. Resident aliens—immigrants—are the issue in citizenship law. For immigrants, the issue is usually not Am I a citizen? (the answer is clearly no) but Can I become one? And how?

The same tendencies that bear on the question Who is a citizen? obviously bear on the question Who can become one? Jus soli countries encourage naturalization much more than jus sanguinis countries. But the subject is complex and has a long history in any country. The United States Constitution (article 1, section 8 [4]) gave Congress the power to "establish an uniform Rule of Naturalization." Congress duly passed its first naturalization law in 1790. An alien who was a "free white person" and had lived in the United States for two years could apply to a court in any state where he had lived for a year or more; on giving "proof" of "good character" and swearing an oath "to support the constitution of the United States," he was to be "considered as a citizen of the United States."[16] This act lasted only a short time. A law of 1795 (still applicable only to free whites) called for a longer residence period—five years. And *three* years before naturalization, the alien had to declare in court an "intention to become a citizen"; the alien also had to renounce "all allegiance and fidelity to any foreign prince, potentate, state or sovereignty whatever." To admit this person to citizenship, the court had to be satisfied that the alien had "behaved" as a person "of a good moral character" and was "attached to the principles of the constitution."[17]

There have been many turns of the wheels since these early, and somewhat restrictive, laws on naturalization. Today, in the United States, resident aliens have a fairly easy time becoming citizens; the real trick is getting in legally. Naturalization is also not a major problem in France—again, once you are legally inside the borders. But in Germany, the law has been, at least as of 1998, quite restrictive for those without proper German blood in their veins. A resident alien can apply for citizenship, to be sure, but the requirements are rather stringent: ten years' residence (at least), a clean record, good command of the German language, and a "free-willed and lasting commitment to Germany." Even if an applicant meets these tests, she is not *entitled* to citizenship. Citizenship is granted only if it is "in the public interest for political, cultural, or economic reasons."

Practically speaking, it has been hard for the resident Turks, all 1,800,000 of them, to be come citizens of the Federal Republic. Supposedly, most of them do not want to. But this may be because of what they sense as the *meaning* of German citizenship—a kind of commitment which perhaps they do not care to make—or perhaps because they do not feel welcome enough. Turkish immigrants in the United States do not shy away from naturalization. Americans treat citizens as citizens—they are used to foreigners, accents, and newly minted Americans. The Germans feel differently.

The Turkish population in Germany might find dual citizenship more to its liking, but it is not available under current law.[18] In fact, many countries, including the United States, have spurned the very idea of dual citizenship.[19] Citizenship has to be a matter of exclusive loyalty—an either-or proposition. In the United States, partly as a result of court decisions, the situation has become a bit less stark.[20] A number of countries have now given up the battle against dual citizenship, and hundreds of thousands of people have two or more passports.

Dual citizenship or dual nationality, whatever it may mean in the legal system, implies some kind of plural equality socially. It rejects the idea that membership in a country is confined to a tightly defined and exclusive group, or that it requires a total commitment of hearts and minds. In other words, under a regime of dual citizenship it is possible to "belong" to two countries at the same time. In horizontal societies, multiple and overlapping identities are not only possible; they are, in fact, the norm. Dual citizenship also reflects the facts of modern life: children of (ethnically) mixed marriages and vastly increased global shiftlessness and mobility.[21]

Germany is, of course, not the only country that made it hard for resident foreigners to become full-fledged citizens. In Spain, a candidate has to show "good civic conduct" and must also demonstrate a "sufficient level of integration into Spanish society," whatever that means.[22] It is also not easy to achieve the exalted status of an Austrian citizen. Ten years of residence is required, along with a spotless record, and even then it is a matter of discretion: the authorities can take into account, among other things, the "public interest."[23] In Switzerland, a notoriously clubby country, federal law required twelve years' residence; many cantons piled on further restrictions—requiring an applicant to demonstrate good character, good health, and some level of assimilation.[24] Rates of naturalization have been extremely low—so much so that in 1992 Switzerland was moved to make the process somewhat easier and to allow foreigners living in Switzerland to keep dual citizenship.[25]

Another restrictive country is (no surprise) Japan. Citizenship law there smacks strongly of jus sanguinis. Japanese children born to Japanese parents are citizens from birth. But it is very difficult to *become* Japanese; this is open only to people of Japanese ancestry. People of Korean ancestry—who number perhaps half million in Japan—are not citizens and cannot become citizens, no matter how many generations have lived in Japan.[26] For a Korean to become a citizen in Japan is even tougher than for a Turk to become a citizen in Germany.

British citizenship law has been complicated and politically charged. Great Britain, like France, though to a much greater extent, struggles with the debris of identities and allegiances left over when the mighty British Empire shuffled offstage. The millions who were once subjects of the empire were potentially citizens, but of course this was not physically possible and certainly not politically tolerable. British law *might* have simply declared all these former subjects ineligible to settle in the homeland and claim citizenship rights. Instead, the law before 1981 drew a sharp line between "patrials" and "nonpatrials."[27] The details were technical, but the basic concept was rather simple: to make it easy, legally speaking, for a nice white Australian or New Zealander to emigrate to London, while shutting the door on Indians, Pakistanis, Africans, and Chinese.

The basic mechanism was to draw a line between descendants of the English, that is, people who had actually lived in the United Kingdom, and those who lacked this heritage. Obviously, white Australians passed the test; dark-skinned Gambians or Sri Lankans did not. The concept of a "patrial" was, thus, a definite nod in the direction of jus sanguinis. On the other hand, the British Nationality Act of 1948 recognized jus soli as well: anybody born in the United Kingdom was a citizen by birth (with trivial exceptions).[28]

An act of 1981 abandoned the concept of the patrial,[29] but the law also retreated from the principle of jus soli. Children born in the United Kingdom would be citizens only if one parent was a British citizen. The government, we are told, was afraid that jus soli "could be abused by those who came to the UK for the express purpose of having their child acquire British citizenship"; it was also "undesirable" for children born in the United Kingdom to have "an indefinite right of re-entry without any substantial connection with the UK."[30] Great Britain is an island state; it has no border with the Third World, and the image of hordes of immigrant women crawling into England to give birth seems ludicrous. The retreat from jus soli will affect only a few people, but its symbolic (and political) import seems obvious.

At the same time, some countries have been moving in the opposite direction—that is, away from jus sanguinis. One example is Belgium. In 1991, an amendment to Belgian law gave citizenship automatically to "third-generation immigrants," that is, children born in Belgium whose grandparents had come as immigrants. "Second-generation" immigrants (children born in Belgium of immigrant parents) could become citizens between eighteen and thirty by "making a *declaration* to that effect." These changes, according to one authority, "must be seen within the scope of the government policy to enhance the integration of immigrants into Belgian society."[31] "Integration" implies assimilation: under Belgian law, if a second-generation immigrant opts to become a Belgian, citizenship is not automatically granted. For one thing, the public prosecutor can raise objections if the immigrant has a criminal record (this is understandable, and a common feature of citizenship laws). But citizenship can also be blocked if there are facts that cast doubt on the person's "will to integrate into Belgian society."[32] The stress on integration at least implies a kind of melting-pot philosophy. Belgian is as Belgian does; an eligible second-generation immigrant, if he feels like a Belgian and chooses to live the Belgian life, can therefore *be* a Belgian.

Of course, clashing conceptions of national identity lie behind all these rules and concepts, in their various permutations and combinations. In an immigration country, becoming a citizen is, more or less, like joining a club. The club belongs primarily to people *born* in the country; they are in fact automatically members. Ethnic identity is (at least in theory) of lesser importance. Clearly, the Japanese feel otherwise. Nobody can choose to be Japanese; being Japanese is entirely ascriptive—part of a closed world, a private club with no nonmembers admitted. Japan, like Germany, has something vaguely reminiscent of the Israeli Law of Return. Brazilians of Japanese descent (many of whom speak not a word of Japanese) routinely get permits to enter Japan and to work as foreign laborers.[33] This is the exception that proves the rule—these "foreigners" look Japanese, and in the minds of their hosts, they *are* Japanese—perhaps fallen-away Japanese, half-formed Japanese, but Japanese nonetheless. In a way, the principle of jus soli is just as ascriptive as jus sanguinis: the emphasis on birth is the same; only the principle is different, that is, where you were born, instead of to whom. This stress on the land, the territory, the soil, is more compatible, conceptually, with a theory of choice. It is an accident whether one is or is not born within the borders of a particular country. Still, if you have this kind of luck, you are accepted; you are welcome to stay in the club; you are a member, regardless of blood or ethnicity. And a person legally inside the country, wherever his or her place of birth, can choose freely to stay and become an equal member of the club. That is most definitely not the case in Japan. In Japan, citizenship only goes to those with a Japanese inner essence.

Conceptions of national identity therefore make or break the law of citizenship and naturalization and, as we will see in the next chapter, the law of immigration as well. The two fields are of course closely related. Citizenship laws, on the whole, have to do with people who are already inside the country; immigration laws guard the doors. But both are, in fact, connected with ruling ideas about the nature of the nation and the soul, as it were, of the national community. In a country that defines the nation in terms of blood and Volk, immigration will be hedged about with restrictions, and naturalization will be frowned upon; it will be the exception, not the norm.

It is important, too, to recognize that *all* these principles are solutions to distinctly modern problems—problems of the horizontal society. They are problems that arise in a mobile, shifting world, a world in which affiliation is not fixed and unchangeable. Germany and Japan are, perhaps vainly, trying to lock the doors, to define a kind of nationalism of the blood and hold back the forces that a horizontal society has set loose. Immigrant countries face similar problems, but their solutions, as we will see, are necessarily more complex, because they do not have the luxury of defining membership solely in terms of some precious stock of blood.

National Identity: The Case of the United States

Theories of national identity are an aspect of the culture of any community; that culture is the parent and progenitor of the community's *legal* culture, which, in turn, is the source of law, formal and informal.[34] Indeed, law is what results when general culture gets refracted through the prism of legal minds and legal institutions. The law, in its own right, has a certain feedback effect on the general culture—though how much, and to what extent, are hotly disputed questions.

The United States is a rather extreme case of jus soli; it is also the immigration nation par excellence. It seems to occupy one pole on the continuum of national identity. In this section, we will trace, in broad brush strokes, the way social forces and general culture have molded a sense of national identity. Norms and concepts of national identity are the blueprints and templates out of which laws of citizenship and naturalization are crafted. Some influence may also flow in the other direction. That is, citizenship and naturalization laws, once they are in place, may influence the way people think about these subjects; what *is* has a certain ideological impact on what people think *ought* to be.

"National identity" refers, of course, to an aspect of political and legal culture, that is, an aspect of public opinion. Legal culture refers to attitudes about law—values, expectations, ways of thinking about the subject—

which bend social forces toward or away from the law.[35] National identity is also an aspect of general culture: it is the answer to the question What does it mean to be a real American (or Frenchman or Japanese, and so on)?

Public opinion and legal culture are slippery concepts that can mean different things in different contexts; in addition, they are extremely hard to measure. How can we arrive at a coherent picture of political or legal culture? One way is to stitch together stray writings, newspaper articles, quotations from famous and not-so-famous books, and whatever else we can get our hands on; another is to interpret the (supposed) inner meaning of events, situations, and incidents and to infer political or legal culture from behavior. There are better methods—survey research, for example—but these also have problems and were simply not available before recent times. Still, we have to be careful when we reconstruct culture out of bits and pieces. Such data do not lend themselves to scientific rigor, and there is no sense pretending that they do.

We also have to ask: *Whose* political or legal culture? The answer, for most of American history—or French history, for that matter—is that there are many dialects of legal culture. The prevailing one, the one that gets itself noted and recorded, is the culture of elites—those segments of the population that call the tune in society. Throughout most of the history of the United States, this has meant white males who are middle-class and above. This leaves a lot of people out, a fact that historians have been forced to come to grips with more and more. But it also leaves a lot of people *in*—de Tocqueville, whatever his blind spots, was not really wrong in his assessment of the United States: compared to European nations, this was an extraordinarily democratic country in the context of the nineteenth century.

The United States was, in fact, the first truly middle-class country, and the white middle-class was large and inclusive. This was a country of extraordinary mobility—perhaps the first horizontal society. It was the first major Western country in which land was widely held, in which millions owned a farm, a house, a lot. It was the first country in which a middle-class mass had a stake in the economy, and not as peasants or serfs; in which ordinary people had voting rights and a share in shaping and molding the law; and in which the culture of the middle class, not the culture of the elites, was dominant.[36] Everybody else in the Western world, and elsewhere (Japan, for example), has been rushing to catch up.

Not that everybody within the mega-group that counted in the United States was, or is, of one mind on any particular subject. Nor have issues of citizenship, naturalization, and national identity always been high on the national agenda or central to political culture. Sometimes these issues were dim, implicit, hardly a matter of debate; at other times, they emerged from the shadows and provoked alarm and great political noise.

The culture of national identity went through three general stages. We will call these toleration, assimilation, and plural equality.[37] The stage of *toleration* lasted roughly from the Revolution to the late nineteenth century.[38] During this period, elites and leaders (and probably the general mass of solid citizens as well) had a sense, conscious or unconscious, of a single regnant national identity. There was, after all, a dominant religion (or cluster of religions), that is, Protestant Christianity; there was also a dominant moral code, dominant customs, and a dominant normative order. America was an offshoot of northern European Protestant culture.

But there were also other people living in the American republic after independence. There were scattered populations that did not fit into the dominant mold—Catholics and Jews, for example. For these minority identities—especially minority religions—and for their cultures, the majority culture adopted (on the whole) a stance of quiet tolerance. This was particularly clear in the case of religion. Constitutionally and legally, this country was free, democratic, and tolerant; minorities of all sorts could live in peace and pursue their own visions of good. Yet this benign tolerance was at best skin-deep. Black slavery was one radical exception.[39] Even free blacks in the slave states were lower than second-class citizens: they were subject to legal and social humiliations and denied many fundamental rights. In northern states, too, free blacks were barely tolerated, and in most places, they were denied the vote.[40] The native peoples (Indians) were another major exception to American tolerance. In this case, the racial element in the struggle between the settlers and the native peoples was probably less decisive than the clash of cultures—and the white man's hunger for the land.

Tolerance in fact rested (implicitly) on the assumption that people outside the mainstream were only a wee bit different from the mainstream: Swiss or Swedish instead of English or German. The United States was a nation that came close to Jefferson's ideal—a union, as Rogers Smith describes it, of "smallish agrarian republics, populated by self-supporting, educated white yeomen."[41] An influx of people who were very different—Turks or Chinese, for example—might have strained tolerance to the breaking point. But there was no such influx in the early nineteenth century. In fact, the population was overwhelmingly Protestant and northern European—at least until the great rush of Irish Catholics in the 1840s, driven by hunger and poverty from Ireland to the promised land. Irish Catholics indeed faced hatred and discrimination on this side of the Atlantic; they were considered ignorant savages and were the target of rabid, anti-Catholic propaganda.[42]

The Irish influx was perhaps the first substantial test of the limits of toleration. The Constitution and the Bill of Rights, of course, made an established church or state religion impossible—certainly on the federal level.[43] Congress could not make any religion official, nor could it interfere with the "free exercise" of religion. People could follow the dictates of whatever religion they wished. Catholics lived more or less in peace with the Protestant majority (itself divided into many different denominations). A handful of Jews coexisted with the mass of Christians—they were unloved, perhaps, but there were no American ghettos or pogroms; Jews voted and had full civil rights. The religious minorities built their churches and synagogues. Nobody interfered with their religious life. The republic had no laws against heresy and burned nobody at the stake.[44] Still, Catholics, Jews, and Moslems were guests, as it were, in a house that did not really *belong* to them; it belonged to the dominant Protestants, and nobody else had genuine title or ownership.

Throughout American history, intolerance, nativism, and bigotry were always there, simmering darkly under the surface.[45] During the Jacksonian period, in the turbulent cities, there were frequent riots and disorders against Irish Catholics.[46] The burning of the Ursuline Convent, near Boston, was a famous outrage based on religious intolerance.[47] No one in authority defended these riots; and, indeed, they frightened the comfortable and respectable. In fact, urban turbulence led to demands for an army of domestic order—that newfangled English innovation, the police.[48]

Even with regard to religion, there were limits to *official* tolerance. This was amply demonstrated by the fate of a new and disturbing religion, the Church of Latter-day Saints (the Mormons, as they have always been familiarly called). In the early years of the church, Mormons faced continuous persecution, sometimes violent: a mob killed Joseph Smith, founder of the religion.[49] The Mormons ultimately sought refuge in "Deseret," their new home in far-off Utah. There they were able to create an independent society, free from the suspicions and anger of the Gentiles.

Remote as it was, Utah was not, as it turned out, quite far enough away from the rest of the United States. The Mormons practiced polygamy, and this practice evoked horror and rage in the rest of the country to a degree that seems hard to imagine today. Congress thundered down prohibitions against the practice; the Supreme Court, in *Reynolds v. United States,* gave its stamp of approval to draconian laws against this vile habit.[50] The decision was drenched in the language and thought of Anglo-conformity. Polygamy, the court said, had always been "odious" to the "northern and western nations of Europe." It was, in fact, a "feature of the life of Asiatic and of African people." In 1878, this was quite enough to condemn the practice. The reference to Asiatic and African people speaks volumes. Nobody in this country dreamed of a welcome mat for Asiatics and Africans; people assumed, like the Court, that this was a country by and for Europeans. Despite the freedom, democracy, and tolerance, features of the lives of Asiatic and African people were not acceptable in the United States. As the Reynolds case demonstrated, the government was determined to stamp out polygamy. During the moral crusade against this practice, hundreds of Mormons were put in prison for the crime of "unlawful cohabitation."[51] The persecutions continued until the Mormon church, in 1890, bowed to the inevitable and recanted; from then on, the faithful were not allowed more than one wife.

The rise and fall of the crime of *blasphemy* tells an instructive story. Blasphemy was, in essence, the crime of defaming Christianity. It was considered a serious offense in the seventeenth and eighteenth centuries. In eighteenth-century Maryland, for example, if anyone dared to "blaspheme or curse God, or deny our Saviour . . . or . . . the Holy Trinity," the offender was liable to be "bored through the tongue"; punishment for second offense was branding on the forehead with the letter B; punishment for a third was death.[52] There were, in fact, not many prosecutions, and actual punishments were less savage than those the statutes prescribed. Still, cases did occur; in one interesting episode in Maryland, in 1658, a Jewish doctor, Jacob Lumbrozo, was accused of blasphemy. He let slip, among Christians, that he did not believe in Christ as the Messiah or in the Resurrection. He was ordered to stand trial, but a general amnesty saved him from this fate.[53]

Despite the official credo of tolerance—and the First Amendment to the Constitution—blasphemy remained a crime in many states during the nineteenth century. As before, law and practice confined this crime strictly to acts that derided or defamed Christianity. It was never blasphemy to denounce or ridicule other religions—Judaism or Islam or Buddhism. Some judges defended the blasphemy laws, on the grounds that they were simply rules for keeping the peace. As a Delaware judge put it, there was a distinction between a "religion preferred by law," that is, an established religion (forbidden by the Constitution), and a "religion preferred by the people"; such a religion was entitled to the "protection of law."[54]

People v. Ruggles, decided in 1811, was one of the best-known blasphemy cases of the republican period.[55] Chancellor James Kent of New York put the matter bluntly: yes, the state was entitled to punish blasphemy against Christianity, even though it did not punish "the like attacks upon the religion of *Mahomet* or of the great *Lama*." And why? For the "plain reason, that . . . we are a christian people, and the morality of the country is deeply ingrafted upon christianity, and not upon the doctrines or worship of those imposters."

Of course, Kent had no intention of actually harassing or persecuting people who did in fact worship "imposters." There is no reason to doubt Kent's sincerity or his belief in religious freedom. All religions had rights in the United States; all religions could live in peace. But only Christianity was entitled to recognition as *the* religion of the country; only Christianity was entitled to dominance and to the protections of laws of blasphemy. Christianity, in short, was the norm. All other religions were deviations from the norm.

The blasphemy statutes were not in themselves particularly significant, but they are a symptom, a bit of evidence about national identity in the nineteenth century. This evidence suggests a cultural domination that went almost unquestioned and was hardly even noticed by most people in the country—it was as natural as the air they breathed. I say "almost unquestioned" and "hardly noticed"; religious minorities certainly noticed it and, in secret, probably, questioned it. As the Roman Catholic population grew, it became acutely aware that the public schools were really Protestant schools; they were not truly neutral and nondenominational. In these schools, Catholic children were "forced to read the Protestant version of the Bible, to study explicitly anti-Catholic texts, to sing Protestant hymns." This sense of alienation gave Catholics a powerful incentive to found their own, separate system of schools; and they did so, beginning in the mid-nineteenth century.[56]

In the latter part of the nineteenth century, the emphasis in the general culture shifted subtly, as far as we can tell, from tolerance to *assimilation*. This was a period of heavy immigration into the United States. Earlier human waves had come mostly from northern Europe and from Great Britain, except for the mass migration from Ireland before and after the great potato famine. By and large, immigration had been Protestant, comfortable, familiar—and, from the standpoint of the majority, eminently desirable. The new immigrants who poured into the United States toward the end of the nineteenth century were a different breed. They included hordes of Catholics, Jews, and Eastern Orthodox from southern and eastern Europe. Culturally, these new immigrants seemed exotic, remote from American ways. Old-line Americans looked at them with deep suspicion. They considered them ignorant, dirty, morally inferior; their languages, customs, and food evoked disgust. And there were so many of them! This army of newcomers, with their primitive, foreign ways, threatened to overwhelm the normative order and to elide the established culture.

Assimilation implied that immigrants had a duty to "Americanize" as rapidly and completely as possible. But what did this mean? In one crude sense, it meant imitating or conforming to the patterns of people already here. It meant fitting "unobtrusively into the American scene," shedding the old identity completely, embracing Americanism, and thus advancing national unity as "true Americans," that is, joining the mainstream.[57] Assimilation, then, meant conformity; it meant molting the old skin and putting on the new. Assimilation demanded complete loyalty to what was assumed to be the American standard. There were to be no "hyphen-Americans" (that is, no "Italian-Americans" or "Armenian-Americans"); immigrants and their children were supposed to get rid of the rags and tatters left over from the old country and become 100 percent American as quickly as possible.

What was new about assimilation, what made it marginally different from the era of tolerance, was that it imposed a positive duty on immigrants to change their behavior. Tolerance at least implied a right to live in one's own obscure little corners; it was appropriate so long as discordant cultures were rare, exotic, dispersed, and few in number. Tolerance also assumed that minorities would be humble and grateful and make no noise. A defiant minority, like the Mormons, was therefore not accepted. And tolerance became a luxury when millions of unwashed peasants, the huddled masses, poured into the country.

The message for these masses was: become as we are. Leave your ghettos, learn English, join the great American civilization. Some immigrants, however, put a slightly different spin on assimilation. They believed in America as a melting pot. This striking phrase comes from the title of a play by Israel Zangwill (1908), himself a Jewish immigrant. "American," he wrote, rather breathlessly, "is God's crucible, the great Melting Pot where all the races of Europe are melting and re-forming. . . . Germans and Frenchmen, Irishmen and Englishmen, Jews and Russians—into the Crucible with you all! God is making the American."[58]

Americanism thus was something special, something unique; American identity, American culture, was not a dialect or mixture of European or British cultures and identities but something distinctive in its own right. The national character was not fixed and unchanging, a set pattern into which immigrants were supposed to blend. Rather, it was a culture that changed as one added ingredients; it was a new light made up of all the colors of the rainbow.

The melting-pot idea did not mean less devotion to America. It simply defined America a bit differently. This new country, after all, was God's creation—God was a celestial chef, devising a new and tastier dish. Immigrants were not expected to discard absolutely everything about their past; as they Americanized, they kept some bits of culture, some norms, some ways of life, and as they melted into the pot, they added their unique contribution to the American version of stone soup.

Of course, they had a duty to become citizens. Germany was quite willing to keep Turkish residents at arm's length and to discourage them from becoming Germans. But Americans consider it anomalous, and even insulting, if someone lives years and years in this country and never bothers to become a citizen. In the land of the melting pot, everyone has a duty to melt. This responsibility rests on a "rock-bottom belief" that Americans generally hold—a belief that, first of all, it is "better to be an American" and that "anyone can become an American"; in short that it is a matter of free choice—and a free choice that, in a way, a person who lives in the United States *should,* indeed *must,* make.[59]

The two notions of assimilation (which were not, after all, that far apart) continued to coexist into the twentieth century. Ultimately, they parted company over the issue of immigration and over the "American dilemma" of race.[60] Plenty of old-line Americans were far from enthusiastic about the melting-pot idea, not particularly keen on embracing or welcoming the likes of Zangwill. They doubted whether the new immigrants would or could become real Americans. The Levantine rabble pouring into the country was simply too different—or downright inferior by birth. As we have noted, the late nineteenth and early twentieth centuries were the climactic age of the poisonous pseudoscience of race. To eugenicists and others, some races were plainly superior to others: notably the white race, and within that group, its northern branches in particular.[61] Darwinian theories of evolution seemed to support the idea. Some races were further along on the route from ape to humanity than others. Many solid citizen prided themselves "on the superiority of older stock"; they were afraid that assimilation "into the homogeneous whole would result in a loss of the finer qualities of their national identity."[62]

In particular, the newcomers were a threat to moral purity—to the high ethical standards and respectability of the American bourgeoisie. For-- eigners were presumed to be hostile or indifferent toward these delicate val- ues. In 1922, just before the passage of a restrictive immigration act, Pro- fessor Brander Matthews denounced "unassimilated aliens" as "outlanders" whose "racial hatred for England . . . leads them to resent those aspects of American civilization which we have been in the habit of calling 'Anglo- Saxon.'" These outlanders, or some of them, were not bathed in the cold clear water of American morality: their "impulses seem to be phallic rather than cephalic"; they were "outspoken in their hostility to the Puritan tra- dition and vaunt themselves as Impuritans, so fierce is their rancor against the ideals of decorum and of decency which are part of the Anglo-Saxon inheritance."[63]

This screed defined the American way strictly in terms of English and northern European culture. The moralism is striking and characteristic. Americans had reached some kind of high plateau of civilization. The dirty peasants, pouring in by the thousands at Ellis Island, did not know or care about American values, and they would end up polluting and debasing those values. In their most extreme form, ideas like Matthews' played into the hands of racists; these ideas bolstered the eugenics movement, provided intellectual support for restricting Asian immigration, and propped up the "Southern way of life," with all that implied for black Americans. Ulti- mately, they helped produce the national quota system, in the Immigra- tion Act of 1924.[64]

These old ideas never quite die, nor do they exactly fade away; but they face a strong rival in our day. We have now entered a third phase in the evo- lution of national identity. In this phase, many people reject the various di- alects of assimilation. They espouse what might be called *plural equality*.[65] This is not a philosophy in the formal sense. It does not come from the academy or from the thin layer of intellectuals at the top of American so- ciety. It is a cluster of ideas, fairly crude, shapeless, and inchoate, that seem to arise spontaneously out of the mélange of events, situations, and talk in America. In fact, what fathered plural equality is the mature horizontal society. In particular, what gives it energy and pulse is the formation of a pride of subnations. This new norm insinuates itself, unconsciously, as a taste, a habit, a way of thinking, in the minds of people living in the country.

It is easier to define what plural equality is not, and what it is against, than what it is for. It is against the idea that there is or can be or should be a single canon, a single hierarchy, a single form of identity in this country. Its goal for the nation is not assimilation, not the melting pot, but diversity within a multicultural state.[66] In other words, the country is or ought to be a kind of coalition or federation of distinct groups and cultures, each with its rightful share of genuine power. No group or set of norms dominates (in theory).[67] Castles and Miller describe the multicultural model of citizenship as a "definition of the nation as a political community . . . with the possibility of admitting newcomers to the community, providing they adhere to the political rules, while at the same time accepting cultural difference and the formation of ethnic communities."[68] Without the political rules, in fact, no multicultural state is possible. When the South was a one-party state, when blacks were driven and harassed from the polling places, there was no multiculturalism there.

These political rules, then, are a prerequisite. But the cultural differences and the ethnic communities are the essence of the multicultural state. It represents the breakdown of the old hegemony; what replaces it are the virtual communities, the subnations, linked through ideology and technology in the new and sharply horizontal state.

Many people think plural equality is a good in and of itself. Others argue that, good or bad, it is unavoidable in a country with so many different nations inside its borders. Ethnic purity is not an option in the United States. A multicultural society was not freely chosen; in fact, it was forced on the country by the power of circumstance; it exists more or less by default.

But this is only partly correct. True, the United States does have a mix of races, religions, and peoples. Nonetheless, many people who say they are in favor of a multicultural society, in fact, do not really like the idea. Frankly, they do not care much for any of the cultures except their own, or for any of the colors in the "rainbow coalition" except theirs. But all those other colors and cultures exist, and each wants equality, each wants a fair share of power and prestige. The multicultural state, then, is something people settle for, a lesser of various evils. They are passengers trapped on a long ocean voyage, on the same boat.

But the sheer intensity of race feelings, like concepts of national identity, is a product of the forces that produced the horizontal society; in any event, these forces are distinctively modern. They all reflect a loose, mobile, fluid, self-forming society. They are all children of TV, of jet airplanes, of the movies, of advertising and the consumer society. Nationalism, as we saw, is a movement that insists on the primacy of one horizontal group, the nation, which outranks all the other constituent groups. Plural equality and multiculturalism are fragmented forms of nationalism—splinter nationalisms, so to speak. Yet in the strict sense they are also enemies of nationalism. They elbow themselves to the foreground with allegiances that compete with national loyalty.

Historically, a fairly narrow elite formed the heart and soul of nationalism; it helped define a national identity. What was left out of the definition was as significant as what was left in. But in our times, the out-groups are no longer content to skulk at the margins. They reject the main-line tradition and the concepts of tolerance and assimilation, since these, each in its own way, embody a narrow brand of nationalism, a nationalism of exclusion. What plural equality does is dissolve the nation, that is, the ideology of a single, overarching unity. For the pluralists, there is no America. There are only sub-Americas.

There is nothing new under the sun, and it is easy to find precursors of plural equality here and there, as far back as one cares to go. But only recently has it become a strong political force. In some ways, it is very much the child of the civil rights movements of the 1950s and 1960s, as well as the other liberation movements that the civil rights movement encouraged or inspired—the new feminism; movements of the handicapped, senior citizens and sexual minorities; prisoners' and students' rights; the right of adopted children to find their biological parents, and so on. Very prominent have been movements of ethnic minorities—especially Hispanics, who represent a growing and powerful panethnicity. Equally striking are the new claims of various Native American peoples for land, recognition, tribal law, and even autonomy. Many of these groups reject assimilation outright or condemn it as a threat to true pluralism and equality. Assimilation, in fact, is a dirty word for some, a form of discrimination—something "more insidious than outright exclusion and hence possibly more dangerous."[69]

Thus, in this age of plural equality, many of the nations inside American are overtly and blatantly opposed to goals that once seemed self-evident—for example, assimilation itself. Public education, which is locally controlled, is particularly apt to become a battleground. The new national cultures have, in a way, turned the aims, methods, and content of education upside down. In the nineteenth century, the ethos of education was frankly assimilationist. Education was a way to train citizens; in particular, it was a way to turn polyglot urchins into "real" Americans. In the age of the melting pot, education *was* the melting pot.

To be sure, assimilation was popular with many immigrant parents. They wanted the best for their children, and Americanism looked like the yellow brick road to success. Many immigrants hated the old country— they had run away from oppression or grinding poverty. They were eager to embrace America, if it would only embrace them. Undoubtedly, many immigrants today feel exactly the same way. They know that it pays to speak English, for example. Spanish-language TV stations are full of ads on how to master English as painlessly and rapidly as possible.

But one now often hears another tune entirely. One hears that assimilation is not a virtue at all, but rather a kind of cultural genocide (for Native Americans, it literally was). More and more, one hears voices rejecting assimilation; as one scholar argued, assimilation can be "psychologically damaging" when it is "forced" on a group. Schools should therefore never try to cram Americanism down the throats of children. Rather, school should try to "heighten" a child's "consciousness" of its "ethnic heritage."[70] Such an idea would have been almost unthinkable a century ago.

There is no question that the dogma of plural equality is politically and culturally prominent, in ways that were not true in the past. Where does it come from? It is, in the first place, a product of the horizontal society. The horizontal society makes plural equality *structurally* possible. The individual movements that together make it a reality depend very much on the miraculous ways in which we can talk and communicate and visit across great spaces. In our times, people who are horizontally separate can join together and spread their message far and wide.

But there is more to plural equality than structure; it is, essentially, a cultural phenomenon. To me, it seems clearly related to the specific twentieth-century brand of individualism. The United States in the nineteenth century, for all its talk about freedom, simply assumed domination by men, by whites, by Protestant Christians, and by English speakers. That was the essence of "Anglo-conformity." We have already spoken of the legal and social position of blacks. Women did not vote, and they lost many of their property rights when they married. Gays and lesbians not only lacked rights and recognition but were guilty of the "infamous crime against nature" and could be severely punished if caught in the act.

Nineteenth-century theorists talked obsessively about individual freedom, but what they meant was political and economic freedom. Western countries made, in fact, considerable progress toward these ends. By the middle of the nineteenth century, almost all adult white men in the United States could vote; after the Civil War, blacks too had the franchise;[71] and in the first decades of the twentieth century, women as well won the vote. Slavery was abolished in 1865. Married women gained the right to own property, to enter into contracts, and to buy and sell as they wished—the ancient sovereignty of their husbands was finally overthrown (legally, at least).[72] In the nineteenth century, there was a good deal of what most people today would consider progress in human rights. The twentieth century has added its own gloss to the notion of individual freedom, a gloss that is much more expressive, much more concerned with lifestyle, personality, sexuality, and intimacy, leisure and entertainment.[73] The emphasis in the culture is on the individual as a free agent, as a person who crafts his or her own unique talents and life.

Paradoxically, however, this individualism encourages the formation of horizontal groups. It allows and indeed supports a person's search for his or her peers in whatever regard a person finds most salient. If one becomes a passionate body-builder or a bird-watcher, one can pivot one's life, indeed, one's very identity about this passion. The same person can form or join horizontal identity groups organized in terms of race, gender, or (more rarely) class or around ethnic lines, sexual identity, or some other fragment of life experience. One can shed these identities, too, in favor of a more meaningful identity—perhaps even an accidental one (parents of handicapped children or winners of the lottery or people who suffer from breast cancer).

Many of these identity groups are purely social or informational. Others cut closer to the bone. What minorities really want are not, realistically speaking, *group* rights, although it might seem that way, but the removal of group disabilities and a place at the table for their members. Plural equality seems to be the only way to achieve these ends in this country. For one type of group—those that are geographically compact, small, and based on ethnic ties—separation or independence within a country is a reasonable alternative to plural equality. In fact, independence often seems downright essential. No Estonian can be really free except in a free Estonia. That seems to be the lesson of decades of Russian hegemony. Francophones in Quebec can also imagine, not irrationally, that nothing can be done in the way of cultural liberation and equality, surrounded as they are by the vast mass that is Anglophonic Canada, except through autonomy or downright independence.

Note that, in both cases, what happens to Estonia or Quebec—or rather to the people in these places—once the yoke is removed, is left wide open. For some people, nationalism is an end in itself; it is their chosen cause in life. But for most people, to sing songs of glory and wrap themselves in the flag is not the be-all and end-all of life. To them, nationalism is only a *prerequisite,* the foundation of a life in which the citizen is free to choose a life without discrimination. Russian or Anglophone domination was wrong precisely because it gave some people unfair advantages and blockaded others. If you are not allowed to speak your own language or follow your own customs, without disadvantage, then you are not truly free. The idea is certainly far from fanciful. Estonians are now free to watch American sitcoms in Estonian and to live "normal" lives. A similar point can be made about the American subnations. It is not fanciful for a black American to imagine that there is no way to "get a life" unless blacks achieve a kind of subnational autonomy, or at the very least plural equality. The goal is to be like everybody else in the context of difference. For this reason, plural equality is a matter of *individual* rights; group demands, group rights, and the like are only a means to an end.

The history of the civil rights movement is, in one sense, a flowering of the notion of plural equality. The same can be said for the feminist movement and for all the movements that stress ethnicity or religion or race; and each of these (the civil rights movement most dramatically) has helped to encourage, or even to give birth to, all the new "nations" within the borders of America.

Plural equality takes many forms. Plural equality can also be heard in the call for more research funds for Parkinson's disease. It echoes in demands for bilingual education, for the revival or preservation of Native American languages, and for the recognition of sign language at schools for the deaf.[74] It fosters separatist movements and separatist elements in movements that are not, in themselves, particularly separatist. It builds arguments for women's colleges and black academies. Of course, each movement, and each strategy in each movement, has its own special history and, very often, mixed motives. One can argue in favor of, say, women's colleges without believing that women are or should form some kind of separate nation. A lot depends on whether separation is considered a stage, a chrysalis, a pit stop, or an end in itself. The subject is too complicated to be summed up in a single formula.

Plural equality is not, of course, uniquely American at all. There are similar movements and tendencies everywhere, each with its separate twist. The big heterogeneous countries are most like the United States. There are, after all, rumblings and uprisings from indigenous peoples in Canada, in southern Mexico, and elsewhere in the Western hemisphere; Russia has its Chechens, and China its Tibetans and its Turkic minority. But even the smaller countries—the Estonias and Icelands of the world—have their subnations. Feminism, to take one example, has made a mark, or tried to, in almost every country in the world. Country after country has experienced demands for plural equality, in one form or another. All this suggests, as our analysis would indeed predict, that the underlying causes are worldwide in nature. All of these movements are, in fact, children of the horizontal society.

Stresses and Strains

Plural equality, as we mentioned, is only a *tendency,* a shift in emphasis; it does not command total respect in any society. Indeed, it is bitterly contested on almost every front. In many ways, it remains an aspiration, and an embattled one at that. It competes for public attention with older theories of national identity; it does not supplant them. Assimilation and toleration are still important cultural factors. At present, it would be hard to say which of the three tendencies is the most powerful.

The older theories are not mere survivals, vestiges of the past that are certain to die out. They are active movements in their own right. Defenders of ancient cultural faiths, adherents of the classic themes of national identity, fight on, sometimes violently. In many circles, nobody uses the word *multicultural* except with a sneer. Most Americans say they are in favor of racial equality—in fact, in favor of equality altogether. They think they are sincere. Yet they also claim to be against affirmative action; many people believe the law has gone too far. Programs of affirmative action are in jeopardy. An anti-affirmative action referendum passed in California in 1996. Affirmative action has also taken a blow or two in the Supreme Court,[75] and an important decision in Texas struck down affirmative action in higher education in that state and in neighboring states.[76]

The religious right is strong, well organized, and militant on a number of issues. One of them is gay rights. If you believe that same-sex relations are not just another lifestyle but a mortal sin, or a threat to civilization as we know it, you are not likely to embrace tolerance or agree quietly to demands for equal rights. Americans, by large majorities, say they are worried about the state of the family.[77] "Traditional values" is a common phrase of the day. Gay rights *seems* to some to be a threat to these values.[78]

It is tempting, but dangerous, to pin labels on movements, calling some progressive, others reactionary, some modern, others antimodern. In the first place, even the antimodern has to wear the clothing and styles of modernity—a point we have often made. In the second place, many movements are themselves mixed and ambiguous. The religious right tends to oppose gay rights, but religious groups are also, on the whole, liberal with regard to issues of immigration and, in the past two generations at least, on race. Black leaders tend to be socially liberal, though black Muslims like Louis Farrakhan are not easily labeled in this way.

The opposition to this or that aspect of plural equality, in short, is and remains quite strong. Plural equality is a goal that is nowhere near fulfillment. As Kenneth Karst points out, "none of the groups claiming their equal citizenship consider those claims fully vindicated." Moreover, new groups clamor for inclusion "in an increasingly pluralized polity"; in the process, they create new constituencies, united around "themes of cultural counterrevolution."[79] The noise that results is at the very heart of modern American politics.

The plain fact is that in some ways plural equality *cannot* be realized. It is one thing for a minority to ask for a share of power or wealth. Hard as that may be, the majority may, in the end, give way, however grudgingly. Some demands, however, are flatly in conflict; other demands are for shares in goods that no Solomon could ever succeed in dividing. A high school curriculum cannot teach tolerance for all sorts of life-styles and traditional biblical values at the same time. A history book cannot call Columbus a hero in one paragraph and a genocidal scoundrel in the next. The best one can hope for here is a kind of wishy-washy blandness that brings no peace or satisfaction to either side.

Intertribal War

Plural equality can be painted in rosy colors—as a solution to oppression, as a way of sharing, a way to build community, a way to a world that looks like a Benetton ad, with its rainbow of smiling colors. The reality is quite different. As we have just pointed out, some goods *cannot* be shared. In other cases, the haves do not much feel like giving to the have-nots. Moreover, the rainbow people do not necessarily get along with each other. They compete as much as they share.

The United States has been spared the worst of tribal and intertribal warfare in this century. It is far from a Bosnia. The worst excesses of the past have receded into history. Lynching is at an end. There is no longer any serious attempt to kill off native peoples, either physically or culturally. But there is plenty of racism left—enough for everyone to share, including black anti-Semitism, Jewish intolerance of Arab-Americans, Korean hatred of blacks, and so on:

Charles Lawrence, for one, attributes much or all of this to the "belief systems of the dominant white culture." He thinks these pathologies are the legacy of "white supremacy." As he vividly puts it, in intentionally paradoxical language, "When a Vietnamese family is driven out of its home in a project by African-American youth, that is white supremacy. When a Korean store owner shoots an African-American teenager . . . that is white supremacy. . . . When over 40 percent of African-American voters in California support [an] . . . antiimmigrant initiative, that too is white supremacy."[80]

Obviously, Lawrence has a point; racism and its associated ideas have become, in a way, part of the culture in the United States—a country that, as we saw, is almost obsessively race conscious. But white supremacy hardly explains why (for example) the Japanese in Japan seem so racist, why they mistreat Koreans, why they look down on blacks and even whites. White supremacists did not invent nationalism; and white supremacy is not much of an explanation for ethnic cleansing in Bosnia or Rwanda or for the troubles in Sri Lanka or Fiji. In fact, white people have never had a monopoly on racist ideas. Racism is not an infectious disease that spreads from person to person. It is not particularly new, and it may not even be radically different from similarly negative feelings toward strangers, outsiders, and other varieties of "them" or "the others." Racism is, in some ways, only a dialect of nationalism—a way of defining insiders and outsiders. These distinctions and definitions have become sharper, and in some ways more sinister, in a horizontal society.

Racism, to be sure, has had a particularly evil and perverse influence in certain countries where various races live together. The United States is one of these countries. South Africa is another. Great Britain has become yet another. Plural equality, and the political conditions of modern life, make it possible for suppressed people to express their emotions and attitudes in public forums. That was not so easy in the past—at least not overtly. Perhaps the Chinese in nineteenth-century California were prejudiced against whites, Native Americans, blacks, and everybody else, but this hardly mattered. They were themselves so disadvantaged that their own bundle of hatreds, such as they were, had no way to reach, and touch, the outside world. Over and over again in human history, it has been the case that victims who come to power immediately forget what it was like to be a victim. They eagerly grasp the chance to do unto others what others had been doing unto them.

Plural equality and multiculturalism certainly do not *cause* racism. Some conservatives like to blame these movements for pitting Americans against each other, for destroying national unity. But they are, I am afraid, misreading history and tradition and misinterpreting culture. They are confusing domination with consensus—a common mistake. If you liberate people, then they behave like . . . people. They do not become angels or saints. Not all of what comes out of the mouths of the liberated will be to other people's liking. Not all of it will be noble. Not all of it will be good.

On the other hand, multiculturalism is a fact as well as an ideology. More and more in a horizontal society, people are in fact all mixed together. They work together, shop together, meet each other in parks and on beaches. Whether this contact rubs the wounds raw or heals them is an empirical question. But the age of tribal warfare is also the age of universal human rights and of societies that, at their best, are more understanding of human diversity than any societies we know of in the past.

Rewriting History

Every nation, as we have seen, develops a standard story—a standard historical drama. It is this story that gets adopted, is taught in schools, and gains official status. This standard history takes the form of a kind of national myth; it was produced along with the imagined community as the imaginary history of that community.[81] Popular history is almost always mythic; but professional history—historian's history—has by no means been immune from these ills. Quite the contrary. Official history, and mainstream history, have tended to be heroic, one-dimensional, and nationalistic to the core. They have been a celebration of the past. They are stories about "us" and "them." If history treats outsiders at all, it is as enemies; if the outsiders are inside the borders, then the message is one of tolerance or assimilation at best.

This kind of history becomes controversial in the age of plural equality. The history books have to be rewritten in a (vain) attempt to satisfy everybody's demands. The myths of origin get deflated; the roster of heroes gets pruned and rearranged. New stories come to be written; the new writers bespatter the old heroes with mud and melt their bronze statues into scrap. New heroes (or hero groups) emerge.

One dramatic illustration of how plural equality changes the story of the past was the celebration—or anticelebration—in 1992 of the arrival of Columbus in the Western hemisphere five hundred years earlier. (Calling his trip the "discovery" of America will no longer do; there were people here already, and they did not need to be discovered.) A shrill chorus of complaining voices strangled any attempts to *praise* Columbus for what he accomplished. On the contrary, native groups heaped insults on the head of the dead white admiral. They angrily denounced the crimes of Spaniards and other interlopers. They deplored the cultural and physical destruction of their cultures. A leader of the American Indian Movement "compared the legacy of Columbus to the legacy of Hitler."[82] The five hundred years following Columbus' landfall were described as years of genocide and oppression.[83]

When the city of San Jose, California, commissioned a bronze statue of Captain Thomas Fallon, who rode into San Jose during the Mexican War and put up the American flag, a firestorm of protest erupted, mostly from the large community of Mexican Americans.[84] To calm things down, Captain Fallon was exiled to a warehouse, and the city spent half a million dollars on a sculpture of Quetzalcoatl, the Aztec serpent god. But this set off yet another storm of protest: Christian fundamentalists vehemently denounced the statue on the grounds that Quetzalcoatl was a pagan god "associated with human sacrifice."[85] Would *any* statue be free of controversy?

The battle of the statues was, of course, largely symbolic. But symbols seem to matter to people, and symbols, if they are strong enough and meaningful enough, can actually transcend the symbolic realm and turn into concrete power and wealth. The battle of the statues was in some ways a cultural echo of struggles for political office, jobs, and economic power. Much the same could be said about battles over the Confederate flag in the southern states. In New Orleans, in November 1997, the Orleans Parish

School Board voted to change the name of George Washington Elementary school to Dr. Charles Richard Drew Elementary (Drew was a black surgeon). Washington lost out because the father of our country also owned slaves.[86]

A National Language?

English has never been proclaimed the national or official language of the United States.[87] In a way, there was never any need to. The primacy of English was simply taken for granted. During the age of assimilation, Americans expected immigrants to shed their native languages as rapidly as possible, outside the home at any rate. Nobody demanded that public schools teach little children in Italian or Yiddish or Greek. Some language groups had the strength of numbers—notably German speakers—and these groups did achieve some recognition. There was serious debate about bilingual education (English and German) in nineteenth-century Pennsylvania, but the tendency has been to put English first and not to allow any rivals.[88]

Immigrants probably agreed, by and large. In the age of assimilation, immigrants wanted their children to learn English, to become Americans, and to blend into the mainstream as soon as possible. It was the way to get ahead—the only way. For this reason, language tended not to be a political issue in American history (with a few egregious exceptions). Now, in the late twentieth century, it has become one. Plural equality, and the demographics of immigration in our times, have redefined the language issue; and the redefinition, in turn, has evoked backlash and hostility.

In the period following the First World War, a palmy era of nativism, a number of states, including Nebraska, passed laws to stamp out the teaching of foreign languages in school. Nebraska, by statute, made it an offense for a teacher to "teach any subject . . . in any language other than the English language" or to teach any foreign language at all until after a "pupil shall have attained and successfully passed the eighth grade." The Supreme Court struck down this law in 1923, in *Meyers v. Nebraska*. The statute, said the Court, was an infringement of "liberty," and the Fourteenth Amendment to the Constitution condemned it.[89]

The language at issue in the Meyers case was German; fifty years later, a language question again came up before the Supreme Court, but now the language was Chinese, and the question was strikingly different. This case, *Lau v. Nichols,* was brought on behalf of schoolchildren in San Francisco who spoke Chinese and were unable to read or understand English. The claim was that the school system did nothing special for these children and their language problem. Did they have a *right* to receive some sort of help, some sort of bilingual education? The Supreme Court said they did, under the existing web of civil rights laws and regulations. The school authorities had to devise a program to take care of the language problem.[90] For generations, no doubt, there had been schoolchildren in a similar fix; the state's response had always been, on the whole, sink or swim. But in the age of cultural pluralism, rights consciousness, and judicial activism, sink or swim was no longer an adequate response. Or so the Supreme Court (and the plaintiffs) felt.

In the 1980s and 1990s, the language issue flared up again, this time in a furious controversy over bilingual education. For the most part, this was an issue between speakers of English and speakers of Spanish.[91] There is a thriving "English-only" movement—a movement to give the English language official status at last. There are some precedents at the state level. Nebraska, as early as 1920, declared English the "official language of the state," to be taught in all schools and used for all "official proceedings, records and publications."[92] Nebraska, of course, is hardly a border state; it would be hard to think of a place where English was less threatened. But this was, as we have seen, a period of ferocious nativism. Illinois, in 1923, declared "American" the official language of the state, whatever that might mean; the law was later amended to substitute "English" for "American"; the statute says nothing about what, if anything, follows from the status of English as the official language of Illinois; and it appears on the books together with statutes making the square dance the official state folk dance and designating *Tullimonstrum gregarium* the official state fossil.[93]

These state laws do not seem terribly consequential; the recent English-only movement is more vehement; but whether it has more bite remains to be seen. The movement has gained some important political victories: California voters, for example, solemnly enthroned English as *the* language of the state in 1986; other states have done the same.[94] Whether these declarations have any practical meaning is open to doubt, but the symbolic significance is unmistakable. There was no great need for "English only" in the good old days when immigrants knew their place. Equally symbolic, but on the other side—and perhaps an example of what the English-only movement is fighting against—is the action of Hawaii. In that state native Hawaiians have formed a strong movement to demand *their* share of plural equality (some are even asking for sovereignty). Since 1978, the Hawaiian Constitution has stated that English *and* Hawaiian (a language spoken by only a few thousand people and struggling to survive at all) are "official languages" of the state.[95]

7

Immigration and Its Discontents

IN THE LAST CHAPTER, I talked about the law of citizenship and naturalization; in this chapter I will continue with a brief discussion of immigration law and policy. The two subjects are closely connected; in a way, it is artificial to separate them.

Politically speaking, the subject of immigration is highly charged in our times. I will briefly trace the history of American immigration law, with some glancing references to other countries. Then I will talk about how social facts, in the horizontal society, transform the problem of immigration.

The laws and rules of immigration guard the gates of the nation-state. They decide who can come in and who must stay out. It is a tough, concrete body of rules, a field of law of daunting complexity, but underlying it, and ultimately shaping it, are malleable, changeable norms and concepts—ideas about race, nationality, and kinship in the minds of the people who live in immigration countries.

The law of naturalization is closely linked to the law of immigration. Immigrants who have spent the required time as residents and who have the necessary qualifications can apply to become citizens.[1] Closely related, too, are laws and practices about asylum and refugee status, since these are essentially annexes to the laws about ordinary immigration; in some countries, asylum seekers and refugees supply most of the legal immigrants.

Immigration is a *political* problem today for one simple reason. Strong cultural barriers once limited the movement of peoples in a horizontal world; these have irretrievably broken down. As a consequence, a flood of immigrants presses against the borders of the richer countries of the world. These receiving countries react in panic and prejudice. Some are more or less successful in stemming the tide. But in other countries, it is impossible to seal the borders. Hence, like it or not, many modern countries have become much more "plural"; this brute social fact has significant consequences for their very conception of nationhood and identity.

American Immigration: A Thumbnail Sketch

Immigration has had a complex history in the United States, as it has elsewhere.[2] The United States is, to begin with, a nation of immigrants. The land was thinly populated when settlers began to arrive in the seventeenth century. Native peoples lived in the forests and on the plains, but white settlers defined them as "savages" and never took their culture seriously. More to the point, as we have seen, they never recognized native rights to possess and use the land. Native Americans were simply an obstacle, people who stood in the way of progress. They were incapable, it was thought, of developing the land. The Indian tribes were "fierce savages, whose occupation was war," and the land—so rich in possibilities for crops, industry, commerce, and wealth—would be nothing but "wilderness" if left in their hands.[3]

It would be hard to think of a word whose emotional meaning has changed so thoroughly as *wilderness*. Today, wilderness is good, pure, unsullied, noble, majestic. There are wilderness societies and wilderness areas; thousands of men and women claim they love wilderness and are dedicated to preserving it. Indeed, many people would like to return great sections of the land to a state of wilderness. In the past, however, wilderness did not evoke images of beauty. Rather, wilderness was foul and dangerous; it meant wasted opportunities and barriers to settlement; it implied obstacles to economic growth.

For the colonists, America was a land of golden chances, and wilderness, like the native tribes, stood in the way. By the same token, immigration was considered desirable, on every count. Immigrants would swell the population, push up land values, provide markets, help overwhelm the native population, and foster the production of wealth. Before independence, the colonies were at odds with the mother country over immigration and naturalization. England had an age-old distrust of foreigners, of people who were not subjects of the crown. Naturalization was not a normal process. Legally, only the king and Parliament could grant citizenship—a cumbersome arrangement, which the colonies tended to ignore.[4]

The United States, as far as formal law was concerned, seemed to welcome immigrants with open arms for much of the nineteenth century. There were no overt restrictions, no quotas. The official policy was to encourage immigration. Still, there were assumptions about *who* would be encouraged, and these assumptions underlay the statutes on naturalization.[5] Throughout the republican period, there were eruptions of nativism from time to time, like outbreaks of some noxious disease. Indeed, the 1795 law on naturalization, itself rather restrictive,[6] was replaced by a law of 1798, which set up a long resident time (fourteen years); the whole text of the law was suffused with hostility toward aliens. Moreover, the Alien Act of 1798 authorized the president to deport "dangerous" aliens.[7] The law was repealed in 1802, when Thomas Jefferson was president, but naturalization was still confined to "free white persons."[8]

The specter of the evil or degenerate alien continued to haunt segments of the population. In the early nineteenth century, there was certainly no notion of a rainbow of races. This was plainly a white man's country, and blacks were slaves or, if free, a pariah caste. Almost all Americans were Protestants from the north of Europe, in various sectarian shades. Until the influx of the Irish, Catholics constituted a tiny minority. There was a tiny handful of Jews. Immigration laws were fairly open; they did not represent any sort of commitment to act as a haven, an asylum, for the world's oppressed. Indeed, in the nineteenth century, "foreigners were generally regarded with suspicion, if not outright hostility"—at least this was true of really "foreign" foreigners, that is, those unlike white Protestant Americans.[9]

In short, when people thought "immigrant," they did not think of refugees from misery, the wretched of the earth. They conjured up an image of people who were basically more of the same—the right sort of people, those of good stock, like those already here. The Irish invasion stirred up a witch's brew of resentment, as we have seen. In fact, in the 1840s and

1850s, "antipathy between immigrant and native-stock Americans" was one of the "most disruptive forces" in the country, a fertile source of riots and unrest in city after city.[10] The lust for new citizens was always selective in the United States (and in other countries that advertised for bodies). Nobody wanted Chinese coolies or starving Hindus. This was the social reality, whatever the text of the law had to say. The best immigrants, as far as the United States was concerned, were white, English-speaking Protestants from northern Europe.

In the latter part of the century, the character of immigration changed dramatically. Millions of immigrants poured into the United States, and these immigrants were not "more of the same." They seemed, in fact, radically different. They hailed from southern and eastern Europe: Italians, Greeks, Poles, Jews from Russia. The Statue of Liberty, that colossus erected on an island in New York harbor, was a symbol of America the welcomer: as Emma Lazarus put it in her famous poem engraved on the statue, the statue was an invitation to the poor, the "huddled masses," inviting them to a home, a refuge, an opportunity in the promised land. But respectable public opinion in the late nineteenth century was by no means as keen on huddled masses as Ms. Lazarus imagined.

This was the age of assimilation. At least that was the goal or ideal. Assimilation meant, as we have seen, two rather different ideas. To many it connoted, in essence, Anglo-conformity. To others, it meant an enrichment, a flavoring, a modification of the basic culture. But many "regular" Americans were, in fact, appalled by the flood of immigrants. They hated the squalid, big-city slums, with their foreign-born masses; they were suspicious of the miserable tenements, where nobody spoke English, where people cooked funny foods and strange smells were in the air, where exotic gods were worshiped and dirt and poverty prevailed. "Real" Americans felt as alien in such districts as they would in a foreign country. The melting process—the process of assimilation—seemed excessively slow. Perhaps it was worse than slow: perhaps the foreigners would cling stubbornly to their Old World ways and *never* change. And there were so many of them: more and more were arriving all the time. Old-line Americans had the sense that some foreign force was overwhelming them, that they were occupied by an alien culture.

In such a climate, nativism became more powerful politically. At the extremes, it fed the growth of radical, even violent groups. The Ku Klux Klan, modeled after the racist Klan of the Reconstruction era, sprang back into life in the 1920s, making war on foreigners, Catholics, and Jews, as well as on blacks, their historic enemy.[11] The Klan was also hostile, generally speaking, toward "aliens" and did not believe they could be turned into true Americans. In the words of Hiram W. Evans, the Imperial Wizard and Emperor of the Klan in the 1920s, these immigrants were "unalterably fixed in . . . instincts, character, thought and interests by centuries of racial selection and development."[12] So much for the melting pot.

The Klan was the right-wing fringe, but milder forms of these sentiments were shared by millions in the late nineteenth and early twentieth centuries. In short, the political climate for immigrants became distinctly chillier. In addition, important changes in the structure of immigration law were taking place. The turmoil that led to these changes may have been rooted, in part, in the economy or, rather, in structural changes in the industrial order.[13] But perhaps the heart of the problem was race and culture. No one had ever much doubted that immigrant Swedes could be turned into good, strong, loyal Americans, but mainstream Americans also firmly believed that there were groups and sorts of people who were so different from the standard that they would not and could not assimilate. They were doomed to remain unmelted lumps at the bottom of the crucible. A sprinkling of German Jews was one thing, millions of *Ostjuden* from Polish and Russian villages another. In the rather bizarre opinion of Evans, American Jews were "not true Jews, but only Judaized Mongols"; they showed "a divergence from the American type so great that there seems little hope of their assimilation."[14]

American blacks were, of course, the paradigm case—and not merely in the eyes of racists and the wizards and kleagles of the Klan. In the southern states, segregation laws created an American system of apartheid, which the Supreme Court (to its eternal dishonor) upheld in 1896, in the famous case of *Plessy v. Ferguson*.[15] But millions of blacks were, of course, native-born citizens, and their citizenship was guaranteed by the Fourteenth Amendment; blacks had lived in the United States for centuries and were obviously going to remain. Movements to ship blacks back to Africa had surfaced from time to time, but nobody thought deportation was a real so-lution to the "problem." Moreover, the South badly needed—and ex-ploited—their labor, whatever their legal and social status.

The Chinese, another racial minority, were more recent immigrants. They were mainly concentrated on the West Coast. Their numbers were not large, and they had arrived in the late nineteenth century. From the 1870s on, they were the object of severe repression.[16] The rabble-rousers of the West Coast, in their vitriolic attacks on the Chinese, always stressed how foreign and exotic they were, how impossible it was to imagine Chi-nese assimilation. Millions of Americans agreed: the Chinese were so in-herently other, so alien, so strange, that it was pointless even to think about mixing them into the American mélange. And, according to a standard cliché, the Chinese did not *want* to assimilate.[17] This might or might not have been true; in any event, the public never gave them the chance. The problem here was defined in terms of both culture and race. Unlike the blacks, the Chinese were hardly essential to the economy; organized labor in California definitely wanted them gone. At the very least, their numbers had to be controlled. In 1882, Congress passed a law that prohibited im-migration of Chinese laborers for a ten-year period; moreover, no state or federal court was to "admit Chinese to citizenship." In 1888, the Scott Act prevented any Chinese laborer who temporarily left the country from ever returning. A further act, of 1892, "to prohibit the coming of Chinese per-sons into the United States," suspended immigration for another ten years. By the turn of the century, Chinese exclusion was final and permanent.[18]

This was, after all, the period of "scientific" racism and the age of eu-genics.[19] White supremacy had been elevated to the rank of scientific truth. Scientific racism lasted well into the twentieth century: the Third Reich is a melancholy and horrific example. Nazi ideology, of course, was extreme, but plenty of ordinary Americans, who perhaps rejected the most flagrant aspects of white supremacy, did feel that races were unmixable and that people had better stick with their own. In all southern states, and many northern ones, marriage between a black and a white was a criminal act. In the light of such attitudes, it should come as no surprise that immigration laws took a racist turn.

A case decided by the United States Supreme Court in 1923 can be taken as diagnostic. The plaintiff, a "high caste Hindu of full Indian blood" claimed to be a "white person" for purposes of naturalization. The Supreme Court disagreed. Justice George Sutherland, speaking for the court, pointed out that "children born in this country of Hindu parents" would "retain indefinitely the clear evidence of their ancestry." This was a matter of "racial difference," not "racial superiority or inferiority," he said—a difference of "such character and extent that the great body of our people instinctively recognize it and reject the thought of assimilation."[20]

This instinct not only fed the anti-Chinese movement (or, for that matter, the segregation of American blacks), it also complicated the issue of the expanding American empire. At the end of the nineteenth century, the United States fought a brief and highly successful war against Spain. The country then found itself, lo and behold, in possession of a colonial domain. Millions of people in Puerto Rico and the Philippines were now under the domination of the American flag, and they were certainly not European whites. What was to be done with them? They were now American subjects: were they also to enjoy all the rights and privileges of mainland Americans?

One way of phrasing the question was to ask whether the Constitution, and its basic guarantees, "followed the flag." In a famous series of cases (the insular cases), the Supreme Court said no.[21] The actual issue in these cases had to do with such matters as a tax on oranges and lemons, but the principle ran much deeper. The language of argument in these cases was stained with ideas of race. Distinctions of culture, development and—above all—race divided Filipinos and Puerto Ricans from the mainstream.[22] Justice Henry Brown, in one of the crucial cases, referred to these people as "alien races," whose "religion, customs, laws . . . and modes of thought" constituted such a barrier that it would be "impossible" to administer "government and justice, according to Anglo-Saxon principles"—at least for the time being.[23]

Many people, and perhaps Brown himself, were sure that the alien races would *never* be ready for self-rule or assimilation. It was probably only empty politeness to suggest that the imperial period was temporary. Hawaii, which fell or was pushed into American hands in the late nineteenth century, was another island paradise spoiled by the presence of alien races. Partly because of its racial mix, statehood eluded Hawaii for a good half-century, even though the territory seemed to have all the other requirements. Hawaii was and is the first and only state in the Union in which white people are not a clear majority. The largest ethnic group, in fact, is Japanese.

Of course, Puerto Rico, Hawaii, and the Philippines were not issues of immigration as such. They merely added to the sense of a fortress America, threatened and beleaguered by billions of lesser beings swarming on the face of the earth. In the early twentieth century, immigration no longer seemed a source of strength—a way to boost the economy, guarantee growth, and populate the wilderness. The frontier was closing, literally and figuratively.[24] Immigration was now a danger—a source of social pollution. American culture seemed fragile and corruptible. The new immigrants were potential spoilers. They were too crude, too ignorant, for the delicate machinery of Anglo-Saxon civilization. For this reason, the country had to close the gates on immigration.[25] Control of immigration would act like a tariff on imported goods: a wall against foreign competition and corruption.

Nativists of this century smeared immigrants with two distinct charges: political radicalism and moral corruption. In the first place, they were labeled as Bolsheviks, anarchists, and general bomb throwers. During the so-called Red Scare, immediately after the First World War, loads of undesirable aliens, of the leftist variety, were unceremoniously dumped back into their native lands.[26] Congress also passed laws to keep out foreign prostitutes; terror over this kind of traffic in sex was one of the key ideas behind the Mann Act of 1910 (the law against "white slavery"). Under this law, it was a crime to import a woman, or to "transport" her across state lines, for prostitution or for other "immoral" purposes.[27]

The movement to restrict aliens reached a climax in 1924, when American immigration law was completely revamped.[28] At the core of the complex new law was the so-called national quota system. The law fixed an overall ceiling on the number of immigrants who could enter the United States each year. Every exporting country had a quota: it was limited to no more than 2 percent of that country's share of the American population—based on figures for 1890, not 1924. The earlier date was picked because it came *before* the greatest influx of Italians, Jews, Slavs, and Greeks. The national quota system, in other words, was strongly tilted in favor of old American stock—people from northern Europe and the British Isles—and against the new immigrants from eastern and southern Europe.[29]

Curiously enough (in the light of what is happening today), this *very* restrictive law had no effect on, and set no quota for, Mexican immigration, or, for that matter, any immigration from Latin America. Laws relating to Mexican immigration have their own, complex history. In the 1930s, in the midst of the Depression, Latin Americans were kept out through more informal means: consuls in Latin countries were instructed to exclude immigrants if they were likely to become "public charges."[30] Mexican labor immigrants were a special case. The so-called bracero program allowed an elastic, fluctuating supply of seasonal labor; men and women were brought in to pick the crops of American growers and then sent home when the harvest was done.[31] (The Germans had had a similar arrangement for Polish farmworkers during an earlier period.) Growers and farm owners in the Southwest, a powerful lobby, wanted and needed this supply of Latin labor.

Despite this, it is striking that the 1924 act, on its face, did nothing to control Latin American immigrants. In theory, all of Mexico or Guatemala could walk in the door. Not that this omission went entirely unnoticed. There were those who warned of a "deluge-like stream" of Mexicans, people of "markedly low-powered intellect," far below "American stock, ranking with the negro, the Portuguese, the Sicilian"—all of whom, obviously, were among the lowest of the low. Besides, Mexicans were a "fecund" group; they multiplied like rabbits. To introduce "a low-powered but rapidly breeding group into our population mass" was "profoundly serious"; it was, in fact, a "eugenic menace."[32] Congressmen who shut the door on Greeks or Italians or Jews may have been willing to tolerate Mexican braceros but were certainly not eager to see hordes of Dominicans, Panamanians, or Bolivians stampeding across the border.

Why, then, the emphasis on Greeks or Italians or Jews? The answer is obvious: Greeks and Jews were actually entering the country; Latin Americans were not. It was the Greeks, Italians, and Jews who threatened America—not Bolivians or Panamanians.

But what kept out the peasantry of Latin America—and the millions of Bengalis or Africans or Malays, for that matter? To be sure, the sheer cost of travel barred the poor in the nineteenth and early twentieth centuries. Indeed, the invention of the steamship, which made it easier to cross the Atlantic, was a major factor in the upsurge of emigration from southern and eastern Europe in the late nineteenth century.[33] But travel was still beyond the reach of the desperately poor. Then again, for many groups (say, Bolivians), there was no welcoming community of people from home already here. Most immigrants go where they can find relatives, townspeople, or people who speak their language. It is no accident that Algerians and Tunisians go to France, or Pakistanis to England, or that 70 percent of the migrants from Portugal between 1900 and 1959 went to Brazil.[34] The enclaves of familiar people are rich sources of social support for immigrants.[35] Immigrants are much less eager, and less likely, to settle in places where these communities do not exist.

The United States, however, has long since lost any form of ethnic virginity. Today it would be hard to imagine an ethnic group of any size without a colony in the United States. For the largest groups—Poles, Italians, Greeks, Jews, Chinese, Mexicans, and Cubans—the United States is *the* diaspora, for all practical purposes. For many other non-Europeans, developing their own colonies in the States took time. In 1924 there was basically no community of Koreans, Hondurans, Bengalis, or Vietnamese.

But another factor is perhaps the most significant of all. Immigration by and large is an offshoot of modernization. Immigration is a current political issue in large part because of global restlessness. All over the world, people are on the move. Millions of refugees stream across borders; many of them were uprooted by wars and civil disturbances. When Rwanda dissolved into a caldron of blood, hundreds of thousands of men, women, and children ran for their lives into Tanzania, Burundi, or what was then called Zaire. When Liberia, in turn, disintegrated, great masses of frightened and desperate people fled to neighboring countries. Anti-Castro Cubans piled ashore in Florida. East Germans found haven in West Germany; after unification, they were joined by a sad army of Bosnians. And so it goes.

There are millions of economic refugees as well. The population explosion is partly to blame.[36] The land can no longer feed the mouths of indigenous peoples. Waves of these men and women dash against the high walls of developed countries; they come by boat, by plane, by cars, by bus, and on foot; they seep into the lands of the rich through every crack and crevice in the border. They hide in the hulls of ships and in cargo containers; they crowd onto rusty, leaky boats and navigate dangerous waters, always hoping for a favorable landfall. They pay their last pennies to unscrupulous men who promise to smuggle them into the lands of opportunity. As of 1993, by one estimate, between 80 and 100 million people were living outside their native country.[37] From year to year the numbers grow.

Immigration is not a nineteenth-century invention. People have been moving, shifting, fleeing, resettling, and wandering since the dawn of time. But most such movements have been by and in groups. Twentieth-century migration cannot be compared to the movements of the Vandals or Huns, the Angles or Jutes, or their victims. There is still mass immigration and the shifting of peoples (sometimes coerced), but today the norm is *individual* migration. Modern, individual immigration demands a certain level of awareness, a certain degree of sophistication, a certain amount of exposure to the big wide world. This is what it takes to elicit, among traditional peoples, the desire and the willingness to leave home for the promised land. Only people who have this minimum awareness will deracinate themselves, the way that millions did in the nineteenth century, crowding into the belly of boats leaving European ports, never expecting to see their home, their place, their roots, again.

Thus it is the horizontal society—or, to be more accurate, what the horizontal society consists of, its ease in spreading news about the world, its technological toys (movies, radio, and television)—that, more than anything else, has set immigration in motion. The horizontal society is also responsible, in part, for the national and ethnic upheavals that create so many refugees. But beyond this, it has evoked in countless millions living in societies once sealed off from the outside world the urge to seek a fortune, or at least a living. It has fed the need to see, feel, and experience the world—to have a better, or richer life—in the only places where this seems possible, that is, in the golden lands so far away geographically, yet so close at hand on the screen.

Life in self-contained, provincial communities was isolated; it was a life that taught fatalism and humble acceptance of one's lot. Traditional society did not give rise to the itchy restlessness so crucial to modern migration. Traditional Chinese, as Alex Inkeles has pointed out, "expanded their human bonds through kinship" and the "cult of ancestors"; they almost never "became explorers"; and "no Chinese . . . went to foreign lands to spread the Chinese way of life or Chinese religion."[38] Nor did they go abroad to seek their fortune, except for a few people, nearly all from southern, coastal China. Almost all the Chinese simply stayed put.

Rapid population growth is also a factor, as we noted. Driven off the land by poverty, people stream into provincial capitals and then to the metropolis. Millions crowd into Mexico City or Calcutta or Shanghai. Others go beyond: over the borders. History is full of village suffering and rural despair, of floods, famines, plagues, and other disasters. Millions died hopelessly in China and India in centuries past, almost unnoticed by the outside world. They died without a sense that they could have found salvation in some far-off country. But many of the starving Irish, in the 1840s, had a different dream—America. Thus, as society becomes more horizontal, hunger takes on a different dynamic.

What kept immigration under control in the past was poverty and isolation. It seems paradoxical to mention poverty at all; poverty, for so many migrants, is what pushed them from their original homes. Yet these migrants are never totally destitute, unlike the pitiful refugees of central Africa, for example. Migrants have to make a long, arduous trip. For this they have to scrape together at least enough money for the journey.

The ultimate barriers have been ignorance and tradition, and these are breaking down. Traditional society tied men and women with invisible ropes to their soil and their way of life. But the village is no longer closed off from the world; it is bombarded with messages that come in like cosmic rays from outer space. People hear news of magic places, places with jobs, at the end of the yellow brick road. Most of course never leave home; but enough set out on the journey to make a real difference to the world.

The new messages are everywhere. In the middle of New Guinea, tribespeople wear blue jeans and T-shirts. There are still backwaters, to be sure, pockets untouched by electricity and hamburgers. But more and more people in places like Guatemala or Kenya or Cambodia have some access to television, radio, and movies. Many villagers have cousins or nephews or sons who have gone to the city, who have seen the world; their onetime neighbors or relatives may now live in Los Angeles or London or Berlin. A relative in Oslo or El Paso or Rome, who has a little money saved from a dishwashing job, is the incentive that pulls the young and the desperate into the whirlpool of global wandering. The cousin writes from the big city about his job, his bicycle, about chances for work. Somehow there is just enough money to buy passage. The cousin offers a bed to flop on and hot meals for a while. Moreover, travel to another country is not so apocalyptic as it once was—the village knows that people do come back, for visits or even to resettle with their bundle of cash. And so the journey begins. It is a kind of journey that the men who drafted the 1924 U.S. immigration act never dreamt of; a trip to countries that, in a way, never existed in the past.

The rich, receiving countries are, as we said, aghast at this nomadic army. The public sees the strangers (rightly or wrongly) as an economic burden, as a threat to wage rates and a drain on the treasury; they see them, too, as threats to culture, to ethnic purity, to the very soul of the country. When the foreigners come in critical numbers, they cling more easily to their language, religion, and customs. They became less digestible. When they demand rights (including cultural rights), they become a danger to the national image, the national heritage, even the national soul. Or so it seems. The laws of immigration then became weapons in the war to save the nation from these foreign invaders.

The text of the 1924 immigration act still tacitly assumed that people of the Third World would not come, and in large part it ignored what we now call the Third World. Its main focus was on the immigrants who would and had come: the peasants and villagers of southern and eastern Europe who had gotten the message of America. The act clearly supposed that the wrong mix of immigrants would put American society at risk. The debates in Congress show this clearly. Of course, all but the most dyed-in-the-wool nativists had to concede that some immigrants—or many immigrants or perhaps most immigrants—were not a threat of any kind; this included the Jews, Italians, Greeks, and Slavs who were so prominent in the waves of immigration. On the contrary, these were hardworking and law-abiding people. Not to mention grateful, docile, and willing to work long hours for low pay.

Then why should anybody care about how many of these people came in by way of Ellis Island? Organized labor had some reasons to distrust cheap labor, but immigrants were also the backbone of the unions. Still, many people, even those who were quite tolerant and free of the worst forms of racism, were uneasy about the flood of foreigners. They were afraid that immigrants, who spoke other languages, followed different customs and religions, and ate strange food, would swamp the country. Exactly what is it that so frightened the American soul? What is still frightening people today—both in the United States and in all receiving nations?

One might as well as ask what upsets people when their children move to a different country or marry someone who speaks a different language or convert to some strange religion. Most people seem to loathe the idea of cultural extinction. They cling to their own customs and habits, their way of life, as if the survival of their norms, their language, and their way of doing things will guarantee them a kind of immortality. One confronts here some sort of deep, primordial fear, like the fear of actual, physical death. Immortality is found in "the idea of posterity," in children and children's children, in a "chain of . . . deeds and memories, which stretch back into the mists of obscure generations of ancestors and forward into the equally unknowable generations of descendants."[39]

But immigrants are human beings, too. They often have to suffer the pain of rejection by an alien culture. They raise their families in a place that makes their children virtual strangers to them. For millions of these immigrants, this pain was surely great. But before the emergence of plural equality, this was, for the most part, hidden pain, silent and subterranean pain; the rush to assimilate submerged it. Assimilation, after all, was the key to making it in the new country; adjustment, estrangement, dislocation, were all part of the price that had to be paid for the better life America offered and the opportunities you were buying for your children.

This fear of cultural death is by no means confined to America. It is found all over the world, and not only in immigrant communities. Nationalism has only made it more powerful. The fear of extinction was a major theme in the nationalist revivals of the nineteenth century and in the liberation movements of the twentieth. Why else does Quebec want to be free? There are no political prisoners in Quebec; Canada is not an oppressive country, by any stretch of the imagination; the Québecois enjoy all the conventional freedoms; there are no armies poised on the border; the enemy, if there is one, is the language of Shakespeare and Chaucer—and, more to the point, the language of Hollywood, of movies and TV.

The deep fear of cultural extinction leads countries—even democratic and peaceful countries—to limit the rights of national minorities. Estonians insist that *their* Russians have to learn Estonian, have to function in Estonian. Estonians live in a small country; and the Russians are a substantial minority who speak a major world language. Without drastic moves, how can this small nationality—about a million in all—preserve its language and culture?[40]

In the age of plural equality, as we have seen, the subgroups—immigrants, minorities, and others—assert their claim to cultural survival, their right to sit at the table alongside the majority (in the United States, this would be the old-line Americans). In this phase—very imperfectly realized, to be sure—assimilation as formal policy is abandoned, the melting-pot metaphor disappears, and what replaces it is a kind of coalition of nations. Each member nation keeps and nurtures its own culture; each shares powers and prestige with the dominant culture (if there is one). There is in theory no hierarchy of norms and customs. Every group is equal to every other group; each is, if possible, sovereign in its own sphere. If *possible*. It rarely is.

A working, living, breathing country practicing plural equality in a fully developed way hardly exists—and may never exist. But some plural states move cautiously (and with a lot of resistance) in this general direction. This is true of the United States. The civil rights laws embody something of this spirit. From about 1950 on, the equality of the races has been official policy, strongly buttressed by law. There are also official equalities of religions, ethnic group, ages, and genders; and, in many parts of the country, sexual preference is fighting for a place on the list. All of these become newly created subnations (more on this in Chapter 8). Immigration law, too, responds to the national mood. Change did not come overnight.

In 1952, Congress passed (over the president's veto) a new immigration law, the rather retrograde McCarran-Walters Act. McCarran-Walters dropped the absolute ban on the Chinese—who were, after all, our allies in the Second World War. But it replaced the ban with highly restrictive quotas on Asians and kept, in essence, the national quota system.[41]

Still, the days of this system were numbered. In the 1960s, in a burst of liberalism, Congress eliminated quotas.[42] The results have been dramatic. The traditional European ports of embarkation no longer supply the bodies of immigrants; instead, the newcomers come from Asia and Latin America. They are Mexicans, Dominicans, Guatemalans; they are Chinese, Vietnamese, Koreans, Pakistanis; they speak Samoan or Tongan or one of the Philippine languages. We have already discussed the reasons why. The volcanic forces of the horizontal society lie behind the new immigration. Cultural isolation has ended; the pull of rich countries and the push from poor countries have become irresistible forces.

When a Dominican, a Bengali, or a Cambodian community gets established in Detroit or Phoenix—or an Ethiopian enclave in Milan—another barrier to immigration from the homeland breaks down. Also, there are now cousins and brothers and aunts who send postal money orders to the people back home. This is yet another incentive for relatives and country folk to come. Cultural pluralism, then, begins to reinforce itself. America has come to look and feel even more diverse than in the past, and France, Italy, and Germany become plural societies, almost despite themselves. In the United States, the minorities even look forward to a time, in the not too distant future, when they will be, in the aggregate, a kind of majority. Some states—California, very notably, with its huge Asian and Latin populations—will get there sooner than others. Meanwhile, the new communities start to flex their muscles. They become politically more powerful, demanding voices in government, elective offices, and rights, including cultural rights. *Assimilation* has become, as we have seen, a dirty word. Kwanzaa and Hanukkah elbow their way toward parity with Christmas. But these, and other alternative rituals, have been corrupted by Christmas—while Christmas itself, and other rites of the majority, have themselves been reshaped in the light of modernity, capitalism, and the imperatives of a consumer society. Historical narrative, too, becomes irrevocably altered. And the ghosts of dead Aztecs and Iroquois haunt the children of Columbus.

Down Under: The Rise and Fall of White Australia

I have given, of course, the merest sketch of American immigration history. Each of the other immigration countries has its own special story. Yet there are important parallels in all of them. In Australia, for example, there was very little in the way of immigration control in the nineteenth century, and the bulk of the immigrants were of British stock. Here was a white enclave within shouting distance of Asia's impoverished masses, but the impoverished masses stayed away. Here, too, the Chinese had the dubious honor of earning the first overt restrictions. In 1901, the Immigration Restriction Act, in essence, locked out all non-Europeans. It established what came to be known as the "white Australia" policy.[43] Australian law held tightly to this policy until fairly recent times.[44] Similarly, New Zealand, in 1908, excluded anyone who was not British or Irish and who was unable to "write out and sign" an application in "any European language." In this outpost of European life, the Chinese once again were the object of special restrictions: they had to be able to "read a printed passage of not less than one hundred words of the English language."[45]

Australian policy toward the native Aborigines also runs in gruesome parallel to policy and practice in North America. Aboriginal policy was, in a word, extraordinarily ruthless. When the natives were no longer a threat, official policy turned toward assimilation, though this carried with it its own brand of callousness. Natives were torn out of their cultural context—some children were literally kidnapped and placed with white families[46]—and could gain citizenship rights (in their own country) only if they had achieved a certain "standard of development and intelligence," which meant, in effect, that they were no longer Aborigines at all.[47]

This period is now history. The "white Australia" policy has been officially abandoned, and a New Zealand act of 1987 is race-neutral on its face.[48] The original policies—there is no point denying it—were frankly racist. But *if* we were to try to defend them, it would be along such lines as these: an immigration country, too, has the right to ask newcomers to assimilate and to defend itself culturally. How far can it go in doing this? The answer depends, in part, on "how great the differences are between the country of origin and the country of immigration."[49] If the new immigrants seem a lot like the old immigrants (in language and culture), then absorbing them is no trick at all. An immigration policy that is nonracist— a policy that does not give points to people who come from the "mother country" (England) or similar nations—may make it harder to absorb the newcomers. The process has got to be slower.

In fact, when the "white Australia" policy died, the country had, in effect, given up quick assimilation as a goal. Homogeneity was no longer as high on the scale of values as it once had been. Cultural pluralism had gained, if not the upper hand, more of an influence. If Australia lets in more Chinese, Vietnamese, East Indians, and other foreign nationals, the Britishness of Australia becomes somewhat attenuated—no question. An Australian "National Policy on Language," adopted in 1987, expresses warm hospitality toward the languages of immigrant communities, especially Asian languages. In 1989, the prime minister, with "great fanfare," announced a "National Agenda for a Multicultural Australia," which included the right of "all Australians . . . to express and share their individual cultural heritage, including their language and religion."[50] Very clearly, this included native cultures as well. The rights of Australia's native people—and of the Maoris in New Zealand—are, in general, high on the national agendas. The parallels to the American and Canadian experiences are striking indeed.

More Stresses and Strains

As is obvious to everyone, the new waves of immigration, legal and illegal, have not gone uncontested. In country after country, immigration has evoked anger, repression, reaction. In today's world, the waves of poor immigrants and refugees pounding on the gates or boring in from the outside have touched off something akin to panic among members of the club of rich countries. There is a heavy, unmistakable overlay of bigotry and racism in many countries. In Germany, in August 1981, a "manifesto," signed by fifteen professors, warned that immigrants were undermining Germany;

that immigrants would overwhelm German culture, language, and national character; and that a multicultural society would be an "ethnic catastrophe."[51] In 1996, there was a rumpus in Italy when a naturalized citizen from the Dominican Republic was chosen "Miss Italy" (her mother had married an Italian). To make matters worse, she was black. How, then, could she represent Italian standards of beauty? What was the symbolic message—how did this choice of "Miss Italy" bear on the question of what it means to be an Italian?[52] In France, the far Right secretes hateful messages about foreigners and gains ominously at the polls; the center, in fright, reacts with appeasement and a dash of harshness—directed mostly at Muslims from North Africa. One hears anti-immigrant rumblings in Belgium as well: in 1995, the Flemish Bloc, which calls for mass expulsion of immigrants, received 13.1 percent of the vote in Flanders; its Walloon counterpart, the National Front, won 7.6 percent of the vote in Francophone sections of the country.[53]

The United States has its "English only" movement. Despite vehement denials, the bigotry here lies barely beneath the surface. In California, immigration, especially illegal immigration, is political dynamite: nobody is really worried about Canadians—it is Mexicans and Central Americans that evoke the fear and the wrath. It is hard, of course, to defend illegal aliens. But many people seem to think there are too many *legal* ones. Under the welfare reform law of 1996, perfectly legal aliens lost their rights to food stamps and the like.[54] The Republican party platform of 1996 suggested getting rid of the rule of jus soli. Why should everybody born inside the borders be automatically a citizen? Children of illegal aliens or short-term visitors, it was felt, should not quality.[55] Vivid pictures were painted of pregnant women crawling over the border from Mexico for the dastardly purpose of producing citizen-babies. Because the Fourteenth Amendment enshrines jus soli, the Republic plan would require a constitutional amendment. This is almost surely out of the question. But that a major political party put this plan in its platform tells us something—something ominous.

In Europe, immigration and asylum laws have fallen victim to the politics of panic. The stresses and strains have become unusually visible in Germany in recent years. To be sure, there are forces pulling at both ends of the rope. On one side are the young skinheads and neo-Nazis, pouring out their bile against foreigners; there have been, indeed, some nasty incidents of bloody violence.[56] But the dirty little secret is that the skinheads are not really alone. Their worldview finds at least a muted echo in the hearts and minds of millions of others, respectable people, people who despise the tattoos, shaven heads, and Nazi paraphernalia of the brutal right wing. The solid bourgeoisie dislikes and distrusts most foreigners, especially those from the Third World or places like Romania.[57] They feel only contempt for these odd and discordant newcomers who (as they see it) threaten to undermine the cozy Gemütlichkeit of German society and to impair its Wirtschaftswunder.

The bloody incidents aimed at foreigners shocked millions of people inside and outside Germany. They were extremely bad for the image and reputation of the republic. They led to a backlash against backlash, official clucks of disapproval, and a sincere outburst of parades and demonstrations. Germany is, after all, Hitler's country; Nazi skeletons rattle about in its neat, orderly closets; like an ex-convict on parole, Germany cannot afford too many blots on its current record. This puts pressure on the German government to adopt a humanitarian posture with regard to refugees and asylum seekers; there are severe pressures, in short, pushing in both directions.

Pressures in France have been mostly in the direction of toughening up laws and enforcing them rigorously. The right-wing parties win votes by bashing immigrants and demanding an end to the alien invasion. Millions of ordinary French people seem to agree. About 6.5 percent of the population is made up of foreigners; 68,000 foreigners migrated to France in 1995 (a substantial decline since 1992); and about 100,000 foreigners a year acquire French nationality.[58] Thus in France many people of foreign stock are citizens. They vote in elections; and there are also many liberals, or people worried about what the world might think of France, so that here too politics is pulled in both directions at once. In February 1997, "tens of thousands" of opponents of tough immigration laws "took to the streets . . . in protest."[59] In December 1997, a bill to soften immigration laws and laws concerning migrant workers and refugees was on the table in Parliament.[60]

In France it is the Muslim minority that puts the most strain on French policy. To many French people, Algerians are simply outside the pale. They are too different from the ordinary French citizen. Algerians and other North Africans are not likely to assimilate—at least not on terms the French can appreciate. A minor issue—the right of Muslim girls to wear head scarves in class—touched off a national uproar in 1993.[61] The girls were suspended from school; a Turkish imam was deported; and France seemed gripped by the kind of paranoia usually reserved for war, the influx of American movies, and other major threats to the national soul. A wave of terrorist bombings in 1995 in Paris—perhaps an echo of the struggle in Algeria between the government and Islamic extremists—made matters worse.[62] These sad events only reinforced the views that Algerians were a source of trouble and national pollution—and a danger to safety, to boot.

The state of the economy makes the political problems of immigration in Europe worse. Many people are out of work in France, Germany, Italy, Spain, and other countries. It is easy to pin some of the blame on foreigners who, it is said, come in and steal the jobs. On the other hand, the forces that led Germany to import millions of workers in the past have not entirely spent themselves. Of course, there are plenty of local unemployed who could, if they wanted to, do the dirty work that foreigners do. But there is a pool of jobs that citizens simply will not take. And why? Because these jobs, compared to welfare benefits, are literally not worth the trouble. Hence, openly or covertly, these societies come to terms with foreign workers, legal or illegal, who form a fluid underclass.

This is, more and more, one world—a "global village." Migrant labor—in the West Indies, in Germany, in the United States—is an old phenomenon, but never before has there been so much of it—so great a floating population of men and women at the bottom of the pay scale. In Europe and Japan, birthrates are pathetically low; in Europe, welfare benefits are generous. This combination creates a labor shortage in the midst of unemployment—at least a shortage of people willing to wash dishes and scrub toilets and make beds. Many countries, then (including the United States), still have a large demand for cheap workers. In Japan, perhaps the most xenophobic of all the advanced countries, the police close their eyes to a rather substantial number of foreign workers who overstay their visas.

Immigration control is, in theory, strict and unyielding, but in practice this is more and more of an illusion.[63]

Structural, cultural, and economic factors have propelled modern immigration; they have also given rise to the movements that oppose modern immigration. We can, if we want to, call the opposition reactionary, racist, misguided. But this counterrevolution, like all the rest, is organically related to the revolution that it claims to despise. All the rich societies are certain to put a lid on immigration. The question is how the lid will be put on: should immigration be based on culture and race? That seems backward and bigoted—and indeed it is. Yet culture and race are themselves relatively modern ideas. So is nationalism. So is ethnicity. Ethnic cleansing is unthinkable without a sense of ethnicity.

Thus resistance and backlash are genuine movements. They represent real social forces, they are not anomalies, and they cannot be dismissed as primitive and doomed to die. Their importance goes far beyond immigration and citizenship laws. One can speak of cultural counterrevolution in the United States—and in many other countries as well. The counterrevolution, as Kenneth Karst reminds us, is "primarily a contest for influence among social groups over dominance of expression in public, a contest over the meanings attributed to behavior."[64] In short, counterrevolution is not simply a struggle for revival of the past; it is a struggle for domination in the present. And it operates to a large degree on the plane of meaning and symbol. At any rate, a society is lucky if it can *keep* the struggle on that plane. The danger comes when the struggle leaves the world of symbols and politics and enters the world of murder, death squads, and bombs. That has happened, alas, all too frequently in the recent past.

A struggle on the plane of meaning and symbol is not merely a matter of words. Karst is surely right that symbols are weapons in a battle for power, domination, and material goods. But it would be equally wrong to dismiss symbols as unimportant. Similarly, struggles over religion, sexual behavior, moral values, and the like cannot be totally reduced to money and power. Religious fundamentalism, for example—a powerful force today—is certainly a reaction to what many people see as moral decay and normative breakdown in modern society. It is modernity and its technology, and in particular the horizontal society, that have weakened traditional ways of thinking and behaving. By the same token, these forces have inspired a strong countermovement among the faithful.

Another form of backlash reacts to the real, or imagined, establishment of rival nations within the political nation: separatism, raucous disunity, the rejection of the melting pot, the decline of patriotic zeal. Raucous disunity is certainly no figment of the imagination. Conservatives tend to cite obsessively some kind of golden-age benchmark in the past—an age of glorious consensus—though no such golden age ever existed. What seemed like consensus was in fact domination.[65] Nevertheless, what they decry *is* real; it is something that is actually happening. The backlashers try to defend monopolies of power and prestige—monopolies of status, moral dominance, economic power, and (above all) recognition of this or that as the One True Way. These monopolies were also real. Plural equality threatens the webs of control and prestige that used to govern in society. This was in fact a white man's country, a Christian country, and so on.

The theme of lost unity—or endangered unity—is strong, for example, in the "English only" movement.[66] This movement also gives off a strong odor of prejudice, directed above all at Hispanics. Its leaders deny this; they argue that they are simply defending the precious English language. They mourn the passing of assimilation. According to a fund-raising letter of the organization "U.S. English Only," immigrants once "took it as a source of pride and fundamental necessity" to learn English and through English to become "successful, contributing citizens." Now the cause of multilingualism is leading to "disintegration and growing disharmony." America might become "a jumble of competing languages"; if so, its unity will be damaged, and it will fragment "along language-lines."[67]

Counterrevolutionaries always sing the song of lost unity. The golden age was a *united* age, an age in which everybody subscribed to the same cozy code of norms and warmed themselves before the same hearth of principles. Of course, nobody is really against unity and consensus. A society needs some kind of minimum agreement on norms and principles, or else it will fall apart; it needs legitimacy. But how much *national* unity and consensus is needed? How much flag waving, how many parades and marching bands, how many national holidays, and how much patriotic whoop-de-do? A country can tolerate quite a bit of disunity, so long as there is at least a truce among factions and a decent amount of agreement about procedures, elections, respect for minorities, and the other aspects of political life that make a country safe and democratic.

Modern democratic societies are committed to pluralism, at least as a matter of theory; they allow a range of cultures, manners, and opinions, though obviously only up to some invisible limit. In big countries like the United States, no solution on the model of Iceland is possible. Diversity is a fact. Plural equality *is* a solution to the problem of diversity, but only a partial one. For true believers—and there are true believers right, left, and center—there comes a point where plural equality simply has to give way. Almost all of us are true believers on some questions. Millions of people support rights for sexual minorities. But pedophilia? Millions more support religious pluralism. But what about snake worshipers or cults devoted to human sacrifice?

The communitarian movement in the United States has attracted quite a bit of attention in recent years. Communitarians decry the rootlessness, the anomie, of modern life. They want to "shore up" the "moral, social, and political environment."[68] They pit the "allegedly alienated individualism of late-twentieth-century capitalist society against the supposed security and personal rootedness of life in the collectivity."[69] The search for community is, in some ways, a search for the lost unity and consensus of the golden age, before it was destroyed by the big city and modern technology.[70] Genuine community is not to be sneezed at; but the movement does give off more than a hint of backlash. The nostalgia is inconsistent with plural equality, and communitarians are at least somewhat hostile to the multicultural state. Any community of memory and longing is unlikely to appeal to those who never really belonged, those who were forcefully excluded from the club of the golden past.

As Richard T. Ford has pointed out, America's various racial and cultural groups "refer to themselves as 'communities,'" but the "community" of the communitarian movement is one that "stands alone, without any specific physical location or normative boundaries."[71] It does, I think, *imply* a physical community; it invokes images of small towns, Norman Rockwell paintings, neighbors helping with the barn and the harvest, smiling people working together for common goals. It is, then, an attempt to recreate the nation that existed, if only in imagination, before it splintered into all the different subnations. It also harks back to the prehorizontal age. One image of a community is an image of loving people standing in a circle and holding hands. It is a yearning for Main Street, for small-town life, for the village.

Of course, these physical communities still exist, but they are supplemented by the "virtual" communities of our contemporary world. The communities made up of racial and cultural groups are organized (to a large extent) on a nonspatial and very horizontal plane. Not entirely: there are, after all, ghettos and ethnic neighborhoods. But the real community, even of the minorities, is the virtual community—the psychological community, the community of dedication. Under present circumstances, it is hard to see how anything else is possible.

Deaf People and Others: The Limits of Backlash

The nation of the deaf is one of the most interesting of the "nations" within America's borders. One of its major issues is languages: specifically, sign language, as opposed to English, lip reading, and the like. The issue of sign language does not evoke strong reactions in the general public. Most Americans know nothing about the issue at all. Yet, basically, the sign-language movement makes a claim as radical as any that Hispanics (or any other minority) have ever made with regard to language. The "English only" people do not utter a peep about sign language and pay no attention to the deaf nation at all.

Some of the reasons are perfectly obvious. After all, everybody knows that Spanish is a foreign language, but many people in the United States have no idea what sign language is. They think it is people making hand gestures in English. Moreover, the deaf are a fairly small group; they are scattered here and there; they do not pose any threat to the rest of the population—the people with hearing. Deafness can occur in any family. There are no deaf neighborhoods or enclaves (except for certain specialized schools and colleges). Hence the deaf do not seem to fragment the unity of the country.

In addition, people think of the deaf as genuine victims; they can't help

being deaf. Of course, blacks and other minorities are also victims of circumstance, and (with much justice) so consider themselves. But large numbers of majority people hate to admit this, or at least like to flatter themselves that the age of oppression, like slavery itself, is gone and forgotten.
Blind people or people in wheelchairs also seem like real victims, not
phoney ones with trumped-up historical claims. For this reason, even in a
period of backlash against civil rights, the claims of the handicapped meet
surprisingly little opposition. In 1990, a law forbidding discrimination
against people with handicaps in the United States sailed easily through a
fairly conservative Congress.[72] Potentially at least, such a law could be far
more intrusive and expensive for businesses, universities, and other institutions than affirmative action for blacks or women—a program that is
under severe attack.[73] Yet hardly anybody said boo in opposition, and President Bush signed it triumphantly, remarking that handicapped people
could now pass through "once-closed doors into a bright new era of equality, independence, and freedom."[74]

It seems likely, too, that workers do not see much threat from disabled
people. They do not think that the blind are stealing their jobs or that children with handicaps are squeezing their own children out of good schools
and, later, out of Harvard or Berkeley. Some claims—of Native American
tribes for sovereignty and shares of land, for example—are also far more
radical than the claims of blacks for affirmative action. But these claims are
geographically limited, and the groups involved are relatively small. Moreover, Anglos *perhaps* do not really think of Native Americans as quite so
alien as blacks. In any event, Native Americans have been successful in ways
that would be impossible for a larger group or for a movement that might
threaten the dominance of established majorities.

These various examples suggest some of the limits of backlash and in
so doing shed more light on movements which *do* generate strong, even violent reactions. Clearly, the size and strength of a movement affect the sense
of threat. When a majority feels beleaguered, its status questioned, its privileges assaulted, it is most prone to fight back in what it sees as self-defense.
The majority can afford to be generous when the minority is tiny and weak.
Equally important is the factor of (perceived) justice: Do the demands seem
right or wrong? Of course, *how* these judgments are formed is a complex

social question. There seems little doubt that millions of white people have been converted from faith in absolute Caucasian supremacy (at least up to a point) in the years since 1950.

Assimilation and Convergence

The pressure to keep people out, and the resistance to the demands of the subnations that are already inside, take on, as we have seen, the character of a culture war, a battle for the national soul. But there is a real paradox here. Assimilation is for many people an unacceptable, even oppressive, goal. Yet assimilation is not only still possible; it is quite inevitable. Take the issue of the Chinese in Australia. The Chinese are no longer excluded, and (as we have seen) official Australia calls itself diverse and multicultural. But is it really? The Chinese white-collar worker or small businessperson is perfectly capable of becoming a real Australian. These newcomers do not fit the image that so haunted the minds of Australians in the last century— that of Chinese who were exotic, incredibly alien, and totally unable or un-willing to become one of the crowd. The new Chinese immigrants are more or less modern; they are far more like Australians than their grandparents were. Assimilation is mostly a question of language, a few customs, and nothing more: it is a matter of acquiring the habits of a particular *dialect* of modernism.

This paradox of plural equality can be put more generally. The de-mands become more strident even as the distance between the contending groups grows shorter and shorter. Not only do the Chinese immigrants share modernity with their Australian hosts, those hosts have, in addition, become more cosmopolitan. The Chinese restaurants of Sydney and Mel-bourne are crowded with white Australians using chopsticks. Australians travel more and are (one hopes) much less xenophobic.

Consider, once more, the great battle over Muslim head scarves in French schools. This looks like a "clash of cultures"; and the Muslim girls seem more traditional than the modern French. But *is* this correct, and in what sense? The Muslim girls watch TV, shop in supermarkets, listen to rock music, and are no less modern in most ways than many French girls. Some French girls wear crosses instead of scarves. These French girls cannot enter some churches in shorts, while the Muslim girls, in their demure outfits, would find easy entré if they wished. In any event, the Muslim girls are *mostly* modern, like the French girls; the only problem, if it is a problem, is that in a mobile, horizontal society, they have come to roost in Paris, along with a lot of other foreigners, and they have evoked in some of their hosts a fear of cultural danger or death. The threat, if there is one, comes from the fact that the Muslim girls are too much *like* the French; if they were truly different, truly marginal and unassimilated, there would be less of a sense of siege.

The children of Chinese immigrants in Australia are probably less jarring than the Muslim girls. They may look a little different from the great-great-grandchildren of British convicts, but they will speak English without an accent, and they will share in the culture of their adopted country to the core. Generation by generation, their Chinese ethnicity slowly retreats to some peripheral corner of their lives. They come to *think* like Australians, and even when they insist on the right to preserve their culture, it is like preserving culture in a museum; their real culture, which they share with the other Australians, is the culture of modernity. The timid deference of their grandparents is long gone. They even come to *look* more like Australians: they become taller and subtly and unconsciously blend in with the rest of the community. They walk like Australians and they talk like Australians.

In fact, assimilation is the experience almost everywhere. It is true of militant Mohawks in Canada or black nationalists in the United States. It helps immeasurably that *all* the groups are, so to speak, fluent in the core dialect of modernity. It is an enormous irony that covert assimilation triumphs precisely in a period that has come to reject assimilation as cultural genocide.

Plural equality, then, does not mean quite what some people think it means. It does not mean tolerance of extreme diversity. Truly diverse people—nonmodern people—would find Western societies impossible to live in, and they in turn would simply not be tolerated. Nobody would be allowed to roam about Italy naked, hunting animals and conducting "primitive" rituals. Nonetheless, plural equality is meaningful, within its limits. And it comes to feed on itself. The Chinese who arrive in Vancouver are not only less Chinese than the Chinese of the past; they come to a society in which they find people of Chinese descent already living there—people in every stage and instar of assimilation. This makes it easier for the newcomers; the transition is less painful in every way. At the same time, the *theory* of plural equality means that the immigrants can raise their heads proudly; it means never having to say you are humble and grateful to Canada and will take whatever crumbs fall from the national table.

Can Plural Equality Work?

Japan and a few other countries are struggling to keep themselves ethnically pure. For many other countries, immigration and internal subnations are simply facts of life. There are two polar solutions to the problem: ethnic cleansing, at one end of the scale, and plural equality, at the other.

It is obvious which one of these two is morally superior. But the question is, can plural equality work? We must remember that culture is not the only issue. There are, in most countries, other, salient motives: jobs, positions, money, power. This fact is obvious in countries as dissimilar as Canada and Latvia. At stake are such things as control of the civil service and jobs for school teachers and post office workers; even jobs in department stores may hinge on the results of struggles over language and culture. And in many countries, the very ownership of the land is at stake.

There is, in short, a lot of jockeying for position, in universities, government offices, the job market, the media, and society in general. It would be naive to ignore the raw greed that lies behind *some* national strivings. Some nations might disintegrate, or at least weaken, without the demands of self-interest. Who can blame a Native American tribe for suing the fork-tongued Anglos over land, water rights, and enough sovereignty to run a casino? In their view, after all, the Anglos cheated and murdered and stole the land.

Land can be restored; fishing rights can be restored; sacred mountains and old bones can be given back. What cannot be restored is the past. There is nothing in anybody's tradition about running a casino. The *way* the claims are asserted, the texture of the claims, and the structural and cultural results all reflect modernity and the horizontal society that modernity generates. Moreover, Native Americans were once divided by language and way of life; but now they tend to come together (for certain purposes) and form a new panethnicity.

Yet despite panethnicity, the groups (if not the subgroups) are, in some ways, highly competitive. On college campuses it is popular to talk about a rainbow coalition made up of all the minorities. For the most part, this is nothing but talk. For some purposes, many of the groups can indeed form coalitions—blacks and Hispanics in favor of affirmative action, for example; in other regards they may be clearly at loggerheads.

In part, this is because many of the games subnations play are zero-sum games. Jobs and seats in Parliament can be parceled out in a more or less equitable way. Plural equality at the level of culture and ideology is more difficult. Columbus can be a hero to Italian-Americans and a genocidal devil to Hispanics; but the two images cannot coexist in the history books. It is fair to ask: Can any country deal successfully with a fully ripe system of plural equality, with its incessant demands, its constant proliferation of new subnations?

In country after country, small, submerged ethnic groups have awakened from centuries of sleep. Some of these were once clearly on the road to cultural extinction: Bretons, Basques, Welsh, Sardinians, Faroe Islanders; and many native peoples of the United States, Canada, Brazil, Australia, and Taiwan. Some subnations want home rule; some even want separation and independence. At the very least, they want plural equality. What results is what Anthony Smith has called "concentric loyalties."[75] There are countries that have hammered out a kind of accommodation, which actually seems to work. Spain has given the Basques and Catalans a large measure of autonomy. Italy has done the same for its German speakers in the snowy Alps.

A few countries seem to have done rather well in power sharing among ethnic groups. Singapore may possibly be a working example; Switzerland might be another. Switzerland, structurally, is a federal republic. Federalism is a possible solution to pluralism, at least when the various peoples can be sorted out geographically. Belgium and Spain are examples of what Koen Lenaerts has called "devolutionary federalism."[76] In each case of success, the rainbow coalition is bound together by some overarching sense of nationality. Some emotion, or some substitute for an emotion, must tie German, French, Italian, and Roman speakers together into Swissness—concentric loyalty, in other words. (Perhaps the Swiss are united in looking down on everybody else. This may be true of Singaporeans as well.) Certainly, many Americans have strong feelings about American identity, although it is not clear *how* many people have it, and exactly what it entails. All the plural nations have to work hard to create their own sort of imagined community, and the job is harder than in countries like Japan, where the ethnic core of nationality seems much more obvious.

Stirrings for autonomy have sometimes led to civil unrest. In big, multiethnic countries, like India or Nigeria or Russia, it is hard to see how a true or lasting accommodation can ever be worked out. In some countries, coexistence has broken down completely—Rwanda, Liberia, Sri Lanka. Actually, the question of identity is raised in every country, and in some it is extremely problematic, even when no blood is shed. Is there such a thing as a strong Canadian identity? Certainly not in Quebec; it is an open question whether "Canada" will survive as such another twenty years. Even among the English speakers, Canadian identity is a problem. As one scholar put it, "Canada's identity is its identity crisis"; the country is condemned to "endless, inconclusive attempts at self-definition."[77] Each country has its own mix of failure and success at creating a sense of nationhood; each has its own grade of insistence on loyalty or patriotism. The United States, for example, has seemed at times more virulently patriotic than, say, Canada or Australia, more prone to flag waving and xenophobia.

Each country has its own chemical reaction to plural equality. In each case of a country that actually holds together, there must be, perhaps, some kind of minimal but binding identity. This sense of identity may come from simple, brute cultural facts about the country: from people living in the same place, climbing the same mountains, swimming in the same rivers, shopping at the same stores, singing the same songs, enduring the same bouts of weather.

The sense of nationhood that people talk about refers, of course, to something much more intense—patriotism, loyalty, devotion to the flag. But this sense varies in strength, from society to society, and within societies. Some people lack attachment to *any* group; they drift, like plankton, on the sea of loyalty. Others may be deeply loyal to the country and its symbols. In most countries, citizens are pushed and pulled in different directions. They can be part of movements that ask for, or demand, the loyalty of their members, and this loyalty to a movement can be in addition to patriotism or a substitute for it. Can you be a good American and, at the same time, a fervent feminist or black nationalist?

Every country asks for patriotism, though not all of them get it. A lot depends on what country it is. There is, as Monroe Price has put it, a "market" for loyalties—a "competition for allegiances."[78] Nations (countries as a whole) are among the competitors. They use their control of the media to try to maintain their regimes through "myths, ideas, and narratives." They try to foster patriotism—devotion to the country, loyalty that goes beyond all other loyalties. Nations, or the dominant groups within them, try to create "cartels of allegiances where possible"; they aim to shut out competing voices and gain a monopoly on the allegiances of their members.[79] Control of the marketplace of allegiances is not easy, even in countries like mainland China or Iran. Satellites and modern equipment make cultural borders more porous than ever. This is on the physical side: on the invisible, cultural side, mass tastes, habits, songs, and practices spread mysteriously, through invisible networks. These make a state monopoly of allegiance highly insecure. Of course, it is not just nations that compete for loyalty; the same is true of every horizontal group. The competition may be overt, or it may be implicit. Feminists do not *literally* demand that women give the movement their undivided or primary allegiance. But unless *some* women do so, the movement will falter.

Michael Ignatieff has drawn a distinction between what he calls "civic nationalism," and "ethnic nationalism."[80] Civic nationalism "maintains that the nation should be composed of all those . . . who subscribe to the nation's political creed"; it is a nationalism, in other words, of shared values. It is, he says, "necessarily democratic." "Ethnic nationalism," on the other hand, is the nationalism of roots, of common descent, of blood.

Obviously, immigrant countries tend to fall into the camp of civic nationalism—at any rate, they seem to talk the language of civic nationalism. But can we believe them? I suppose we can imagine these two categories as polar types or ideal types. In a sense, all nationalism is, more or less, ethnic; all of it implies brotherhood and sisterhood, as we have seen. Probably nationalism carries at least a flavor of civic nationalism, that is, it assumes that all Germans or Tongans or Latvians are not only kin but share an allegiance to common ideals and virtues—ideals and virtues that, ultimately, flow from the kinship of the Volk. Complete civic nationalism, as Ignatieff defines it, is too noble to exist in the real world. No country simply opens its doors to everybody willing to subscribe to some credo or body of beliefs; too many millions would rush forward to subscribe to the credo of America or France.

As we have said before, immigrant countries do have a problem of national identity. They have to stitch together a single flag, so to speak, out of many different patches of cloth. The *idea* of a common creed—of civic nationalism—is a useful element in the process. But we can ask, How successful are the efforts today? In the United States, do blacks or Chinese Americans born in Seattle or members of the Navajo nation feel particularly American? How much kinship do they feel with the people whose ancestors came over on the *Mayflower*? Or, for that matter, with urban Greeks, Jews, or Italians? Do the people of Puerto Rico or Guam feel "American"? In each case, it is hard to answer the question. Indeed, the same question can be asked about descendants of the *Mayflower*, who do they feel a kinship with, and why? As we have noted, other identities have become increasingly powerful, in the minds of many, and threaten to trump national identity.

Paradoxically, there probably *is* an American identity, an American nationality, whether people are conscious of it or not. What is common to almost all Americans is a certain popular culture. Americans watch the same TV programs, sing the same songs, watch the same basketball games, listen to the same political babble. There is even an American creed, or a collection of ideas, concepts, norms, and the like, which Americans tend to share. The differences among the "nations" inside American are differences of dialect. The differences seem, of course, utterly crucial and fundamental, but this is precisely because they are *not*. Americans are acutely aware that British English and Jamaican English and Australian English "sound funny"; or that black English has a distinctive ring; or that people in Mississippi use some words and phrases that are not heard in Wichita or

Boston. But all these idiosyncrasies are variations of *English*, and not some other language. Chinese, for example, is entirely different; and most Americans cannot fathom a word of it. Hence they never bother about the ways in which Chinese and English are unalike.

Indeed, one of the themes of this book is a theme of convergence. What is true of the United States, and its "nations," is also true on a global scale. All nationalisms are, in a way, dialects of a single vast language, so to speak: the language of horizontal modernity. In every country, to be sure, history has written a special story, and the mixture of components is unique. But common themes exist in abundance, uniting all countries; a kind of common global culture seems to be developing, and even the first stirrings of a common language.

Would it be cynical to suggest a *third* category to add to Ignatieff's two types of nationalism? There is also citizenship based not on blood or creed but on skills or cold hard cash. Citizenship (or residency) is for sale. Canada, for example, is willing—indeed eager—to entice rich Chinese from Hong Kong. Permanent residence in Canada costs an investment of $250,000. Australia is more expensive: $365,000. The American green card is the most expensive of all: it takes $1 million.[81] The excuse offered—in America at least—is jobs. A newcomer with a spare million or two is supposed to invest and make jobs for *Americans*.[82] On a less crass basis, many countries welcome immigrants, no matter who they are, if they have certain skills. Immigration law in the United States makes special provision for aliens "with extraordinary ability in the sciences, arts, education, business or athletics." At the other end of the spectrum, there are special provisions for "qualified immigrants who are capable . . . of performing unskilled labor . . . for which qualified workers are not available in the United States"—the floating pool of migrant workers we have mentioned before.[83] In any event, this business of selling nationality can be found in the immigrant countries, which are less fixated on blood and Volk. It is not to be found in Japan or Germany. If taken to an extreme, it would mean that, in the end, loyalty and identity do not matter that much; or perhaps that identity is just another market commodity. This is, however, too marginal an aspect of citizenship and identity to make much difference.

Beyond Ethnicity

IN EARLIER CHAPTERS, I DISCUSSED how the horizontal society gradually emerged out of primal ooze. That led us to discuss one of its cultural consequences: nationalism. And nationalism, we remarked, always has at least some ethnic component. The great national movements worked to define a nationality or ethnic group, to find a homeland for that group, or, in immigrant countries, to generate national feeling, a unity, a loyalty, a patriotism, based on creed and ideology (more or less).

For both immigrant and nonimmigrant nations, the movement of peoples generates crisis, as we explored in the last chapter. Ethnic and racial minorities *inside* the country also may generate crisis. Some subnations go so far as to demand autonomy; others are willing to settle for plural equality—if they can get it.

In a horizontal society, there are all kinds of identity; not all of them are racial or ethnic. Identities are complicated and overlapping. Identity is, as we have said, the label a person attaches to the self. Identity seems to us partly a matter of choice and partly something handed us by fate. I am what I was born as, but I am also what I make of myself and what others have made of me. Race, gender, and family heritage come about as part of our personal destiny, without anybody asking us. Sexual preference, wherever it comes from, is tough and tenacious and has a powerful grip on the self. Religion is partly given, partly chosen. These feelings may be (as we discussed) objectively false—what *is* race?—but are subjectively, and socially, powerful.

All these factors, and a host of others—age, occupation, political persuasion—are important markers of identity. In fact, society more and more tends to dissolve and fragment into a host of "virtual" subnations, which become, in a way, forms of ethnicity—not only the nation of Islam but the nation of feminists or even, perhaps, the nation of cancer victims. Some of these nations can become extremely greedy or extremely seductive, so that for members, they suck up the whole stock of meaningful territory—militant feminism or black separatism, for example. When this happens, of course, the real or imagined unity of the nation-state is at risk.

In a sense, as we have seen, all identities are socially constructed, even gender and race. We see the world, necessarily, through a social lens; culture, history, and personality bend the light prismatically. The classical social scientists and anthropologists taught this lesson to the scholarly world. How far we want to carry this idea, and to what end, is another question. For present purposes, it is pretty much irrelevant whether, say, gender and race are socially constructed; what matters, at this point, is how people see themselves. The strong identities in society *seem* rooted in reality; all of them *compete* with national or ethnic identity for first place inside the mind.

They also very often overlap: a young man born in London of West Indian parents may see himself as primarily black or English or for that matter West Indian; he may assign himself to any number of nations. He can also *choose* to give something else top priority: perhaps gender or sexual identity, perhaps religion, even a hobby, occupation, or activity, a sport or a way of life. There is, theoretically, no limit to the number or kind of nations a person can belong to.

From Nationalism to Ethnicity—and Beyond

The social movements of contemporary times—all the strands in the social fabric, and all the groups that claim rights to plural equality—are organically connected. They all bubble up out of the culture of modernity; they all reflect the power of expressive individualism; they are all aspects, too, of the horizontal society. Technology has totally unsettled the known world; it has disestablished tradition and prepared the stage for mobile, shifting, impetuous, interconnected identities and relationships. The forces of modernity—of communication and transportation, above all—created the nation-state. They made peasants into French people, and also into Russians, Chinese, and Bolivians. But the nation-state no longer seems able to control its unity; the very forces that brought it about seem to gnaw away at its foundations like termites.

The communications revolution bears the heaviest burden of responsibility—television above all. The significance of the Internet may be equally great in the future. At one time, it was the family and other intimate insiders who made the self what it was and came to be. A child grew up in a hut or a palace, surrounded, in either case, by powerful agents of socialization. These agents have lost at least some of their force. The self today is the product of a bigger, broader world. Seductive images and voices burst in on the baby self, practically from childbirth on. Television "bypasses the filters of adult authority"; it makes the "child's physical isolation in the home" less important.[1] In Western societies, TV and the media reach into every house, every day, at almost every hour; they permit, and encourage, as we have said, the formation of horizontal groups. In other words, they allow or foster the creation of an infinite number of nations, subnations, and subsubnations.

In one sense, each modern liberation movement demands the same social goods: each wants acceptance, power, respect, a place in the sun. In short, they all want plural equality. They also want their share of the dominant imagery. This, they think, may be just as important as votes or representatives in Parliament. They want to see black faces on TV, women in male roles in advertising; they want the movies to get rid of stereotypes about old people or gay people or Spanish-speaking people; they want positive images. They want programs broadcast in Welsh or Breton or Catalan. They want employers to hire people in wheelchairs and to put these new workers in visible spots. They want deaf people to run their own colleges.

These demands are far from irrational. In our times, images are as important as reality; they *are* reality. Imagery, in the modern state, is as vital an aspect of power as the number of seats in Parliament. Without a share of national imagery, there is no hope for other kinds of power; nice little dialects, unless they have access to schoolrooms and broadcasters, go quickly extinct. Television, *within* its catchment area, is a ruthless leveler. What does not get broadcast is doomed. A language without a TV station is a language on its way to the morgue.

Language is, in some ways, an obvious case, but an important one. Language is a vital carrier of ethnicity and cultural independence. But feminism, too, would be threatened with doom if it could not make a dent in the media or if women were seen only in subordinate positions, or never seen at all. It is not just a question of role models; it is a question of power and survival.

The movements share another key feature. Being a woman or a gay or a handicapped person has become a kind of ethnicity; each status, each identity, has become, as it were, a type of nation, community, or tribe. The horizontal society makes all this possible. Perhaps the idea is best expressed by turning it around: that is, ethnicity has dissolved into yet another way of life, another aspect of self, *like* gender or religion or sexual preference. For many people, there are definite choices to be made: Shall I put religion, gender, language and culture, or some other identity at the center of my being: What shall I make the pivot of my personal struggle for meaning? One can hardly be a Basque nationalist, a feminist, an ardent Catholic, and a battler for the rights of the blind all at once. Each of these then becomes a kind of ethnic choice.

In the United States, although ethnicity and religion have been important themes in history, the jagged line that divides black from white has been of supreme significance. The civil rights movement—a movement for black equality and black empowerment—paved the way and presented a model for other victim groups to emulate. Plural identity is a palette of clashing colors in the United States. It is far more complicated than standard ethnicity. It covers many markers of identity. Women, gays, the elderly, Latinos, students, prisoners, the handicapped—these are all highly visible groups, all more or less organized, all clamoring for recognition, power, and a share of symbolic goods. Modern politics revolves to a large extent around these horizontal interest groups.

Although there is a wide band of choice, for most people, social understandings create impassable boundaries that prevent some options. I can decide *not* to be a committed Jew, but I cannot decide not to be a Jew if that is what the world chooses to call me. The Nazi regime carried this process of labeling to the point of madness; the Nazis considered Jews a race, a genetic condition, which could not be eradicated even by renouncing the religion and becoming a priest or a nun. When we say a status or a condition is socially constructed, that statement is ambiguous. We have not said *who* socially constructed it. If we say Welsh ethnicity is socially constructed, we usually mean the Welsh people constructed it themselves. But many categories are, in fact, constructed by the outside world or the larger society. The Welsh do not create Welshness in a vacuum—they create it as part of a historic process, against a specific social background. The others—the outsiders—are always important, indispensable in fact. It is white people who decided, as an initial matter, who was black and who was not; then, to fill out the picture, the attitudes of white people induced black people to construct their own categories in a specific way. Before the white colonists arrived, the various peoples of the Americas did not think of themselves as Indians or Native Americans or as any kind of unity. I doubt that people in Europe, in the seventeenth century, thought of themselves as "white people," or in fact as "Europeans."

Panethnicity, which we have mentioned several times, is a rather new, and important, phenomenon. It refers to an "imposed category," which comes about because the majority public lumps together "diverse peoples in a single, expanded 'ethnic' framework"; the units "may have nothing in common except that which the categorizer uses to distinguish them." New categories—Asian-American is one—have sprung up thus in the United States.[2] Chinese, Japanese, Koreans, and Vietnamese had little enough in common in Asia, but they all look alike to many Americans, and pretty soon a new category emerges.

There are, of course, limits—external realities. One can stitch together Romance dialects and create something called French, but one cannot weave Basque speakers into this particular fabric. Most of us think that race is something real (more than is justified biologically). As a matter of social fact, nobody can decide to be black unless she fits the current and agreed-upon definition. Nor can a black decide *not* to be black (unless she is able to pass). All this seems common sense.

But there is less here than meets the eye. One can imagine a sort of sci-

ence-fiction world in which people are able to choose whether to be Belgians or Peruvians, men or women, old or young—and make the choice
stick. In the days when America had few obvious limits on immigration, a
white person from Europe who could scrape together the cash needed for
the trip could literally *choose* to be an American. Sex-change operations are
(today) rare, difficult, and highly stigmatized, but this could change some
day. Similarly, what we consider markers of race (skin color, hair type)
could fade into insignificance—replaced by something quite different or
by nothing at all.

Religion and the Horizontal Society

Religion is, and has been historically, one of the most significant ways in
which people stamp their identity. Like every other major institution, its
form and function have changed over time. Officially, religion today is a
matter of individual choice. Most of the religious groups (or nations) are
only too happy to gain new recruits; this is true of all forms of Christianity, Islam, and many of the Eastern religions. Indeed, many religions actively fish for souls.

In modern society, religion has become *less* a matter of ethnicity, more
a matter of choice. Once upon a time, it was rare to leave the religion one
was born into. At most, a person shifted from one brand of Christianity to
another or from Orthodox to Conservative Judaism. Or one simply lapsed
and became a nonpracticing member of one's religious group. A century
ago, people would have thought it very strange if an American became a
Muslim or a Buddhist.[3] This is no longer now the case. Garden-variety
white folks now take up Eastern religions, and many blacks have been attracted to types of Islam. Most people, to be sure, stick like glue to the religion they got from their mother and father. They may lapse, but they will
not switch. The differences between then and now are probably marginal,
but they are still significant.

The horizontal society has weakened two pillars of religious identity:
first, that religion is truly a heritage, something given as a birthright and
not to be abandoned casually—an ethnicity in an almost literal sense; and
second, that one's religion is the One True Faith. The latter is still official

dogma in some religions, but it is not what many people really believe. The chief dogma of the horizontal society is individual choice. This dogma runs very deep. It is an age of easy divorce—not just from spouses but from churches as well. No-fault divorce allows a man or woman to get rid of a partner and to look for a companion that better fills his or her needs. No-fault religion allows, and in a sense encourages, getting rid of one's religion at will and taking up another one that brings more *personal* satisfaction.

In a plural society, where people of many different religions live side by side, it is hard to think that *your* religion is the one true faith. It is hard to accept that millions of people are going to hell, when these doomed souls are all around you—at work, on the streets, in school, and on TV. And even harder if you are Catholic, but your sister marries a Jew and your brother a Baptist. Religion, then, gets redefined as a matter of personal choice. There *is* no one true religion. There is only the one that is true for you, just as there is a mate or a hobby for you; just as some people look better in brown or orange, some better in lavender or blue. Americans, compared to people in most Western countries, are believers and churchgoers. But they also believe that there are many paths to salvation or inner peace. No one path is right for everybody. You pick the one that suits you best. This may be hard to justify in terms of theology, but ordinary people are not theologians. Rather, they are citizens of the horizontal society, and their minds are shaped thereby.

How does this square with the fact that in many places—in Israel and Palestine, in Northern Ireland, in the former Yugoslavia, in Algeria and Iran—people kill in the name of religion? In part, the answer is simply that some people, in some countries, are in revolt against pluralism, which they define as heresy or worse. In part, the answer is that these are wars of ethnic cleansing and not religious wars at all. The aim is not to conquer and convert, not to gain new souls, but to annihilate and expel the other side.

You Are What You Eat

Mobility and individual choice are key concepts in a horizontal society; people can and do learn about other religions, other habits, other ways of life. Life gives them, they think, the chance to molt one's skin.

Indeed—paradoxically—ethnicity itself has become less ethnic in our times. Partly this reflects the restlessness of the world's populations—the migrations of our day—and even more, perhaps, the explosion of tourist travel. Populations are more mixed than ever. This is most true of immigration countries but is also true of semi-immigration countries, like Britain and France. And even countries like Japan, which (officially) refuses immigrants, are affected by travel into Japan and by travel out of it by the Japanese. No matter how much the Japanese travel in groups, cocooned by interpreters, and whisked about in charter busses, they still absorb the smells and colors and flavors of all the other lands they experience.

In some parts of the world, borders are melting away. The European Union is groping toward a new-fangled supercitizenship. Of course, it still makes a huge difference whether you are Irish or Greek or Italian, but if goods and people flow effortlessly across borders, the borders inevitably mean a *little* less than before. Language is and remains a barrier, and a tough one. But culture in general loses a lot of its narrow grip on the population in an age of satellite TV and modems.

Identity is vastly more fluid than it once was. Identity is "self-created," and it is "indeterminate."[4] A rather minor case in point is the gourmet revolution. At one time, you were what you ate, in the ethnic sense. You were born into a tradition that told you whether or not you ate snails or pork or raw fish; whether you had cabbage or beets or bok choy. Now people find it exciting to try Cambodian food, visit a sushi bar, or snack on Polish sausage. In a global uniculture, the (fashionable) word about certain foods spreads like lightning: people become open to the idea that raw fish actually tastes good, if you give it half a chance. American yuppies are something of an extreme case—they will try anything; while Italians (for example) stubbornly resist most non-Italian food. In many countries of the West, immigrants encourage a taste for their foods. In London and Paris, even if you are totally ignorant of history, you can make good guesses about the lost empires by counting ethnic restaurants. The ex-colonial subjects cook the food, at first, for themselves. Then the natives get the hang of it. Nor is this only a matter of high culture. It is enough to mention hamburgers, french fries, and pizza.

The spread of sushi and pizza is thus a sign that identity, in small matters as well as large, has become positively liquid in the contemporary world. The horizontal society expands the menu of eating habits enormously. In the case of clothing, the forces at work are the same, but the result is almost the opposite: local ways of dressing are vanishing as rapidly as rain forests. Kimonos and wooden shoes do not spread to the rest of the world; they simply disappear. The global uniculture imposes a kind of uniform, especially on the young and on businesspeople. Kimonos and wooden shoes retreat to small ceremonial corners of their cultures.

Ethnicity and the Fragmentation of Nations

To sum up: ethnicity and its relatives, quasi-ethnicity, pseudo-ethnicity, and the like, are highly complex phenomena, but they are always shaped, as they must be, by the exigencies of the horizontal society. Modern life brings about what seems to be a paradox. On the one hand, nationalism burns with a fiery flame all over the world; the world is cursed with ethnic wars; countries like Czechoslovakia crack into pieces along the fault lines that divide it into ethnic groups. Yet, at the same time, the whole idea of a nation comes under attack and threatens to disintegrate, in ways that have nothing to do with the boundaries (social and spatial) between orthodox ethnic groups. Some militant gays in the United States call themselves the "Queer Nation"; the choice of the word *nation* is meaningful. There is, indeed, a whole crowd of new nations in the United States—the feminist nation, the elderly nation, the deaf nation, and so on. Each is an imagined community in much the same sense as the orthodox and traditional nations. Each has its traditions, invented or real. Each builds up a collective memory, a collective ideology, a collective pantheon of heroes. Each, as Soysal points out, uses the idea of the nation as a "trope of convenience for claims to collective rights and identity."[5]

Indeed, the number of new nations seems to be constantly on the rise. A famous black gang in Chicago calls itself the "Blackstone Nation." Gangs are certainly nothing new. They grow up out of the disintegration of the family and other vertical structures. As early as the nineteenth century, youth gangs prowled the streets of the big American cities. In the 1920s, Thrasher studied dozens of Chicago gangs.[6] But gangs seem to proliferate in the horizontal society; they seem tougher, fiercer, more competitive, more demanding of allegiance; some have branches in many cities, which Thrasher's gangs of apple-stealing, hookey-playing kids most certainly did not. The black Muslim movement also refers to itself as a nation, the "Nation of Islam." We have mentioned at various points what we might call a nation of the deaf; it would be easy to imagine the growth of a nation of blind people, stamp collectors, or bird-watchers. Stranger things have happened.

A horizontal group becomes a kind of nation when it generates a strong sense of belonging and demands a high level of commitment. The subnations are competitors in the market for allegiance and the market for identities. The nations, on the whole, recruit vigorously within some defined catchment area. Some define that area broadly, some narrowly; some subjectively, some in terms of criteria that are clean, clear, and objective. Every nation wants to gather up as many members as possible, but always with some sense of limits or boundaries. There is a continuum, from the most to the least open of groups. They are all dependent on *voluntary* action; you cannot get rid of membership in the black nation or the deaf nation, but you can certainly choose to do nothing about it. Apathy is a possible choice—and probably the most popular one. Some religions are willing to recruit anybody, anywhere in the world. Ethnic groups, because they put stress on kinship and blood, tend to recruit only within that sphere. Any black can join the Nation of Islam, but it would be hard, or at least awkward, for whites to belong. The nation of, say, the deaf requires deafness, though of course not all the deaf really join. The handicapped do not recruit outside their domain, and, despite the paranoid nightmares of the far Right, neither do most lesbians and gays. It is a heated question as to whether membership in the sexual minorities is a matter of choice, but to come out of the closet, to join active groups, to center your life on this membership, most certainly *is* a matter that people choose or refuse, according to conscience and will.

Age Groups and the Youth Culture

In modern society, we hear a great deal about the youth culture. We hear, too, about age cohorts and peer groups. The media love to talk about "generation X," "baby-boomers," and other real or imaginary cohorts. Age cohorts are no surprise to anthropologists, who find them in all sorts of societies, often with elaborate customs that mark passages from one stage of life to another.[7] But these are face-to-face societies. The modern age cohort is made up of members who may, and often do, live at great distances from each other.

In some ways, the concept of a youth culture is misleading. Contemporary society, to be sure, places emphasis on the young in popular culture—their tastes, their habits, their way of life. Sports stars are always young; so too (on the whole) are movie stars and rock stars. But what makes modern culture a youth culture is precisely the fact that you do not have to be young to belong. You can *join* the youth culture at any age—just as you can join a religion—by imitating its taste in music, its way of walking, talking, dressing, and cutting your hair. In the horizontal society, styles of life, at least at the surface level, are amazingly fluid. Fast communication makes this possible. A style that starts among gangs in Los Angeles can end up, six months later, influencing fashions in Paris. Styles are not only fluid; they are open to everybody. Just as you no longer need to be Japanese to eat sushi, you no longer need to be young to wear youthful clothing. Nor do you need to be rich. Blue jeans are, in a way, quite democratic.

The youth culture also means (paradoxically) that nobody needs to get old these days. (Of course, you do need your health and some money.) The old can now choose to act as if they were young. There is, in a way, a senior culture, just as there is a youth culture, though nobody who is not in the golden years ever willingly chooses it. In other words, nobody respects the elderly—except politicians, who are forced to. This is because the old are devout voters, form a powerful lobby, and exert considerable power in the economy and the polity. Not that most old people are Gray Panthers or even active in public affairs. But enough of them are to form a genuine interest group. That group fought for the end of mandatory retirement, among other issues. What old people want, above all, are pensions and health care, but enough of them also want the right to *choose* to do whatever young people do. Hence all the literature on sex in the golden years and the like. In a horizontal society, as long as the body does not give out, the elderly have many options that were denied them in social orders based on rigid age grades.

Not many old people are members of the Woodstock Nation—that group of young people obsessed with rock-and-roll music and, generally speaking, of the hippie persuasion. (By now, of course, some of the original members of this nation are approaching middle age and beyond). "Nations" of this kind form horizontally; the word spreads through the media, snowballing as it goes. The Woodstock Nation is only a metaphor; nobody has a passionate allegiance to this nation, at least compared to most of the other nations in a multicultural society. People who meet at a rock concert are certainly not a *stable* group. Indeed, they interact less with each other than with the performers howling and screeching on the stage. (They are not as isolated as watchers of MTV.) What binds them together is not the concert experience but a culture, a frame of mind. Nations differ in modern society in the degree of stability and the amount of commitment. The Woodstock Nation may be at one pole; secret societies, with blood oaths, strange rituals, and mystic bonds, might be at the other.

Separatism

In some ways, separatism is the exact opposite of recruitment: it is the urge to isolate the group, to set it off from the rest of the world. Many ethnic groups are eager both to recruit and to separate. They want to attract every possible soul they can, within the space of their definition—every Serb, every Basque, every Chechen. Then, once they have gotten as far as they can toward this goal, they want to split off from the body in which they are imbedded. This, indeed, describes the strategy of many national movements. Nationalism, at its core, always involved an ingathering; then it asserted an overarching identity that, for better or worse, trumped other forms of identity. Nationalism had an implicit ideology of centralism. It aimed to squash the local and the tribal, to suffocate all competitive dialects, to destroy competing loyalties. This was done by force, if necessary—ideally by applying enough gentle pressure to make the periphery join with the core.

Separatism is attractive, too, to some subnations. Here again the idea is, first, to gather as many potential members as possible (to make all women feminists, for example), and then, in some cases, to lead the faithful to some promised land. On the recruitment side, there are two general strategies. One might recall here Ignatieff's distinction between civic and ethnic nationalism.[8] Feminism would be "civic" if it welcomed men in its ranks, provided they pledged allegiance to the principles of the movement. And many feminist organizations *are* civic in this sense. The NAACP also is civic; whites can and do join when they believe in the cause and want to help out. But nobody can "join" an ethnic group (at any rate, not easily); some subnations are "ethnic" in this sense too: no men, whites, straights, or other outsiders are allowed to join.

Most forms of nationalism are not very civic. Nor is the mainstream necessarily civic either. In the United States, as we saw, not every group had the option to assimilate—certainly not the African-American population. For them, especially in the South, there was a kind of forced separatism— the segregation system. Hitler had no interest in assimilating the Jews or the Gypsies. But where assimilation was the ideology, it *was* a kind of civic goal, within its sphere. Every man, woman, and child within the nation was supposed to be enlisted for the same adventure, enrolled as a passenger on the same great ship of state. The multicultural society, on the other hand, has no such mighty ocean liner; instead, it seems at times like a fleet of small, hostile dinghies, battling for space in a limited or shrinking pond.

The fading star of assimilation creates an opening for new forms of separatism. The point is perhaps clearest with regard to race in the United States. During the long and bitter struggle to gain racial justice, many liberals (black and white) argued for discarding race as a marker of identity. Race was trivial, race was nothing; it was merely "pigmentation of the skin." And, by virtue of the one-drop rule, it was sometimes not even that.[9] But much has happened since the 1950s and 1960s. Race relations seem to have turned acrid, sour. Many blacks no longer think in terms of integration or assimilation. Integration, they believe, is not possible, and probably not even desirable. Race is not just skin color; rather, it is culture, it is destiny; it defines the Afro-American nation. These blacks no longer consider a color-blind society the ideal. In fact, as one critic put it, a color-blind society would abolish black culture and amount to a kind of "cultural genocide."[10] Black separatism is once more in vogue, in certain circles; there are calls for Afrocentric curricula in schools—schools that will be deliberately all-black, that will be vessels for imparting self-respect and for teaching the national (that is, black national) culture.[11]

Separatist leanings occur, to a degree, in other subnations as well. San Francisco and other cities, for example, have distinctly gay neighborhoods, and there are rumblings among some feminists, deaf people, and other groups for some form of separate physical spheres. Would it be too fanciful to see traces of separatism among the elderly too? Obviously, some older people enjoy life in retirement communities for all sorts of reasons, and homes for the aged have been around for a long time. But the idea of a retirement *community* is, indeed, a mild form of separatism; in these communities, members of the gray nation withdraw from the rest of society and commune instead with people who, they imagine, both think and act like them.

Subnations: A Look at the Larger World

In this chapter, we have been talking mostly about the United States. But in every Western country—and non-Western ones as well—there are versions of the politics of identity; each has its own distinctive constellation of nations and subnations. If the nation is an imagined community, so too are each of these groups and their various subgroups. They are all more or less artificial, all more or less socially constructed; this does not in the least detract from their emotional power when they explode into consciousness. The sense of solidarity among people in wheelchairs is something radically new in the world. Handicapped people were at one time the most isolated and detached of human beings—as they still are in parts of the world (Japan, for example).[12] In the horizontal society, however, thanks to technology, there is no limit to the number of imagined communities that can be built up; the handicapped are only one of these.

The horizontal society, as we have noted, both splits and unites—in either case, along lines of horizontal force. And the social factors that create this kind of society, as we have argued consistently, are not American or European; they are modern and global. Each country has its own recipe of ingredients, its own minority movements. Some subnations are more universal than others. Feminism, for example, is everywhere, though it would be ludicrous not to note vast differences between say, Japan, and Sweden, let alone Saudi Arabia.[13] Still, the *idea* of gender equality has made its mark everywhere. It can be found in dozens of constitutions and in most legal systems—in laws that protect against sex discrimination, laws that guarantee equal pay, and more woman-friendly laws concerning rape.[14] Whether these laws are effective in the real world is another story.[15] Nonetheless, they attest to the growing power of the feminist nation.

Of course, most women are not active feminists. Of those that are, probably only a few have any sense of nationhood in the most extreme (separatist) sense. Still, in many ways, the fringes or extremes in social movements push the center and, after a while, sometimes *become* the center. How many Slovaks or Basques were active in the national movement? How many old people are militant and politically active? Not many. But how many does it take?

The revolt of the so-called sexual minorities has also made its mark on many Western countries. In the United States and elsewhere, many of the old, punitive laws (against sodomy and the "crime against nature") have been repealed.[16] This has not been a smooth or easy development. There remains bitter opposition to gay rights, much of it religiously based, not to mention backlash. President Clinton, after his election in 1992, tried to abolish one of the most obvious forms of discrimination: the ban on gays in the armed forces. He unleashed a whirlwind and soon had to run from the storm.

The saliency of race has been obvious in the United States and in South Africa as well. Race and ethnicity overlap to create political and social issues in many countries—Guyana, Trinidad, Fiji, Malaysia; the list is long. Historically, race has not been a salient issue in Europe, but this is no longer the case, especially in Great Britain. Recent emigrations from Africa have brought race to the surface in France, Italy, and other European countries. At one time, a black face on the streets of Rome was a novelty; no longer.

Indigenous peoples, once only helpless victims, are now flexing their muscles in the United States, Canada, Australia, and New Zealand, not to mention Brazil, Russia, Guatemala, and elsewhere. In some countries, native peoples have won significant *legal* victories—the recognition of land rights, for instance, in Australia[17] and in Canada. In some Latin American countries, the Indian issue is more a question of language and culture—and money and power—than of race, strictly speaking. But race is an element nonetheless.

In the United States, very notably, the elderly have emerged as one of the most powerful lobbies, and in some ways they too constitute a nation. As a pressure group, senior citizens have won a long string of victories. Since the late 1960s there have been laws protecting men and women over forty from discrimination in hiring and firing;[18] thousands of claims were brought every year under these laws. Congress also abolished mandatory retirement. A company can dismiss a worker who "can't cut the mustard" but cannot adopt a *rule* that everyone must go at age sixty-five or seventy—or at any age for that matter.[19] Congress enacted a drastic law in 1990 outlawing workplace discrimination against people with disabilities.[20] The law floated through Congress with surprisingly little opposition. The handicapped have won legal victories in other countries too, among them Canada, Australia, and New Zealand. In Australia, for example, Parliament enacted a Disability Discrimination Act in 1992; its purpose was to eliminate, as much as possible, discrimination in work, education, accommodations, "access to premises, clubs and sport" and to "promote a recognition and acceptance within the community of the principle that persons with disabilities have the same fundamental rights as the rest of the community."[21]

Each movement of an underdog group has its own complicated history; and each complicated history is different in its complications in each country. But it is surely no coincidence to find history grinding out similar results in nation after nation—laws on women's rights, race, or the handicapped. In the horizontal society, news travels fast and effectively. Networks of opinion cross borders with ease, and no border guards can keep them out. But the root causes of these worldwide movements lie deeper. The Australian law, just quoted, talked about "fundamental rights."

This reminds us of a point we made earlier. The horizontal society believes strongly in equality and individualism. People think about rights and entitlements as natural, inherent, universal. They are the patrimony of the whole human race. They are "rights across borders"[22]—rights without boundaries, without limits, without exceptions or deviations.

This newly developed consciousness of right is, indeed, a crucial facet of modern legal culture.[23] It transcends particular codes of law. Even despised and downtrodden people—guest workers in European countries, for example—tend to have a feeling of entitlement, based not on "national citizenship" but on a "more universal model of membership," which, as we have noted, is anchored in "deterritorialized notions of persons' rights."[24] Yet this universalism does not exclude *group* activity; indeed, it fosters it. Our Turkish guest worker in Germany, for example, even if he rejects German identity and does not want German citizenship, may feel conscious of his natural rights. How can he make sure the state recognizes these rights? How can he translate them into action? Only by joining with other people similarly positioned in social space—other Turks, primarily. Hence, by affirming his Turkishness, his allegiance to Islam, and his cultural heritage, he makes it more likely that his basic human rights will gain respect in the German polity. It is not fanciful to imagine that some similar urge animates, say, handicapped people in Australia or women with feminist consciousness in Brazil or whatever the group that is searching for a better life or a larger package of human dignity. It is this paradoxical mix of universality and particularity that characterizes the horizontal society.

9

Some Concluding Remarks

IN THIS BOOK, I HAVE described what I call the horizontal society. What I mean by this term is simple. In the modern world, for a number of reasons, vertical authority has weakened: the authority of parents, bosses, heads of state, the local priest or elder—people who are above us. Modern society, compared to past societies, is much more horizontal. There is a much more important place for groups that are voluntarily formed, for groups that do not meet face-to-face but that join together through the miracles of modern technology. Of course, I did not mean that a society, no matter how modern, is *absolutely* horizontal. Take, for example, the noise about the decay of the family. It does have a basis in fact. But the family (in various senses) is still the basic unit of human organization. Fathers and mothers have lost some authority, and broken homes are on the increase, but parents still mean a lot, are still the foundation of life, and still influence the lives of most people. The same is true of many other vertical aspects of human life—religion, the state; they will not enter the twenty-first century intact, but there's a tremendous amount of life left in them. The point I am trying to make here is relative, a point about tendencies, changes at the margin. It is often the case that a small shift produces large results. How many burglars does it take to make a crime wave? How many terrorists or skyjackers does it take to throw a society, or an air-travel system, into chaos?

The basic propositions about horizontal societies are, perhaps, most vividly true in the Western democracies. But they are probably true (to a degree) elsewhere as well. In modern society, people tend to form and re-form horizontal groups—groups whose members are on a level; groups joined by a sense of commonality; groups whose unity does not have to be spatial or geographic; groups made possible by modern communication and transport. Even modern dictatorships—even Hitler's Germany or more recent autocracies—tend to be strongly horizontal. They rely heavily on mass movements, control of the media, propaganda. Every aspect of modern life is affected by the technologies that have created the horizontal society—the mass media, above all—and by the social and structural forces they unleashed.

In this small book, I have tried to track some of the consequences of the horizontal society. All human societies have pyramids of authority; in the horizontal society, authority tends to merge with celebrity status; the rulers are not Gods or heroes but people "just like us." We get bound to them in a complex, reciprocal, interactive relationship, quite unlike the old vertical relationship between women and their husbands, between people and their kings.

Most important, a horizontal society affects, at the deepest level, a person's sense of self. A horizontal society is a society of individuals—and individualists. People in society are taught, and come to believe, that they have the right and the power to construct a life, a meaning, an identity for themselves as unique individuals. The groups that make up society are different from the groups within traditional societies. They are socially constructed, they are complex, and they are voluntary—*chosen*—in significant ways. In a sense, one even chooses (within limits) a race, a gender, a form of sexuality. one can also choose *not* to be counted as part of any particular group, though this is sometimes more difficult, because the outside society does not always go along with one's choice.

I do not ignore the fact that choice is often an illusion. People are firm believers in free will. But they choose their politics, their dress, their manners, their very identity, from a menu they had no hand in writing. They are constrained by forces they do not understand and are not even conscious of. But even the *illusion* of choice is of enormous social significance.

And how is it, we asked, that a horizontal society, a society of individuals, is also a society of strong, even extreme ethnic nationalism? Why do we see so many wars of hate in so many parts of the world? Why is it that even peaceful countries, the smug Western democracies, are riven with conflicts and clashes rooted in identity politics? The answers to these questions lie, basically, in the nature of horizontal groups and the way they form allegiances. The modern nation is the creation of mass education and literacy; it comes about, as we have seen, when roads connect little villages to provincial capitals, when the children in the village go to school, and when the grown-ups serve in the army, read newspapers, and are drawn into a centralized culture. Later come the movies, TV and, lastly, the Internet. The nation becomes a kind of extended family, but it also puts up boundaries, it excludes, it assimilates, it grinds down those who do not share in the national culture. The same forces that create the nation—the horizontal group above all horizontal groups—set the stage for its rivals, the subnations, the ethnic minorities, the imitation nations, the identity groups. Plural equality is an attempt to sort things out and reach a kind of peaceful accommodation. But it does not always work. In some places, in fact, it never even gets a chance. To be sure, there is peaceful Switzerland, there are societies like the United States (warts and all) struggling for a kind of pluralism and a rainbow of cultures; on the other side, however, there is the horror of Lebanon, Bosnia, Rwanda, Sri Lanka, and East Timor.

A horizontal society is a society on the move. The messages of modernity get spread to remote villages. These messages dissolve vertical identities and traditional ways of life—not totally, of course, but enough to remove many of the significant cultural barriers to emigration. The consequences for identity and allegiance are vast. They are also vast in regard to immigration and citizenship, and they set off deep, hostile reactions in the receiving countries.

One key aspect of the horizontal society, as we have said, is its division into identity groups. Nations are only one of these groups. Or, to put it another way, there are many ways to constitute a "nation," and ethnic identity is only one of these. Each of the major identity groups can be considered a kind of nation. Or, to rephrase this, each nation is only a kind of identity group. Some of these groups are large, some are small. Some are fervent, some are weak. Some are based on inborn characteristics (race, gender), others on more ambiguous traits (religion, sexual preference). Very striking in the modern world is the declining significance of class as a form of solidarity and allegiance. Marx would be surprised, and shocked, to see how little is left of the international brotherhood of the oppressed and suffering masses, how little consciousness of class there is among workers and peasants.

In this book, I have raised some questions and suggested some answers. I probably did little more than scratch the surface. I had to deal, necessarily, in broad generalities. Statements about human societies are never *absolutely* true; no description of how people behave can even remotely approach the iron laws that make the sun rise and set or control the reaction of two chemicals in a beaker. I tended, deliberately, to stress samenesses rather than differences among the passengers on the ship of modernity. I was concerned with big, global happenings—tendencies that make it possible to compare, say, Finland, Canada, and sometimes Japan; sometimes even the Third World is thrown into the bargain. Obviously, modernity affects different countries in different ways. Nobody could mistake Japan for Belgium, and certainly not for Honduras or Nepal. It would be incredibly instructive to figure out why these differences occur *among* nations, what determines their precise dialect of modernity. There are all sorts of reasons in history, social structure, culture, geography, climate, and religion. All of these would be worth exploring. But that would be another book.

The horizontal society—the society created by mass media, by modern forms of transportation, by modernity itself—is relatively new, and it is hard to know where its paths are leading us. We already see a few of the consequences. Some are worrisome; others seem, on the whole, quite benign. It is hard to criticize the idea of universal human rights. One can quibble with details, but the core concept seems incredibly decent. Even people who carp at radical feminism, for example, will accept—grudgingly perhaps—the basic idea that women are people and that they deserve more control of their lives and a better share of what the world has to offer than they have gotten previously. As for racism, the United States and South Africa, two prominent sinners in the past, have outlawed overt racism, and the worst forms of it now hide in dark corners and among fringe communities. Of course, racism is still alive in the United States, but the worst excesses (segregation and lynching) are ancient history, one hopes. All over the world, there are organizations devoted to human rights, and they may be having some effect. Perhaps, at long last, the plague of dictators is beginning to recede—in Latin America, in Africa, in Asia. All this is to the good.

Plural equality, too, strikes me on the whole as a worthwhile goal—hard to carry out and with some nasty side effects but still worthwhile. Political correctness can be annoying; even at its worst, however, it is not nearly as bad as the blatant and violent racism, anti-Semitism, Paki-bashing, homophobia, and other monstrous evils that are its opposite. Alas, only a few lucky countries are able and willing to go down the road of plural equality. The dark alternative—a battle to the death—is far too prevalent; too many wars and massacres disfigure the world today; there is too much hatred, too much "ethnic cleansing." Too many hopeless refugees, barefoot, hungry, diseased, and desperate, roam across borders, crawling through culverts to find a place of refuge—*any* place of refuge—or die in hostile, parched tent cities far from home.

Many people find the new, the modern, the horizontal society not to their taste. They mourn the passing of a cluster of values they call traditional. They are dismayed by the crime, poverty, and social disorganization so evident in modern society. They are upset by hedonism, consumerism, the shallowness of modern life—the rootlessness of it all. They are disgusted by pornography, divorce, rock-and-roll music, body piercing and by the slovenly and hollow values they see in the young. They long for the age of faith. Indeed, it is possible to lay many pathologies at the door of the horizontal society. Specifically, it is easy to blame the media for many of the sicknesses of the horizontal society. The media spread messages that are offensive to many people—respectable, churchgoing people, decent, hardworking people, people who believe in traditional values.

But the sins they denounce and the images that disgust them thrive because they are genuinely popular. And is there really an option? Even if we want to, is there any way to turn back the clock? This is a rapid, mobile world. Even people who sit still and watch TV are mobile in the psychological sense; if they do not go out to meet the new world, it comes into their huts to meet them. The process changes the way they think, their belief patterns, their view of life and of destiny.

The media *are* to blame, in a sense, for violence, family decay, drug addiction, and the whole litany of modern woes. But they are not to blame in the way many people assume. In my view, what erodes traditional values is not a few dirty words on TV or a bare breast or a pile of dead bodies on a cop show. It is the very *fact* of TV, its ubiquity, its power, its messages of mobility and consumption, that erodes traditional values. Or, to put it more bluntly, it is the horizontal society itself that makes the past forever impossible.

A Brief Note on Power

This book has been, among other things, an essay about law, governance, and authority. I wondered out loud about how a celebrity society affects government and structures of authority. At many places in the discussion—on the subject of immigration, for example—politics and politians, responding to what they considered public opinion, inevitably figured in the story.

Yet, on the whole, I emphasized citizens, not rulers; I underscored areas of life that fall under that domain which I have elsewhere called the republic of choice.[1] There was an assumption running through the text—or one might think so—that in the horizontal society people make choices for themselves: choices to affiliate with identity groups, to practice a religion, to immigrate, and so on. But I have been careful to point out that these choices may be imaginary. People are naive about, and unaware of, the many constraints that guide and limit their choices. The constraints I spoke about were mainly social and cultural—the kind of invisible but powerful forces that make kids wear baggy pants or adults buy sports cars.

Did I pass over or omit the problem of power? Should I have said more about dominance and manipulation? In other words, could I tell the same general story, but in terms of ruthlessness and superior force? Take nationalism, for example: Isn't it imposed from the top? The national movements of the nineteenth century were, in fact, led by elites. The peasants neither knew nor cared. Who sets school curricula? Who writes the history books? Who imposes the dictatorship of a standard language? Surely not the proletariat. Moreover, the twentieth century will go down in history as a century of ferocious tyrants—men who mobilized their nations for evil and war; men who devised the most efficient killing machines ever known and used them to the hilt. Even today, at the end of the century, tyrants are hardly an endangered species.

There is continuing debate over who was guilty of the immense slaughters during the Third Reich. Was it just the Nazi regime, or were the Germans as a whole Hitler's eager accomplices? In either case, nobody can deny that the regime was run by murderers. They ordered the killings and marshaled every tool of propaganda and deceit to advance their sickening ideology. Stalin killed millions; Gorbachev refused to prop up the Soviet empire with corpses. Leadership makes a difference. In almost every instance of genocide or brutal civil war—whether in Rwanda or Sri Lanka or elsewhere—one can find, in the background, an evil government or evil governors pulling many of the strings.[2] The history of the war in Bosnia is, unfortunately, a perfect example. Everybody talks about the ancient ethnic hatreds at work. But they are not, in fact, ancient at all. They were concocted and fomented and stirred into life, within the last decade or so, by ruthless and designing leaders.[3]

All this is true enough. But to take full account of power and dominance would be another, and a different, book. I would nonetheless like to add a word or two to this plea of confession and avoidance. First of all, modern dictatorship is, after all, just as modern as modern democracy. Its *ways* of mobilizing and dominating and tyrannizing are, in other words, distinctly modern. Modern dictatorship presupposes the horizontal society. Technology makes modern dictatorship possible. A feudal society had to rule indirectly, through layers of (vertical) authority, because nothing else was possible at the time. Louis XIV and other autocrats never used mass propaganda, never ranted and raved in public meetings like Hitler did. All forms of government today, and all forms of domination, are necessarily rooted in contemporary life. Computers, TV, the radio, public opinion polls—not to mention wiretapping, electronic surveillance, automatic weapons, bombs and missiles—are available to all governments. Both demagogues and democrats appeal to the horizontal masses with themes and slogans that are appropriate to the times.

In short, power and the holders of power are certainly relevant to our story; but what we focus on here is not power itself but ways in which the forms and uses of power reflect the trends and forces in society that we have been trying to describe. So we ask: Which buttons do the authorities push when they want to mobilize and command? Which themes lend themselves to propaganda and manipulation? Which slogans can rouse blood and enthusiasm? What resonates with the mass public and what does not?

Just as it would be naive to ignore power, it would be naive to assume that power is absolute, that it has only to command for its will to be done. As I mentioned in discussing the celebrity society, the public and government are locked in an embrace of reciprocity. It is too simple, then, to treat legal authority as a blunt, irresistible force, a force united with an ideology that paralyzes the people through an "aggregate of socio-cultural-political forces that generate consent and induce acquiescence to power." The subjects of power are not helpless slaves; the power above them is "always . . . contestable" and is in fact "contested at various points."[4] In important ways the powers are themselves dependent on their subjects. Big Brother may be watching *you*, but you are also watching Big Brother, at least on the evening news.

In modern society, everyone—at the top, middle, and bottom—is wrapped in the folds of a culture he or she cannot escape. It is a culture that technology created, but from there it takes over and has almost a life of its own. This culture affects different strata, and different individuals, in different—and unpredictable—ways. One woman becomes a rabid fan of Elvis Presley; another becomes a militant feminist; another takes up Asian cuisine; still another throws bombs. Some choose to run for office; others do not even bother to vote—they stay home and watch soap operas on election days. Some are impervious to politics or religion; some become obsessed with these. How power affects people, how it is distributed, how it is used and abused in horizontal societies, are rich subjects only hinted at in these pages.

What Is to Be Done?

I am not sure I can answer this question. Is there a problem? Of course there is. But what is it? There are many definitions of the problem, or problems, of modern society. What some people consider problems, other people define as solutions—sexual freedom, for example, or the global economy.

I am not *required* to ask, what is to be done? or to answer the question. I wrote this book to describe what I think is going on in the world and to offer some words of explanation. I did not set out to change the world or to show how others might change it. But an author finds it hard to resist a chance to preach or recommend.

Unfortunately, I can do very little along those lines. What technology has wrought in the world cannot be undone. A transformed society will never get untransformed. There is no way to go back, ever. Nobody can put the genie back into the bottle.

I have presented an argument—a strong one, I hope—about certain social trends in the contemporary period. What happens next? Nobody really knows. A trend can continue, get stronger, or peter out totally. Prices of stocks and bonds can go up, stay put, or go down. Any trend can reverse itself.

In some senses, of course, the past *seems* to be alive (but only seems). What is, is always new. Even old things are, in reality, as new as the new. An antique chair has a different *meaning* from the meaning it had when it was first made; it is not the same chair, even if physically it is exactly the same. Religious fundamentalism is not the same as the religious orthodoxy of five centuries ago, even when it claims to be. It is inevitably and irreversibly modern, or tinted with modern ideas and modern forms. History, like time, travels in only one direction. We laugh at the Luddites. "Progress" cannot be stopped. Neither can movements that appear to be going backward. The forces at work are much too powerful to be trapped and caged and diverted and tamed, let alone reversed. As far as future trends are concerned, then, the only certainty is that the future will not be like the past. But *what* it will be like is unknown—as yet.

Mooning over the past, over a lost golden age, is itself a sign of modernity, as we pointed out. It is almost always an exercise in futility as well. In the first place, the golden age was never so golden as we think. Would anybody who thought about it really want to live as an ordinary person (rather than as a noble, king, or queen) in the fourteenth century? I am referring here to the *real* fourteenth century, with its ignorance, dirt, misery, plagues, and catastrophes, not the Disneyland version. Does anybody really regret the invention of antibiotics, air conditioning, and the fax machine? In the past—even fairly recently—life was, from our perspective, like Hobbes' state of nature, that is, nasty, brutish, and short. But for good or ill, we are stuck with the world as it is.

On the other hand, the march of technology and the development of the horizontal society do not do away with ideas about good and bad, justice and injustice. There is plenty of room for improvement and reform *within* the horizontal society, even if that society cannot be fundamentally altered or reversed. Whatever our problems, however you define them, they are rooted in the present, in our times, and in our culture. If people were more aware of causes and effects, if they were more sophisticated about the world, they might be willing to take small, halting steps toward improvement. Official policy in many countries, and on so many issues, is a jumble of inconsistencies, a combination of pandering and punishment, directed at the wrong people, at the wrong time, and in the wrong way.

What people need is something to cling to in the wreckage, perhaps those concepts, habits, and values that are distinctively modern yet unquestionably good: tolerance, pluralism, respect for one another, freedom. Many people would agree, and would add that it would be nice if these could be joined with the best that remains from earlier strata of time—the work ethic, a sense of civic responsibility, reverence for beauty and high culture, religious faith, and morality. Many things operate to undermine all these values in modern society. Our very successes work to destroy the qualities that produced these successes. Men and women of brilliance and incredible diligence work killing hours to produce fantastic machines, miracles of technology—and then they and others fill those machines with nothing but mindless, numbing entertainment. Computer games and TV shows are amazing achievements of the human race, but the *content* (as opposed to the technology) is something else again. The content peddles values that go to destroy the habits, values, and inclinations that made the machines possible in the first place. Perhaps the market thus sows the seeds of its own destruction. In a horizontal society, image and entertainment come to play a decisive role in the lives of millions of people. The media act as missionaries for a specific brand of modernism.

Mobility and individualism have both benefits and costs. Never before, perhaps, have there been so many disconnected people—people unplugged from the sources of human power and light. The men and women who live in cardboard boxes under viaducts in London and New York are extreme examples of rootlessness and despair, but there are millions who are "homeless" in a less visible and literal sense. There is good reason to worry about crime rates and family disorganization in Western societies and about unchecked population growth and the fouling of the earth. The problem is not sexual freedom or people who don't go to church or refuse to salute the flag. The problem is the restlessness that modernity produces—a hungry, global, devouring culture. The culture has accomplished a lot of good things, but it has side effects as well. It accentuates quick, glitzy, empty success. It *de*emphasizes what many enlightened people feel are good, sound values.

Enlightened education might help to neutralize the void at the heart of the culture. But the public does not seem willing to pay for this investment. So much for the domestic front. On the global front, one can hope for a stronger international community and the strength of will to oppose, with guns and bombs if necessary, intolerance, hatred, and aggression. These too are pathologies of the horizontal society.

The good society is, in some ways, easy to describe. It is a society of true pluralism, as far as that is possible. It is a society with respect for other people and their ways of life—their languages, religions, lifestyles. It is multicultural in the best sense of the word: different cultures and values mingle and enrich each other. This goal seems far off indeed—and further off in some countries than in others. Prejudice and ignorance are powerful enemies of the good society. Mix these old diseases with modern technology and modern communications, and you let loose a horror on the earth. What follows is Hitler—or Rwanda. So we come back, in the end, to where we started.

NOTES

Introduction

1. On the events in Rwanda, see, e.g., *New York Times,* Apr. 15, 1994, p. A3. The crisis went on for months and was extensively reported in the press. See also Prunier, *The Rwanda Crisis, 1959–1994.*

2. See Philip Gourevitch, "Letter from Rwanda: After the Genocide," *New Yorker,* Dec. 18, 1995, pp. 78–95.

3. This is not to say that people are incapable of killing other people within ethnic groups, though sometimes what is at root here is a subethnic group—a clan, family, or other agglomeration with a strong sense of identity. There are also many inglorious examples of persecutions on other bases by dictators and their cliques.

4. On this general subject, see Human Rights Watch, *Slaughter among Neighbors: The Political Origins of Communal Violence,* with chapters on Rwanda, India, the West Bank (Israel), South Africa, Romania, Sri Lanka, Kenya, the former Yugoslavia, Lebanon, and Armenia-Azerbaijan.

5. Taylor, *Sources of the Self,* p. 27.

6. See, e.g., Giddens, *Modernity and Self-Identity.*

7. Berger, Berger, and Kellner, *The Homeless Mind,* p. 77.

8. Lifton, *The Protean Self,* p. 1.

9. Isaacs, *Idols of the Tribe,* p. 38.

10. Lifton, *Protean Self,* p. 103.

11. On this point, see O'Neill, *Divorce in the Progressive Era.*

12. Although the Catholic Church, for example, is much more horizontal—more democratic, in fact—in the twentieth century than it was in the Middle Ages. This is true of most religious groups: what makes "sects" and "cults" so deviant is the fact that they control their members so tightly.

13. Berger, Berger, and Kellner, *The Homeless Mind,* p. 9.

14. On this point, see, e.g., Giddens, *Modernity and Self-Identity.*

15. See Friedman, *The Republic of Choice.*

16. See Barber, *Jihad vs. McWorld,* p. 179.

17. On the perils and dangers from the global economy, see Greider, *One World, Ready or Not.*

18. Barber, *Jihad vs. McWorld,* p. 16.

19. See, e.g., Martin Shapiro, "The Globalization of Law," *Indiana Journal of Global Legal Studies* 1: 37 (1993).

20. Friedman, *American Law,* p. 271.

Chapter 1: The Way We Live Now

1. Postman, *Amusing Ourselves to Death*, p. 74.

2. Ibid., p. 107.

3. Berger, Berger, and Kellner, *The Homeless Mind*, p. 67.

4. Berger, *Individualisierung*, p. 11; Berger, Berger, and Kellner, *The Homeless Mind*, p. 113.

5. Manchester, *A World Lit Only by Fire*.

6. One point should be made: change and instability are not the same. Indeed, in many of the rich Western countries, the public expects constant change in their lives, but not insecurity and instability. On this point, see Friedman, *Total Justice*.

7. As I write this, in the United States and many Western countries there is a backlash against big government, whose day (according to President Clinton) is over. Except for a handful of ideologues, however, most people in Western countries are perfectly happy with many aspects of big government and grumble only about marginal programs. Conservatives would like less regulation of the economy, but many want more regulation of morality and more vigorous attention to drugs, crime, and other social phenomena. The average person wants lower taxes but shows no inclination to give up the welfare state. True libertarians are a rare breed indeed.

8. Barber, *Jihad vs. McWorld*, p. 18.

9. See *New York Times*, Jan. 12, 1997, p. 1.

10. Alex Inkeles, "Linking the Whole Human Race: The World as a Communications System," in Sawyer, *Business in the Contemporary World*, pp. 133, 159, 160.

11. Before the dominance of what he calls "McWorld," as Barber points out, "the Swedes drove, ate, and consumed Swedish; the English drove, ate, and consumed English," and the rest of the world "either mirrored their colonial masters or developed domestic consumption economies around native products and native cultures" (Barber, *Jihad vs. McWorld*, p. 52).

12. Pells, *Not like Us*, p. 306.

13. Friedman, "Is There a Modern Legal Culture?" Of course, vast differences in legal culture remain and must be taken into account, despite "globalization" and "harmonization" of legal institutions; see Gessner, "Global Legal Interaction and Legal Cultures."

14. See, e.g., the discussion in Röhl and Magen, "Die Rolle des Rechts im Prozess der Globalisierung."

15. This definition is from Putnam, *Making Democracy Work*, p. 167; on the decline of social capital in the United States, see Putnam's article "Bowling Alone"; see also Putnam's "The Strange Disappearance of Civic America." Francis Fukuyama defines social capital as "a capability that arises from the prevalence of trust in a society or in certain parts of it. It can be embodied in the smallest and most basic social group, the family, as well as the largest of all groups, the nation, and in all the other groups in between" (Fukuyama, *Trust*, p. 26).

16. See Putnam's two articles, cited in the previous note. Putnam's facts and conclusions have not gone without challenge; see Lemann, "Kicking in Groups."

17. Tocqueville, *Democracy in America*, p. 513.

18. Nathaniel C. Nash, "For the Love of Elvis, a Tug-of-War," *New York Times,* Aug. 26, 1995, p. 4.

19. It must be constantly emphasized, of course, that all this is a matter of trends. The changes discussed are, perhaps, changes at the margins. This does not make them the less significant, to be sure.

20. Boorstin (*The Image,* p. 57) remarks that a celebrity is a "person who is known for his well-knownness. . . . He is the human pseudo-event." A "pseudo-event" is a "happening" that is "not spontaneous, but . . . planned" and that is "planned primarily . . . for the immediate purpose of being reported or reproduced" (p. 11). On celebrity culture, see Schickel, *Intimate Strangers* (1985); Friedman, *The Republic of Choice,* ch. 7.

21. Rein, Kotler, and Stoller, *High Visibility* (1987), pp. 5–15. This book is primarily a study of the way celebrity status is "manufactured." It stresses the fact that celebrity "generates substantial rewards for celebrities and their support systems" (p. 15).

22. There are signs that the role of the emperor has changed since the accession of the new emperor in the 1990s. The current emperor and his wife, for example, traveled to the United States in 1994, where they talked to ordinary people, and behaved very much like a European monarch would. See below, n. 45.

23. When the emperor of Japan, in 1945, broadcast to the Japanese public the announcement of Japan's imminent surrender, it was the first time anybody outside a small court circle had ever heard his voice.

24. The process began, perhaps, with Hollywood stars. They "had to be people who were acceptable in the home. An air of unapproachable mystery . . . might have worked well in the older medium, but not in the newer" (Fowles, *Starstruck,* p. 35).

25. Michelmore, *Einstein,* p. 24: "Young Albert was a flop as a schoolboy"; to the same effect, Wise, *Albert Einstein,* p. 7. Leithäuser, *Albert Einstein,* p. 7: "Einstein war alles andere als ein 'Wunderkind'"; but see Pais, *"Subtle Is the Lord,"* p. 37.

26. This was one of the themes of the 1995 movie *To Die For,* a black comedy about the desperate search of a young woman for celebrity status.

27. Fowles, *Starstruck,* p. 12.

28. The media frenzy in this case may have provoked a kind of backlash. The judge presiding over the retrial of the notorious trial of the Menendez brothers—who killed their parents—decided to get rid of the courtroom cameras (*New York Times,* Oct. 6, 1995, p. 9). The first trial had ended in a hung jury (none of the jurors thought the "boys" were innocent, but they could not agree on what they were guilty of). In the retrial, they were convicted (*Los Angeles Times,* Mar. 21, 1996, p. A1).

29. *Estes v. Texas,* 381 U.S. 532 (1965). A year later, the Court decided *Sheppard v. Maxwell,* 384 U.S. 333 (1966), which came up out of a sensational murder trial; here too the Court reversed because, in the Court's view, publicity and broadcasting had deprived the defendant of any chance at a fair trial.

30. The announcement of the verdict in the O. J. Simpson case drew one of the largest TV audiences in history; it was a day "the country stood still" (*New York Times,* Oct. 4, 1995, p. A1).

31. "O.J's Men about Town," *Newsweek,* Mar. 27, 1995, p. 55. One could ask, too, why Kaelin had even been invited to such a party, with members of the cabinet and other important people. But celebrities are, apparently, very important people themselves and can mix with any level of society.

32. Paul Gray, "What Price Camelot?" *Time,* May 6, 1996, pp. 66–73.

33. See Fine, "Scandal, Social Conditions, and the Creation of Public Attention."

34. There were many factors that help explain why the level of indignation against Simpson remained so low. The media treated the case as if it was a murder mystery; and in a murder mystery, the key item is puzzlement and suspense, not moral condemnation. In addition, many people, especially African Americans, were all too ready to believe that white people had framed Simpson, a black who had risen above his station, or that the police, who were notoriously racist, had planted the damning evidence.

35. Jack Curry, "Fallen Stars Rise Again," *New York Times,* June 25, 1995, sec. 4, p. 2. The other "fallen star" discussed in this article was a baseball player, Darryl Strawberry, who was suspended for sixty days for "substance abuse" and has been charged with income tax evasion. The New York Yankees "fervently pursued" him nonetheless and "made him the 11th-highest paid Yankee."

36. There were important precursors in the nineteenth century, with the rise of mass magazines and newspapers. Noteworthy were such rags as the *National Police Gazette,* a periodical devoted to sports figures and accounts of lurid crimes, with a hint of sex. The *Gazette* began to appear in the 1840s and lasted until the twentieth century.

37. Fowles, *Starstruck,* p. 165.

38. Perhaps, then, the point is rather one about the ranking of celebrities, since religious and political leaders have themselves become celebrities. Conceivably, the pope or the Dalai Lama might have made the list, but never the emperor of Japan. One does not "admire" a God.

39. Gamson, *Claims to Fame,* p. 189. "Like entertainers, politicians are coached, handled, wardrobed, made up, carefully lit. Publicity practitioners have a central role, often building a conventional celebrity sell."

40. Watson, *The Expanding Vista,* p. 2

41. Gamson, *Claims to Fame,* p. 190.

42. Meyrowitz, *No Sense of Place,* pp. 270–71. The "great leader image" depends on "mystification," but through television "we see too much of our politicians."

43. For data, see Hunter, *The State of Disunion.*

44. "German Tabloid Publishes Photo of Nude Prince Charles," *Los Angeles Times,* Sept. 8, 1994, p. A4.

45. Catherine S. Manegold, "In Japan's Imperial Roadshow, Signs of a More Relaxed Era," *New York Times,* June 27, 1994, p. A10.

46. *New York Times,* July 11, 1995, p. A5. A truck driver is quoted in this article as saying that Martinez was "a man of the people and a real leader" who could do "better" than the "professional politicians," who "haven't been worth a dime and haven't kept any of their promises."

47. Meg Greenfield, "Imitation Everything," *Newsweek,* Mar. 13, 1995, p. 82.

48. Of course, there is also a long tradition of radical egalitarianism in the United States, which foreign visitors continually noticed and remarked upon. This was not necessarily the kind of egalitarianism that, say, Marx had in mind but an egalitarianism of *manners*—what Americans despised was not people with money or power but people who acted "superior." De Tocqueville claimed that the wealthy in America were "almost entirely outside politics," that wealth was a disadvantage in politics. The rich man "goes to work in a dusty den in the middle of a busy town, where everyone is free to accost him. He meets his shoemaker passing in the street and they stop to talk to each other" (Tocqueville, *Democracy in America,* p. 179).

49. Millionaires can also throw around their own money, which, as campaigns come to be more and more dominated by television, is no small advantage. In addition, they either have or can buy name recognition, which is a vital ingredient of success.

50. Another example is the fate of the referendum and initiative system, whose most baroque development is in California. The elephantine ballot in California is crammed with "propositions" that the people have to vote on. This whole system was supposed to advance direct democracy. But you can only reach "the people" by billboards, direct mailings, and (above all) TV; hence the referendum system is just as much a prisoner of media politics and money, as the elections themselves—if not more so.

51. See, e.g., for the United States, Tomlins, *Law, Labor, and Ideology in the Early American Republic.*

52. Barber, *Jihad vs. McWorld,* p. 77.

53. Some political figures—notably Patrick Buchanan, during the American presidential campaign of 1996—did make some headway by complaining about corporate greed, loss of jobs, downsizing, and so on. But the enemy for Buchanan and other populists was not wealth or corporate power as such; the enemy was the global economy and a lack of patriotism, which allowed these corporations to export jobs to Mexico and Malaysia. The remedy was protectionism, not a politics of redistribution; see Chapter 3, this vol.

54. The leading American case is *Griswold v. Connecticut,* 381 U.S. 479 (1965), which struck down a Connecticut statute restricting birth control.

55. Spanish Constitution of 1978, art. 18 (i). I am indebted to Rodrigo Bustos Sierra for this and other citations on the European developments in privacy law.

56. Section 9 of the Civil Code protects the right to privacy. This section was added by way of an act of July 17, 1970. It reads: "Everyone has the right to respect for his private life"; judges are empowered to prescribe any measures, including injunction, "for the prevention or cessation of encroachment on the intimacy of private life."

57. See Ely, "The Wages of Crying Wolf."

58. The right of action is often traced to a famous article by Brandeis and Warren, "The Right to Privacy." Many courts are leery about granting such a right to people who have, voluntarily or unvoluntarily, gotten into the limelight; see *Haynes v. Alfred A. Knopf, Inc.,* 8 F. 3d 1222 (1993).

59. *Virgil v. Sports Illustrated,* 424 F. Supp. 1286 (D.C. S.D. Cal., 1976).

60. See, arguing for a narrower, more rigorous use of the term, Gavison, "Privacy and the Limits of Law."

61. See, e.g., Stuart Hall, "The Local and Global: Globalization and Ethnicity," in King, *Culture, Globalization and the World-System,* pp. 18, 27.

62. Barber, *Jihad vs. McWorld,* pp. 299–300.

63. See Willett, *The Americanization of Germany, 1945–1949;* Maase, *BRAVO Amerika.*

64. Blurring the lines between classes does not mean that there are no markers of status; Americans, Robert Wiebe argues, "came to rely" in judging people "upon shorthand devices that sort people by their surface characteristics: their skin color, their demeanor, their public habits" (Wiebe, *The Segmented Society,* p. 21).

65. See Price, "The Market for Loyalties," p. 667.

66. See "Strains in the Global Village," *Financial Times,* Feb. 16, 1996, p. 21; for an earlier discussion of the problem, see Josef Joffe, "Protection Isn't a Workable Remedy for Europe's Audiovisual Deficit," *International Herald Tribune,* Mar. 22, 1995, p. 8.

67. Howard Schneider, "Canada Drops U.S. Shows in Effort to Build Identity," *Washington Post,* Sept. 29, 1996, A30.

68. Barber, *Jihad vs. McWorld,* p. 83.

Chapter 2: A Revolution of Rights

1. On these points there is, of course, an enormous literature; on the idea of equality in the United States, see Pole, *The Pursuit of Equality in American History.*

2. Glendon, *Rights Talk,* p. 12. Glendon is critical of the American infatuation with entitlements and rights, which she thinks has dangerous consequences for American political and social life.

3. On differences between conceptions of rights in the two halves of Europe (before the collapse of the Soviet empire), see Markovits, "Law or Order: Constitutionalism and Legality in Eastern Europe."

4. On this point, see the striking differences in attitudes toward law between the former East Germany and the rest of the country, in Noelle-Neumann, "Rechtsbewusstsein im wiedervereinigten Deutschland."

5. See, in general, An-Na'im, ed., *Human Rights in Cross-Cultural Perspectives.*

6. See Obiora, "Bridges and Barricades."

7. Koh, *The United States and East Asia,* pp. 100–101.

8. Bauböck, *Transnational Citizenship,* p. 239.

9. Santos, "Toward a Multicultural Conception of Human Rights."

10. Seth Mydans, "Do Rights Come First? Asia and Europe Clash," *New York Times,* Mar. 1, 1996, p. A8.

11. See the perceptive essay by Panikkar, "Is the Notion of Human Rights a Western Concept?" approving *and* critiquing, from a Indian perspective, the notion of universal human rights.

12. Huntington, "The West," p. 28. Huntington argues that the West is unique and lists a number of "distinguishing characteristics" (pp. 30ff.) which set it apart from the rest of the world, including the "classical legacy," Christianity, separation of church and state, the rule of law, and "social pluralism and civil society."

13. Donnelly, *Universal Human Rights in Theory and Practice*, p. 61.

14. Weber, *Peasants into Frenchmen*.

15. Danielus, "The International Protection against Torture and Inhuman or Degrading Treatment," pp. 157–58.

16. See Langbein, *Torture and the Law of Proof*.

17. John Rockwell, "The New Colossus: American Culture as Power Export," *New York Times*, Jan. 30, 1994, sec. 2, p. 1.

18. This, of course, was the thesis of Max Weber's famous book *The Protestant Ethic and the Spirit of Capitalism*, which identified Protestantism as a crucial factor in the rise of capitalism. Much has been written about Weber's thesis, which is by no means universally accepted; see Eisenstadt, *The Protestant Ethic and Modernization*.

19. To be sure, missionaries are still active, but they have to tread much more carefully, and with more sensitivity to other cultures and religions, than they did in the nineteenth century.

20. Soysal, *Limits of Citizenship*, p. 116.

21. Quoted in Hollinger, *Postethnic America*, pp. 75–76.

22. Soysal, *Limits of Citizenship*, pp. 2, 3.

23. Jacobson, *Rights across Borders*, p. 133.

24. Indeed, it is now "widely accepted that the right to territorial integrity does not include the right to treat one's citizens as one pleases" (Gurr and Harff, *Ethnic Conflicts in World Politics*, p. 151). Of course, one can ask: "widely accepted" by whom? Certainly not by the government of mainland China or by the leaders in countries like Iraq and the Sudan.

25. Loescher and Scanlan, *Calculated Kindness*, p. 171.

26. See Wooldridge and Sharma, "International Law and the Expulsion of Ugandan Asians."

27. In fairness, it has to be pointed out that the United States, after 1945, accepted more than two million "aliens . . . outside of regular immigration channels" (Loescher and Scanlan, *Calculated Kindness*, p. 209); and of course more come in every year.

28. The German asylum provision is *Grundgesetz*, art. 16 (2): "Politisch Verfolgte geniesen Asylrecht." See Knopp, *Die Deutsche Asylpolitik* (1994).

29. See, e.g., Grubb, "Dealing with the Hate"; Knopp, *Die Deutsche Asylpolitik*.

30. See, e.g., Guild, *The Developing Immigration and Asylum Policies of the European Union*. A less noble witness is the fact that citizenship in many countries is, in a way, for sale: a person who has enough money to invest can become a permanent resident and eventually a citizen, regardless of quota or nationality.

31. Bierbrauer, "Rechtskulturelle Verständigungsprobleme," pp. 197, 199.

32. Ibid.

33. Rosenfeld, "Modern Constitutionalism as Interplay between Identity and Diversity," p. 3.

34. The several Soviet constitutions are translated and reproduced in Unger, *Constitutional Development in the USSR*.

35. There is, of course, a large literature on constitutionalism and the spread of judicial review. See, e.g., Jackson and Tate, *Comparative Judicial Review and Public Policy*.

36. See, e.g., Kommers, *The Constitutional Jurisprudence of the Federal Republic of Germany;* see Nevil Johnson, "Constitutionalism in Europe since 1945: Reconstruction and Reappraisal," in Greenberg et al., *Constitutionalism and Democracy,* p. 26.

37. Carl Baar, "Social Action Litigation in India: The Operation and Limits of the World's Most Active Judiciary," in Jackson and Tate, *Comparative Judicial Review and Public Policy,* p. 77.

38. *Marbury v. Madison,* 5 U.S. (1 Cranch) 137 (1803). On this case and the debates over judicial review which preceded it, see Haskins, *History of the Supreme Court of the United State,* vol. 2, *Foundations of Power: John Marshall, 1801–1815,* pp. 182–204.

39. See Friedman, *A History of American Law,* pp. 344–45; Gillman, *The Constitution Besieged.*

40. Two landmarks, of course, were *Brown v. Board of Education,* 347 U.S. 483 (1954), which outlawed racial segregation in public schools; and *Roe v. Wade,* 410 U.S. 113 (1973), which interpreted the "right of privacy" (itself a recent construct) as including a woman's right to an abortion, at least in the early months of pregnancy.

41. See the essays collected in Tate and Vallinder, *The Global Expansion of Judicial Power.*

42. See Barak-Erez, "From an Unwritten to a Written Constitution." The author sees a kind of "fundamental constitutional change" in Israel, which consists of the acceptance of the "concept of judicial review as applied to the legislature, including invalidation of statutes."

43. Maurice Sunkin, "The United Kingdom," in Tate and Vallinder, *Global Expansion of Judicial Power,* pp. 67, 69.

44. See Doris Marie Provine, "Courts in the Political Process in France," in Jacob et al., *Courts, Law, and Politics in Comparative Perspective,* p. 177.

45. See Liss, "A Mandate to Balance."

46. Berger, Berger, and Kellner, *The Homeless Mind,* p. 79.

47. Boorstin, *The Americans,* p. 89. Boorstin argues that the "old world . . . the world of the neighborhood community, was slipping away. In its place there was forming a world where more of the communities to which a man belonged were communities of the unseen" (p. 136). On the rise of consumerism, see Sandel, *Democracy's Discontent,* ch. 7.

48. I have expanded on this theme in *The Republic of Choice;* for the concept of expressive individualism, and its place in American culture, see Bellah et al., *Habits of the Heart.*

49. Similarly, though we hear a lot of talk about conformity, that in itself (paradoxically) testifies to the vigor of individualism; traditional societies did not worry about conformity—they gloried in it. And conformity always implies a *choice* to conform or not to conform. See Friedman, *Republic of Choice,* p. 128.

50. The literature is growing—on such questions as "litigiousness" and "claims-consciousness" and their relationship to culture and structure. See, e.g., Markesinis, "Litigation-Mania in England, Germany and the USA"; Robert A. Kagan, "Do Lawyers Cause Adversarial Legalism?"; Blankenburg, *Prozessflut?*

51. Berger, Berger, and Kellner, *The Homeless Mind,* p. 135.

52. Stokes, "A Theory of Slums."

53. On the shifting meaning of marriage, and consequently of divorce, in the United States, see O'Neill, *Divorce in the Progressive Era*.

54. On divorce in the United States, see Riley, *Divorce;* O'Neill, *Divorce in the Progressive Era*. On divorce in Europe, see Glendon, *The Transformation of Family Law*.

55. On the progress of divorce in the United States, see Friedman, "Rights of Passage."

56. On this law, see D'Antonio, *Il Divorzio*.

57. On the origins of the California developments, see Jacob, *Silent Revolution*.

58. E.g., California Civil Code, sec. 4056, which allows "dissolution" of a marriage (the word *divorce* is avoided) if there are "irreconcilable differences" between the parties, causing the "irremediable breakdown of the marriage." Practically speaking, this means divorce at the free and uncontestable option of either man or wife.

59. Riley, *Divorce,* p. 163.

60. Glendon, *Abortion and Divorce,* pp. 75–76; Glendon, *The Transformation of Family Law,* pp. 182–88.

61. Glendon, *Abortion and Divorce,* pp. 68–69.

62. Tamar Lewin, "Family Decay Global, Study Says," *New York Times,* May 30, 1995, p. A5.

63. Ibid.

64. "Speaking Of: The Changing Family," *Los Angeles Times,* July 3, 1990, p. H7.

65. Beck, *Risikogesellschaft.*

66. Beck, *Gegengifte,* p. 9.

67. See Nuclear Energy Agency, *Chernobyl—Ten Years On: Radiological and Health Impact* (1995).

Chapter 3: A Wealth of Nations

1. There is, of course, an enormous literature on nationalism and related concepts. Some of the works will be cited in the notes. Of particular interest are Hobsbawn, *Nations and Nationalism since 1780,* and Gellner, *Nations and Nationalism.* See also Pfaff, *The Wrath of Nations.*

2. Charles A. Kupchan, "Introduction: Nationalism Resurgent," in Kupchan, *Nationalism and Nationalities in the New Europe,* p. 1.

3. Harold Isaacs distinguishes between the "cultural" and the "political" definitions of a nation or nationality but points out, correctly, that these two views "do not appear or develop separately, but . . . wind in and out of the design, making different patterns as they go" (*Idols of the Tribe,* p. 177).

4. "As an ideological movement, nationalism seeks to attain and maintain the autonomy, unity and identity of a social group, some of whose members conceive it to constitute an actual or potential 'nation.' The aim of nationalism is always the creation of 'nations' or their maintenance and reinforcement." Nationalism refers, then, to the "existence of an identifiable community of culture" (Anthony D. Smith, *The Ethnic Revival,* p. 18).

5. Van den Berghe, *The Ethnic Phenomenon,* p. 25. Van den Berghe calls this kind of group an "ethny."

6. Gellner, *Nations and Nationalism,* p. 1; see also Hobsbawm, *Nations and Nationalism,* p. 9.

7. Anderson, *Imagined Communities,* p. 6. See also Roosens, *Creating Ethnicity.*

8. Weber, *Peasants into Frenchmen.*

9. Ibid., p. 486.

10. Baycroft, "Peasants into Frenchmen?"

11. See Ford, *Creating the Nation in Provincial France.*

12. Dittrich and Radtke, "Einleitung," pp. 11, 22.

13. On the role of such organizations as rifle clubs in Graubünden, Switzerland, see Jäger, *Bündnerisches Regionalbewusstsein und nationale Identität.*

14. The Russian government, however, has been reluctant to let the process of disintegration go any further. Within Russia itself, there are many large and small "autonomous republics" and "autonomous regions." Some of the larger ones have made noises about more autonomy—or outright independence. The basis of autonomy is, primarily, ethnic. The most troublesome case has been Chechnya—a region quite distinct in history, language, and religion. The Russians moved in an army to stamp out the independence movement, at great cost in blood, money, and prestige. They did not succeed. Chechnya won a kind of creeping independence, although the Russians do not openly admit the fact.

15. Gellner, *Nations and Nationalism.*

16. Ibid., pp. 140–41.

17. Gellner, *Encounters with Nationalism,* p. 42. Gellner stresses language here, but not only language: "An Englishman is expected not merely to speak the language of Shakespeare, but also to be white. . . . Poles or Croats are meant to be Catholic" (pp. 42–43).

18. See the discussion in Fishman, Mayerfeld, and Fishman, "'Am and Goy' as Designations for Ethnicity in Selected Books of the Old Testament."

19. Anthony D. Smith, *The Ethnic Origin of Nations;* the quote is from p. 216.

20. It is also a fact that many of these Magyars and Slavs—especially Magyars—live *inside* Romania and hence have a different slant on Romanian nationalism.

21. Isaacs, *Idols of the Tribe,* p. 123.

22. Hobsbawm, *Nations and Nationalism since 1780,* p. 54.

23. For Europe, see, e.g., Haarman, *Soziologie und Politik der Sprachen Europas.*

24. A similar process can be found elsewhere in Europe. Portuguese is a language, but Gallego, trapped inside Spain, is struggling to survive and gain recognition. It obviously is helpful to a stranded linguistic minority to have a powerful homeland elsewhere, but it would be hard to predict whether Germanic speechways will survive in northern Italy and in Alsace-Lorraine.

25. The same is true for Macedonian and Bulgarian and for Moldovan and Romanian; no doubt there are other examples. Whether these end up as languages or dialects will depend entirely on political events in the future.

26. Quoted in Isaacs, *Idols of the Tribe,* p. 103.

27. Ibid., p. 109.

28. Each of these, in turn, is a synthesis—Spanish is really Castillian (as indeed it is

often called by its speakers), the survivor in a battle of many competing versions of Iberian Latin.

29. Weber, *Peasants into Frenchmen,* p. 67.

30. Vos, "Shifting Nationalism," pp. 136–137.

31. Mencken, *The American Language.*

32. Chris Hedges, "In the Balkans, Three Languages Now Fight It Out," *New York Times,* May 15, 1996, p. A4.

33. Hardgrave, "India," pp. 71, 73.

34. On these points, the fundamental book is Hobsbawm and Terence Ranger, *The Invention of Tradition.*

35. See *Texas v. Johnson,* 491 U.S. 397 (1989); Johnson had burned a flag as a political protest and was arrested and convicted under a Texas law against desecrating the flag. The Supreme Court threw out his conviction, on free-speech grounds. See Alan Brinkley, "Old Glory: The Saga of a National Love Affair," *New York Times,* July 1, 1990, sec. 4, p. 2.

36. Eric Hobsbawm, "Introduction: Inventing Traditions," in Hobsbawm and Ranger, *Invention of Tradition,* p. 14.

37. Anthony D. Smith, *The Ethnic Origins of Nations,* p. 24. These are myths of "spatial and temporal origins, of migration, of ancestry and filiation, of the golden age, of decline and exile and rebirth" (p. 25).

38. Van Evera, "Hypotheses on Nationalism and War."

39. Fitzgerald, *America Revised.*

40. Anthony D. Smith, *The Ethnic Origins of Nations,* p. 180.

41. Carrillo, "Surface and Depth."

42. Israeli history in general glorifies ancient Israel and largely ignores the long history of the Jews in the Diaspora—not to mention the centuries when Israel (Palestine) was mostly a country without many Jews at all. And see the discussion of Romanian history, Chapter 2, this vol.

43. Slotkin, *Gunfighter Nation,* pp. 5–6.

44. See Anderson, *Imagined Communities,* pp. 199–206; Hobsbawn and Ranger, *Invention of Tradition.*

45. Thus the enormous hoopla over the "history standards," prepared by a task force at the National Center for History in the Schools, at the University of California at Los Angeles; these standards were flayed by conservatives as too negative or as having a "non-Western," politically correct slant. The United States Senate rushed to condemn the standards. See John Patrick Diggins, "History Standards Get It Wrong Again," *New York Times,* May 15, 1996, A21; *New York Times,* Apr. 5, 1995, p. B1.

46. Horowitz, *Ethnic Groups in Conflict,* p. 57. Horowitz goes on to say that "group members often call each other brothers and call distantly related groups cousins."

47. Possibly, too, the "highly fragmented political culture" is partly to be blamed on the deliberate policy of the colonial powers, who sought to "institutionalize conflicts and to strengthen centrifugal forces rather than to nurture and cement national unity" (Okoth-Ogendo, "Constitutions without Constitutionalism," pp. 65–69). Certainly, it was not in

the interests of, say, France or England to advance a sense of national unity in African colonies.

48. Davidson, *The Black Man's Burden,* p. 201.

49. Perez-Perdomo, "La Organización del Estado en Venezuela en el Siglo (1830–1899)," pp. 389–92.

50. On this point, see Weber, *Peasants into Frenchmen.*

51. On the rise of Honduras, see, in general, Perez-Brignozi, *A Brief History of Central America.* There were other formative elements, some fairly mundane, such as petty squabbles over power. The American Revolution was a potent example, of course, in Latin America. The nation of Honduras, it must be remembered, does not necessarily mean much to some of the people who live there, especially indigenous people.

52. This statement was made at a press conference, *United Nations Monthly Chronicle,* Feb. 1970, p. 36.

53. Mayall, *Nationalism and International Society,* p. 122.

54. Isaacs, *Idols of the Tribe,* p. 176.

55. But what kind of a nation? Although virtually everybody in Austria, according to a poll, thought Austria was in fact a nation, almost half (45 percent) would not rule out another *Anschluss* with Germany. Austrian nationalism is both "late" and "forced" (Menasse, *Das Land Ohne Eigenschaften,* pp. 91–92). See also Burghardt and Matis, *Die Nation-Werdung Österreichs.*

56. See, e.g., Heidt, *Mass Media, Cultural Tradition, and National Identity.*

57. Conzen et al., "The Invention of Ethnicity," pp. 3, 9.

58. There are, of course, new ghettos—the term now refers almost exclusively to black neighborhoods; the more recent immigrant groups, like the older ones, tend to cluster in distinctive, compact districts.

59. See, e.g., Espiritu, *Asian American Panethnicity.*

60. An article in the *New York Times* describes how an immigrant from the Philippines, in 1969, "began to realize he was Asian" after encountering discrimination (Norimitsu Onisha, "Merging Identity—a Special Report: New Sense of Race Arises among Asian-Americans," May 30, 1996, p. 1). Before that he had "identified himself only as a Filipino"; prejudice turned his sense of ethnicity into one of race.

61. Hinnenkamp, "'Gastarbeiterlinguistik' und die Ethnisierung der Gastarbeiter," p. 277.

62. Castles, *Here for Good,* p. 96.

63. See, e.g., the discussion in Nassehi, "Der Fremde als Vertrauter: Soziologische Beobachtungen zur Konstruktion von Identitäten und Differenzen."

64. For this incident, see Christiansen and Barnartt, *Deaf President Now!*

65. The literature, of course, is enormous. See, among other things, Burleigh and Wippermann, *The Racial State.*

66. Moynihan, *Pandaemonium,* p. 5.

67. On these, see Upham, *Law and Social Change in Postwar Japan,* ch. 3.

68. Not to mention the Revolutionary War itself. A large part, to be sure, came peacefully, through buying and selling: the Louisiana Purchase and Alaska.

69. On the Kurds, see Gurr and Harff, *Ethnic Conflict in World Politics*, pp. 27–43 and passim.

70. Even Hitler does not quite fit the traditional imperialist mold. He justified his conquests in terms very different from, say, a medieval king; he claimed to speak on behalf of the German nation, and the conquered people were to be, in part, annihilated and in part simply used as slaves of the German people. Even the worst colonialists of the nineteenth century had some dim notion of bringing civilization or religion to the heathens. See Winthrop D. Jordan, *The White Man's Burden*.

71. The "political cohesion necessary for democracy cannot be achieved without the people determining themselves to be 'the nation'" (Nodia, "Nationalism and Democracy," pp. 3, 8).

72. For a particularly insightful discussion, see Heller, "Modernity, Membership, and Multiculturalism."

73. Disraeli, *Sybil*. Interestingly, the phrase has been used to refer to the racial divide in the United States (Hacker, *Two Nations*).

74. See, e.g., Gellner, *Encounters with Nationalism*, ch. 1.

75. Quoted in ibid., p. 13.

76. See Robert Kaplan, "The Coming Anarchy," *New Yorker*, Feb. 1994, p. 44.

77. See Berger, "Vom Klassenkampf zum Kulturkonflikt," p. 119.

78. Thus Hayek described nationalism as nothing but "tribal sentiments"; quoted in Miller, *On Nationality*, p. 5.

79. Lipset, "Predicting the Future of Post-Industrial Society," pp. 9–11.

80. Robertson, "Social Theory, Cultural Relativity and the Problem of Globality," pp. 69, 77.

81. Though it should be pointed out that the *extreme* nationalists do form a kind of subnation—and a dangerously disloyal one at that. In the name of national patriotism, the fringe groups seem willing to destroy what is left of national unity. They are certainly sworn enemies of a pluralism which, whatever its ideological position, is a demographic *fact*.

Chapter 4: Big Fish and Little Fish

1. Berger, Berger, and Kellner, *The Homeless Mind*, p. 177.

2. Gurr and Harff, *Ethnic Conflict in World Politics*, p. 15.

3. This group is discussed in ibid., pp. 43–52.

4. See, e.g., Levy, "Classifying Cultural Rights," p. 22. Levy is mainly interested in the rights that fall short of secession, such as "exemptions" (allowing Sikhs to wear turbans instead of motorcycle helmets; p. 25).

5. In Estonia, almost a third of the population in the 1990s was made up of ethnic Russians; few of these people spoke Estonian. But the Russian language had "lost any official standing" and was "being phased out as a main language for education" ("Baltics: Them and Us," *Economist*, Aug. 17, 1996, p. 67).

6. And within the European Union, a "separatist" group does not have to separate from

Europe—after all, if Luxembourg can be independent but tied in to its neighbors, why not Catalonia? Thus Catalonia can "boast" that it is a "country in Europe"; it can integrate "itself into Europe precisely by segregating itself from Spain," by insisting that its people were not Spaniards, but Catalonians—yet Catalonians "*are* Europeans—better Europeans than the Spanish!" (Barber, *Jihad vs. McWorld,* p. 174).

7. There is an organization, Iatiku, which concerns itself with endangered languages; some of this information is derived from the newsletter of this organization.

8. See, e.g., Miller, *God Has Ninety-Nine Names;* Choueiri, *Islamic Fundamentalism.*

9. American and other Western fundamentalists do not, of course, reject the West, but they do reject many aspects of modernity.

10. See Hobsbawm and Ranger, *Invention of Tradition.*

11. Berger and his colleagues argue that a "congregation of Tibetan Buddhist monks, let us say, transplanted to the United States, can start using electric razors without thereby altering the character of their social relations" (*The Homeless Mind,* p. 183). True enough; but the electric razors and all the other technological tools will, in the end, alter consciousness—this *has* to be the case. The current Dalai Lama, a genuinely spiritual and deeply religious man, is nonetheless different in important ways from his predecessors.

12. See, e.g., Pommersheim, *Braid of Feathers,* esp. ch. 3, "The Crucible of Sovereignty," pp. 61–98; on an earlier period, see Harring, *Crow Dog's Case.*

13. Pub. L. No. 90–284, 82 Stat. 77 (codified at 25 U.S.C. secs. 1301–41, 1988).

14. *Santa Clara Pueblo v. Martinez,* 436 U.S. 49 (1978); see Christofferson, "Tribal Courts' Failure to Protect Native American Women."

15. Ibid., p. 59.

16. See, e.g., Gluckman, *The Ideas in Barotse Jurisprudence.*

17. There is an enormous literature on the subject; see, e.g., Asiedu-Akrofi, "Judicial Recognition and Adoption of Customary Law in Nigeria"; Obiora, "Reconsidering African Customary Law." For general overviews, see Kuper and Kuper, *African Law;* Morse and Woodman, *Indigenous Law and the State.*

18. See Cutshall, *Justice for the People,* pp. 1–5.

19. Innes, *Creating the Commonwealth,* p. 97.

20. On this point, see Chanock, *Law, Custom, and Social Order;* Obiora, "(En)gaging Nationalism, Traditionalism, and Gender Relations."

21. Obiora, "(En)gaging Nationalism," p. 587.

22. *Benally v. The Navajo Nation, The Navajo Reporter Series* 5: 209, 213 (1986).

23. Matsuda, "Law and Culture in the District Court of Honolulu, 1844–1845." .

24. G. Grasmann, quoted (with disapproval) in Baum, "Rechtsdenken, Rechtssystem und Rechtswirklichkeit in Japan," pp. 259–260.

25. For an insightful discussion, focusing mainly on Korea, of the relationship between law and "culture," see Yoon, *Law and Political Authority in South Korea,* ch. 1.

26. See the essays collected in Eisenstadt and Ben-Ari, *Japanese Models of Conflict Resolution.*

27. See Landa, "A Theory of the Ethnically Homogeneous Middleman Group: An Institutional Alternative to Contract Law," ch. 5 of *Trust, Ethnicity, and Identity.*

Chapter 5: Insiders and Outsiders

1. Espiritu, *Asian American Panethnicity.*

2. On this process in general, and particularly its legal aspects, see Minow, *Making All the Difference.*

3. See Pool, *Eve's Rib;* Rhode, *Theoretical Perspectives on Sexual Difference.*

4. Herrnstein and Murray, *The Bell Curve.*

5. On this point, see Friedman, *The Republic of Choice.*

6. *Race,* of course, is an extremely slippery term. I use it in its modern sense; in the nineteenth century, the Irish and the Italians—and most of what we call nationalities—were often called races. This fact has had legal consequences in the United States—see, e.g., *St. Francis College v. Al-Khazraji,* 481 U.S. 604 (1987) (discrimination against an Arab-American as race discrimination); *Shaare Tefila Congregation v. Cobb,* 481 U.S. 615 (1987) (the same question with regard to Jews).

7. See, in general, Burleigh and Wippermann, *The Racial State,* esp. the chart on p. 47.

8. The quote is from Galanter, *Competing Equalities,* p. 7 n; see also Pandey, *The Caste System in India.*

9. Gould, *Mismeasure of Man.*

10. See Haller, *Eugenics;* Pickens, *Eugenics and the Progressives.* On these sterilization laws, see Friedman, *Crime and Punishment in American History,* pp. 335–39.

11. An important early study was Dugdale, *"The Jukes."* See also Rennie, *The Search for Criminal Man.*

12. Quoted in Rennie, *The Search for Criminal Man,* p. 67.

13. Hooton, *Crime and the Man,* pp. 212, 230, 367, 374.

14. Davis, *Who Is Black?* p. 21.

15. See Lawrence Wright, "One Drop of Blood," *New Yorker,* July 25, 1994, p. 46.

16. The rest of the states presumably did not care or did not define the term. See Spickard, *Mixed Blood,* pp. 374–75.

17. Under a Virginia statute of 1662, children were to be "bond or free only according to the condition of the mother" (*Hening's Virginia Statutes,* vol. 2, p. 170).

18. There was also some traffic the other way: white women who had sexual relations with black men; this was surely less common, and more highly stigmatized—even murderously so—after the Civil War (Hodes, *White Women, Black Men*).

19. Paine, *Six Years in a Georgia Prison,* pp. 155–56.

20. See, e.g., Daniel A. Novak, *The Wheel of Servitude.*

21. See Wright, "Who's Black, Who's White, and Who Cares."

22. Ibid.; see also Tom Morgenthau et al., "What Color Is Black?" *Newsweek,* Feb. 13, 1995, p. 62, which mentions that an organization known as the Association of MultiEthnic Americans is "lobbying Washington to add a multiracial category to the questionnaire for the next census."

23. S. L. Bachman, "California Leads Nation in Mixed-Race Marriages," *San Jose Mercury News,* June 22, 1996, p. 20A.

24. At one time there were signs of a third category, mulatto; and shades of color have made a considerable difference *within* the black community. On this point, see Spickard,

Mixed Blood, pp. 271–72, 317–22; on a colonial Virginia definition of mulattoes, see Morris, *Southern Slavery and the Law, 1619–1860,* pp. 22–23.

25. See "New Rules for Marking Racial Identity," *San Francisco Chronicle,* Dec. 26, 1997, p. 1.

26. Goldin, *Making Race;* Jacobson, *The Cape Coloured.* For a look at the position of coloreds in the new era, see James, *Now That We Are Free.*

27. Degler, *Neither Black nor White,* pp. 102–3.

28. Karen de Witt, "Black Unity Finds Voice in Colombia," *New York Times,* Apr. 18, 1995, p. A4.

29. Office of Management and Budget, Statistical Policy Directive 15, "Race and Ethnic Standards for Federal Statistics and Administrative Reporting," 43 *Federal Register* 19,260 (1978). The directive contemplates two ways of collecting data: the best way, according to the directive, is to "separate race and ethnic categories," so that a black Hispanic, for example, would be recorded as both black and Hispanic, and a white of Scandinavian descent as both white and "Not of Hispanic origin." The other method is to combine the two criteria, so that there would be a category "Black, not of Hispanic origin," another called "Hispanic," and a third, "White, not of Hispanic origin." Basically, then, there is a five-fold classification which, as David Hollinger puts it, has "come to replicate the popular color-consciousness of the past: black, white, red, yellow, and brown." He refers to this as "today's ethno-racial pentagon" (Hollinger, *Postethnic America,* p. 32). For a discussion of Directive 15, see National Research Council, Committee on National Statistics, *Spotlight on Heterogeneity: The Federal Standards for Racial and Ethnic Classification: Summary of a Workshop* (Washington, D.C.: National Academy Press, 1996).

30. Office of Business and Management, Statistical Policy Directive 15. There are a number of technical problems with this definition—where does it leave native Hawaiians, for example? Do they fit in with Native Americans, or are they Pacific Islanders?

31. Indian General Allotment (Dawes) Act, 24 Stat. 388, chap. 119 (1887); see, e.g., Parman, *Indians and the American West in the Twentieth Century,* on the dismal results of the Dawes Act and what followed.

32. See Chapter 4, this vol.

33. Recognition may come from a treaty or from some other action of the executive branch of government. The Bureau of Indian Affairs, in 1978, laid down rules to determine whether or not a tribe would be recognized. See Kim, "The Indian Federal Recognition Administrative Procedures Act of 1995."

34. On this case, see Torres and Milun, "Translating Yonnondio by Precedent and Evidence"; Carrillo, "Identity as Idiom"; Minow, *Making All the Difference,* pp. 351–56. The case is *Mashpee Tribe v. Town of Mashpee,* 447 F. Supp. 940; aff'd sub nom. *Mashpee Tribe v. New Seabury Corp.,* 592 F2d 575 (1st Cir.), cert. denied, 444 U.S. 866 (1979).

35. Torres and Milun, "Translating Yonnondio by Precedent and Evidence"; see Carrillo, "Riverrun," pt. 3.

36. National Research Council, *Spotlight on Heterogeneity,* p. 33.

37. Minow, *Making All the Difference,* p. 355.

38. Although, as we have seen, this is much less a matter of biology than of (complex)

social constructions. And David Hollinger, in *Postethnic America,* p. 124, has argued that "the religious model" might be usefully applied "for ethno-racial cultures," rather than the other way around.

39. Hollinger, *Postethnic America,* p. 7. Hollinger in fact would like to replace the word *identity* with *affiliation,* to get away from the idea of "fixity and givenness"; and he distinguishes between "prescribed and chosen affiliations." As he puts it, the black writer Alex Haley, in his book *Roots,* "might have chosen to trace his father's ancestry back to Ireland rather than his mother's back to Gambia. But this choice was phony, of course, for the blackness in Haley's skin was understood to rule his white heritage inconsequential" (pp. 7–8). This, then, is "prescribed" affiliation.

40. Of course, socially it may matter a great deal; and whether one was Muslim, Catholic, or Orthodox in Bosnia mattered legally and in every other way, including life and death.

41. Hollinger, *Postethnic American,* p. 124.

42. The Germans never adopted a "one-drop" rule for Jews (corresponding to the American "one-drop" rule for blacks), and it was not fatal to have *some* Jewish blood, so long as one did not actively practice the religion and did not identify with the Jewish community. But of course even priests and nuns who had too much "Jewish blood" were in danger of ending up in the death camps.

43. Israel's Law of Return (1950) states that "every Jew has the right to come to this country as an *oleh.*" (An "oleh," meaning literally "one who goes up," is a person who makes "aliya," that is, who immigrates to Israel.) The Law of Return did not define Jew but did grant to the Minister of Immigration the right to exclude anyone "engaged in an activity directed against the Jewish people" or "likely to endanger public health or the security of the State." This English version of the text is from Oscar Kraines, *The Impossible Dilemma,* p. 95.

44. On this point, see Lahave, *Judgment in Jerusalem,* ch. 12. In Israel, after independence was gained, "the secular and religious camps achieved a cease-fire, known as the status quo" (ibid., p. 197). Religious and family matters went to religious courts, all other matters to the secular courts.

45. The "Brother Daniel" case is *Rufeisen v. Minister of the Interior* (1962), reprinted (in English) in Asher F. Landau, ed., *Selected Judgments of the Supreme Court of Israel* (special vol., 1971), p. 1; see Eisenstadt, *Israeli Society,* pp. 314–15. Questions have also been raised as to whether certain groups who are outside the mainstream of Jewish life but define themselves as Jews are to be so considered in Israel. There are, for example, the Benei Israel, a small group from India; on this problem, see Eisenstadt, pp. 312–14; Dominguez, *People as Subject, People as Object,* pp. 174–77.

46. On this case, see Lahav, *Judgment in Jerusalem,* chap. 12.

47. On the "Russlanddeutsche" in general, see Dietz, *Zwischen Anpassung und Autonomie.* There were some two million of these "Russian" Germans at the time of the breakup of the Soviet Union; only a minority of them actually spoke German.

48. See Douglas B. Klusmeyer, "Aliens, Immigrants, and Citizens," pp. 99–101.

49. "Baltics," *Economist,* Aug. 17, 1996, p. 67.

50. Stephen Kinzer, "Fretful Latvians Turn to German with a Racist Past," *New York Times,* Oct. 17, 1995, p. A13.

51. On this point in American history, see Wiebe, *The Segmented Society,* p. 53.

52. Vetterling-Braggin, *"Femininity," "Masculinity," and "Androgyny,"* pp. 33, 36.

53. On the panethnic feeling of Asians, see Chapter 3, this vol.

Chapter 6: Citizens and Strangers

1. On this point, see Soysal, *Limits of Citizenship.*

2. The notary public case is *Bernal v. Fainter,* 467 U.S. 216 (1984). The other cases are *In Re Griffiths,* 413 U.S. 717 (1973) (nonresidents practicing law); *Sugarman v. Dougall,* 413 U.S. 614 (1974) (state civil service); *Examining Board of Engineers v. Flores de Otero,* 426 U.S. 572 (1976) (civil engineers); *Graham v. Richardson,* 403 U.S. 364 (1971) (welfare benefits for resident aliens). Technically, the issue is whether or not, and to what extent, the Fourteenth Amendment protects aliens, or to be more precise, how much of the mantle of "equal protection" covers aliens as well as citizens.

3. In *Ambach v. Norwick,* 441 U.S. 68 (1979), a bare majority of the United States Supreme Court held that states "may refuse to employ as elementary and secondary school teachers aliens who are eligible for United States citizenship but who refuse to seek naturalization"; *Foley v. Connelie,* 435 U.S. 291 (1978); *Cabell v. Chavey-Salido,* 454 U.S. 432 (1982).

4. See Soysal, *Limits of Citizenship;* Jacobson, *Rights Across Borders.*

5. "Information on Norwegian Citizenship" (English version of a pamphlet given out by the Norwegian government), p. 6. The brochure is from the 1990s but is undated. I am indebted to Brian Pearce for this brochure.

6. White, *The Roman Citizenship.*

7. The Fourteenth Amendment states: "All persons born . . . in the United States . . . are citizens of the United States and of the State wherein they reside."

8. Solberg, *Immigration and Naturalization.* Most immigrants to Argentina were from Italy and Spain.

9. The exceptions are children of foreigners who are in Chile in the service of their government and children of foreigners who are in Chile temporarily; even the latter can choose Chilean citizenship. Roberto Mayorga, "Die Rechtsstellung von Ausländern nach staatlichem Recht und Völkerrecht in Chile," in Frowein and Stein, *Die Rechtsstellung von Ausländern nach staatlichem Recht und Völkerrecht,* vol. 1, pp. 187, 189.

10. On French citizenship law, see Brubaker, *Citizenship and Nationhood in France and Germany;* see also Guendelsberger, "Access to Citizenship for Children Born within the State to Foreign Parents."

11. See Bade, *Vom Auswanderungsland zum Einwanderungsland? Deutschland, 1880–1980,* pp. 29–32.

12. See Chapter 4, this vol.

13. The phrase is "deutsche Volkszugehörigkeit" (*Grundgesetz,* art. 116). See Knopp, *Die Deutsche Asylpolitik,* pp. 15–18.

14. Hailbronner, "Citizenship and Nationhood in Germany," in Brubaker, *Immigration and the Politics of Citizenship in Europe and North America*, pp. 67, 73. Hailbronner also points out that the Federal Republic wanted to "accommodate the millions of ethnic Germans who were driven out of Eastern Europe in the years immediately following" the Second World War. This led them to a blood-line definition of "German." The rule was supposed to be "transitional"; but it is significant that it survived the transition period and remained in full flower.

15. Swedish Citizenship Act (1950); unofficial translation. I am indebted to Brian Pearce for this reference.

16. 1 Stat. 103–4 (act of Mar. 26, 1790). Resident children of the new citizen, under the age of twenty-one, automatically became citizens as well. For the debates on this act, see Franklin, *The Legislative History of Naturalization in the United States,* ch. 3.

17. 1 Stat. 414–15 (act of Jan. 29, 1795). The new citizen had to renounce "any hereditary title" or "orders of nobility." The act did not apply to aliens then resident in the United States, for whom the old two-year residence rule still applied. On the debates, see Franklin, *Legislative History,* chap. 5.

18. The basic principle of German citizenship law is that dual citizenship is "to be avoided and decreased." See Ziemske, *Die deutsche Staatsangehörigkeit nach dem Grundgesetz,* pp. 140–47.

19. See Tan, "Dual Nationality in France and the United States," p. 447. .

20. At one time, the United States insisted that a naturalized citizen lost his or her citizenship if the citizen voted in a foreign election, served in a foreign army, and so on—an obvious example of an "either-or" mentality. The Supreme Court, however, refused to denaturalize a naturalized American who voted in an Israeli election (*Afroyim v. Rusk,* 387 U.S. 253 [1967]).

21. To be sure, the development of the European Union implies, in the first place, a kind of dual citizenship; on the implications of community law for dual citizenship, see Evans, "Nationality Law and European Integration," pp. 194–97.

22. Spain: Civil Code, art. 22 (4); see Garcia, *La Reforma de la Nacionalidad,* p. 77.

23. StbG 1985 (Austria), sec. 11: "Die Behörde hat sich bei der Ausübung des ihr . . . eingeräumten freien Ermessens von Rücksichten auf das allgemeine Wohl, die öffentlichen Interessen und das Gesamtverhalten der Partie leiten zu lassen" (The authorities are to be guided, in the exercise of their discretion, by considerations of the general good, the public interest, and the overall behavior of the person in question). I am indebted to Kurt Wagner for this reference.

24. DeGroot, *Staatsangehörigkeit in Wandel,* pp. 168–69; on Swiss immigration policy and related matters, see Hoffman-Nowotny, "Switzerland," in Hammar, *European Immigration Policy,* p. 206.

25. Ireland, *The Policy Challenge of Ethnic Diversity,* pp. 198–99.

26. Foote, "Japan's Foreign Workers' Policy," pp. 707, 710, 725.

27. See Immigration Act of 1971, secs. 1 (1), 2 (6).

28. Macdonald and Blake, *Immigration Law and Practice in the United Kingdom,* pp. 93–109.

29. British Nationality Act of 1981, sec. 39.

30. Macdonald and Blake, p. 109.

31. Alen, *Treatise on Belgian Constitutional Law,* p. 349.

32. Ibid., p. 350: the "procureur du Roi" can object, under article 15 of the Nationality Law, "s'il y a des raisons . . . d'estimer que la volonté d'intégration du déclarant est insuffisante" (if he has reason to believe that the declarant's intent is insufficient).

33. Cornelius, "Japan: The Illusion of Immigration Control," in Cornelius, Martin, and Hollifield, *Controlling Immigration,* pp. 375, 395–97.

34. On legal culture, see Friedman, *The Legal System,* pp. 193 ff. See also Goldberg and Attwooll, "Legal Orders, Systemic Relationships and Cultural Characteristics: Towards Spectral Jurisprudence," in Örücü, Attwooll, and Coyle, *Studies in Legal Systems,* p. 313.

35. Legal culture is thus closely related to the concept of "legal consciousness" and perhaps also to "legal ideology," see, e.g., Merry, "Everyday Understandings of the Law in Working-Class America."

36. See, in general, Friedman, *A History of American Law;* Potter, *People of Plenty.*

37. Cf. Milton M. Gordon, *Assimilation in American Life,* esp. p. 89; Gordon lists three "philosophies" of "assimilation," which he calls "Anglo-conformity," the "melting pot," and "cultural pluralism." The three phases I describe in the text differ in many details from Gordon's three philosophies. In particular, I think it makes sense to treat the "melting pot" phase as the only phase that can genuinely be called assimilationist. Nonetheless, I want to express my debt to this wise and important book.

38. The chronologies, of course, are not to be taken too literally.

39. There is an enormous literature on slavery, growing all the time. A recent comprehensive account of the law of slavery is Morris, *Southern Slavery and the Law, 1619–1860.*

40. On the status of free blacks, see, e.g., Litwack, *North of Slavery.*

41. Rogers Smith, *Civil Ideals,* p. 165.

42. Ibid. p. 210.

43. The states, by and large, had similar guarantees in their own constitutions.

44. Heresy had been a crime in some colonies—Massachusetts Bay, for example. Anabaptists and Jesuits were liable to be banished for their "damnable heresies, tending to the subversion of the . . . Faith" (Friedman, *Crime and Punishment in American History,* p. 32).

45. Milton M. Gordon, *Assimilation in American Life,* p. 88, feels that Anglo-conformity—under which "the English language, and English-oriented cultural patterns" were "dominant and standard," was intimately bound up with nativism. He refers, for example, to the "fever" of Americanization during the period of the first World War, and the movement to "strip the immigrant of his native culture . . . and make him over into an American along Anglo-Saxon lines" (p. 99).

46. See Feldberg, *The Turbulent Era;* Gilje, "The Baltimore Riots of 1812 and the Breakdown of the Anglo-American Mob Tradition."

47. Hennessey, *American Catholics,* pp. 118–27.

48. See, e.g., Wilbur Miller, *Cops and Bobbies.*

49. On the legal travails of the Mormons, see Firmage and Mangrum, *Zion in the Courts.*

50. *Reynolds v. United States,* 98 U.S. 145 (1878).

51. Sarah Barringer Gordon, "The 'Twin Relic of Barbarism.'"

52. Quoted in Friedman, *Crime and Punishment in American History,* p. 480*n.*

53. The incident is recounted in Levy, *Blasphemy,* p. 255. On blasphemy laws and prosecutions in the American colonies in general, see Levy, pp. 238–71.

54. *State v. Chandler,* 2 Del. (2 Harr.) 553 (1837).

55. *People v. Ruggles,* 8 Johns. 290 (N.Y., 1811); see Levy, *Blasphemy,* pp. 401–6.

56. Bryk, Lee, and Holland, *Catholic Schools and the Common Good,* pp. 24–25.

57. Nelson, "The Changing Meaning of Equality in Twentieth-Century Constitutional Law," p. 54.

58. Quoted in Milton M. Gordon, *Assimilation in America,* p. 120.

59. Glazer, "Reflections on Citizenship and Diversity," in Jacobsohn and Dunn, *Diversity and Citizenship,* pp. 98–99.

60. I owe this phrase, of course, to Gunnar Myrdal's famous book *An American Dilemma: The Negro Problem and Modern Democracy* (1944).

61. Gould, *The Mismeasure of Man;* Smedley, *Race in North America,* chap. 11.

62. Pole, *The Pursuit of Equality in American History,* p. 288.

63. Matthews, quoted in "Are We Still Anglo-Saxons?" p. 32.

64. Immigration Act of 1924, 43 Stat. 153, ch. 190 (act of May 26, 1924).

65. The term *plural equality,* as I use it, has a certain similarity to Milton Gordon's third theory of assimilation, which he calls "cultural pluralism." He defines it as a notion which "postulated the preservation of the communal life and significant portions of the culture of . . . immigrant groups" (Gordon, *Assimilation in American,* p. 85).

66. One might perhaps distinguish, as Adeno Addis does, between two types of pluralism. "Paternalistic pluralism" tolerates and actively tries to protect the culture of minorities—protecting this culture mostly from its "own actions which threaten to annihilate the minority"; but the majority culture does not seriously engage in a "creative and constant dialogue" with the minority culture. The minority culture is treated as a kind of endangered species. "Critical pluralism," on the other hand, commits resources to "enable the minority culture to flourish" but takes that culture seriously—as an equal partner in cultural "dialogue" (Addis, "Individualism, Communitarianism, and the Rights of Ethnic Minorities," pp. 620–21).

67. See Minow, *Making All the Difference.* Minow criticizes the assumptions underlying the idea that some people are "different"; this implies a norm, from which they deviate (e.g., black people are not white). She proposes instead treating differences as "relational." "Who or what should be taken as the point of reference for defining differences is debatable. There is no single, superior perspective" (pp. 52–53). This is, on the whole, the philosophy behind plural equality.

68. Castles and Miller, *The Age of Migration,* p. 39.

69. Nomi Maya Stolzenberg, "He Drew a Circle that Shut Me Out," p. 666.

70. Jones, *American Immigration*, p. 276.

71. In practice in the northern states; only in theory in the southern states. In many ways, enfranchisement of blacks in, say, Mississippi was a product of the 1960s.

72. On this development, see Friedman, *A History of American Law*, pp. 209–11.

73. See Friedman, *The Republic of Choice*.

74. And, specifically, for a pure form of sign language, which does not simply ape English word order but uses the "grammatical markers and sentence structure" of sign language itself. See Christiansen and Barnartt, *Deaf President Now!* p. 201. At Gallaudet University (for the deaf), after the 1988 "revolution" (see above, Chapter 3), sign language policy at the school changed, so that now most staff positions, even "secretaries, cafeteria workers, or security officers," would be required to have a certain "minimal skill level" in sign, although the implementation of this rule has been somewhat problematic (ibid). The resemblance of this "language policy" to that pursued by, say, Estonians with regard to Russians is obvious and striking.

75. See *Adarand Constructors, Inc. v. Pena*, 115 S. Ct. 2907 (1995).

76. The case is *Hopwood v. State of Texas*, 78 F3d 932 (C.A. 5, 1996). This federal case technically applies only in the Fifth Circuit, which includes Texas. The Supreme Court refused to hear an appeal from this decision.

77. Hunter, *State of Disunion*, vol. 2, table 46a.

78. There are strong reactions, though less strident, to prisoners' rights, and even to students' rights.

79. Karst, *Law's Promise, Law's Expression*, p. 202.

80. Lawrence, "Race, Multiculturalism, and the Jurisprudence of Transformation," p. 829.

81. See Chapter 2, this vol.

82. Ransby, "Columbus and the Making of Historical Myth," p. 86.

83. See, e.g., Strickland, "Strangers in a Strange Land."

84. Maass, "San Jose's Latinos Howl about Plans for a 'Conquest Statue,'" *Los Angeles Times,* July 14, 1990, p. A28.

85. Jane M. Adams, "Aztec Serpent Sculpture Has Opponents Baring Fangs," *Chicago Tribune*, Oct. 10, 1993, p. 23. The opponents even took the matter to court (see *San Francisco Examiner*, Nov. 17, 1994, p. B4), claiming the statue "violated the First Amendment ban on government establishment of religion", but the court was not sympathetic.

86. See *New York Times*, Nov. 12, 1997, p. A1. Of course, any dramatic change in regime brings about wholesale renaming of streets, pulling down of monuments, and the like. Thus Leopoldville became Kinshasa, St. Petersburg became Leningrad and then St. Petersburg again. See also Eckert, "Strassenumbenennung und Revolution in Deutschland," in Jesse and Löw, *Vergangenheitsbewältigung*, p. 45.

87. On the history and present controversy over the status of English in the United States, see Baron, *The English-Only Question*.

88. Ibid., pp. 74–83.

89. 262 U.S. 390 (1923). In the companion case, *Bartels v. Iowa*, 262 U.S. 404 (1923), the Supreme Court also struck down the statutes of Iowa and Ohio; the Ohio statute specif-

ically prohibited use of the German language. The Nebraska situation is discussed at length in Ross, *Forging New Freedoms.*

90. *Lau v. Nichols,* 414 U.S. 563 (1974).

91. For an overview of the legal complexities, see Moran, "The Politics of Discretion."

92. Nebraska Constitution, art. 1, sec. 27.

93. The current language statute is Illinois Compiled Statutes Annotated (ICSA) 5:460/20; the square-dance law is ICSA 5:460/65; the fossil law is ICSA 5:460/60. There is also, for example, an "official State prairie grass" ("Big Bluestem"; ibid., 460/55), not to mention state slogans, birds, trees, and fish.

94. California Constitution, art. 3, sec. 6, making English the official language, was adopted as an initiative ballot measure. I note, however, as a California resident, that the state sends out a booklet in both Spanish and English as a guide to voters and that the written test for drivers may be taken in Spanish as well as English.

95. Hawaii Constitution, art. 15, sec. 4. But "Hawaiian shall be required for public acts and transactions only as provided by law."

Chapter 7: Immigration and Its Discontents

1. For the most part, these residents must be *legally* in the country. However, the "amnesty" provisions of the American immigration law of 1986, 100 Stat. 3359 (act of Nov. 6, 1986) made it possible for illegal aliens—there are millions in this category—to convert themselves into regular citizens.

2. There is a huge literature on immigration and immigration law. See, e.g., Archdeacon, *Becoming American;* Calavita, *U.S. Immigration Law and the Control of Labor, 1820–1924;* Jones, *American Immigration.* There are also works on specific ethnic groups—e.g., Hing, *Making and Remaking Asian America through Immigration Policy, 1850–1990.*

3. The words are those of Chief Justice John Marshall, in *Jefferson v. McIntosh,* 21 U.S. (8 Wheat.) 543, 590 (1823), an important case on Native American land rights. The "subsistence" of the tribes "was drawn chiefly from the forest. To leave them in possession of their country, was to leave the country a wilderness."

4. See Reed Ueda, "Naturalization and Citizenship," in Easterlin et al., *Immigration,* p. 106.

5. But in immigration and naturalization law (and practice), there were racial restrictions and provisions on criminals, paupers, and the diseased, so that at least one author has described the idea of "open borders" as a "myth" (Neuman, *Strangers to the Constitution,* p. 3). For a comprehensive overview of the history of citizenship law, see Rogers M. Smith, *Civil Ideals.*

6. See Chapter 5, this vol.

7. The Alien Act was 1 Stat. 570 (act of June 25, 1798); it gave the president authority to order out of the country such aliens as he might "judge dangerous to the peace and safety of the United States," or against whom he might have "reasonable grounds" to suspect of

involvement in "treasonable or secret machinations against the government." The act of June 18, 1798, 1 Stat. 566, stiffened the rules of naturalization.

8. 2 Stat. 153 (act of April 14, 1802), setting up new procedures for naturalization, and repealing all the prior laws.

9. Steinberg, *The Ethnic Myth*, p. 11.

10. Archdeacon, *Becoming America*, pp. 80–81.

11. Lowe, *Ku Klux Klan;* Chalmers, *Hooded Americanism.*

12. Evans, "The Klan's Fight for Americanism," p. 40. According to Evans, "the Nordic Americans" realized that "the melting pot was a ghastly failure" and remembered "that the very name was coined by a member of one of the races—the Jews—which most determinedly refuses to melt."

13. For a stimulating exposition of such a viewpoint, see Heller, "Immigration and Regulation," in Bustamante et al., *U.S.–Mexico Relations*, p. 41.

14. Evans, "The Klan's Fight for Americanism," p. 60.

15. On the rise of segregation, see the classic study by Woodward, *The Strange Career of Jim Crow; Plessy v. Ferguson* is 163 U.S. 537 (1896). Here the Supreme Court approved of segregation, that is, the separation of the races, provided the facilities were "equal." This was, of course, always a myth. On the *Plessy* case, see Lofgren, *The Plessy Case.*

16. See Tsai, *The Chinese Experience in America;* Heizer and Almquist, *The Other Californians,* ch. 7.

17. Thus Justice Field, in *Chae Chan Ping v .United States,* 130 U.S. 581 (1889), upholding the law of 1888, remarked that the Chinese "retained the habits and customs of their own country . . . without any interest in our country or its institutions." He agreed that "the presence of foreigners of a different race in this country, who will not assimilate with us," was "dangerous to . . . peace and security."

18. The laws in question are 22 Stat. 58 (act of May 6, 1882); 25 Stat. 476 (act of Sept. 13, 1888); 27 Stat. 25 (act of May 5, 1892); and 32 Stat. 176 (act of Apr. 29, 1902). See, in general, Hing, *Making and Remaking Asian America through Immigration Policy;* Salyer, *Laws Harsh as Tigers.*

19. On this movement, see Haller, *Eugenics;* Pickens, *Eugenics and the Progressives.*

20. *United States v. Bhagat Singh Thind,* 261 U.S. 204 (1923).

21. Notably *Downes v. Bidwell,* 182 U.S. 244 (1901) (on the Revenue Clause of the Constitution and its applicability to Puerto Rico). See Kerr, *The Insular Cases;* Thompson, *The Introduction of American Law in the Philippines and Puerto Rico, 1898–1905,* ch. 7.

22. See Cabranes, *Citizenship and the American Empire.*

23. *Downes v. Bidwell,* 182 U.S. 244, 287 (1901).

24. In 1893, Frederick Jackson Turner published his famous essay "The Significance of the Frontier in American History," which argued for the influence of the frontier on American character and society—and also proclaimed that the frontier was dead.

25. On the immigrant as "villain," see Calavita, *U.S. Immigration Law and the Control of Labor,* pp. 103–13. Calavita argues that the "New England elite" were the spearheads of the anti-immigrant movement, and that "race-minded eugenicists . . . provided it with a

pseudoscientific basis"; it was financed by "leading capitalists." But the politics of immigration control were more complex. Many businessmen were, in fact, happy with imported labor. And the labor unions were, on the whole, enemies of immigration, as Calavita herself points out.

26. See, in general, Preston, *Aliens and Dissenters;* Murray, *Red Scare;* Polenberg, *Fighting Faiths.*

27. The Mann Act is 36 Stat. 825 (act of June 25, 1910); for a comprehensive study of the background and interpretation of this law, see Langum, *Crossing Over the Line.*

28. On the background of this act, see Daniels, *Not Like Us.* Congress passed an immigration law in 1917, over President Wilson's veto, which imposed a literacy test on immigrants (ibid., p. 80).

29. Archdeacon, *Becoming American,* chs. 6 and 7.

30. Lieberman, *Are Americans Extinct?* p. 101.

31. On this program, see Calavita, *Inside the State,* p. 180. For an analogous program in Germany, with regard to Polish labor, see Bade, *Vom Auswanderungsland zum Einwanderungsland?* ch. 2.

32. Goethe, "Other Aspects of the Problem," pp. 767, 768. The "problem" was Mexican immigration; Goethe's article appeared in *Current History* immediately after an article by Stowell, "The Danger of Unrestricted Mexican Immigration."

33. Steinberg, *The Ethnic Myth,* p. 34.

34. Krane, *International Labor Migration in Europe,* p. 169. The only other country to absorb a significant number of Portuguese emigrants was the United States.

35. See Fukuyama, *Trust,* pp. 295 ff. Fukuyama finds a high level of "trust" among Asian immigrant groups and explains the economic success of these groups largely in these terms.

36. See Hans-Joachim Hoffmann-Nowotny, "Weltmigration—Eine Soziologische Analyse," in Kälin and Moser, *Migrationen aus der Dritten Welt,* p. 29.

37. Collinson, *Europe and International Migration,* p. 3. As of 1996, there were more than 24 million foreign born in the United States (U.S. Bureau of the Census, *Statistical Abstract of the United States, 1997,* U.S. Department of Commerce, Washington, D.C., table 55, p. 53).

38. Inkeles, *National Character,* p. 216.

39. Anthony D. Smith, *The Ethnic Origins of Nations,* p. 176. "In our descendants' memory lies our hope," he adds (p. 208).

40. See Chapter 3, this vol.

41. Immigration and Nationality Act of 1952, ch. 477, sec. 201(a), 66 Stat. 163, 175 (act of June 27, 1952, usually referred to as the McCarran-Walter Act).

42. Immigration and Nationality Act Amendments of 1965 (act of Oct. 3, 1965), 79 Stat. 911; see also Gabriel J. Chin, "The Civil Rights Revolution Comes to Immigration Law."

43. Freeman and Jupp, "Comparing Immigration Policy in Australia and the United States," p. 4.

44. See Immigration Restriction Act (1901); see also Willard, *A History of the White Australia Policy to 1920.* The "white Australia" policy was abandoned only in the 1970s. See Gibney, *Open Borders? Closed Societies?*

45. New Zealand, Immigration Restriction Act, 1908, no. 78, sec. 14, sec. 42; Wearing, *Immigration Law in New Zealand and the USA.*

46. See Philip Shenon, "Darwin Journal: Bitter Aborigines Sue for Stolen Childhoods," *New York Times,* July 20, 1995, p. A4.

47. Marilyn Lake, "The Meaning of 'Self' in Claims for Self-Government: Re-claiming Citizenship for Women and Indigenous People in Australia," in Arup and Marks, *Cross Currents,* pp. 9, 11.

48. New Zealand enacted a national quota system in 1920, a few years earlier than the United States. All persons of British or Irish stock had free entry, but others needed an "entry permit," and these were doled out in accordance with the quota system.

49. Joseph H. Carens, "Nationalism and the Exclusion of Immigrants: Lessons from Australian Immigration Policy," in Gibney, *Open Borders? Closed Societies?* pp. 41, 55.

50. Stephen S. Castles, "Australian Multiculturalism: Social Policy and Identity in a Changing Society," in Freeman and Jupp, *Nations of Immigrants,* pp. 184, 190.

51. Quoted in Castles, *Here for Good,* pp. 204–5.

52. On this story, see Celestine Bohlen, "Italians Contemplate Beauty in a Caribbean Brow," *New York Times,* September 10, 1996, p. A3.

53. "Belgium: Holding Together," *Economist,* May 27, 1995, p. 44; Tyler Marshall, "Voter Disillusionment a Boon to European Fringe Parties," *Los Angeles Times,* May 23, 1995, p. 6; John Palmer, "Far Right has Limited Gains in Belgian Poll," *The Guardian,* May 22, 1995, p. 10. I am indebted to Peter Bouckaert for these references.

54. Personal Responsibility and Work Opportunity Reconciliation Act of 1996, Public Law 104–93, 110 Stat. 2105, sec. 402(a) (act of Aug. 22, 1996).

55. The platform was adopted Aug. 12, 1996. It reads in part: "We support a constitutional amendment or constitutionally-valid legislation declaring that children born in the United States of parents who are not legally present in the United States or who are not long-term residents are not automatically citizens."

56. See, e.g., *New York Times,* May 8, 1995, p. A4; Michael Janofsky, "Skinhead Violence Is Worldwide and Growing, a Report Finds," *New York Times,* June 28, 1995, p. A11. On the mushrooming growth in the 1990s of skinhead violence in Germany, see Jaschke, *Rechtsextremismus und Fremdenfeindlichkeit,* especially p. 79.

57. The end of the cold war may have contributed to the problem, at least in the opinion of some scholars; that great event led to the loss of a clearly defined enemy; at this point, the foreigners become the enemy and the scapegoat (Löchte and Sill, *Rechtsextremismus bei westdeutschen Jugendlichen,* p. 14).

58. Barry James, "Immigration to France Unchanged in Twenty Years," *International Herald Tribune,* Feb. 28, 1997, p. 6.

59. "150,000 Protest in France against Immigration Clampdown," *Agence France Presse,* Feb. 22, 1997.

60. John Litchfield, "Coalition Survives as France Eases Strict Immigration Curbs," *Independent* (London), Dec. 18, 1997, p. 16.

61. Alan Riding, "France, Reversing Course, Fights Immigrants' Refusal to Be French," *New York Times,* Dec. 5, 1993, p. 1. An earlier "crisis" occurred in 1989, when three Moroccan girls insisted on their scarves; this led to an uproar that was defused when the King of Morocco "ordered the girls to remove the offending scarves" (James F. Hollifield, "Immigration and Republicanism in France: The Hidden Consensus," in Cornelius et al., *Controlling Immigration,* pp. 143, 166).

62. See, e.g., "New Terrorist Bomb in Paris," *New York Times,* Oct. 18, 1995, p. A2.

63. Cornelius et al., *Controlling Immigration.*

64. Karst, *Law's Promise, Law's Expression,* p. 3.

65. By "domination" I do not refer necessarily to physical domination—certainly not for a country like the United States, which was fragmented politically, had no real ruling class in the English or French sense, and was decentralized with a vengeance. "Domination" in this country was "spread throughout America. An elite monopolized power segment by segment . . . and almost always received their exceptional benefits piece by piece. If they made the system work for them, they did so side by side, not together" (Wiebe, *The Segmented Society,* pp. 134–35).

66. See Chapter 6, this vol.

67. Fund-raising letter from U.S. English, Inc., dated July 18, 1995, received by the author (and thousands of others no doubt). One Mauro E. Mujica signed the letter—presumably a Hispanic, who insisted that it was not his purpose "to ban Spanish or any other language from being spoken. I myself speak Spanish at home and in some of my business dealings."

68. Etzioni, *The Spirit of Community,* p. 247.

69. Howard, *Human Rights and the Search for Community,* p. 109. Howard claims that this view "ignores the liberating aspects of individualism and forgets that collectivities can be highly oppressive social entities."

70. See, on the historical meaning of "community," Bender, *Community and Social Change in America;* Wiebe, *The Segmented Society.*

71. Ford, "The Repressed Community: Locating the New Communitarianism," *Transition,* issue 65 (1995).

72. 104 Stat. 327 (act of July 26, 1990). For a history of the origins and adoption of this law, see Burgdorf, "The Americans with Disabilities Act."

73. California voters, for example, voted in favor of "Proposition 209" in November 1996, a referendum to ban affirmative action in the public sector of California.

74. Quoted in Burgdorf, "The Americans with Disabilities Act," p. 414*n*3.

75. Anthony D. Smith, *The Ethnic Revival,* pp. 163–64.

76. Koen Lenaerts, "Constitutionalism and the Many Faces of Federalism," p. 237.

77. Keith Spicer, "Canada: Values in Search of a Vision," in Earle and Wirth, *Identities in North America,* p. 13; Hugh Donald Forbes, "Canada: From Bilingualism to Multiculturalism," in Diamond and Plattner, *Nationalism, Ethnic Conflict, and Democracy,* p. 88.

78. Price, "The Market for Loyalties."

79. Ibid., p. 670.

80. Ignatieff, *Blood and Belonging*, pp. 6–7.

81. Rose, "Fixing the Wheel," p. 616.

82. 8 U.S.C.A., sec. 1153 (5). Visas are to be made available to "qualified immigrants" who seek to enter the United States "for the purpose of engaging in a new commercial enterprise . . . which will create full-time employment for not fewer than 10 United States citizens or [lawful resident] aliens"; under a subsection of this section, the "capital" required is a minimum of one million dollars. The alien entrepreneur cannot "buy an apartment worth $1 million, which produces income solely in rents" or "buy stocks and bonds worth a million." You have to put ten people to work (Lewis, *How to Get a Green Card*, sec. 20, p. 3).

83. 11 U.S.C.A., sec. 1153 (b) (1) (A); 11 U.S.C.A., sec. 1153 (b) (1) (C).

Chapter 8: Beyond Ethnicity

1. Meyrowitz, *No Sense of Place*, p. 238. "What a young child knew about the world was once determined primarily by where the child lived and was allowed to go," but in the world of TV, this is no longer the case (p. 237).

2. Espiritu, *Asian American Panethnicity*, p. 6.

3. To be sure, nobody would have considered it surprising to move in the opposite direction—that is, from Buddhism to Christianity; and the missionaries of the West spent enormous amounts of time, money, energy, and propaganda to make this happen.

4. Seel, "Reading the Post-Modern Self," p. 39.

5. Soysal, *Limits of Citizenship*, p. 161.

6. Thrasher, *The Gang*.

7. Spencer, "Age-Sets, Age Grades and Age-Generation Systems" p. 25.

8. Ignatieff, *Blood and Belonging*, pp. 5–9.

9. Arguing *Brown v. Board of Education* before the United States Supreme Court, Thurgood Marshall also made the point that "there are Negroes as white as the drifted snow, with blue eyes, and they are just as segregated as the colored man." Quoted in Amsterdam, "Thurgood Marshall's Image of the Blue-Eyed Child in *Brown*," p. 232.

10. Gotanda, "A Critique of 'Our Constitution Is Color-Blind,'" p. 60.

11. See Richard Cummings, "All-Male Black Schools"; Jarvis, "*Brown* and the Afrocentric Curriculum."

12. Nicholas D. Kristof, "Outcast Status Worsens Pain of Japan's Disabled," *New York Times*, Apr. 7, 1996, sec. 1, p. 3.

13. See, e.g., Olsen, "Legal Responses to Gender Discrimination in Europe and the USA."

14. The literature, of course, is very large. On the United States, see Rhode, *Justice and Gender*; on the EU, see Darmon and Huglo, "L'egalité de traitement entre les hommes et les femmes dans la jurisprudence de la Cour de justice des Communautés européenes: un

univers en expansion." Article 119 of the EEC Treaty requires each member state to "maintain . . . the principle that men and women should receive equal pay for equal work." See Ellis, *European Community Sex Equality Law.*

15. See, e.g., Lucke, "Der Gesetzgeber und die Frauen."

16. Some states—e.g., California—have dropped from the penal code all laws against same-sex relationships, at least for consenting adults. In 1986, the Supreme Court of the United States refused to declare sodomy laws unconstitutional, in *Bowers v. Hardwick,* 478 U.S. 186, 106 S. Ct. 2841 (1986). But there is a clear trend toward decriminalization. In 1992, the Kentucky Supreme Court joined the list, striking down the sodomy laws of that state (*Commonwealth v. Jeffrey Wasson,* 842 S. W. 2d 487 [Ky., 1992]).

17. See Edwards, "Australia," p. 53.

18. The Age Discrimination in Employment Act was enacted in 1967, 81 Stat. 602 (act of Dec. 15, 1967); 29 U.S.C., sec. 621. See Friedman, *Your Time Will Come,* on the origins and social significance of this statute.

19. Age Discrimination in Employment Amendments of 1986, 100 Stat. 3342, 3344 (act of Oct. 31, 1986); 29 U.S.C., secs. 623, 624. The abolition of mandatory retirement was effective Jan. 1, 1987, though tenured university faculty did not come under the act until Jan. 1, 1994. Few countries, if any, besides the United States and Canada seem to be serious about age discrimination; and pressure in most European countries, plagued by high unemployment, is for *lowering* the retirement age, in order to spread the work.

20. The Americans with Disabilities Act is 104 Stat. 328, 42 U.S.C. 1210 (act of July 26, 1990). A disability is defined as a "physical or mental impairment that substantially limits one or more of the major life activities" of a person (42 U.S.C., sec. 12102 [2] [A]).

21. 1992 Aust. Act. 135, sec. 3.

22. The phrase was used by Jacobson, *Rights across Borders.*

23. See Friedman, "Is There a Modern Legal Culture?"

24. Soysal, *Limits of Citizenship,* p. 3.

Chapter 9: Some Concluding Remarks

1. Friedman, *The Republic of Choice.*

2. See Human Rights Watch, *Slaughter among Neighbors.*

3. See V. P. Gagnon, Jr., "Serbia's Road to War," in Diamond and Plattner, *Nationalism, Ethnic Conflict, and Democracy,* p. 117.

4. McCann, *Rights at Work,* pp. 304, 306.

BIBLIOGRAPHY

Addis, Adeno, "Individualism, Communitarianism, and the Rights of Ethnic Minorities," *Notre Dame Law Review* 67: 615 (1992).

Alen, André, *Treatise on Belgian Constitutional Law*. Deventer: Kluwer Law and Taxation Publishers, 1992.

Amsterdam, Anthony G., "Thurgood Marshall's Image of the Blue-Eyed Child in Brown," *New York University Law Review* 68: 226 (1993).

An-Na'im, Abdullahi Ahmed, ed., *Human Rights in Cross-Cultural Perspectives: A Quest for Consensus*. Philadelphia: University of Pennsylvania Press, 1992.

Anderson, Benedict, *Imagined Communities: Reflections on the Origin and Spread of Nationalism*. Rev. ed. London: Verso, 1991.

Archdeacon, Thomas J., *Becoming American: An Ethnic History*. New York: Free Press, 1983.

"Are We Still Anglo-Saxons? *Literary Digest*, Sept. 9, 1992, p. 31.

Arup, Christopher, and Lee Ann Marks, eds., *Cross Currents: Internationalism, National Identity and Law*. Melbourne: La Trobe University Press, 1996.

Asiedu-Akrofi, Derek, "Judicial Recognition and Adoption of Customary Law in Nigeria," *American Journal of Comparative Law* 37: 571 (1989).

Baar, Carl, "Social Action Litigation in India: The Operation and Limits of the World's Most Active Judiciary," in Donald W. Jackson and C. Neal Tate, eds., *Comparative Judicial Review and Public Policy*. Westport, Conn.: Greenwood Press, 1992, p. 77.

Bade, Klaus J., *Vom Auswanderungsland zum Einwanderungsland? Deutschland, 1880–1980*. Berlin: Colloquium-Verlag, 1983.

Barak-Erez, Daphne, "From the Unwritten to a Written Constitution: The Israeli Challenge in American Perspective," *Columbia Human Rights Law Review* 26: 309 (1995).

Barber, Benjamin R., *Jihad vs. McWorld*. New York: Times Books, 1995.

Baron, Dennis, *The English-Only Question: An Official Language for Americans?* New Haven: Yale University Press, 1990.

Bauböck, Rainer, *Transnational Citizenship: Membership and Rights in International Migration*. Brookfield, Vt.: E. Elgar, 1994.

Baum, Harald, "Rechtsdenken, Rechtssystem und Rechtswirklichkeit in Japan," *Rabels Zeitschrift für ausländisches und internationales Privatrecht* 59: 258 (1995).

Baycroft, T. P., "Peasants into Frenchmen? The Case of the Flemish in the North of France, 1870–1914," *European Review of History* 2: 31 (1995).

Beck, Ulrich, *Gegengifte: Die organisierte Unverantwortlichkeit*. Frankfurt: Suhrkamp, 1988.

———, *Risikogesellschaft*. Frankfurt: Suhrkamp, 1986.

Bellah, Robert, et al., *Habits of the Heart: Individualism and Commitment in American Life*. Berkeley: University of California Press, 1985.

Bender, Thomas, *Community and Social Change in America.* New Brunswick, N.J.: Rutgers University Press, 1978.

Berger, Hartwig, "Vom Klassenkampf zum Kulturkonflikt—Wandlungen und Wendungen der westdeutschen Migrationsforschung," in Eckhard J. Dittrich and Frank-Olaf Radtke, eds., *Ethnizität: Wissenschaft und Minderheiten.* Opladen: Westdeutcher Verlag, 1990, p. 119.

Berger, Peter A., *Individualisierung: Statusunsicherheit und Erfahrungsvielfalt.* Opladen: Westdeutcher Verlag, 1996.

Berger, Peter L., Brigitte Berger, and Hansfried Kellner, *The Homeless Mind: Modernization and Consciousness.* New York: Random House, 1973.

Bierbrauer, Günter, "Rechtskulturelle Verständigungsprobleme: Ein rechtspsychologisches Forschungsprojekt zum Thema Asyl," *Zeitschrift für Rechtssoziologie* 11 :197 (1990).

Blankenburg, Erhard, ed., *Prozessflut?* Cologne: Bundesanzeiger, 1988.

Boorstin, Daniel J., *The Americans: The Democratic Experience.* New York: Vintage, 1973.

———, *The Image: A Guide to Pseudo-Events in America.* New York: Atheneum, 1961.

Brandeis, Louis, and Samuel Warren, "The Right to Privacy," *Harvard Law Review* 4: 193 (1890).

Brubaker, Rogers, *Citizenship and Nationhood in France and Germany.* Cambridge: Harvard University Press, 1992.

Brubaker, William Rogers, ed., *Immigration and the Politics of Citizenship in Europe and North America.* Lanham, Md.: University Press of America, 1989.

Bryk, Anthony S., Valerie E. Lee, and Peter B. Holland, *Catholic Schools and the Common Good.* Cambridge: Harvard University Press, 1993.

Burgdorf, Robert L., Jr., "The Americans with Disabilities Act: Analysis and Implications of a Second-Generation Civil Rights Statute," *Harvard Civil Rights-Civil Liberties Law Review* 26: 413 (1991).

Burghardt, Anton, and Herbert Matis, *Die Nation-Werdung Österreichs: Historische und Soziologische Aspekte.* Vienna: Österreichische Gesellschaft für Wirtschaftssoziologie, 1976.

Burleigh, Michael, and Wolfgang Wippermann, *The Racial State: Germany, 1933– 1945.* Cambridge: Cambridge University Press, 1991.

Bustamante, J., et al., *U.S.–Mexico Relations: Labor Market Interdependence.* Stanford: Stanford University Press, 1992.

Cabranes, José A., *Citizenship and the American Empire: Notes on the Legislative History of the United States Citizenship of Puerto Ricans.* New Haven: Yale University Press, 1979.

Calavita, Kitty, *Inside the State: The Bracero Program, Immigration, and the I.N.S..* New York: Routledge, 1992.

———, *U.S. Immigration Law and the Control of Labor, 1820–1924.* London: Academic Press, 1984.

Carens, Joseph H., "Nationalism and the Exclusion of Immigrants: Lessons from Australian Immigration Policy," in Mark Gibney, ed., *Open Borders? Closed Societies? The Ethical and Political Issues.* New York: Greenwood Press, 1988, p. 41.

Carrillo, Jo, "Identity as Idiom: Mashpee Reconsidered," *Indiana Law Review* 28: 511 (1995).

————, "Riverrun: Three Essays about the Uses of History in Legal Problems concerning Native Americans," J.S.D. diss., Stanford University School of Law, 1996.

————, "Surface and Depth: Some Methodological Problems with Bringing Native American-Centered Histories to Light," a review of Oren Lyons et al., *Exiled in the Land of the Free: Democracy, Indian Nations, and the U.S. Constitution, New York University Review of Law and Social Change* 20: 405 (1993).

Castles, Stephen S., "Australian Multiculturalism: Social Policy and Identity in a Changing Society," in Gary P. Freeman and James Jupp, eds., *Nations of Immigrants: Australia, the United States, and International Migration.* New York: Oxford University Press, 1992, p. 184.

————, *Here for Good: Western Europe's New Ethnic Minorities.* London: Pluto Press, 1984.

Castles, Stephen, and Mark J. Miller, *The Age of Migration: International Population Movements in the Modern World.* New York: Guilford Press, 1993.

Chalmers, David, *Hooded Americanism: The First Century of the Ku Klux Klan.* Garden City, N.Y.: Doubleday, 1965.

Chanock, Martin, *Law, Custom, and Social Order: The Colonial Experience in Malawi and Zambia.* Cambridge: Cambridge University Press, 1985.

Chin, Gabriel J., "The Civil Rights Revolution Comes to Immigration Law: A New Look at the Immigration and Nationality Act of 1965," *North Carolina Law Review* 75: 273 (1996).

Choueiri, Youssef M., *Islamic Fundamentalism.* Boston: Twayne Publishers, 1990.

Christiansen, John B., and Sharon N. Barnartt, *Deaf President Now! The 1988 Revolution at Gallaudet University.* Washington, D.C.: Gallaudet University Press, 1995.

Christofferson, Carla, "Tribal Courts' Failure to Protect Native American Women: A Reevaluation of the Indian Civil Rights Act," *Yale Law Journal* 101: 169 (1991).

Collinson, Sarah, *Europe and International Migration.* London: Pinter Publishers, 1993.

Conzen, Kathleen N., et al., "The Invention of Ethnicity: A Perspective from the U.S.A.," *Journal of Ethnic History* 12: 3 (1992).

Cornelius, Wayne A., "Japan: The Illusion of Immigration Control," in Wayne A. Cornelius, Philip L. Martin, and James F. Hollifield, eds., *Controlling Immigration: A Global Perspective.* Stanford: Stanford University Press, 1994, p. 375.

Cornelius, Wayne A., Philip L. Martin, and James F. Hollifield, *Controlling Immigration: A Global Perspective.* Stanford: Stanford University Press, 1994.

Cummings, Richard, "All-Male Black Schools: Equal Protection, the New Separatism, and *Brown v. Board of Education,"* *Hastings Constitutional Law Quarterly* 20: 725 (1993).

Cutshall, C. R., *Justice for the People: Community Courts and Legal Transformation in Zimbabwe.* Mount Pleasant, Harare, Zimbabwe: University of Zimbabwe Publications, 1991.

D'Antonio, Adriana, *Il Divorzio.* Padua: Cedam, 1983.

Daniels, Roger, *Not Like Us: Immigrants and Minorities in America, 1890–1924*. Chicago: Ivan R. Dee, 1997.

Danielus, Hans, "The International Protection against Torture and Inhuman or Degrading Treatment," in *Collected Courses of the Academy of European Law*, vol. 2, bk. 2. Dordrecht: M. Nijhoff, 1991, p. 151.

Darmon, Marco, and Jean-Guy Huglo, "Legalité de traitement entre les hommes et les femmes dans la jurisprudence de la Cour de justice des Communautés européenes: Un univers en expansion," *Revue Trimenstrielle de Droit Européen* 28: 1 (1992).

Davidson, Basil, *The Black Man's Burden: Africa and the Curse of the Nation-State*. New York: New York Times Books, 1992.

Davis, F. James, *Who Is Black? One Nation's Definition*. University Park: Pennsylvania State University Press, 1991.

Degler, Carl, *Neither Black nor White: Slavery and Race Relations in Brazil and the United States*. New York: Macmillan, 1971.

DeGroot, Gerard-René, *Staatsangehörigkeit im Wandel*. Cologne: Carl Heymanns Verlag, 1989.

Diamond, Larry, and Marc F. Plattner, eds., *Nationalism, Ethnic Conflict, and Democracy*. Baltimore: Johns Hopkins University Press, 1994.

Dietz, Barbara, *Zwischen Anpassung und Autonomie: Russlanddeutsche in der vormaligen Sowjetunion und in der Bundesrepublik Deutschland*. Berlin: Duncker and Humblot, 1995.

Disraeli, Benjamin, *Sybil: or, the Two Nations*. London: Oxford University Press, 1985. Originally published in 1845.

Dittrich, Eckhard J., and Frank-Olaf Radtke, "Einleitung: Der Beitrag der Wissenchaften zur Konstruktion ethnischer Minderheiten," in Dittrich and Radtke, eds., *Ethnizität: Wissenschaft und Minderheiten*. Opladen: Westdeutcher Verlag, 1990, p. 11.

Dittrich, Eckhard J., and Frank-Olaf Radtke, eds., *Ethnizität: Wissenschaft und Minderheiten*. Opladen: Westdeutcher Verlag, 1990.

Dominguez, Virginia R., *People as Subject, People as Object: Selfhood and Peoplehood in Contemporary Israel*. Madison: University of Wisconsin Press, 1989.

Donnelly, Jack, *Universal Human Rights in Theory and Practice*. Ithaca: Cornell University Press, 1989.

Dugdale, R. L., *"The Jukes": A Study in Crime, Pauperism, Disease, and Heredity*. New York: Putnam, 1877.

Earle, Robert L., and John D. Wirth, eds., *Identities in North America: The Search for Community*. Stanford: Stanford University Press, 1995.

Easterlin, Richard A., David Ward, William S. Bernard, and Reed Veda, *Immigration*. Cambridge: Harvard University Press, 1980.

Eckert, Rainer, "Strassenumbenennung und Revolution in Deutschland," in Eckhard Jesse and Konrad Löw, *Vergangenheitsbewältigung*. Berlin: Duncker and Humblot, 1997, p. 45.

Edwards, Charles, "Australia: Accommodating Multi-Culturalism in Law," in Esin Örücü, Elspeth Attwooll, and Sean Coyle, eds., *Studies in Legal Systems: Mixed and Mixing*. London: Kluwer Law International, 1996, p. 53.

Eisenstadt, S. N., *Israeli Society*. London: Weidenfeld and Nicolson, 1967.

———, *The Protestant Ethic and Modernization: A Comparative View*. New York: Basic Books, 1968.

Eisenstadt, S. N., and Eyal Ben-Ari, eds., *Japanese Models of Conflict Resolution*. London: K. Paul International, 1990.

Ellis, Evelyn, *European Community Sex Equality Law*. Oxford: Clarendon Press, 1991.

Ely, John Hart, "The Wages of Crying Wolf: A Comment on *Roe v. Wade*," *Yale Law Journal* 82: 920 (1973).

Espiritu, Yen Le, *Asian American Panethnicity: Bridging Institutions and Identities*. Philadelphia: Temple University Press, 1992.

Etzioni, Amitai, *The Spirit of Community: The Reinvention of American Society*. New York: Crown Publishers, 1993.

Evans, Andrew, "Nationality Law and European Integration," *European Law Review* 16: 190 (1991).

Evans, Hiram Wesley, "The Klan's Fight for Americanism," *North American Review* 223: 33 (1926).

Feldberg, Michael, *The Turbulent Era: Riot and Disorder in Jacksonian America*. New York: Oxford University Press, 1980.

Fine, Gary Alan, "Scandal, Social Conditions, and the Creation of Public Attention: Fatty Arbuckle and the 'Problem of Hollywood,'" *Social Problems* 44: 297 (1997).

Firmage, Edwin Brown, and Richard Collin Mangrum, *Zion in the Courts: A Legal History of the Church of Jesus Christ of Latter-Day Saints, 1830–1900*. Chicago: University of Illinois Press, 1988.

Fishman, David E., Rena Mayerfeld, and Joshua A. Fishman, "'Am and Goy' as Designations for Ethnicity in Selected Books of the Old Testament," in Joshua A. Fishman et al., eds., *The Rise and Fall of the Ethnic Revival*. Berlin: Mouton, 1985, p. 15.

Fishman, Joshua A., et al., eds., *The Rise and Fall of the Ethnic Revival*. Berlin: Mouton, 1985.

Fitzgerald, Francis, *America Revised: History Schoolbooks in the Twentieth Century*. Boston: Little, Brown, 1979.

Foote, Daniel H., "Japan's Foreign Workers' Policy: A View from the United States," *Georgetown Immigration Law Journal* 7: 707 (1993).

Forbes, Hugh Donald, "Canada: From Bilingualism to Multiculturalism," in Larry Diamond and Marc F. Plattner, eds., *Nationalism, Ethnic Conflict, and Democracy*. Baltimore: Johns Hopkins University Press, 1994, p. 88.

Ford, Caroline, *Creating the Nation in Provincial France: Religion and Political Identity in Brittany*. Princeton: Princeton University Press, 1993.

Ford, Richard T., "The Repressed Community: Locating the New Communitarianism," *Transition*, 5: no. 1 (issue 65) (1995).

Fowles, Jip, *Starstruck: Celebrity Performers and the American Public*. Washington, D.C.: Smithsonian Institution Press, 1992.

Franklin, Frank G., *The Legislative History of Naturalization in the United States*. 1906; reprint, New York: Arno Press, 1969.

Freeman, Gary P., and James Jupp, "Comparing Immigration Policy in Australia and the United States," in Freeman and Jupp, eds., *Nations of Immigrants: Australia, the United States, and International Migration.* New York: Oxford University Press, 1992, p. 4.

Freeman, Gary P., and James Jupp, eds., *Nations of Immigrants: Australia, the United States, and International Migration.* New York: Oxford University Press, 1992.

Friedman, Lawrence M. *American Law: An Introduction.* 2nd ed. New York: Norton, 1998.

————, *Crime and Punishment in American History.* New York: Basic Books, 1993.

————, *A History of American Law.* 2d ed., New York: Simon and Schuster, 1985.

————, "Is There a Modern Legal Culture?" *Ratio Juris* 7: 117 (1994).

————, *The Legal System: A Social Science Perspective.* New York: Russell Sage Foundation, 1975.

————, *The Republic of Choice: Law, Authority and Culture.* Cambridge: Harvard University Press, 1990.

————, "Rights of Passage: Divorce Law in Historical Perspective," *Oregon Law Review* 63: 666 (1984).

————, *Total Justice.* New York: Russell Sage Foundation, 1985.

————, *Your Time Will Come: The Law of Age Discrimination and Mandatory Retirement.* New York: Russell Sage Foundation, 1984.

Frowein, Jochen, and Torsten Stein, eds., *Die Rechtsstellung von Ausländern nach staatlichem Recht und Völkerrecht.* Berlin: Springer-Verlag, 1987.

Fukuyama, Francis, *Trust: The Social Virtues and the Creation of Prosperity.* New York: Free Press, 1995.

Gagnon, V. P., Jr., "Serbia's Road to War," in Larry Diamond and Marc F. Plattner, eds., *Nationalism, Ethnic Conflict, and Democracy.* Baltimore: Johns Hopkins University Press, 1994, p. 117.

Galanter, Marc, *Competing Equalities: Law and the Backward Classes in India.* Berkeley: University of California Press, 1984.

Gamson, Joshua, *Claims to Fame.* Berkeley, University of California Press, 1994.

Garcia, Nieves Diaz, *La Reforma de la Nacionalidad.* Madrid, Spain: Editorial Civitas, 1991.

Gavison, Ruth, "Privacy and the Limits of Law," *Yale Law Journal* 89: 421 (1980).

Gellner, Ernest, *Encounters with Nationalism.* Oxford: Blackwell, 1994.

————, *Nations and Nationalism.* Ithaca: Cornell University Press, 1983.

Gessner, Volkmar, "Global Legal Interaction and Legal Cultures," *Ratio Juris* 7: 132 (1994).

Gibney, Mark, ed., *Open Borders? Closed Societies? The Ethical and Political Issues.* New York: Greenwood Press, 1988.

Giddens, Anthony, *Modernity and Self-Identity: Self and Society in the Late Modern Age.* Stanford: Stanford University Press, 1991.

Gilje, Paul A., "The Baltimore Riots of 1812 and the Breakdown of the Anglo-American Mob Tradition," *Journal of Social History* 13: 547 (1980).

Gillman, Howard, *The Constitution Besieged: The Rise and Demise of Lochner Era Police Powers Jurisprudence*. Durham: Duke University Press, 1993.

Glazer, Nathan, "Reflections on Citizenship and Diversity," in Gary J. Jacobsohn and Susan Dunn, eds., *Diversity and Citizenship: Rediscovering American Nationhood*. Baltimore: Johns Hopkins University Press, 1996, p. 85.

Glendon, Mary Ann, *Abortion and Divorce in Western Law: American Failures, European Challenges*. Cambridge: Harvard University Press, 1987.

———, *Rights Talk: The Impoverishment of Political Discourse*. New York: Free Press, 1991.

———, *The Transformation of Family Law: State, Law, and Family in the United States and Western Europe*. Chicago: University of Chicago Press, 1989.

Gluckman, Max, *The Ideas in Barotse Jurisprudence*. New Haven: Yale University Press, 1965.

Goethe, C. M., "Other Aspects of the Problem," *Current History* 28: 766 (1928).

Goldberg, David, and Elspeth Attwooll, "Legal Orders, Systemic Relationships and Cultural Characteristics: Towards Spectral Jurisprudence," in Esin Örücü, Elspeth Attwooll, and Sean Coyle, *Studies in Legal Systems: Mixed and Mixing*. London: Kluwer Law International, 1995, p. 313.

Goldin, Ian, *Making Race*. London: Longman, 1987.

Gordon, Milton M., *Assimilation in American Life: The Role of Race, Religion, and National Origins*. New York: Oxford University Press, 1964.

Gordon, Sarah Barringer, "The 'Twin Relic of Barbarism': A Legal History of Anti-Polygamy in Nineteenth-Century America," Ph.D. diss., Princeton University, 1995.

Gotanda, Neil, "A Critique of 'Our Constitution is Color-Blind,'" *Stanford Law Review* 44: 1 (1991).

Gould, Stephen Jay, *The Mismeasure of Man*. Rev. ed. New York: Norton, 1981.

Greenberg, Douglas, and Stanley N. Katz, eds., *Constitutionalism and Democracy: Transitions in the Contemporary World*. New York: Oxford University Press, 1993.

Greider, William, *One World, Ready or Not*. New York: Simon and Schuster, 1997.

Grubb, Steven F., "Dealing with the Hate: The Changing Face of German Asylum Law," *Dickinson Journal of International Law* 12: 497 (1994).

Guendelsberger, John W., "Access to Citizenship for Children Born within the State to Foreign Parents," *American Journal of Comparative Law* 40: 379 (1992).

Guild, Elspeth, *The Developing Immigration and Asylum Policies of the European Union*. The Hague: Kluwer Law International, 1996.

Gurr, Robert, and Barbara Harff, *Ethnic Conflicts in World Politics*. Boulder: Westview Press, 1994.

Haarmann, Harald, *Soziologie und Politik der Sprachen Europas*. Munich: Deutscher Taschenbuch-Verlag, 1975.

Hacker, Andrew, *Two Nations: Black and White, Separate, Hostile, Unequal*. New York: Scribner's, 1992.

Hailbronner, Kay, "Citizenship and Nationhood in Germany," in William Rogers

Brubaker, ed., *Immigration and the Politics of Citizenship in Europe and North America*. Lanham, Md.: University Press of America, 1989, p. 67.

Haley, Alex, *Roots*. Garden City, N.Y.: Doubleday, 1976.

Hall, Stuart, "The Local and Global: Globalization and Ethnicity," in Anthony D. King, ed., *Culture, Globalization and the World System*. Binghamton: State University of New York, 1991, p. 18.

Haller, Mark H., *Eugenics: Hereditarian Attitudes in American Thought*. New Brunswick, N.J.: Rutgers University Press, 1963.

Hammar, Tomas, *European Immigration Policy: A Comparative Study*. Cambridge: Cambridge University Press, 1985.

Hardgrave, Robert L., Jr., "India: The Dilemmas of Diversity," in Larry Diamond and Marc F. Plattner, eds., *Nationalism, Ethnic Conflict, and Democracy*. Baltimore: Johns Hopkins University Press, 1994, p. 71.

Harring, Sidney L., *Crow Dog's Case: American Indian Sovereignty, Tribal Law, and United States Law in the Nineteenth Century*. Cambridge: Press Syndicate of the University of Cambridge, 1994.

Haskins, George Lee, *History of the Supreme Court of the United States*, vol. 2, *Foundations of Power: John Marshall, 1801–1815*. New York: Macmillan, 1981.

Heidt, Erhard U., *Mass Media, Cultural Tradition, and National Identity: The Case of Singapore and Its Television Programmes*. Saarbrucken: Breitenbach, 1987.

Heizer, Robert F., and Alan J. Almquist, *The Other Californians*. Berkeley: University of California Press, 1971.

Heller, Thomas, "Immigration and Regulation: Historical Context and Legal Reform," in J. Bustamante et al., eds., *U.S.-Mexico Relations: Labor Market Interdependence*. Stanford: Stanford University Press, 1992, p. 41.

———, "Modernity, Membership, and Multiculturalism," *Stanford Humanities Review* 5: 2 (1997).

Hennessey, James J., *American Catholics: A History of the Roman Catholic Community in the United States*. New York: Oxford University Press, 1981.

Herrnstein, Richard J., and Charles Murray, *The Bell Curve: Intelligence and Class Structure in American Life*. New York: Free Press, 1994.

Hing, Bill Ong, *Making and Remaking Asian America through Immigration Policy, 1850–1990*. Stanford: Stanford University Press, 1993.

Hinnenkamp, Volker, "'Gastarbeiterlinguistik' und die Ethnisierung der Gastarbeiter," in Eckhard Dittrich and Frank-Olaf Radtke, eds., *Ethnizität: Wissenschaft und Minderheiten*. Opladen: Westdeutcher Verlag, 1990, p. 277.

Hobsbawm, E. J., *Nations and Nationalism since 1780: Programme, Myth, Reality*. 2d ed. Cambridge: Cambridge University Press, 1992.

Hobsbawm, Eric, and Terence Ranger, eds., *The Invention of Tradition*. Cambridge: Cambridge University Press, 1983.

Hodes, Martha, *White Women, Black Men: Illicit Sex in the Nineteenth-Century South*. New Haven: Yale University Press, 1997.

Hoffman-Nowotny, Hans-Joachim, "Switzerland," in Tomas Hammar, ed., *European*

Immigration Policy: A Comparative Study. Cambridge: Cambridge University Press, 1985, p. 206.

Hollinger, David A., *Postethnic America: Beyond Multiculturalism.* New York: Basic Books, 1995.

Hooton, Earnest A., *Crime and the Man.* Cambridge: Harvard University Press, 1939.

Horowitz, Donald L., *Ethnic Groups in Conflict.* Berkeley: University of California Press, 1985.

Howard, Rhoda E., *Human Rights and the Seach for Community.* Boulder: Westview Press, 1995.

Human Rights Watch, *Slaughter among Neighbors: The Political Origins of Communal Violence.* New Haven: Yale University Press, 1995.

Hunter, James D., *The State of Disunion: 1996 Survey of American Political Culture.* Ivy, Va.: In Medias Res Educational Foundation, 1996.

Huntington, Samuel P., "The West: Unique, Not Universal," *Foreign Affairs* 75, no. 6: 28 (1996).

Ignatieff, Michael, *Blood and Belonging: Journeys into the New Nationalism.* New York: Farrar, Straus and Giroux, 1994.

Inkeles, Alex, *National Character: A Psycho-Social Perspective.* New Brunswick, N.J.: Transaction Publishers, 1997.

Innes, Stephen, *Creating the Commonwealth: The Economic Culture of Puritan New England.* New York: Norton, 1995.

Ireland, Patrick, *The Policy Challenge of Ethnic Diversity: Immigrant Politics in France and Switzerland.* Cambridge: Harvard University Press, 1994.

Isaacs, Harold R., *Idols of the Tribe: Group Identity and Political Change.* New York: Harper and Row, 1975.

Jackson, Donald W., and C. Neal Tate, eds., *Comparative Judicial Review and Public Policy.* Westport, Conn.: Greenwood Press, 1992.

Jacob, Herbert, *Silent Revolution: The Transformation of Divorce Law in the United States.* Chicago: University of Chicago Press, 1988.

Jacob, Herbert, Erhard Blankenburg, Herbert N. Kritzer, Doris Marie Provine, and Joseph Sanders, *Courts, Law, and Politics in Comparative Perspective.* New Haven: Yale University Press, 1996.

Jacobsohn, Gary J., and Susan Dunn, *Diversity and Citizenship: Rediscovering American Nationhood.* Lanham, Md.: Rowman and Littlefield, 1996.

Jacobson, David, *Rights Across Borders: Immigration and the Decline of Citizenship.* Baltimore: Johns Hopkins University Press, 1996.

Jacobson, Evelyn, *The Cape Coloured.* Rondebosch, South Africa: University of Cape Town Library School, 1945.

Jäger, Georg, *Bündnerisches Regionalbewusstsein und nationale Identität.* Basel: Nationales Forschungsprogramm 21, 1991.

James, W., *Now That We Are Free: Coloured Communities in a Democratic South Africa.* Boulder: L. Rienner, 1996.

Jarvis, Sonia R., "*Brown* and the Afrocentric Curriculum," *Yale Law Journal* 101: 1285 (1992).

Jaschke, Hans-Gerd, *Rechtsextremismus und Fremdenfeindlichkeit.* Opladen: Westdeutscher Verlag, 1994.

Johnson, Nevil, "Constitutionalism in Europe since 1945: Reconstruction and Reappraisal," in Douglas Greenberg et al., eds., *Constitutionalism and Democracy: Transitions in the Contemporary World.* New York: Oxford University Press, 1993, p. 26.

Jones, Maldwyn Allen, *American Immigration.* 2d ed. Chicago: University of Chicago Press, 1992.

Jordan, Winthrop D., *The White Man's Burden.* New York: Oxford University Press, 1974.

Kagan, Robert A. "Do Lawyers Cause Adversarial Legalism? A Preliminary Inquiry," *Law and Social Inquiry* 19: 1 (1994).

Kälin, Walter, and Rupert Moser, eds., *Migrationen aus der Dritten Welt: Ursachen und Wirkungen.* Bern: P. Haupt, 1989.

Karst, Kenneth L., *Law's Promise, Law's Expression: Visions of Power in the Politics of Race, Gender, and Religion.* New Haven: Yale University Press, 1994.

Kerr, James E., *The Insular Cases: The Role of the Judiciary in American Expansionism.* Port Washington, N.Y.: Kennikat Press, 1982.

Kim, Jackie J., "The Indian Federal Recognition Administrative Procedures Act of 1995: A Congresssional Solution to an Administrative Morass," *Administrative Law Journal of American University* 9: 899 (1995).

King, Anthony D., ed., *Culture, Globalization and the World-System.* Binghamton, N.Y.: State University of New York, 1991.

Klusmeyer, Douglas B., "Aliens, Immigrants, and Citizens: The Politics of Inclusion in the Federal Republic of Germany," *Daedalus* 122, no. 3: 81 (1993).

Knopp, Anke, *Die Deutsche Asylpolitik.* Munster: Agende Verlag, 1994.

Koh, Tommy T. B., *The United States and East Asia: Conflict and Co-operation.* Singapore: Institute of Policy Studies, 1995.

Kommers, Donald P., *The Constitutional Jurisprudence of the Federal Republic of Germany.* Durham: Duke University Press, 1989.

Kraines, Oscar, *The Impossible Dilemma: Who Is a Jew in the State of Israel?* New York: Bloch, 1976.

Krane, Ronald E., *International Labor Migration in Europe.* New York: Praeger, 1979.

Kupchan, Charles A., "Introduction: Nationalism Resurgent," in Kupchan, ed., *Nationalism and Nationalities in the New Europe.* Ithaca: Cornell University Press, 1995, p. 1.

Kupchan, Charles A., ed., *Nationalism and Nationalities in the New Europe.* Ithaca: Cornell University Press, 1995.

Kuper, H., and L. Kuper, eds., *African Law: Adaptation and Development.* Berkeley: University of California Press, 1965.

Lahav, Pnina, *Judgment in Jerusalem: Chief Justice Simon Agranat and the Zionist Century.* Berkeley: University of California Press, 1997.

Lake, Marilyn, "The Meaning of 'Self' in Claims for Self-Government: Re-claiming Citizenship for Women and Indigenous People in Australia," in Christopher Arup and Lee Ann Marks, eds., *Cross Currents: Internationalism, National Identity and Law.* Melbourne: La Trobe University Press, 1996, p. 9.

Landa, Janet Tai, *Trust, Ethnicity, and Identity.* Ann Arbor: University of Michigan Press, 1994.

Langbein, John, *Torture and the Law of Proof.* Chicago: University of Chicago Press, 1977.

Langum, David, *Crossing Over the Line: Legislating Morality and the Mann Act.* Chicago: University of Chicago Press, 1994.

Lawrence, Charles R., III, "Race, Multiculturalism, and the Jurisprudence of Transformation," *Stanford Law Review* 47: 819 (1995).

Leithäuser, Joachim G., *Albert Einstein.* Berlin: Colloquium-Verlag, 1965.

Lemann, Nicholas, "Kicking in Groups," *Atlantic Monthly,* April 1996, p. 22.

Lenaerts, Koen, "Constitutionalism and the Many Faces of Federalism," *American Journal of Comparative Law* 38: 205 (1990).

Levy, Jacob T., "Classifying Cultural Rights," in Ian Shapiro and Will Kymlicka, eds., *Ethnicity and Group Rights.* New York: New York University Press, 1997, p. 22.

Levy, Leonard W., *Blasphemy: Verbal Offense against the Sacred, from Moses to Salman Rushdie.* New York: Knopf, 1993.

Lewis, Loida Nicholas, *How to Get a Green Card.* Berkeley: Nolo Press, 1993.

Lieberman, Jethro K., *Are Americans Extinct?* New York: Walker, 1968.

Lifton, Robert Jay, *The Protean Self: Human Resilience in an Age of Fragmentation.* New York: Basic Books, 1993.

Lipset, Seymour Martin, "Predicting the Future of Post-Industrial Society: Can We Do It?" in Lipset, ed., *The Third Century: America as a Post-Industrial Society.* Stanford: Hoover Institution Press, 1979, p. 2.

Lipset, Seymour Martin, ed., *The Third Century: America as a Post-Industrial Society.* Stanford: Hoover Institution Press, 1979.

Liss, Franklin R., "A Mandate to Balance: Judicial Protection of Individual Rights under the Canadian Charter of Rights and Freedoms," *Emory Law Journal* 41: 1281 (1992).

Litwack, Leon F., *North of Slavery: The Negro in the Free States, 1790–1860.* Chicago: University of Chicago Press, 1961.

Löchte, Anita, and Oliver Sill, *Rechtsextremismus bei westdeutschen Jugendlichen.* Münster: Lit, 1994.

Loescher, Gil, and John A. Scanlan, *Calculated Kindness: Refugees and America's Half-Open Door, 1945 to the Present.* New York: Free Press, 1986.

Lofgren, Charles, *The Plessy Case: A Legal-Historical Interpretation.* New York: Oxford University Press, 1987.

Lowe, David, *Ku Klux Klan: The Invisible Empire.* New York: Norton, 1967.

Lucke, Doris, "Der Gesetzgeber und die Frauen," *Zeitschrift für Rechtssoziologie* 10: 236 (1989).

Lynn-Jones, Sean M., and Steven E. Miller, eds., *Global Dangers: Changing Dimensions of International Security.* Cambridge: Massachusetts Institute of Technology Press, 1995.

Maase, Kaspar, *BRAVO Amerika: Erkundungen zur Jugendkultur der Bundesrepublik in den fünfizer Jahren.* Hamburg: Junius, 1992.

Macdonald, Ian A., and Nicholas J. Blake, *Immigration Law and Practice in the United Kingdom.* 3d ed. London: Butterworths, 1991.

Manchester, William, *A World Lit Only by Fire: The Medieval Mind and the Renaissance.* Boston: Little, Brown, 1992.

Markesinis, Basil, "Litigation-Mania in England, Germany and the USA: Are We So Very Different?" *Cambridge Law Journal* 49: 233 (1990).

Markovits, Inga, "Law or Order: Constitutionalism and Legality in Eastern Europe," *Stanford Law Review* 34: 513 (1981).

Matsuda, Mari J., "Law and Culture in the District Court of Honolulu, 1844–1845: A Case Study of the Rise of Legal Consciousness," *American Journal of Legal History* 32: 16 (1988).

Mayall, James, *Nationalism and International Society.* Cambridge: Cambridge University Press, 1990.

Mayorga, Roberto, "Die Rechtsstellung von Ausländern nach staatlichem Recht und Völkerrecht in Chile," in Jochen Frowein and Torsten Stein, eds., *Die Rechtsstellung von Ausländern nach staatlichem Recht und Völkerrecht.* Berlin: Springer-Verlag, 1987, p. 187.

McCann, Michael W., *Rights at Work: Pay Equity Reform and the Politics of Legal Mobilization.* Chicago, Illinois: University of Chicago Press, 1994.

Menasse, Robert, *Das Land Ohne Eigenschaften: Essay zur Österreichischen Identität.* Vienna: Verlag Sonderzahl, 1992.

Mencken, H. L., *The American Language.* New York: Knopf, 1947.

Merry, Sally Engle, "Everyday Understandings of the Law in Working-Class America," *American Ethnologist* 13: 253 (1986).

Meyrowitz, Joshua, *No Sense of Place: The Impact of Electronic Media on Social Behavior.* New York: Oxford University Press, 1985.

Michelmore, Peter, *Einstein, Profile of the Man.* New York: Dodd, Mead, 1962.

Miller, David, *On Nationality.* New York: Clarendon Press, 1995.

Miller, Judith, *God Has Ninety-Nine Names.* New York: Simon and Schuster, 1996.

Miller, Wilbur R., *Cops and Bobbies: Police Authority in New York and London, 1830–1870.* Chicago: University of Chicago Press, 1977.

Minow, Martha, *Making All the Difference: Inclusion, Exclusion, and American Law.* Ithaca: Cornell University Press, 1990.

Moran, Rachel F., "The Politics of Discretion: Federal Intervention in Bilingual Education," *California Law Review* 76: 1249 (1988).

Morris, Thomas D., *Southern Slavery and the Law, 1619–1860.* Chapel Hill: University of North Carolina Press, 1996.

Morse, Bradford W., and Gordon R. Woodman, eds., *Indigenous Law and the State.* Dordrecht: Foris Publications, 1988.

Moynihan, Daniel Patrick, *Pandaemonium: Ethnicity in International Politics.* Oxford: Oxford University Press, 1993.

Murray, Robert K., *Red Scare: A Study in National Hysteria, 1919–1920.* Minneapolis: University of Minnesota Press, 1955.

Myrdal, Gunnar, *An American Dilemma: The Negro Problem and Modern Democracy.* New York: Harper and Bros., 1944.

Nassehi, Armin, "Der Fremde als Vertrauter: Soziologische Beobachtungen zur Konstruktion von Identitäten und Differenzen," *Kölner Zeitschrift für Soziologie und Sozialpsychologie* 47: 443 (1995).

National Reserach Council, Committee on National Statistics, *Spotlight on Heterogeneity: The Standards for Racial and Ethnic Classification.* Washington, D.C.: National Academy Press, 1996.

Nelson, William E., "The Changing Meaning of Equality in Twentieth-Century Constitutional Law," *Washington and Lee Law Review* 52: 4 (1995).

Neuman, Gerald L., *Strangers to the Constitution: Immigrants, Borders, and Fundamental Law.* Princeton: Princeton University Press, 1996.

Nodia, Ghia, "Nationalism and Democracy," in Larry Diamond and Marc F. Plattner, eds., *Nationalism, Ethnic Conflict, and Democracy.* Baltimore: Johns Hopkins University Press, 1994, p. 3.

Noelle-Neumann, Elisabeth, "Rechtsbewusstsein im wiedervereinigten Deutschland," *Zeitschrift für Rechtssoziologie* 16: 121 (1995).

Novak, Daniel A., *The Wheel of Servitude: Black Forced Labor after Slavery.* Lexington: University Press of Kentucky, 1978.

Nuclear Energy Agency, *Chernobyl—Ten Years On: Radiological and Health Impact.* Paris: OECD, 1995.

O'Neill, William L., *Divorce in the Progressive Era.* New Haven: Yale University Press, 1967.

Obiora, Leslye A., "Bridges and Barricades: Rethinking Polemics and Intransigence in the Campaign against Female Circumcision," *Case Western Reserve Law Review* 47: 275 (1997).

———, "(En)gaging Nationalism, Traditionalism, and Gender Relations," *Indiana Law Review* 28: 575 (1995).

———, "Reconsidering African Customary Law," *Legal Studies Forum* 17: 217 (1993).

Okoth-Ogendo, H. W. O., "Constitutions without Constitutionalism: Reflections on an African Political Paradox," in Douglas Greenberg et al., eds., *Constitutionalism and Democracy: Transitions in the Contemporary World.* New York: Oxford University Press, 1993, p. 65.

Olsen, Frances, "Legal Responses to Gender Discrimination in Europe and the USA," in *Collected Courses of the Academy of European Law,* vol. 2, bk. 2. Dordrecht: M. Nijhoff, 1991, p. 199.

Örücü, Esin, Elspeth Attwooll, and Sean Coyle, *Studies in Legal Systems: Mixed and Mixing.* London: Kluwer Law International, 1996.

Paine, Lewis W., *Six Years in a Georgia Prison.* New York: n.p., 1851.

Pais, Abraham, *"Subtle Is the Lord . . . ": The Science and the Life of Albert Einstein.* Oxford: Oxford University Press, 1982.

Pandey, Rayendra, *The Caste System in India.* New Delhi: Criterion, 1986.

Panikkar, R., "Is the Notion of Human Rights a Western Concept?" *Diogenes* 120: 75 (1982).

Parman, Donald L., *Indians and the American West in the Twentieth Century.* Bloomington: Indiana University Press, 1994.

Pells, Richard, *Not like Us.* New York: Basic, 1997.

Perez-Brignozi, Hector, *A Brief History of Central America.* Berkeley: University of California Press, 1989.

Perez-Perdomo, Rogelio, "La Organizacion del Estado en Venezuela en el Siglo (1830–1899)," *Politeia* 14: 349 (1990).

Pfaff, William, *The Wrath of Nations: Civilization and the Furies of Nationalism.* New York: Simon and Schuster, 1993.

Pickens, Donald K., *Eugenics and the Progressives.* Nashville, Tenn.: Vanderbilt University Press, 1968.

Pole, J. R., *The Pursuit of Equality in American History.* 2d ed. Berkeley: University of California Press, 1993.

Polenberg, Richard, *Fighting Faiths: The Abrams Case, the Supreme Court, and Free Speech.* New York: Viking, 1987.

Pommersheim, Frank, *Braid of Feathers: American Indian Law and Contemporary Tribal Life.* Berkeley: University of California Press, 1995.

Pool, Robert, *Eve's Rib: The Biological Roots of Sex Differences.* New York: Crown, 1994.

Postman, Neil, *Amusing Ourselves to Death: Public Discourse in the Age of Show Business.* New York: Viking, 1985.

Potter, David M., *People of Plenty.* Chicago: University of Chicago Press, 1954.

Preston, William, Jr., *Aliens and Dissenters: Federal Suppression of Radicals, 1903–1933.* Cambridge: Harvard University Press, 1963.

Price, Monroe E., "The Market for Loyalties: Electronic Media and the Global Competition for Allegiances," *Yale Law Journal* 104: 664 (1994).

Provine, Doris Marie, "Courts in the Political Process in France," in Herbert Jacob et al., eds., *Courts, Law and Politics in Comparative Perspective.* New Haven: Yale University Press, 1996, p. 177.

Prunier, Gerard, *The Rwanda Crisis, 1959–1994.* London: Hurst, 1995.

Putnam, Robert D., "Bowling Alone: America's Declining Social Capital," *Journal of Democracy* 6: 65 (1995).

———, *Making Democracy Work: Civic Traditions in Modern Italy.* Princeton: Princeton University Press, 1993.

———, "The Strange Disappearance of Civic America," *American Prospect* (Winter 1996): 34.

Ransby, Barbara, "Columbus and the Making of Historical Myth," *Race and Class* 33: 79 (1992).

Rein, Irving J., Philip Kotler, and Martin R. Stoller, *High Visibility*. London: Heinemann, 1987.

Rennie, Ysabel, *The Search for Criminal Man: A Conceptual History of the Dangerous Offender*. Lexington, Mass: Lexington Books, 1978.

Rhode, Deborah L., *Justice and Gender*. Cambridge: Harvard University Press, 1989. Lexington, Mass.: Lexington Books, 1978.

Rhode, Deborah L., ed., *Theoretical Perspectives on Sexual Difference*. New Haven: Yale University Press, 1990.

Riley, Glenda, *Divorce: An American Tradition*. New York: Oxford University Press, 1991.

Robertson, Roland, "Social Theory, Cultural Relativity and the Problem of Globality," in Anthony D. King, ed., *Culture, Globalization and the World-System*. Binghamton, N.Y.: State University of New York, 1991, p. 69.

Röhl, Klaus F., and Stefan Magen, "Die Rolle des Rechts im Prozess der Globalisierung," *Zeitschrift für Rechtssoziologie* 17: 1 (1996).

Roosens, Eugeen E., *Creating Ethnicity: The Process of Ethnogenesis*. Newbury Park, Calif.: Sage, 1989.

Rose, Ronald R., "Fixing the Wheel: A Critical Analysis of the Immigrant Investor Visa," *San Diego Law Review* 29: 615 (1992).

Rosenfeld, Michel, "Modern Constitutionalism as Interplay between Identity and Diversity," in Michel Rosenfeld, ed., *Constitutionalism, Identity, Difference, and Legitimacy: Theoretical Perspectives*. Durham: Duke University Press, 1994, p. 3.

Rosenfeld, Michel, ed., *Constitutionalism, Identity, Difference, and Legitimacy: Theoretical Perspectives*. Durham: Duke University Press, 1994.

Ross, William G., *Forging New Freedoms: Nativism, Education, and the Constitution, 1917–1927*. Lincoln: University of Nebraska Press, 1994.

Salyer, Lucy E., *Laws Harsh as Tigers: Chinese Immigrants and the Shaping of Modern Immigration Law*. Chapel Hill: University of North Carolina Press, 1996.

Sandel, Michael J. *Democracy's Discontent: America in Search of a Public Philosophy*. Cambridge: Belknap Press of Harvard University Press, 1996.

Santos, Boaventura de Sousa, "Toward a Multicultural Conception of Human Rights," *Sociologia del Diritto* 24, no. 1: 27 (1997).

Sawyer, Herbert L., ed., *Business in the Contemporary World*. Lanham, Md.: University Press of America, 1988.

Schickel, Richard, *Intimate Strangers: The Culture of Celebrity*. Garden City, N.Y.: Doubleday, 1985.

Seel, John, "Reading the Post-Modern Self," *Echoes* (Winter 1998): 39.

Shapiro, Ian, and Will Kymlicka, *Ethnicity and Group Rights*. New York: New York University Press, 1997.

Shapiro, Martin, "The Globalization of Law," *Indiana Journal of Global Legal Studies* 1: 37 (1993).

Slotkin, Richard, *Gunfighter Nation: The Myth of the Frontier in Twentieth-Century America*. New York: Atheneum, 1992.

Smedley, Audrey, *Race in North America: Origin and Evolution of a Worldview.* Boulder: Westview Press, 1993.

Smith, Anthony D., *The Ethnic Origins of Nations.* Oxford: Blackwell, 1986.

————, *The Ethnic Revival.* Cambridge: Cambridge University Press, 1981.

Smith, Rogers M., *Civic Ideals: Conflicting Visions of Citizenship in U.S. History.* New Haven: Yale University Press, 1997.

Solberg, Carl, *Immigration and Naturalization.* Austin: University of Texas Press, 1970.

Soysal, Yasemin N., *Limits of Citizenship: Migrants and Postnational Membership in Europe.* Chicago: University of Chicago Press, 1994.

Spencer, Paul, "Age-Sets, Age Grades and Age-Generation Systems," in David Levinson and Melvin Ember, eds., *Encyclopedia of Cultural Anthropology.* New York: Henry Holt, 1996, p. 25.

Spicer, Keith, "Canada: Values in Search of a Vision," in Robert L. Earle and John D. Wirth, eds., *Identities in North America: The Search for Community.* Stanford: Stanford University Press, 1995, p. 13.

Spickard, Paul R., *Mixed Blood: Intermarriage and Ethnic Identity in Twentieth-Century America.* Madison: University of Wisconsin Press, 1989.

Steinberg, Stephen, *The Ethnic Myth: Race, Ethnicity, and Class in America.* Boston: Beacon Press, 1989.

Stokes, Charles J., "A Theory of Slums," *Land Economics* 38: 187 (1962).

Stolzenberg, Nomi Maya, "'He Drew a Circle That Shut Me Out': Assimilation, Indoctrination, and the Paradox of a Liberal Education," *Harvard Law Review* 106: 581 (1993).

Stowell, Jay S. "The Danger of Unrestricted Mexican Immigration," *Current History,* 28: 763 (1928).

Strickland, Rennard, "Strangers in a Strange Land: A Historical Perspective of the Columbian Quincentenary," *St. John's Journal of Legal Commentary* 7: 571 (1992).

Sunkin, Maurice, "The United Kingdom," in C. Neal Tate and Torbjörn Vallinder, *The Global Expansion of Judicial Power.* New York: New York University Press, 1995, p. 67.

Tan, Simone, "Dual Nationality in France and the United States," *Hastings International and Comparative Law Review* 15: 447 (1992).

Tate, C. Neal, and Torbjörn Vallinder, eds., *The Global Expansion of Judicial Power.* New York: New York University Press, 1995.

Taylor, Charles, *Sources of the Self: The Making of the Modern Identity.* Cambridge: Harvard University Press, 1989.

Teich, Mikuláš, and Roy Porter, eds., *The National Question in Europe in Historical Context.* New York: Cambridge University Press, 1993.

Thompson, Winfred Lee, *The Introduction of American Law in the Philippines and Puerto Rico, 1898–1905.* Fayetteville: University of Arkansas Press, 1989.

Thrasher, Frederic M., *The Gang: A Study of 1,313 Gangs in Chicago.* Chicago: University of Chicago Press, 1963. Originally published in 1927.

Tocqueville, Alexis de, *Democracy in America.* Edited by J. P. Mayer. Translated by George Lawrence. Garden City, N.Y.: Doubleday, 1969. 2 vols.

Tomlins, Christopher L., *Law, Labor, and Ideology in the Early American Republic.* Cambridge: Cambridge University Press, 1993.

Torres, Gerald, and Kathryn Milun, "Translating Yonnondio by Precedent and Evidence: The Mashpee Indian Case," 1990 *Duke Law Journal,* p. 625.

Tsai, Shih-shan Henry, *The Chinese Experience in America.* Bloomington: Indiana University Press, 1986.

Unger, Aryeh L., *Constitutional Development in the USSR: A Guide to the Soviet Constitutions.* New York: Pica Press, 1981.

Upham, Frank K., *Law and Social Change in Postwar Japan.* Cambridge: Harvard University Press, 1987.

Van den Berghe, Pierre L., *The Ethnic Phenomenon.* New York: Elsevier, 1981.

Van Evera, Stephen, "Hypotheses on Nationalism and War," in Sean M. Lynn-Jones and Steven E. Miller, eds., *Global Dangers: Changing Dimensions of International Security.* Cambridge: Massachusetts Institute of Technology Press, 1995, p. 251.

Vetterling-Braggin, Mary, ed., *"Femininity," "Masculinity," and "Androgyny": A Modern Philosophical Discussion.* Totowa, N.J.: Roman and Littlefield, 1982.

Vos, Louis, "Shifting Nationalism: Belgians, Flemings and Walloons," in Mikulás Teich and Roy Porter, eds., *The National Question in Europe in Historical Context.* New York: Cambridge University Press, 1993, p. 128.

Watson, Mary Ann, *The Expanding Vista: American Television in the Kennedy Years.* New York: Oxford University Press, 1990.

Wearing, Brian, *Immigration Law in New Zealand and the USA.* Los Angeles: University of California, 1990.

Weber, Eugen, *Peasants into Frenchmen: The Modernization of Rural France, 1870–1914.* Stanford: Stanford University Press, 1976.

Weber, Max, *The Protestant Ethic and the Spirit of Capitalism.* London: Allen and Unwin, 1930.

White, Sherwin, *The Roman Citizenship.* Oxford: Clarendon Press, 1973.

Wiebe, Robert, *The Segmented Society: An Introduction to the Meaning of America.* New York: Oxford University Press, 1975.

Willard, M., *A History of the White Australia Policy to 1920.* 2d ed. London: Cass, 1967.

Willett, Ralph, *The Americanization of Germany, 1945–1949.* London: Routledge, 1989.

Wise, William, *Albert Einstein, Citizen of the World.* New York: Farrar, Straus and Cudahy, 1960.

Woodward, C. Vann, *The Strange Career of Jim Crow.* 2d. rev. ed. New York: Oxford University Press, 1966.

Wooldridge, Frank, and Vishnu D. Sharma, "International Law and the Expulsion of Ugandan Asians," *International Lawyer* 9: 30 (1975).

Wright, Luther, Jr., "Who's Black, Who's White, and Who Cares: Reconceptualizing the United States's Definition of Race and Racial Classifications," *Vanderbilt Law Review* 48: 513 (1995).

Yoon, Dae-Kyo, *Law and Political Authority in South Korea*. Boulder: Westview Press, 1990.

Ziemske, Burkhardt, *Die deutsche Staatsangehörigkeit nach dem Grundgesetz*. Berlin: Duncker & Humblot, 1995.

INDEX